Cognitive Contact Linguistics

Cognitive Linguistics Research

Editors
Dirk Geeraerts
Dagmar Divjak
John R. Taylor

Honorary editors
René Dirven
Ronald W. Langacker

Volume 62

Cognitive Contact Linguistics

Placing Usage, Meaning and Mind at the Core
of Contact-Induced Variation and Change

Edited by
Eline Zenner
Ad Backus
Esme Winter-Froemel

DE GRUYTER
MOUTON

ISBN 978-3-11-070799-1
e-ISBN (PDF) 978-3-11-061943-0
e-ISBN (EPUB) 978-3-11-061684-2
ISSN 1861-4132

Library of Congress Control Number: 2018950671

Bibliographic information published by the Deutsche Nationalbibliothek
The Deutsche Nationalbibliothek lists this publication in the Deutsche Nationalbibliografie;
detailed bibliographic data are available on the Internet at http://dnb.dnb.de.

© 2020 Walter de Gruyter GmbH, Berlin/Boston
This volume is text- and page-identical with the hardback published in 2019.
Typesetting: Integra Software Services Pvt. Ltd.
Printing and binding: CPI books GmbH, Leck

www.degruyter.com

Contents

Introduction: Placing usage, meaning and mind at the core of contact-induced variation and change —— 1

Part I: Conceptual foundations and categorization principles in contact-induced change

Alexander Onysko
1 Reconceptualizing language contact phenomena as cognitive processes —— 23

Anna Verschik
2 English-Estonian code-copying in blogs: Combining a contact linguistic and cognitive approach —— 51

Esme Winter-Froemel
3 Reanalysis in language contact: Perceptive ambiguity, salience, and catachrestic reinterpretation —— 81

Stefania Marzo, Eline Zenner and Dorien Van de Mieroop
4 When third-wave sociolinguistics and prototype analysis meet: The social meaning of sibilant palatalization in a Flemish Urban Vernacular —— 127

Part II: Associating concepts: Metaphors and cultural models in contact

Stephen Lucek
5 Notions of CONTAINMENT and SUPPORT in Irish English: Implications of language contact on the cognition of space —— 159

Anna Finzel and Hans-Georg Wolf
6 Conceptual metaphors as contact phenomena? The influence of local concepts on source and target domain —— 187

Stefano De Pascale, Stefania Marzo and Dirk Speelman
7 Cultural models in contact: Revealing attitudes toward regional varieties of Italian with Vector Space Models —— 213

Part III: Construction Grammar: Contact in and through more and less schematic form-meaning pairs

Bram Vertommen
8 Language alternation and the state-event contrast: A case-study of Dutch-Turkish and Dutch-Moroccan heritage speakers —— 253

Antje Endesfelder Quick, Ad Backus and Elena Lieven
9 Partially schematic constructions as engines of development: Evidence from German-English bilingual acquisition —— 279

Dirk Noël and Timothy Colleman
10 Constructional renovation: The role of French legal language in the survival of the nominative-and-infinitive in Dutch —— 305

Index —— 339

Introduction: Placing usage, meaning and mind at the core of contact-induced variation and change

Contact between languages nearly always leads to change in at least one of the languages involved (Thomason 2001). This change manifests itself in a whole number of linguistic phenomena, ranging from lexical borrowing and the transfer of specific phonemes over codeswitching to language death. Since Sapir's (1921) and Bloomfield's (1933) landmark studies ignited contact-induced variation and change as a proper research domain in linguistics, each of these phenomena has been subject to extensive empirical research and theoretical description.

In their work on the varied complex outcomes of contact, researchers have often drawn on other linguistic sub-disciplines. MacSwan (2012), for example, draws on Universal Grammar (Chomsky 1965), Gumperz (1982) on discourse analysis (Foucault 1980), and Poplack, Sankoff, and Miller (1988) on variational sociolinguistics (Labov 1970). Given this openness of contact linguistics to the theories and methods developed in other research paradigms, it is surprising that interaction with Cognitive Linguistics and its associated usage-based approach has been highly uncommon, especially considering the broad variety of other cross-fertilizations with the usage-based framework (see e.g. Boers and Stengers 2008 on contrastive linguistics, Ureña and Buendía 2017 on terminology, and cf. the book series *Applications of Cognitive Linguistics* edited by Gitte Kristiansen and Fransisco J. Ruiz de Mendoza Ibáñez).

The collection of papers presented in this volume, which grew out of a theme session organized at the 13th *International Cognitive Linguistics Conference* (Northumbria, UK, July 2015), aims to illustrate the benefits that follow from combining the two paradigms. We specifically make a case for *Cognitive Contact Linguistics* as a framework excellently suited to the integration of psycholinguistic and sociolinguistic inquiry of the bi- and multilingual mind. As such, our volume is oriented more towards exploration than towards specialization: we selected ten papers that together illustrate the wide range of research that can ensue from the interaction of contact linguistics and Cognitive Linguistics, rather than for example digging deep into one area of cross-fertilization (compare e.g. *Constructions in Contact*, Boas and Höder, under review).

In this introductory chapter, Section 1 presents the reasons why we advocate a more profound interaction between the paradigms, after which Section 2 sets forth the main objectives of *Cognitive Contact Linguistics*. Finally, we succinctly introduce the papers in this volume and describe the ways in which they contribute to our understanding of contact-induced variation and change and – as such – to both contact linguistics and to Cognitive Linguistics.

It is not the purpose of this introduction to provide a full-fledged overview of either paradigm: no detailed definition of contact phenomena will be provided, no exhaustive discussion of theoretical concepts and descriptive models of Cognitive Linguistics will be presented, nor will we attempt to synthesize the vast body of empirical research that has been conducted in the respective paradigms over the past decades. Readers who would like to know more about the Cognitive Linguistics framework are referred to general introductions such as Ruiz de Mendoza and Peña Cervel (2005), Geeraerts (2006), Ungerer and Schmid (2006), Evans and Green (2006), Evans, Bergen and Zinken (2007), and of course Geeraerts and Cuyckens (2007a). Readers interested in a general outline of contact linguistics and contact-induced variation and change can consult Thomason (2001), Matras (2009), Hickey (2010), Darquennes, Salmons, and Vandenbussche (forthc.), or the evergreens Weinreich (1970) and van Coetsem (1988). For an overview of contact phenomena from the lens of Cognitive Linguistics, comprehensive accounts are found in this volume in the papers by Onysko and Verschik.

1 Positioning *Cognitive Contact Linguistics*

In presenting our main arguments for cross-fertilizing Cognitive Linguistics and contact linguistics, we start off with a brief introduction of the general principles of Cognitive Linguistics, specifically describing why it is both surprising and unfortunate that it has taken so long for the paradigm to adopt an interest in contact-induced variation and change. Next, we flip the perspective and describe why we deem it beneficial for contact linguistics to pursue a more profound interaction with Cognitive Linguistics.

Cognitive Linguistics emerged in the late 1970s in the work of George Lakoff, Ronald Langacker, and Leonard Talmy as a reaction against existing formal approaches to language. In shaping the paradigm, one of the agreements was to capitalize Cognitive Linguistics as a way to emphasize the distinction with small-caps "cognitive linguistics". The latter serves as a cover term for all approaches studying language as a mental phenomenon, including Generative Grammar (Chomsky 1965) (see Evans and Green 2006 and Geeraerts and Cuyckens 2007b for more history). The differences are however outspoken: the Chomskian emphasis on the innate language faculty and the idea that language, thought and cognition are independent of each other are strongly refuted by Cognitive Linguistics. Instead, the paradigm considers language as "an integrated part of human cognition which operates in interaction with and on the basis of the same principles as other cognitive faculties" (Dirven 2005). The shared quest for these general cognitive principles that structure the way we use language – and as such provide a window to general human conceptual organization (Evans and Green 2006: 5; Geeraerts and Cuyckens 2007b: 3), has over the past fifty years developed into an accommodating framework that hosts a whole number of approaches (Geeraerts and Cuyckens 2007b: 4; Geeraerts 2006). Each of these rely on their own guiding principles of categorization, such as embodiment, image schemas, figure-ground, force dynamics; construction and construal; categorization and conceptual structure, prototypicality, fuzzy boundaries, basic levels and family resemblance, entrenchment and salience; mental spaces, frame semantics, conceptual metaphors and metonymies; idealized cognitive models; and the usage-based approach.

The usage-based approach is one of the most widespread foundations of Cognitive Linguistics. Yet, it is irreconcilable with the unquestioned empirical focus on monolingual competence that has long characterized research activities in the framework. This paradox provides us with the main argument for *Cognitive Contact Linguistics*. The central idea behind the usage-based approach is that language competence is based on language use: competence is grounded in "concrete pieces of language and straightforward generalizations across them" (Tomasello 2003: 5–6). This conviction comes with methodological consequences. If language structure is said to emerge from language use, then language use is what we should study to understand language structure. And if we appreciate that language use is more often than not characterized by contact between languages (in Weinreich's words: "a linguistic community is never homogeneous and hardly ever self-contained"; 1970: vii), then contact-induced variation and change should be at the center of attention. Looking at almost half a century of Cognitive Linguistics research, we are however confronted with a paradigm that has assumed monolingualism to be the default state, often focusing its attention to written data from standardized varieties of major languages and too uncritically adopting approaches from studies on monolingual language use to the study of bi- and multilingualism (compare Vaid and Meuter 2018 in Libben, Goral, and Libben 2018).

The rise of Cognitive Sociolinguistics (Croft 2009; Kristiansen and Dirven 2008; Geeraerts, Kristiansen, and Peirsman 2010) has given visibility to the plea for the integration of social context and, consequently, of variation, into work that relies on a usage-based approach. The interplay between the individual and the community, the tension between language variants and language varieties, and the importance of adequate methods to empirically study these fundamental relations acquired a central position in the study of categorization in and through language. However, contact-induced variation and change largely stayed under the radar, despite the wealth of learning opportunities offered by the bi- and multilingual mind.

The central objective of *Cognitive Contact Linguistics* is thus to explore how the guiding principles of Cognitive Linguistics apply to the bi- or multilingual mind in its dynamic bi- and multilingual environment, how this feeds back to our general understanding of these guiding principles, and how we can as a result better grasp how the interaction between cognition and context results in contact-induced variation and change. As such, perhaps we merely echo Weinreich, Labov, and Herzog (1968), but repeating their pleas is highly relevant as to date many approaches to contact-induced change still too little consider the interaction of meaning, context and the mind (see Winter-Froemel 2011; Backus 2014).

Many opportunities present themselves for research on language contact when we reconceptualize existing contact phenomena through the lens of Cognitive Linguistics. For example, the strict theoretical distinction between lexical borrowing and codeswitching, which has been very prominent in codeswitching research (see amongst others Poplack and Meechan 1998; Myers-Scotton 2002; Muysken 2000), loses much of its importance when embracing insights from Cognitive Linguistics. From a usage-based perspective, a word of foreign origin becomes a loanword if it is used time and time again, so that what can be described synchronically as a codeswitch can at the same time also be the lexical selection of a relatively established word that is ultimately of foreign origin, i.e. a loanword (see Backus 2014). Another fundamental distinction that has led to different paradigms in contact linguistics is the one between lexicon and syntax, which has given rise to separate traditions studying lexical influence (or codeswitching) and structural influence. Here too, Cognitive Linguistics helps reconceptualize this distinction. First, the Cognitive Linguistic emphasis on non-modularity, especially developed in Construction Grammar, frames language as an inventory of units of varying degrees of complexity without making formal distinctions between lexicon and syntax (e.g. Langacker 1987, and see Section 2 of this introduction). Adopting this principle makes it possible to unify research on lexical borrowing, codeswitching and structural borrowing (see Doğruöz and Backus 2009, Boas and Höder, under review, and Heine and Kuteva 2005 as precursors). Additionally, the prototype theoretical emphasis on family resemblance and fuzzy boundaries in categorization (e.g. Geeraerts, Grondelaers, and Bakema 1994, and see Section 2) helps relax the desire for a classical definition of the contact-induced phenomena in terms of necessary and sufficient conditions. A highly convincing account along these lines can be found in Matras (2009: 113–114), who synthesizes results from decades of research on codeswitching and borrowing to arrive at a definition of "prototypical borrowing" and "prototypical codeswitching" respectively, with a continuum of contact phenomena that are part of the linguistic reality positioned between these outer poles.

More examples of the ways in which Cognitive Linguistic categories can help reframe traditional questions in contact linguistics can be found in the chapters in this volume, in previous work of the contributing authors (e.g. Backus 1996 applying the notions of salience and entrenchment to borrowing, Wolf and Polzenhagen 2009 applying cultural models to World Englishes, Winter-Froemel 2011 for a usage-based perspective on loanword integration, Zenner, Speelman, and Geeraerts 2014 applying the notions of onomasiology and entrenchment to the borrowability of core vocabulary, Callies and Onysko 2017 on metaphors in World Englishes) and in other contributions (e.g. Boas, Dux, and Ziem 2016 on frame semantics in second language learning, Serigos 2016 on concepts and semantic specificity, Stefanowitsch 2002 on entrenchment and bilingual punning, and see further examples such as Kecskes 2006; Schmid et al. 2008; Knospe 2016). In the next section, we distil the main objectives that unite these different approaches.

2 Usage, meaning and the mind at the core of contact-induced variation and change

As was noted above, the usage-based hypothesis (viz. the assumption that the mental representation of language structure is derived from the cognitive processing of language use) forms the cornerstone of the *Cognitive Contact Linguistics* approach we would like to propose, which entails that we first and foremost study language use: how speakers rely on language to express their subjective experience of the world, how each such attempt adds to the meaning of a specific unit of language in the speaker's mind and how this meaning lies at the core of how we categorize the units of language in our mental lexicon. These central notions of Cognitive Linguistics hold in a bi- and multilingual environment as well as in a monolingual environment, yet the precise interaction between use, meaning and mind in settings with more than one language presents specific opportunities for our understanding of mental categorization. Below, we present the precise objectives we can as such derive for *Cognitive Contact Linguistics*.

First, if we claim that categorization of linguistic units is usage-based in bi-/multilingual speakers, then we have to determine how varying degrees and types of language contact interact with that categorization: albeit usage-based, "language refers to concepts in the mind of the speaker rather than to objects in the external world" (Evans and Green 2006: 158). As categorization changes through specific usage instances, these mental categories are characterized by flexibility and fuzziness, which manifests itself in prototypicality effects, varying degrees of salience and in the – perhaps in itself somewhat fuzzy – notion of entrenchment (Geeraerts 1997). These phenomena can advance theories in language contact, e.g. explaining which units are borrowed and what type of contact-induced change does or does not occur. It has for instance been argued that variation in the borrowability of linguistic units (viz. the likelihood of an item in language A being borrowed in language B; e.g. Haspelmath 2009) is dependent on the degree of salience (see Backus 1996, 2001; compare Winter-Froemel, this volume) and entrenchment (see Zenner, Speelman, and Geeraerts 2014) of the concept it expresses. These first studies need to be expanded on, if we aim to fully **understand the interaction between mental categorization and contact-induced variation and change**, which is the first objective of Cognitive Contact Linguistics.

If we claim that mental categorization is influenced by contact (and vice versa), then it follows that the conceptual system *eo ipso* becomes a locus of contact (compare Finzel and Wolf, this volume). Our second objective is then to **study contact-induced variation and change below the surface of the linguistic sign**, which can primarily be attested in the way language users blend concepts. Ample evidence has been put forward in Cognitive Linguistics supporting the idea that the human mind constantly makes associations between concepts: meanings and categories interact, with elements of certain concepts and domains being mapped onto and experienced through others. Most notably, such mappings have been studied in Conceptual Metaphor Theory (viz. patterns of "understanding and experiencing one kind of thing in terms of another"; Lakoff and Johnson 1980: 5), in research on metonymy (e.g. Barcelona 2000; Koch 2001), and in research on conceptual blending (Coulson 2006). In addition, recent research on semantic changes that involve a taxonomic reorganization has contributed to our understanding of conceptual hierarchies in the mental lexicon (e.g. Mihatsch 2006; see also Winter-Froemel, this volume). The structure of the mental lexicon in bi- and multilinguals is still a matter of debate, with a lack of clarity on the way languages and lects combine in the mental repertoire (see Kroll and Stewart 1994, Grosjean 2001, Verspoor, de Bot, and Lowie 2011, and Onysko, this volume for a more extensive discussion).

When studying mappings between source and target domains, researchers typically opt for semasiological perspectives (Finzel and Wolf, this volume), rather than onomasiological approaches (Lucek, this volume). The perspectives are, however, two sides of the same coin in the study of meaning. Semasiological approaches take the linguistic sign as point of departure, and study its different meanings and how these are related (the Dutch word *bank*, for instance, refers to (1) a financial institution, English 'bank'; and (2) a piece of furniture, English 'couch'). In onomasiology, the focus is on naming instead of meaning:

the possible lexicalizations for a particular concept are charted (the piece of furniture can in Dutch be lexicalized by *bank, sofa* or *zetel*), as well as how social and stylistic factors, e.g. perspectivization and construal, drive the choice for particular lexical items (see Geeraerts 2010 for a lengthier discussion). As Cognitive Linguistics primarily focuses on how language users *categorize* linguistic units through *meaning*, these semasiological and onomasiological perspectives should be combined in any analysis of variation and change (compare Winter-Froemel 2014). Specifically in contact settings, complementing the traditional semasiological analyses with an onomasiological perspective can be of much use. For instance, as is argued by Onysko and Winter-Froemel (2011) and Zenner, Speelman, and Geeraerts (2012), the inclusion of onomasiological analyses moves the study of lexical borrowing away from lexical items to concepts: instead of only patterning the use of (new) source language material (the English loanword *jeans* in Dutch), possible receptor language alternatives (Dutch *spijkerbroek*) are also included. This allows researchers to arrive at a more thorough theoretical, methodological, and – hence – a more inclusive empirical description of borrowability. In this perspective, for example, objective grounds for the traditional distinction between *luxury* loans and *necessary* loans can be identified based on the number of lexicalizations found for a concept, and the onomasiological success rate for loanwords provides an additional tool for analyses of lexical borrowings (see Zenner, Speelman, and Geeraerts 2012). As third objective we thus put forward is that we aim to **adhere to the combination of semasiological and onomasiological perspectives in the description of contact phenomena.**

This third objective does not only hold for lexical borrowing, but also applies to other, more schematic contact phenomena. As mentioned above, in Cognitive Linguistic theories the basic function of language is to convey meaning, and since words and patterns both contribute meaning, this makes a strict dividing line between lexicon and syntax problematic. The linguistic units language users have recourse to in order to convey meaning are of varying degrees of complexity, and can be placed on a continuum from less to more schematic (see Langacker's 1987 Cognitive Grammar, Goldberg's 1995 Construction Grammar, Croft's 2001 Radical Construction Grammar; for an overview of the similarities and differences between these approaches, see Langacker 2005). Our fourth objective is to rely on the central notions of Construction Grammar to **pursue a unified framework of matter and pattern replication.** Construction Grammar assumes a continuum from the lexical pole of highly specific and conventionalized lexical items (e.g. single content words such as *computer* or completely fixed idioms such as *as good as it gets*) to the syntactic pole of highly schematic patterns based on grammatical roles and word order (e.g. *I called you* instantiates the pattern [S V O], though for any individual speaker the actual sequence *I called you* may be entrenched as a fully specific multiword lexical unit). In between are partially schematic units which have both fixed lexicalized items and open slots that can be filled with a variety of items, ranging from lowly schematic phraseological sequences (such as [*pimp my* N] for *pimp my ride*, *pimp my grandma*) to highly schematic phraseological sequences (such as the V_{intr} POSS $N_{inalienable}$ *off*-construction for *work my butt off*). This approach accommodates both matter and pattern replication: where the former concerns the borrowing of linguistic signs and can hence be placed on the specific (or 'lexical') side of the lexicon/syntax-continuum, the latter concerns the replication of linguistic structures and can thus be placed on the schematic side of the continuum (see Matras and Sakel 2009; Heine and Kuteva 2005). A number of studies have revealed that contact-induced variation and change may manifest themselves through a combination of matter and pattern replication (see e.g. Doğruöz and Backus 2009; Colleman 2016), showing the need for a comprehensive framework. A recent attempt is found in Höder's Diasystematic Construction Grammar (2014), which rests on the assumption that language users have both language-specific and general constructions in their minds. Bi- and multilingual language users are claimed to have a repository of language-specific constructions for each of the codes they master, but also, driven by the innate human need to categorize elements that are similar as forming a category, more schematic constructions that are shared across these codes. More research is however still needed to grasp the cognitive and social triggers for specific lexicalizations in concrete utterances.

Categories exist in people's minds, but we should not forget that "language clearly does exist only by virtue of being used in social interaction between people" (Backus 2014: 97). Any usage-based account of contact-induced variation and change can hence not restrict its attention to psycholinguistic processes in bi- and multilinguals, but should also consider the interactional dimension of communication as well as socio-lectal variation (see Geeraerts 2016). Focusing on acts of communication as acts of speaker-hearer interaction means that linguistic analyses need to take into account both the speaker and hearer and the interactional dynamics of communication (see Winter-Froemel 2011). This defines another main aim of *Cognitive Contact Linguistics* i.e. to provide a framework that allows us **to include the perspectives of the speaker and hearer, the interaction between the codes they have in their respective repertoire, and (ensuing) issues related to the encoding and decoding of messages.**

In social interaction, language varieties and individual language features as such acquire their social meanings. This social meaning ties in with the way we use and store these varieties and variants, which leads to our sixth objective: **to**

incorporate an analysis of the social meaning of contact phenomena when studying their mental representation. Besides the broader framework of Cognitive Sociolinguistics (cf. supra), two specific models in Cognitive Linguistics can help us attain this objective. First, D'Andrade (1987: 112) provides us with a model for the conceptual organization of cultural models, which are "cognitive schemas that are intersubjectively shared by a social group". When one such social group uses different languages, or when different social groups use the same language, the question arises whether the groups' cultural models differ and how these differences can be described. Polzenhagen and Dirven (2008) for instance present a comprehensive overview of the different meanings surrounding the debate on Global English, drawing from the conceptual metaphors LANGUAGE AS A TOOL and LANGUAGE AS AN IDENTITY MARKER (see also Geeraerts 2003, and De Pascale, Marzo, and Speelman, this volume). Second, several models of categorization have been put forward that rely on prototype theory. Although the crucial role of culture in prototype formation has been acknowledged in psychological categorization studies from the very beginning (see Polzenhagen and Xia 2015), linguistic approaches to prototypical categorization have only recently awarded special attention to socio-lectal and contact-related phenomena. Pustka (2009) for instance describes how Southern French is characterized by more and less (proto)typical linguistic variants, visualizing the difference in salience of the categories through radial structures. More work however remains to be done if we want to arrive at the Cognitive Sociolinguistic description of lectal and contact-induced variation described by Polzenhagen and Xia (2015: 262), which rests on the premise that the association of linguistic variants with socio-cultural stereotypes is in essence a metonymic link between two types of prototypes: prototypical allophones (variants that characterize an accent) and social prototypes (see Marzo, Zenner, and Van de Mieroop, this volume).

Obtaining this description of the socio-cognitive reality rests on a solid empirical methodology that allows us to study precisely how categories are constructed through meaning in use. The constant interaction between the mental representation of a category in the individual mind and the conventionalization of meaning at the level of the speech community (see Backus 2014) provides a challenging and volatile object of study. *Cognitive Contact Linguistics* therefore equally aims **to bring together synchronically oriented and diachronically oriented research.** When studying diachronic processes of language contact leading to language change, it is important to bear in mind that language change ultimately goes back to individual instances of language use (as emphasized among others by Croft 2000; see also Winter-Froemel 2011). At the same time, the speakers' individual linguistic behavior is also guided by the existing linguistic convention, and when studying individual contact phenomena in language use, the aim frequently consists in identifying general patterns and potential pathways of diachronic evolution, so that synchronic and diachronic approaches complement and mutually enrich each other. The diachronic focus of analysis also opens up links to previous research on other domains of language change such as semantic change, morphosyntactic change, lexical change, or grammaticalization processes, and permits us to integrate contact linguistic perspectives into these approaches and to contribute to a better understanding of the importance of contact phenomena in different domains of language change.

Our final objective is to **attempt to overcome the methodological issues presented in Cognitive Contact Linguistics, in the tension between use and corpus size, by exploring mixed methods**: designs from different domains of previous research, e.g. lexicology, psycholinguistic studies and sociolinguistic studies need to be combined to fully grasp how contact-induced variation and change occurs and consolidates. Needless to say, none of these approaches are self-evident in contact settings. Where Cognitive Linguistics is gradually making the shift towards large-scale usage-based accounts (see Janda 2013), contact linguistics runs up against barriers of data collection. Collecting large corpora of spoken language use is expensive and in the case of contact varieties it is unlikely that funding will easily be forthcoming for the construction of corpora big enough and representative enough to be suitable to the sophisticated quantitative analyses that are being pioneered in Cognitive Linguistics. Contact varieties lack the social and political significance to make such investments attractive other than for scientific reasons. However, given the ever evolving techniques of corpus analysis to deal with relatively small corpora and the possibilities for data triangulation when several methods are combined, there is undoubtedly much territory left to chart. Nevertheless, there will always remain problems related to a lack of available data for specific analyses (e.g. for diachronic studies), and *Cognitive Contact Linguistics* should therefore also include a thorough and continuous reflection about its proper limits, possible theoretical biases and methodological challenges, and ways to adequately deal with them.

3 Outline of the volume

The ten chapters brought together in this volume illustrate how the objectives described above can be pursued, and as such help advance our understanding of both contact-induced variation and change and of the nature of linguistic competence in general. The papers combine several of the principles outlined above to various contact settings. They rely on a range of empirical methods, but are all united in embracing the usage-based approach. This "family resemblance" between the chapters means that the structure we chose for our volume is up for debate: the classification of papers in sections is a convenient one, but there are many connections and links between the chapters.

3.1 Conceptual foundations and categorization principles in contact-induced change

The first four papers in this volume aim to uncover general conceptual foundations underlying language contact, zooming in on the way categorization principles that have been described in Cognitive Linguistic research apply to contact phenomena. The first two of these chapters ambitiously attempt to provide the reader with an all-encompassing usage-based model of contact. In "Reconceptualizing language contact phenomena as cognitive processes", **Alexander Onysko** addresses the question whether and how processes of language contact are cognitively motivated. Describing four typical and broadly studied outcomes of contact (viz. borrowing, codeswitching, transfer / interference and replication), Onysko marries contact-linguistic research on these phenomena with insights from psycholinguistic studies on multilingual cognition by relying on the usage-based conception of language as a mental network.

Anna Verschik's paper "English-Estonian code-copying in blogs: Combining a contact linguistic and cognitive approach" likewise presents a general model for Cognitive Contact Linguistics, which in her case starts off from Lars Johanson's code-copying framework (2002), a holistic framework that employs the same meta-language for lexical and syntactic contact phenomena. Using data from blogs, Verschik firstly summarizes the six main principles that guide her approach, principles reminiscent of the guidelines for *Cognitive Contact Linguistics* we suggested above. These are then applied to Johanson's framework, illustrating its compatibility with a Cognitive Linguistic framework. Finally, Verschik's resulting model is applied to twenty fashion, beauty and life-style blogs (> 90,000 words) through a qualitative analysis of specific instances of code-copying from English in Estonian.

These two broad approaches that are aimed at outlining the cognitive foundations of the bi- and multilingual mind are followed by two chapters that adopt a more narrow focus on specific contact phenomena. At the same time, the two papers share Verschik's and Onysko's objective to address them from the perspective of mental categorization. Particularly, "Reanalysis in language contact: Perceptive ambiguity, salience, and catachrestic reinterpretation" presents us with a usage-based semiotic model to contact-induced semantic and morphological change. Through a reanalysis of 500 lexical items imported from English into Italian as documented in the etymological dictionary *Dizionario Etimologico della Lingua Italiana*, **Esme Winter-Froemel** focuses on the differences observed between source language (English) and receptor language (Italian) in spelling, semantics and morphology. Acknowledging the limits of her lexicographical approach, Winter-Froemel further foregrounds the need of a usage-based analysis. The paper proposes a semiotic model of semantic reanalysis that could serve as a launching pad for methodological innovation in this time-honored tradition.

The final paper in this section, "When sociolinguistics and prototype analysis meet: The social meaning of sibilant palatalization in a Flemish Urban Vernacular", focuses on sound change in *Citétaal*, a contact variety of Dutch spoken in the Belgian province of Limburg. **Stefania Marzo, Eline Zenner and Dorien Van de Mieroop** present a mixed-method approach to the factors steering *s*-palatalization in the interactions of Limburgian youngsters with and without migration backgrounds. After presenting the results of both variationist and interactional analyses of 20 hours of self-recorded data, the authors zoom in on the mental representation of the factors that steer *s*-palatalization. More particularly, the benefits and drawbacks of a prototype theoretical perspective on the social meaning of the contact phenomenon are discussed.

3.2 Associating concepts: Metaphors and cultural models in contact

As was described above, one of the central areas of research in Cognitive Linguistics concerns the interaction between mental categories. In this section, three papers draw attention to conceptual mappings in contact. The first two rely on Lakoff and Johnson's (1980) Conceptual Metaphor Theory, and consider contact-induced variation and change in conceptualization. The third paper scales up from the individual to the community, applying cultural models (Holland and Quinn 1987) to dialect leveling and standardization.

In "Notions of CONTAINMENT and SUPPORT in Irish English: Implications of language contact on the cognition of space", **Stephen Lucek** studies the conceptualization of the relationship between a structure and the road where that structure is located. Through semi-structured sociolinguistic interviews and questionnaires with 20 Irish English speakers, Lucek reveals variation in Irish English between the road providing a surface for the structure (e.g. "on the road") and the road containing the structure (e.g. "in the road"). Analyzing the data through Conceptual Metaphor Theory, drawing on source domains such as CONTAINERS and SURFACES, Lucek reveals variation that can be linked to contact between Irish and Irish English.

In "Conceptual metaphors as contact phenomena? The influence of local concepts on source and target domain", **Anna Finzel and Hans-Georg Wolf** present the results of an association study, in which the mental associations of British English, Indian English and Nigerian English speakers with the English words *witch*, *woman* and *homosexuality* are compared, as such adopting a semasiological perspective. Through survey data, the authors reveal how speakers from the same speech community to a large degree share associations. Linking their insights to the emerging field of Cultural Linguistics, Finzel and Wolf discuss how local cultural models influence the construal of concepts and reality in varieties of English.

In the final paper of this section, "Cultural models in contact: Revealing attitudes toward regional varieties of Italien with Vector Space Models", **Stefano De Pascale, Stefania Marzo and Dirk Speelman** incorporate state-of-the-art techniques from natural language processing and corpus linguistics to derive cultural models (located at the level of the community) from free response surveys in which speech samples of different varieties of Italian were evaluated by 213 speakers of Italian. Specifically, vector space models are used to automatically cluster the evaluative responses into semantic fields, which helps the authors arrive at empirically driven claims about how Italians attribute social meaning to the variation they perceive in their linguistic environment.

3.3 Construction grammar: Contact in and through more and less schematic form-meaning pairs

Central to Cognitive Linguistics is the conviction that language is an assembly of form-meaning combinations. As described above, the primacy of meaning entails a non-modular approach to language, in which the traditional partitioning of language in lexicon and syntax no longer holds. In turn, the Construction Grammar equivalent of syntax is the inventory of conventionalized non-compositional, mostly schematic units, called 'constructions'. These constructions include traditional syntactic patterns as well as 'partially schematic units', which are constructions built around particular lexical or morphological elements. Constructions have proven to be a useful empirical focus for addressing several issues surrounding contact-induced variation and change (see e.g. Doğruöz and

Backus 2009; Boas and Höder, under review), as is illustrated by the final three papers in this volume.

First, in "Language alternation and the state-event contrast: A case-study of Dutch-Turkish and Dutch-Moroccan heritage speakers", **Bram Vertommen** works on the construction grammatical notion of conceptual scenes ("conventionalized mental scripts designed to categorize and structure thoughts according to the subtype of experiences or generalizations they pertain", Vertommen, this volume, and see Goldberg 1995; Langacker 2008) to explain the link between variation in code choice and different argument structures. After a succinct overview of research on conceptual scenes, Vertommen presents his analysis of code choice between Dutch and Turkish, and Dutch and Moroccan Arabic, respectively, for three conceptual scenes (association, occurrence, and directionality), and the degree to which their realization correlates with patterns of alternational codeswitching. Based on the argument structures in four corpora representative of two heritage communities in the Netherlands he reveals a clear link between code choice and conceptual scene: overall, Dutch is preferred for the verbalization of general states and Turkish or Moroccan Arabic for events. Why Dutch is tied to general states is a question difficult to answer, and Vertommen discusses several avenues for future research to tackle this issue.

The second paper in this set also studies code-switching from a construction grammatical perspective, empirically focusing on bilingual language acquisition. In "Partially schematic constructions as engines of development: Evidence from German-English bilingual acquisition", **Antje Quick, Ad Backus and Elena Lieven** present codeswitching data from a German-English bilingual child who was growing up in Germany with a German mother and an English-speaking father. Using the Traceback Method familiar from work on monolingual child language acquisition, they show that much of the child's output builds on words, word combinations and constructional frames that were already part of the child's grammar at earlier points in his development. While this has been shown by much previous work as well, Quick, Backus and Lieven trace the development of codeswitching patterns in the child's output to developments in his linguistic environment, which is interesting since the parents do not codeswitch. This means that the child's language mixing provides a window on where creativity resides in language use. On the strength of the evidence in the paper, linguistic creativity largely seems to hinge on the use of partially schematic constructions, which can be characterized as a layer of linguistic organization in between lexicon and syntax.

While Quick, Backus and Lieven study constructions in contact as they are being acquired, **Dirk Noël and Timothy Colleman** introduce a diachronic perspective. "Constructional renovation: The role of French legal language in the survival of the nominative-and-infinitive in Dutch" focuses on rather subtle effects of contact on the evolution of a construction. Based on a corpus extracted from the Delpher digital text archive, Noël and Colleman revisit the 19th- and 20th-century history of *geacht worden te* and *verondersteld worden te* (both meaning 'to be supposed to'). Specifically, they debate the role of French influence in the diachronic trajectories of these instantiations of the so-called 'nominative-and-infinitive' construction.

4 Summing up: Towards a *Cognitive Contact Linguistics*

Taken together, the ten papers in this volume serve as prime examples of the promising insights to be gained when combining Cognitive Linguistics with the context-oriented study of contact-induced variation and change. Each research tradition brings crucial ingredients that, when combined, have the potential to advance linguistics. Cognitive Linguistics brings the usage-based approach and its associated theoretical and methodological innovations. This includes an empirical focus on meaning and conceptualization, a tight integration of the synchronic and diachronic planes, an emphasis on usage data, and a mixed-method approach to data collection. The emphasis on usage data it shares with the tradition in contact linguistics, which further brings empirical richness on variation and change and the need to reflect on what language is. A focus on usage automatically implies a focus on the speaker rather than the language, on the social factors that affect how one uses language, and on the demands and affordances of concrete communicative settings. Combining the study of the individual mind with the study of shared context, bridging research on experience and perspective with research on variation and change, and tackling the methodological complexities that this empirical approach to mental categorization entails, will help us determine how the meaningful units that make up language are categorized and structured in the bi- and multilingual mind and, by extension, in any human mind. To achieve this ambitious goal, more research that combines insights from the two perspectives is needed: we hope the current volume will inspire future research exploring the possibilities of the cross-fertilization of two fields we have labelled *Cognitive Contact Linguistics*.

References

Backus, Ad. 1996. *Two in one. Bilingual speech of Turkish immigrants in The Netherlands*. Tilburg: Tilburg University Press.
Backus, Ad. 2001. The role of semantic specificity in insertional codeswitching: Evidence from Dutch Turkish. In Rodolfo Jacobson (ed.), *Codeswitching Worldwide II*, 125–154. Berlin: Mouton De Gruyter.
Backus, Ad. 2014. Towards a usage-based account of language change: implications of contact linguistics for linguistic theory. In Robert Nicolaï (ed.), *Questioning Language Contact: Limits of Contact, Contact at its Limits*, 91–118. Leiden & Boston: Brill.
Barcelona, Antonio. 2000. *Metaphor and Metonymy at the Crossroads*. Berlin: Mouton De Gruyter.
Bloomfield, Leonard. 1933. *Language*. London: George Allen & Unwin Ltd.
Boas, Hans C., Ryan Dux & Alexander Ziem. 2016. Frames and constructions in an online learner's dictionary of German. In Sabine De Knop & Gaetanelle Guilquin (eds.), *Applied Construction Grammar*, 303–326. Berlin & Boston: De Gruyter.
Boas, Hans C. & Steffen Höder (eds.) Under review. *Constructions in Contact*. Amsterdam & Philadelphia: John Benjamins.
Boers, Frank & Helene Stengers. 2008. A quantitative comparison of the English and Spanish repertoire of figurative idioms. In Frank Boers & Seth Lindstromberg (eds.), *Cognitive Linguistic Approaches to Teaching Vocabulary and Phraseology*, 355–374. Berlin & New York: Mouton De Gruyter.
Callies, Marcus & Alexander Onysko (eds.). 2017. *Metaphor Variation in Englishes Around the World*. Special issue of *Cognitive Linguistic Studies* 4(1). 1–158.
Chomsky, Noam. 1965. *Aspects of the Theory of Syntax*. Cambridge (MA): MIT Press.
Colleman, Timothy. 2016. A reflection on constructionalization and constructional borrowing, inspired by an emerging Dutch replica of the 'time'-away construction. *Belgian Journal of Linguistics* 30(1). 91–113.
Coulson, Seana. 2006. *Semantic Leaps. Frame-Shifting and Conceptual Blending in Meaning Construction*. Cambridge (MA): Cambridge University Press.
Croft, William. 2000. *Explaining Language Change: An Evolutionary Approach*. Harlow: Pearson Education.
Croft, William. 2001. *Radical Construction Grammar: Syntactic Theory in Typological Perspective*. Oxford: Oxford University Press.
Croft, William. 2009. Toward a social Cognitive Linguistics. In Vyvyan Evans & Stéphanie Pourcel (eds.), *New Directions in Cognitive Linguistics*, 395–420. Amsterdam & Philadelphia: John Benjamins.
D'Andrade, Roy G. 1987. A folk model of the mind. In Dorothy C. Holland & Naomi Quinn (eds.), *Cultural Models in Language and Thought*, 35–53. New York: Cambridge University Press.
Darquennes, Jeroen, Joe Salmons & Wim Vandenbussche (eds.). Forthcoming. *Language Contact*. Vol. 1. Berlin: De Gruyter.
Dirven, René. 2005. Major strands in Cognitive Linguistics. In Fransisco Ruiz de Mendoza Ibáñez & M. Sandra Peña Cervel (eds.), *Cognitive Linguistics: Internal Dynamics and Interdisciplinary Interaction*, 17–68. Berlin & New York: Mouton De Gruyter.
Doğruöz, Seza & Ad Backus. 2009. Innovative constructions in Dutch Turkish: an assessment of ongoing contact-induced change. *Bilingualism: Language and Cognition* 12(1). 41–63.

Evans, Vyvyan, Benjamin Bergen & Jörg Zinken. 2007. *The Cognitive Linguistics Reader*. London & Oakville: Equinox.
Evans, Vyvyan & Melanie Green. 2006. *Cognitive Linguistics. An Introduction*. Edinburgh: Edinburgh University Press.
Foucault, Michel. 1980. Questions of method. In James. D. Faubion (ed.), *Michel Foucault: Power*, 223–238. New York: The New Press.
Geeraerts, Dirk. 1997. *Diachronic Prototype Semantics: A Contribution to Historical Lexicology*. Oxford: Clarendon.
Geeraerts, Dirk. 2003. Cultural models and linguistic standardization. In René Dirven, Frank Roslyn & Martin Pütz (eds.), *Cognitive Models in Language and Thought. Ideology, Metaphors and Meanings*, 25–68. Berlin & New York: Mouton De Gruyter.
Geeraerts, Dirk. 2006. *Cognitive Linguistics: Basic Readings*. Berlin & New York: Mouton De Gruyter.
Geeraerts, Dirk. 2010. *Theories of Lexical Semantics*. Oxford: Oxford University Press.
Geeraerts, Dirk. 2016. The sociosemiotic commitment. *Cognitive Linguistics* 27(4). 527–542.
Geeraerts, Dirk & Hubert Cuyckens. 2007a. *The Oxford Handbook of Cognitive Linguistics*. Oxford: Oxford University Press.
Geeraerts, Dirk & Hubert Cuyckens. 2007b. Introducing Cognitive Linguistics. In Dirk Geeraerts & Hubert Cuyckens (eds.), *The Oxford Handbook of Cognitive Linguistics*, 1–24. Oxford: Oxford University Press.
Geeraerts, Dirk, Stefan Grondelaers & Peter Bakema. 1994. *The Structure of Lexical Variation. Meaning, Naming, and Context*. Berlin & New York: Mouton De Gruyter.
Geeraerts, Dirk, Gitte Kristiansen & Yves Peirsman. 2010. *Advances in Cognitive Sociolinguistics*. Berlin & New York: Mouton De Gruyter.
Goldberg, Adele E. 1995. *Constructions: A Construction Grammar Approach to Argument Structure*. Chicago: Chicago University Press.
Grosjean, François. 2001. The bilinguals's language modes. In Janet L. Nicol (ed.), *One Mind, Two Languages: Bilingual Language Processing*, 1–22. Oxford: Blackwell.
Gumperz, John J. 1982. *Discourse Strategies*. Cambridge (MA): Cambridge University Press.
Haspelmath, Martin. 2009. Lexical borrowing. Concepts and issues. In Martin Haspelmath & Uri Tadmor (eds.), *Loanwords in the World's Languages: A Comparative Handbook*, 35–54. Berlin & New York: Mouton De Gruyter.
Heine, Bernd & Tania Kuteva. 2005. *Language Contact and Grammatical Change*. Cambridge (MA): Cambridge University Press.
Hickey, Raymond. 2010. *The Handbook of Language Contact*. Chichester: Wiley-Blackwell.
Höder, Steffen. 2014. Phonological elements and Diasystematic Construction Grammar. *Constructions and Frames* 6(2). 202–231.
Holland, Dorothy & Naomi Quinn (eds.). 1987. *Cultural Models in Language and Thought*. Cambridge: Cambridge University Press.
Janda, Laura A. 2013. *Cognitive Linguistics – The Quantitative Turn: The Essential Reader*. Berlin & Boston: Mouton De Gruyter.
Johanson, Lars. 2002. Contact-induced change in a code-copying framework. In Mari C. Jones & Edith Esch (eds.), *Language change. The Interplay of Internal, External and Extra-Linguistics Factors*, 286–313. Berlin & New York: Mouton De Gruyter.
Kecskes, Istvan. 2006. The dual language model to explain code-switching: A cognitive-pragmatic approach. *Intercultural Pragmatics* 3(3). 257–283.

Knospe, Sebastian. 2016. Through the Cognitive looking glass: Studying bilingual wordplay in public signage. In Sebastian Knospe, Alexander Onysko & Maik Goth (eds.), *Crossing Languages to Play with Words: Multidisciplinary Perspectives*, 195–230. Berlin & Boston: De Gruyter.

Koch, Peter. 2001. Metonymy: Unity in diversity. *Journal of Historical Pragmatics* 2(2). 201–244.

Kristiansen, Gitte & René Dirven. 2008. *Cognitive Sociolinguistics: Language variation, Cultural Models, Social Systems*. Berlin & New York: Mouton De Gruyter.

Kroll, Judith F. & Erika Stewart. 1994. Category interference in translation and picture naming: Evidence for asymmetric connections between bilingual memory representations. *Journal of Memory and Language* 33. 149–174.

Labov, William. 1970. The study of language in its social context. *Studium Generale* 23. 30–87.

Lakoff, George & Mark Johnson. 1980. *Metaphors we Live by*. Chicago: University of Chicago Press.

Langacker, Ronald W. 1987. *Foundations of Cognitive Grammar, Vol.I: Theoretical Prerequisites*. Stanford (CA): Stanford University Press.

Langacker, Ronald W. 2005. Construction Grammars: Cognitive, radical, and less so. In Fransisco Ruiz de Mendoza Ibáñez & M. Sandra Peña Cervel (eds.), *Cognitive Linguistics: Internal Dynamics and Interdisciplinary Interaction*, 101–159. Berlin & New York: Mouton De Gruyter.

Langacker, Ronald W. 2008. *Cognitive Grammar. A Basic Introduction*. Oxford: Oxford University Press.

Libben, Maya, Mira Goral & Gary Libben (eds.). 2018. *Bilingualism. A Framework for Understanding the Mental Lexicon*. Amsterdam & Philadelphia: John Benjamins.

MacSwan, Jeff. 2012. Generative approaches to code-switching. In Barbara E. Bullock & Almeida Jacqueline Toribio (eds.), *Linguistic code-switching*, 309–335. Cambridge (MA): Cambridge University Press.

Matras, Yaron. 2009. *Language contact*. Cambridge: Cambridge University Press.

Matras, Yaron & Jeanette Sakel (eds.). 2009. *Grammatical Borrowing in Cross-Linguistic Perspective*. Berlin: Mouton De Gruyter.

Mihatsch, Wiltrud. 2006. *Kognitive Grundlagen lexikalischer Hierarchien untersucht am Beispiel des Französischen und Spanischen* (Linguistische Arbeiten 506). Tübingen: Niemeyer.

Muysken, Pieter. 2000. *Bilingual speech: A typology of code-mixing*. Cambridge (MA): Cambridge University Press.

Myers-Scotton, Carol. 2002. *Contact linguistics: Bilingual encounters and grammatical outcomes*. Oxford: Oxford University Press.

Onysko, Alexander & Esme Winter-Froemel. 2011. Necessary loans – luxury loans? Exploring the pragmatic dimension of borrowing. *Journal of Pragmatics* 43(6). 1550–1567.

Polzenhagen, Frank & René Dirven. 2008. Rationalist or romantic model in globalisation. In Gitte Kristiansen & René Dirven (eds.), *Cognitive Sociolinguistics. Language variation, cultural models, social systems*, 237–299. Berlin & New York: Mouton De Gruyter.

Polzenhagen, Frans & Xiaoyan Xia. 2015. Language, culture and prototypicality. In Farzad Sharifian (ed.), *Routledge Handbook of Language and Culture*, 253–269. New York: Routledge.

Poplack, Shana & Marjory Meechan. 1998. How languages fit together in code-mixing. *International Journal of Bilingualism* 2(2). 127–138.

Poplack, Shana, David Sankoff & Chris Miller. 1988. The social correlates and linguistic processes of lexical borrowing and assimilation. *Linguistics* 26. 47–104.

Pustka, Elissa. 2009. A prototype-theoretical model of Southern French. In Kate Beeching, Nigel Armstrong & Françoise Gadet (eds.), *Sociolinguistic Variation in Contemporary French*, 77–94. Amsterdam & Philadelphia: John Benjamins.

Ruiz de Mendoza Ibáñez, Fransisco & M. Sandra Peña Cervel. 2005. *Cognitive Linguistics: Internal Dynamics and Interdisciplinary Interaction*. Berlin & New York: Mouton De Gruyter.

Sapir, Edward. 1921. *Language: An Introduction to the Study of Speech*. New York: Harcourt, Brace and company.

Schmid, Hans-Jörg, Dymitr Ibriszimov, Karina Kopatsch & Peter Gottschligg. 2008. Conceptual blending in language, cognition, and culture. Towards a methodology for the linguistic study of syncretic concepts. In Afeosemime Unuose Adogame, Magnus Echtler & Ulf Vierke (eds.), *Unpacking the New: Critical Perspectives on Cultural Syncretization in Africa and Beyond*, 93–124. Zürich & Berlin: LIT.

Serigos, Jacqueline. 2016. Using distributional semantics in loanword research: A concept-based approach to quantifying semantic specificity of Anglicisms in Spanish. *International Journal of Bilingualism* 21(5). 521–540.

Stefanowitsch, Anatol. 2002. *Nice to miet you*: Bilingual puns and the status of English in Germany. *Intercultural Communication Studies* 11(4). 67–84.

Thomason, Sarah Grey. 2001. *Language Contact*. Edinburgh: Edinburgh University Press.

Tomasello, Michael. 2003. *Constructing a Language: A Usage-Based Theory of Language Acquisition*. Cambridge: Harvard University Press.

Ungerer, Friedrich & Hans-Jörg Schmid. 2006. *An Introduction to Cognitive Linguistics*. Harlow (UK): Pearson Longman.

Ureña Gómez Moreno, J.M. & Buendía Castro, M. 2017. Semantic and conceptual aspects of volcano verb collocates within the natural disaster domain: A frame-based terminology approach. In Marcin Grygiel (ed.), *Cognitive Approaches to Specialist Languages*, 330–350. Newcastle-upon Tyne: Cambridge Scholars Publishing.

Vaid, Jyotsna & Renata F.I. Meuter. 2018. Languages without borders: Reframing the study of the bilingual mental lexicon. In Maya Libben, Mira Goral & Gary Libben (eds.), *Bilingualism. A Framework for Understanding the Mental Lexicon*, 7–26. Amsterdam & Philadelphia: John Benjamins.

van Coetsem, Frans. 1988. *Loan Phonology and the Two Transfer Types in Language Contact*. Dordrecht: Foris.

Verspoor, Marolijn H., Kees de Bot & Wander Lowie. 2011 (29th edn). *A Dynamic Approach to Second Language Development. Methods and Techniques*. Amsterdam & Philadelphia: John Benjamins.

Weinreich, Uriel. 1970. *Languages in Contact*. The Hague & Paris: Mouton De Gruyter.

Weinreich, Uriel, William Labov & Marvin Herzog. 1968. Empirical foundations for a theory of language change. In Winfried P. Lehmann & Yakov Malkiel (eds), *Directions for Historical Linguistics: A Symposium*, 95–195. Austin: University of Texas Press.

Winter-Froemel, Esme. 2011. *Entlehnung in der Kommunikation und im Sprachwandel: Theorie und Analysen zum Französischen*. Berlin: De Gruyter.

Winter-Froemel, Esme. 2014. Formal variance and semantic changes in borrowing: Integrating semasiology and onomasiology. In Eline Zenner & Gitte Kristiansen (eds.), *New perspectives on lexical borrowing*, 65–100. Berlin & Boston: De Gruyter Mouton.

Wolf, Hans-Georg & Frank Polzenhagen. 2009. *World Englishes. A Cognitive Sociolinguistic approach*. Berlin & New York: Mouton De Gruyter.

Zenner Eline, Dirk Speelman & Dirk Geeraerts. 2012. Cognitive Sociolinguistics meets loanword research: Measuring variation in the success of anglicisms in Dutch. *Cognitive Linguistics* 23(4). 749–792.

Zenner Eline, Dirk Speelman & Dirk Geeraerts. 2014. Core vocabulary, borrowability, and entrenchment: A usage-based onomasiological approach. *Diachronica* 31(1). 74–105.

Part I: **Conceptual foundations and categorization principles in contact-induced change**

Alexander Onysko
1 Reconceptualizing language contact phenomena as cognitive processes

Abstract: This paper explores the possibility of reframing, from a cognitive linguistic perspective, long-standing notions that describe processes of language contact. A usage-based view of language is adopted to recast the definitions of borrowing, codeswitching, transfer, and calquing and to model their relationship to each other. First, a review of important research in contact linguistics and multilingualism provides insight into the most widespread terminological categories used in the field. This is supported by evidence from multilingual cognition, which is discussed on the background of understanding language as emerging from neuronal activation in a mental network. The merging of traditional categories in contact linguistics and their cognitive grounding leads to a new conception of language contact phenomena that is consonant with a cognitive linguistic approach to language.

Keywords: borrowing, codeswitching, transfer, calquing, language mode, multilingual cognition, cognitive language contact model

1 Introduction

> In speech, interference is like sand carried by a stream; in language it is the sedimented sand deposited on the bottom of a lake. [...] In speech, it occurs anew in the utterances of the bilingual speaker as a result of his personal knowledge of the other tongue. In language, we find interference phenomena which, having frequently occurred in the speech of bilinguals, have become habitualized and established. Their use is no longer dependent on bilingualism. (Weinreich 1953: 11)

Studies by Haugen (e.g. 1950) and Weinreich's (1953) concise monograph *Languages in Contact* are frequently considered to mark the advent of modern contact linguistics. Their work has extended the domain of language contact research from the realm of historical linguistics to the synchronic analysis of multilingual speech. The matching of language contact and multilingualism has brought social and cognitive concerns into the limelight, and it has fostered the view that language contact is pervasive in the use, the development, and the

Alexander Onysko, Alpen-Adria Universität Klagenfurt

acquisition of language. Major introductions to the field emphasize the omnipresence of contact in virtually every language and stress its crucial relevance in many linguistic disciplines. Thomason (2001: 8), for example, states that "language contact is everywhere: there is no evidence that any languages have developed in total isolation from other languages." Winford (2003: 2) chimes in when saying that "most, if not all languages have been influenced at one time or another by contact with others". The opening line of Matras' (2009: 1) book reads that "manifestations of language contact are found in a great variety of domains, including language acquisition, language processing and production, conversation and discourse, social functions of language and language policy, typology and language change, and more."

These observations by some of the current researchers in language contact embody the legacy expressed in metaphorical terms by Weinreich quoted at the beginning. His imagery draws on the source domains of BODIES OF WATER and SAND to refer to language and features of language contact (i.e. interference in his use of terminology, 1953: 1). The metaphorical flow of a river, i.e. language use, carries along influences from other languages ('sand') while the still water of a lake, i.e. language metaphorized as a stable entity, can accumulate such influences, which become part of its substance. Essentially, this metaphor reflects the proverbial two sides of the same coin in research on language contact. On the one hand, language contact surfaces in individual acts of language use as a result of cognitive processes occurring in the mind of a speaker; on the other hand, language contact is evident in socially shared conversational habits that become representative of a speech community.

The pervasiveness and complexity of language contact involves a range of linguistic disciplines including historical linguistics, language typology, sociolinguistics, grammatical theory, language acquisition, pragmatics, and the cognitive sciences (psycho- and neurolinguistics) to reiterate some from Matras' list above and to spell out a few other important ones. The ubiquitous relevance of language contact also bears an impact on theory development in linguistics, emphasizing the need for theorizing the interaction of codes and its consequences for language use and development. This demand also holds for Cognitive Linguistics, in particular since recent years have seen a rediscovery of the ties between social and cognitive aspects of language (e.g. Harder 2010; Kristiansen and Dirven 2008; Pütz, Robinson, and Reif 2012; cf. Geeraerts 2016 and Schmid 2016). So far, some first steps have been made to approach language contact from cognitive linguistic perspectives. These highlight a usage-based view (Backus 1996, 2014) and related empirical considerations (Zenner 2013; Zenner, Speelman, and Geeraerts 2012, 2014a, 2014b). In the framework of construction grammar, Höder (2012, 2014a, 2014b, forthc.) has put forward a model of Diasystematic Construction Grammar (see section 3 for more detail), and Winter-Froemel (this volume) provides a detailed analysis of lexical reanalysis in borrowing.

Besides these approaches, cognitive linguistics can also help to elucidate the description of language contact processes, which are referred to by a multitude of terminology in research across different linguistic disciplines and traditions. Rather than adding to the terminological plethora, a combined cognitive and language-systemic perspective can provide underlying motivations for differentiating basic processes of language contact that can be used as cognitively grounded descriptive tools when analyzing crosslinguistic interactions. The current article strives to contribute to theory development on the nexus of contact and cognitive linguistics by differentiating basic phenomena of language contact according to cognitive processes and their language-systemic effects.

On the road towards a cognitively grounded typology of language contact processes, the next section will provide an overview of the most relevant models and terminology of language contact used in the field with the purpose of carving out essential similarities and differences among these categories. Section 3 will focus on aspects of cognition in multilingual language use and reflect these on basic assumptions about language and the mind held in Cognitive Linguistics. Building on that, section 4 will outline a typology that illustrates cognitive characteristics of language contact phenomena and their systemic descriptions as form-meaning units occurring in different languages.

2 Types of language contact phenomena and their terminology in contact linguistics

Research into language contact has had a long history in the discipline of linguistics from the 19th century on as testified by the work of Müller (1861), Paul (1886), Schuchardt (e.g. 1884), and Whitney (1881), among others. As part of historical linguistics, language contact was discussed as an important factor influencing the (metaphoric) classification of languages as "genetic" affiliates, and it became the undercurrent of the emerging field of pidgin and creole studies. In the 20th century, the studies by Haugen (1950) and Weinreich (1953) have marked the beginning of a new era of modern contact linguistics as acknowledged, in retrospect, by a number of scholars (e.g. Clyne 1987; Winford 2003; Matras 2009). Clyne (1987: 456), for example, states that "there was, before Weinreich (1953), no systematized theory of language contact." In line with the foundational role played by Weinreich and his contemporary Haugen to establish modern contact linguistics, the present article takes their theorizing as a starting point.

At the same time, it has to be mentioned that the last six decades since the publication of Weinreich's monograph have seen the development of a great number of terminologies to describe processes and phenomena of language contact. The sheer amount of research in language contact makes it next to impossible to provide a complete account of all terminological distinctions and such an endeavor would definitely exceed the scope of this article. However, in keeping with important studies in the field, the attempt is made to focus on widespread classifications in order to provide a comprehensive mapping of theoretical notions used in the field.

To start with, Weinreich (1953) employs the term interference as a superordinate concept that includes all types of language contact phenomena. As subtypes of interference, he differentiates between interlingual identification and borrowing. The term borrowing is restrictively used for lexical items which are transferred wholesale from a source language (SL) to a recipient language (RL). Weinreich also distinguishes between borrowings as accepted lexical items in speech communities and nonce borrowings as one-off uses of single lexical items in language A that originate from language B (1953: 11). The issue of how to ascertain when a nonce-borrowing turns into a borrowing has remained controversial in the field of contact linguistics as it has implications for the differentiation between codeswitching (as individual features of multilingual speech) and borrowing (as accepted lexical influences in speech communities) (cf., e.g. Poplack and Dion 2012; see section 4 for further discussion).

In contrast to borrowing, the term interlingual identification is employed by Weinreich to account for all types of crosslinguistic interactions in which a multilingual speaker identifies formal and semantic similarities in their language repertoire and can mix the formally and semantically similar units in their speech (1953: 8). The main part of Weinreich's foundational monograph is devoted to discussing interference (as interlingual identification) on the levels of phonology, morphosyntax, and the lexicon. For the latter, he focuses on semantic extensions due to contact, which means that, if languages in contact share an interlingual near homophone with partly overlapping meanings, the different language-specific meanings of the interlingual homophone can influence each other. As an example, Weinreich mentions that the Romance languages in the US have acquired the sense of 'to acquaint, to present formally' of the English term *introduce* in their Romance near homophones of American Portuguese (Amer. Port.) *introduzir*, American Italian *introdurre* and Louisiana and Canadian French *introduire* (1953: 49). In the case of compound words and phrases, Weinreich discusses hybrid compounds that combine a borrowed and a recipient language term as in Wisconsin German (G.) *Grund-floor* from English (E.) *ground floor* (1953: 52) – also note the close formal similarity between G. *Grund* and E. *ground*, which has probably facilitated this creation. Apart from that, Weinreich largely relies on Betz's (1949) distinction of loan formations into loan translation, i.e. literal translations (e.g. Amer. Port. *estar direito* from English *to be right*), loan renditions, i.e. partial translations (e.g. G. *Wolkenkratzer* 'cloudscraper' after E. *skyscraper*), and loan creations, i.e. a new coinage in the recipient language (RL) following a conceptual stimulus from the source language (SL), as in Yiddish *mitkind* from English *sibling* (1953: 51).

Haugen adopted the term borrowing as a hyperonym of all contact influences in bilingual speech. He defines borrowing as "the attempted reproduction in one language of patterns previously found in another" (1950: 212). As subtypes of borrowing, Haugen discusses the same processes as Weinreich but labels them differently. For Haugen, borrowings can be imported into an RL or substituted by language internal means in the RL. Morphemic importation and substitution are taken as measures to distinguish between loanwords, loanblends, and loanshifts (1950: 213–215). Loanwords are characterized as complete morphemic importations of form-meaning units as in E. *Internet* → G. *Internet*, even though some phonetic adaptation in the RL (i.e. phonemic substitution in Haugen's terms) is possible. Loanblends exhibit both morphemic importation and substitution as in Weinreich's examples of hybrid forms, and loanshifts are defined as complete morphemic substitutions. They retain the meaning of the original SL-concept in the RL. Interestingly, Haugen applies this criterion to loan translations (calques) as described in Weinreich and to those instances of interlingual identification that are based on homophony so that formal relations between the languages in contact can facilitate the transfer of meaning from one language to another. Haugen mentions the example of Am.Port. *humoroso* that acquired the meaning of Am.E. *humorous* 'funny'.

In general, Weinreich and Haugen's depiction of language contact phenomena have remained foundational distinctions that have withstood the test of time while a wealth of research on contact linguistics has ensued up to the present day. Although researchers have postulated a range of alternative terminologies and have carved out some more details in individual analyses, the underlying processes of contact influence and crosslinguistic interaction have remained the same. New terminologies have highlighted certain aspects of contact scenarios, which, however, can be related to the processes explained in Weinreich and Haugen's works. For example, Thomason (2001: 61) adopts Weinreich's notion of interference for all types of contact phenomena. In addition, she applies the term 'borrowing' to refer to the integration of lexical units from one language into another language, which is contrasted with 'imperfect learning'. The latter relates to Weinreich's notion of interlingual identification that can lead to the transfer of structural and semantic features of code X into code Z (Thomason 2001: 66–69).

A similar dichotomy between the borrowing of lexical form-meaning units vs. the transfer of structural features is evident in Matras' (2009) distinction between matter replication (i.e. borrowing in Weinreich's sense) and pattern replication (i.e. interlingual identification in Weinreich's sense). As the names imply, matter replication involves the use of form-meaning units (i.e. linguistic matter) from language A in language B while pattern replication refers to the replication of structural features and patterns (or constructions in Matras' sense 2009: 235) in an RL. Matras also extends the notion of pattern replication to instances of contact-induced grammaticalization as discussed in Heine and Kuteva (2005).

Johanson (2002), who criticizes the inappropriate metaphor of borrowing (cf. Haugen for similar criticism 1950: 211), adopts the term 'copying' to describe the use of language material from an SL in an RL (also see Verschik, this volume). In his terminology, 'global copying' refers to the copying of complete linguistic units of form and meaning while 'selective copying' describes the partial transfer of lexical units and grammatical structures, i.e. Weinreich's interlingual identification, Matras' pattern replication, and Haugen's loanblends and loanshifts. Furthermore, Johanson claims that 'copying' can be used as a general label for all types of language contact phenomena, "what is otherwise called 'borrowing', 'diffusion', 'transfer', 'interference', 'replication', etc." (2008: 62).

As major types of "contact-induced linguistic transfer", Heine and Kuteva (2008: 59) draw a bipartite distinction between replication and borrowing. While replication relates to all instances in which a contact-induced structural or lexical stimulus is reproduced in an RL using linguistic material of the RL, borrowing involves the transfer of form-meaning units from an SL to an RL.

Another twofold division into basic processes of language contact is given in Van Coetsem's (2000) model of borrowing (or RL-agentivity) vs. imposition (or SL-agentivity). Van Coetsem's approach pays tribute to the factor of (language) dominance. In a situation where the recipient language is dominant, contact influence will most likely cause the borrowing of lexical items that do not disrupt the structure of the RL. In a scenario of SL dominance (SL-agentivity), on the other hand, lexical items and grammatical features are imposed on an RL which undergoes drastic changes up to the point of language shift towards the SL (cf. Thomason's notion of shift-induced interference 2001: 74). In contrast to other models, Van Coetsem highlights that language dominance is a crucial factor that determines the extent of contact influence in an RL. Winford (2008) applies Van Coetsem's notion of imposition (as the cognitively dominant language of a speaker) to the formation of creole languages. According to him,

> In creole formation, just as in second language acquisition, learners tend to appeal to L1 knowledge to compensate for their lack of proficiency in their L2. This is reflected in their L2 production, which depends to varying degrees on the grammatical encoding procedures of their L1, which is dominant. (Winford 2008: 136)

The field of pidgins and creoles, traditionally regarded as prototypical contact languages, has nourished its own terminological distinctions that can be connected to processes discussed in Weinreich, Haugen, and other contact linguistic research discussed above. The notions of superstratum and substratum reflect a social component as pidgins and creoles are usually held to arise from a hierarchical relation of its input languages. While the notions of substratum and superstratum have a particular relevance in the formation of Romance languages from Latin (cf. Winter-Froemel 2011), the terminology has also been applied to the formation of English-based pidgins and creoles. In these contexts the lexicon of the emerging pidgin and creole is heavily influenced by the superstratum language English. English turns into a lexifier language, (re)lexifying the pidgin/creole language (cf. Muysken 1981 on the concept of (re)lexification). Features of the emerging pidgin/creole grammar, on the other hand, are frequently related to the non-dominant, substratum language. For example, in Kriol, spoken in the Northern Territory in Australia, and in its areally related creoles in the Pacific such as Torres Strait Creole, Tok Pisin and Bislama, the rich pronoun systems of their substratal languages have given rise to structurally similar pronoun systems in the English-based creoles (see Malcolm 2004; Smith 2004; Crowley 2004). The lexical substance that encodes the singular, dual (trial), and plural pronouns as well as their inclusive and exclusive forms, however, has largely been borrowed (i.e. lexified) from English.

The notion of substratum influence has also become used to describe scenarios of contact where multilingual speakers transfer features from one of the languages in their repertoires to an emerging (mixed) contact language. Bao's (2015) analysis of Singlish as a mixed code of Singapore English and Chinese substrate dialects is a case in point. The near synonymous use of substrate influence with the transfer of grammatical and structural features emphasizes the connection between second language acquisition (SLA) research and language contact. In his incisive monograph on language transfer, Odlin defines substratum transfer as "the type of cross-linguistic influence investigated in most studies of second language acquisition; such transfer involves the influence of a source language [...] on the acquisition of a target language." (1989: 12). Investigations of transfer have remained characteristic of research in SLA, but, as Treffers-Daller and Sakel point out, it has also been prominent in "a wide range of fields: language contact and Creole linguistics, bilingual first language acquisition, L2 and L3 acquisition, language attrition and psycholinguistics" (2012: 5). One could add studies on multilingualism and cognition, particularly those concerned with the interaction of languages in the multilingual mind. A book-length overview devoted to that is provided by Jarvis and

Pavlenko (2007), who use the term 'crosslinguistic influence' synonymously with transfer to highlight the psycholinguistic dimension of language interaction in multilingual adults and language learners.

The notion of crosslinguistic influence (transfer) has taken us full circle back to Weinreich's understanding of interlingual identification as a major component of interference. In general, the discussion of some of the major terminologies used in language contact, pidgin and creole languages, and SLA shows that the expanding research in these fields has led to the development of some new labels while the underlying mechanisms of crosslinguistic interaction have remained the same as described in Weinreich's foundational monograph, and in Haugen's typology of borrowing.

As an exception to that, research on the process of codeswitching has developed most strongly, leaving behind Weinreich's early and prescriptively tinted assumption that an 'ideal bilingual' does certainly not switch languages within a single sentence (1953: 73). Academic interest in codeswitching started in the 1970s (e.g. Blom and Gumperz 1972), and ever since Poplack's (1980) groundbreaking study, *Sometimes I'll start a sentence in Spanish Y TERMINO EN ESPAÑOL*, the nature of codeswitching as a variable and not completely predictable process has been established. Research on codeswitching has focused on its use as a discourse strategy (e.g. Gumperz 1982; Auer 1984) and on its relation to identity construction (e.g. Auer 1998). It has also inspired major contact linguistic models such as Myers-Scotton's Matrix Language Frame Model (1993), which was later extended to the 4-M model (2002), and Muysken's (2000) tripartite typology of codemixing as insertions, alternations, and congruent lexicalizations. Furthermore, the substantial number of edited volumes highlighting multidisciplinary approaches to codeswitching (e.g. Isurin, Winford, and De Bot 2009; Jacobson 1998, 2001; Milroy and Muysken 1995), an introduction devoted to the topic (Gardner-Chloros 2009) and a handbook (Bullock and Toribio 2009) are a testimony to the fact that codeswitching has turned into a separate discipline. Particularly from a cognitive point of view, codeswitching has shifted into the prime focus of psycholinguistic and neurolinguistic research on multilingual language use, reinforcing the link between language contact, multilingualism, and the mind as presaged by Weinreich.

Having sketched the relation between processes of language contact and their various terminologies, the next step towards a cognitive typology of language contact processes involves taking a look at cognitive aspects of crosslinguistic interaction. Thus, section 3 will discuss some first cognitive linguistic studies on language contact and, particularly, psycholinguistic approaches to the multilingual mind.

3 Cognitive and psycholinguistic insights into the multilingual mind

Approaching the notion of language contact from cognitive linguistics is particularly challenging since it throws into relief the basic conceptualization of language as a bounded entity. If language is seen as an image-schematic container consisting of experiential boundaries, it makes sense to speak of different languages being in contact and influencing each other (also cf. Nicolaï 2017 on the notion of 'boundary' in language contact). While on the social plane languages can indeed appear as entities belonging to certain groups of speakers, internal separations for different codes in the mind of a speaker are difficult to draw. Cognitive linguistics assumes that the processing and production of language is dependent on activity in a mental network within which there are virtually no boundaries. This means that connections between the neuronal nodes in the network are not inherently limited and solely depend on patterns of activation (i.e. language use). The work of Bybee (1985; also see 2007, 2010) has laid out convincing foundations of that view, which has become fundamental to the field. Patterns of activation in the mental network that represent language behavior can become entrenched by an interplay of repeated activation (i.e. frequency of use) and saliency emerging in specific socio-pragmatic contexts (cf. Schmid 2016 for a comprehensive model of entrenchment).

In light of these observations, the question arises of how we can establish separations between languages in the mental network if there are no *a priori* boundaries for different manifestations of languages, and usage is the sole arbiter of how languages develop and become instantiated in speech acts. In cognitive linguistics, recent work by Höder (2014a, 2014b, forthc.) picks up on that question. He introduces the notion of Diasystematic Construction Grammar, according to which a multilingual or multilectal speaker (i.e. virtually any kind of speaker) holds language-unspecific and language-specific constructions in their constructicons. If constructions (on different levels of schematicity) are shared among the codes making up the repertoire of a speaker, they exist as unspecific to the socio-pragmatic conditions of different language use. Language-specific constructions, on the other hand, are confined to those usage contexts where certain languages, codes or lects are employed. The totality of language-specific and unspecific constructions make up the multilingual/multilectal repertoire of a speaker, which, in Höder's terms "can be conceptualised as a set of linguistic structures consisting of idiosyncratic subsets on the one hand (containing elements that solely belong to one language or variety) and common subsets on the other hand (containing elements that are common to several or all languages within the repertoire; [...])" (forthc.). In line with an "all-inclusive" view of constructions (cf. Goldberg 2006: 18), it can be assumed that language-specific constructions will show more frequently on the segmental stratum of individual languages (i.e. among phonemes and morphemes) rather than on more schematic, grammatical and discourse related patterns (e.g. causative constructions, word order patterns, and so on). The emergence of such specific and unspecific sets of constructions in the mind of a speaker can be cognitively motivated by processing economy as well as by the pervasive process of interlingual identification (Weinreich 1953: 7, see section 2; cf. Höder 2014a: 141). The recognition of similarities between linguistic units from different languages is a consequence of the human instinct to categorize information – in this case to form associative relations based on perceived similarities in the linguistic structures.

The postulate of language-specific and language-unspecific constructions assumes some form of constructional identification in the multilectal repertoire of a speaker. This knowledge can be built up episodically (as tied to certain socio-pragmatic conditions of language use) or it can be acquired as declarative knowledge. Thus, it follows that, on the one hand, growing experience in constructional choices that are adequate for a particular speech situation promotes how episodic knowledge of a 'language' is acquired in the mind. On the other hand, speakers can be told that a certain construction belongs to a certain code, which fosters their conscious, metalinguistic skills of code identification. Without going into this discussion, Diasystematic Construction Grammar involves the identification of language-specific forms, which presupposes the existence of linguistic boundaries in the mind of a speaker. Only if language-specificity is somehow encoded in the neuronal network (e.g. via certain patterns of neuronal activation), will a speaker be able to distinguish between different sets of language-specific forms and between specific and non-specific constructions.

Looking beyond cognitive linguistics, the last few decades have witnessed a wealth of psycholinguistic research into bi- and multilingualism that has been concerned with cognitive aspects of multilingual speech processing and production as well as with the representation of multiple languages in the mind of a speaker. While this type of research is carried out on the background of different cognitive theories, the following discussion will focus on the major strands and findings in psycholinguistic research on multilingualism. These are most relevant to highlight the connection between cognition and language contact. In general, the plethora of psycholinguistic studies converge on presupposing the ontological nature of languages as entities held in a multilingual mind. Even recent efforts in Dynamic Systems Theory acknowledge bounded entities of neuronal activation patterns for specific languages. As Lowie and Verspoor summarize

> The emerging picture thus far is one of the multilingual mind as a multidimensional state space, in which fuzzy subsets of symbolic units, be it words, formulaic sequences or syntactic constructions, are activated in particular contexts and what has traditionally been referred to as language-specific information emerges from the context of use in an embedded and embodied language system. (2011: 282)

This comment is in sync with the view proposed in Diasystematic Construction Grammar, according to which the notion of language is deconstructed into patterns of speech behaviour dependent on specific usage contexts. At the same time, Lowie and Verspoor (2011: 282) employ the metaphor of the multilingual mind as a multidimensional state space that contains "fuzzy subsets of symbolic units". The notion of subsets within a larger neuronal network is thus taking on the role of separate languages held in the mind of a multilingual speaker.

Other psycholinguistic research following network models of language production, processing and representation relies on the metaphor of 'localist networks', which means that certain neuronal nodes (i.e. neurons) hold language-specific information which is represented in lexical items, grammatical constructions and so on. Alternatively, 'distributional networks' claim that language-specific information is encoded via distributional patterns of neuronal activation in the mental network (cf., e.g., Hartsuiker and Bernolet 2017: 229). Again both views need to accommodate locally-bounded groundings of linguistic units in the neuronal network.

A conception of separate codes in a speaker's multilingual repertoire is also evident in major psycholinguistic models of speech production and processing. De Bot's Bilingual Production Model (1992), for example, builds on Levelt's Speaking Model (1989) to outline the production of language as passing through the stages of conceptualization, formulation, and articulation. As an extension to Levelt's monolingual model, De Bot postulates language-specific pathways of formulation and articulation and partially overlapping 'conceptualizers' for the different languages (cf. Hartsuiker and Pickering 2008). This means that conceptual representations can be partially shared in a speaker's multilingual repertoire while some concepts are specific to a certain language. The idea of a largely shared conceptual "store" has remained a dominant view in neuro- and psycholinguistic approaches to multilingual cognition. Paradis (2004) sides with the theory that multilinguals share a common conceptual store but hold language-specific lexicons. The BIA+ (Bilingual Interactive Activation Plus) Model proposed by Dijkstra and Van Heuven (2002) goes one step further and assumes integrated lexical storage in the multilingual mind, allowing parallel activation of lexical items in a speaker's multilingual repertoire. Finkbeiner, Gollan, and Caramazza (2006), on the other hand, propose that lexical selection is language-specific. In that scenario, parallel activation in multiple languages does not lead to a competition in lexical selection. Finally, the Revised Hierarchical Model (Kroll and Stewart 1994; also see Kroll and Hermans 2011) is based on a common conceptual store for a speaker's L1 and L2. Lexical access, however, is guided by asymmetrical relations between L1 and L2. Thus, in initial stages of L2 acquisition, learners supposedly rely on L1 translation equivalents to gain insight into L2 meaning. Increased knowledge of the L2 facilitates the creation of direct links between L2 words and their meaning; however, a speaker's L1 maintains stronger links to the shared conceptual store than her/his L2 (Kroll and Hermans 2011: 17).

These psycholinguistic models arise from vast experimental evidence on crosslinguistic priming, which proves that hypostasized codes in the mind of a multilingual speaker are always co-activated in the mental network (for overviews, see, e.g. Kroll, Gulliver, and Rossi 2013; Kootstra and Muysken 2017). Co-activation (also called parallel activation) is particularly evident in crosslinguistic homonyms and cognates among the languages of a speaker's repertoire (e.g. Arêas Da Luz Fontes and Schwartz 2010; Lemhöfer, Dijkstra, and Michel 2004; Starreveld et al. 2014). Co-activation of languages has also been interpreted as proof of the observation that the languages of a multilingual person are always "switched on" even if operating in a monolingual language mode (Grosjean 2001; cf. Canseco-Gonzalez et al. 2010). Crosslinguistic priming and the resulting cognate effects form a cognitive backdrop to the contact linguistic process that Weinreich labelled interlingual identification and that is also known in the field as transfer or interference. These terms describe the same process according to which similar form-meaning units from different codes tend to become co-activated in the mental network potentially causing lexical-semantic changes or syntactic (constructional) shifts. Furthermore, parallel activation of codes can also surface in spontaneous intrasentential codeswitching, which can be facilitated by textual triggers such as cognates or proper names (cf. Clyne 2003 for the notion of triggering).

Codeswitching also connects to another important research question explored in a range of psycholinguistic studies on multilingual speech production: how does language choice function in multilingual speakers? Tentative answers to that question draw upon the notions of 'inhibition' and, in particular, 'executive control'. As summarized in Bialystok (2009), bilingual children and adults show enhanced capabilities in nonverbal tasks that demand the inhibition of irrelevant stimuli, the switching between task conditions, and the updating of information in working memory. This enhanced cognitive performance of multilinguals compared to monolinguals is explained by the fact that the multilingual mind is constantly engaged in controlling its languages, i.e. in controlling the joined activation that represents different codes in the mental network.

The discussion of cognitive approaches to multilingualism and language contact shows that cognitive linguistics and psycholinguistics operate, on the one hand, with the construct that separate codes/languages are represented in the multilingual mind. On the other hand, it is acknowledged that language emerges from neuronal activity in an associative mental network with no *a priori* boundaries. How can these two views be reconciled?

One attempt is to introduce the idea of 'subsets' within the mental network. They represent neuronal areas which metaphorically correspond to different codes. Another metaphor is the one of language specific 'tags' that would somehow mark neuronal nodes or patterns of activation as belonging to a certain code (see, e.g. Hartsuiker and Bernolet 2017). Both images highlight a form of neuronal grounding of different codes as specific components and patterns of neuronal activation in the mind. As of yet there is no clear experimental evidence that would support such neuronal subsets or language tags (cf. Abutalebi and Green 2008).

While it is difficult to localize different languages in the mind, a reconciliation is perhaps possible on the grounds of socio-pragmatic experience, which builds up awareness on behavioural patterns of language use as part of a speaker's episodic knowledge. Thus, the socio-pragmatic conditions and categories that are imposed on the use of language(s) can create language specific representations (as both conscious, declarative knowledge and implicit, habitualized usage patterns).

In its traditional sense, the notion of language contact relies on explicit (experiential) knowledge that relates to the socio-pragmatic conditions and usage contexts of a specific code. Otherwise, speakers (and linguists) would not be able to discern instances of language use that draw on different codes or discover the provenance of language material from different codes. A lack of such knowledge would render products of language interaction (i.e. contact) ephemeral symptoms of language production and processing.

So, while congruity between the cognitive representation of languages and the descriptive facts of language contact can be built when considering socio-pragmatic conditions of language use, a further essential link between cognition and language contact has not yet been explored. This relates to the question of how language contact phenomena established in descriptive research can be mapped onto our understanding of multilingual cognition. The next section will dig more deeply into that matter.

4 A cognitively grounded typology of language contact phenomena

To make a step towards unearthing the cognitive grounding of language contact phenomena, this section proposes a model of language activation in the mental network that describes four major phenotypes of language contact, as introduced in a different context in Onysko (2016): borrowing, codeswitching (CS), transfer/interference, and replication. These different types of language contact phenomena can be described in language-systemic terms (i.e. as form-meaning units in La and Lb) and find their cognitive grounding in the model laid out below. The model combines insights from language contact theory and multilingual cognition and is couched in a usage-based conception of language as a mental network. As discussed in the previous section, it is important to emphasize again that the notion of language-specificity in the mental network is held to arise from experiential knowledge accumulated from socio-pragmatic contexts of language use, which involve specific codes or modes of combining these codes. Figure 1 provides a visual summary of the model. This will be followed by a description of its components and how they interact.

Figure 1 shows that, in general, the cognitive process of language activation depends on socio-pragmatic conditions, which provide the contextual embedding of any utterance and speech act. As cognitive phenomena, language contact types are tied to two basic dispositions of language activation in the mental network. Conscious and unconscious activation are shown as opposite states on a continuum of attention given to the mental process of language production. In everyday contexts of spontaneous language use, unconscious activation means that people produce language without stopping their flow of speech to actively (i.e. consciously) perform metalinguistic tasks such as searching for and comparing expressions and other linguistic features in several of their repertoires. If, on the other hand, that is the case, it is argued here that the conscious attention to language production and the application of metalinguistic reasoning such as comparisons among the codes in a multilingual repertoire is a qualitatively different process of language activation in the mental network.

The different dispositions of activation play out on the level of language modes. Thus, automatic (i.e. unconscious) activation relates to the continuum of language modes described by Grosjean (2001). In spontaneous language use, a multilingual person can sway between a more monolingual and a more multilingual language mode, depending on the context of the speech situation. In a monolingual mode, activation of neural structures relate to one and the same code while the other codes are suppressed and remain to some extent activated

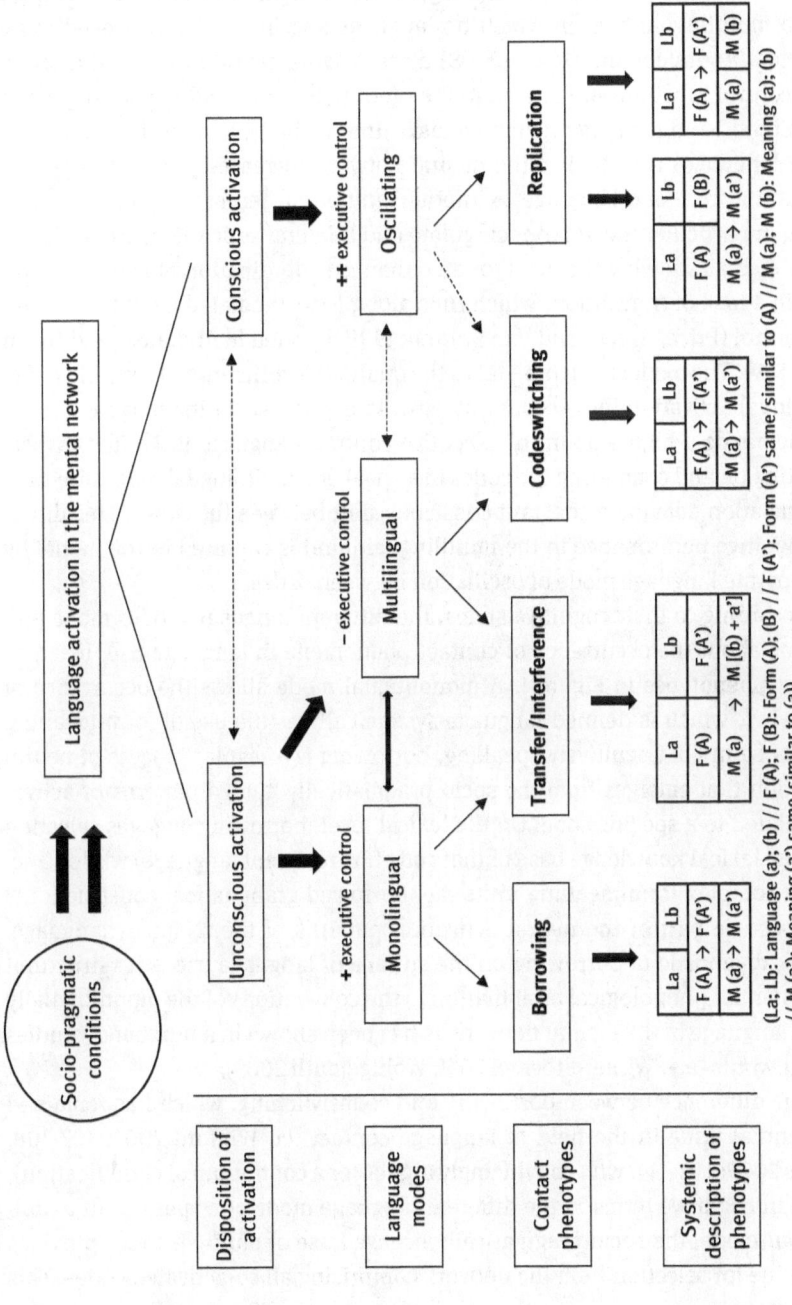

Figure 1: A cognitive model of language contact phenotypes and their language-systemic descriptions.

(La; Lb: Language (a); (b) // F (A); F (B): Form (A); (B) // F (A'): Form (A') same/similar to (A) // M (a); M (b): Meaning (a); (b) // M (a'): Meaning (a') same/similar to (a)) in the background. In a multilingual mode, on the other hand, the appropriate codes are co-activated to a greater extent. Accordingly, it can be hypothesized that a monolingual mode demands a higher degree of inhibitory executive control than a multilingual one, in which no language-specific activations need to be inhibited. Abutalebi and Green (2008) discuss some neural evidence that executive control functions are related to the prefrontal cortex and the basal ganglia in inhibition and language switching tasks. Interestingly, as conscious attention to the languages activated in the mental network increases (e.g. in the task of translating from one language to another), different neural structures become active, in particular the anterior cingulate and bilateral subcortical areas. This is interpreted as showing the need for an enhanced coordination of mental operations in a task of translation, which runs along less automated circuits of cognitive control (Price, Green, and Van Studnik 1999 reported in Abutalebi and Green 2008: 569). The model in Figure 1 takes the qualitative difference of controlled (i.e. conscious) activation into account by postulating an oscillating language mode that demands a high amount of executive control. Language tasks that involve reflecting on and comparing the codes in a speaker's multilingual repertoire such as translation demand a constant conscious shift between the codes. This different cognitive performance in the multilingual mind is captured in the model by the separate language mode of oscillation between codes.

According to their cognitive states, the different language modes make predictions about the occurrence of contact phenomena in language use, listed as contact phenotypes in Figure 1. A monolingual mode allows the occurrence of borrowing, which is defined language-systemically as the use of form-meaning units of La in Lb. Cognitively speaking, borrowing is a regular process of neural activation that emerges from the socio-pragmatically guided patterns of activation related to a specific code. On the lexical level, borrowing engages selection from the lexical knowledge base of that code (i.e. recipient language) while structurally complex form-meaning units (i.e. borrowed grammatical constructions) have become part of the neural activation patterns of the recipient language. A weak diagnostic of borrowing on the surface of language use is its structural and potential phonological assimilation to the conventions of the monolingually active language in the mental network as has been shown in a number of studies on loanwords (e.g. Winter-Froemel 2011; Wohlgemuth 2009).

The difference between borrowing and codeswitching, which has remained a perennial issue in the field of language contact (cf. Winford 2003: 107–108; Matras 2009: 110–114, who convincingly argues for a continuum of classification), is tied in cognitive terms to the different language mode of a speaker. In a multilingual mode, the socio-pragmatically licensed use of multiple codes provides a baseline for selection from the network comprising all co-activated codes. This shows on the surface of language use as a switching of codes, which is possible on all segmental levels of language and can also lead to creations based on substance from different codes (e.g. Weinreich's example of *Grundfloor* as a German/English creation mentioned in section 2). As far as their language-systemic description is concerned, borrowing and codeswitching (CS) follow the same process in that form-meaning units in La are used within a frame of Lb (in line with Myers-Scotton's postulate of a matrix language in codeswitching, cf. 2002). Additionally, high levels of co-activation can also induce codeswitching as an interspersed use of elements in two and more codes without a clear matrix structure (see Muysken's postulate of congruent lexicalization 2000: 122–153; also cf. Gardner-Chloros 2009: 91–116). The cognitive model of language contact phenotypes implies that, even though based on identical language-systemic effects, a difference between these two processes relates to the language mode of activation in the mental network. CS is confined to multilingual modes while borrowing is a typical contact phenomenon of a monolingual mode although it can also occur in a multilingual mode (as an item in one of the co-activated codes).

Being part of the entrenched activation patterns of a specific code, the contact phenomenon of borrowing is not different from other linguistic surface forms arising from code-specific activation patterns. Multilingual speakers of the borrowing's source and recipient languages can identify the origin of a borrowing by building associative connections in their multilingual repertoires. This is more difficult for monolingual speakers of the recipient language, who need to draw on other sources of information to learn about the contact origin of the borrowed unit. Besides the cognitive distinction between borrowing and codeswitching according to language modes, the two contact phenomena can also be differentiated by the sociolinguistic condition that borrowings represent accepted lexical items and grammatical structures across a community of speakers sharing the same code (La) whereas codeswitching involves the use of language units from another code (Lb) that are not part of the habitual forms of expression in La. In other words, the continuum between codeswitching and borrowing is aligned to the question of whether or not a lexical unit or a grammatical construction is habitually used in a speaker community sharing the same code. In practical terms, the variable of 'habitual use' is a fuzzy category as it is difficult to define a hard and fast criterion for when a linguistic form can be held as sufficiently widespread in a speaker community (cf. Deuchar and Strammers 2016).

The distinction between borrowing and codeswitching in terms of language modes and spread among speaker communities bears implications for the concept of 'nonce borrowing' propounded in particular in some of Poplack's work (e.g. Poplack and Meechan 1998; Poplack 2012). If CS is defined as a multilingual speaker operating in a multilingual mode and as the incidental and idiosyncratic use of La units mixed with Lb and not by structural criteria of linguistic integration, 'nonce borrowing' becomes a moot category. Instead, all items of one code used in another code that meet the conditions of multilingual language mode and lack social dispersion appear as codeswitches. This is in line with Strammers and Deuchar's (2012) empirical conclusion on the integration of English verbs in Welsh. Borrowing, on the other hand, is restricted to those uses of La material in Lb that have become part of the shared code in a speaker community. Thus, borrowings can still occur when multilinguals converse in a monolingual mode with their monolingual peers.

If codeswitching is considered to be a symptom of language mode, further types can be distinguished. As a socio-pragmatically adequate conversational tool in a multilingual mode, CS occurs spontaneously, coheres with the contextually conditioned discourse strategies, and carries out multiple functions (e.g. as a marker of identity, as referentially adequate language choice, as an instrument of multilingual language play, and so on). This situation marks the most prototypical occurrences of CS in multilingual communication as investigated in a plethora of research on codeswitching. Apart from that, CS can also sometimes occur spontaneously, interfering with monolingual language use when multilinguals converse in a more monolingual mode. This type of CS is usually restricted to single word switches that have slipped past executive control functions. Discourse markers, conjunctions or single content word switches have been described in the literature as examples of that (e.g. Clyne 2003: 215–232; Matras 2009: 91–99). This type of spontaneous interferential switching is socio-pragmatically marked in the discourse situation. The switches occur unexpectedly for both the speaker and the listener and are frequently repaired and subject to further inhibition. Furthermore, CS can also be employed as a conscious strategy in an oscillating language mode. In this case, switches appear as a controlled (non-spontaneous) act of language use emerging from language conscious activities such as translation, paraphrasing, introducing original language expressions that are explained in another language, and so on.

Unconscious, automatic activation of the language network which is regulated by the socio-pragmatically conditioned language modes leads to another kind of language contact phenomenon that is different on a language-systemic level from borrowing and codeswitching. What is labelled as transfer/interference in the model describes an analogically stimulated activation of language units in code La that influences the production of a formally/semantically related language unit in code Lb. Analogical activation means that formally/semantically related language units or constructions in different codes are co-activated in the mental network. Crosslinguistic priming such as the cognate effect shown in a vast body of psycholinguistic research is direct evidence of that kind of activation. If the analogical activation leads to the use of linguistic substance (form/meaning) of a code La in a code Lb, language contact becomes manifest. The systemic description of transfer/interference in Figure 1 illustrates a typical case of such contact, in which formal similarities between two units in La and Lb can inspire the transfer of meaning and function from the La unit to its similar counterpart in Lb. Examples of transfer/interference have been amply discussed in the literature on language contact as in Weinreich's analyses of interlingual identifications (1953) and Jarvis and Pavlenko's monograph on crosslinguistic interaction (2007) to name just a few. In loanword research, the notion of semantic loan (cf. Haugen 1950: 214) actually refers to instances of transfer/interference based on analogical co-activation in the mental network which has turned into an established feature in the recipient language (see Onysko 2007: 14–21 for discussion). The same process of transfer/interference has been amply studied in the field of second language acquisition. Widely known as true or false friends, transfer/interference can show in learners who apply the meaning and function of a unit in their first language to a formally or structurally similar unit in their learner language. The use of English *sensible* in the meaning of 'sensitive' (following the meaning of the close German formal equivalent *sensibel*) is a case in point. Since transfer/interference happens on the basis of automatic, similarity-based activation in the mental network, it can occur both in a monolingual and a multilingual mode. Following the hypothesis that activation across a speaker's multilingual repertoire is less inhibited in a multilingual mode, it seems reasonable to expect a higher incidence of transfer/interference in a multilingual than in a monolingual mode. This prediction, however, is in need of empirical consolidation.

As shown in Figure 1, conscious language activation in the mental network gives rise to a contact phenotype that is situated on the fuzzy border between contact-induced and intrinsic language change. In the model, the term replication refers to those cases in which either a conceptual stimulus (on all schematic levels of language) from La is replicated in Lb by using linguistic material from Lb, or a linguistic form from La is replicated in Lb assuming a different, unrelated meaning from the similar form in La. These two scenarios of replication give rise to two language-systemic descriptions in the model. To clarify the terminological choice, it needs to be stated that the term replication is similar to Heine and Kuteva (2008: 59) but different from Matras's sense. He applies the notion as a cover term for language contact influence and distinguishes the two basic types of matter and pattern replication (cf., e.g., 2009).

Cognitively speaking, the process of replication in the current model is different from straightforward activation in the mental network. In this case, a speaker performs a process of transmutation; that is, s/he activates code-specific linguistic units whose conceptual content is then rendered in linguistic units specific to another code. In line with neural evidence discussed in Abutalebi and Green (2008: 569), this process is based on conscious attention and is performed along less automated neural pathways of activation. In the cognitive model of language contact phenotypes outlined above, replication is thus restricted to those instances of language production that rely on an oscillating language mode following from conscious and controlled language activation in the mental network. The use of grammatical constructions from La in Lb that are filled with lexical material in Lb are instances of replication if a speaker performs a conscious effort of translating the items in a construction from La to Lb. However, spontaneous occurrences of La constructions fleshed out in the Lb with lexical material of the Lb are also possible. These qualify as instances of transfer/interference. In this case, the constructional meaning of La is mapped onto a related constructional pivot in Lb (see Matras 2009: 240–243), which triggers the selection of the corresponding linguistic surface form in Lb. An example of that process is discussed in Matras (2009: 25–26, 240–243), where the multilingual child Ben produces German and Hebrew existential constructions that mirror his English model of *I am cold*.

Loan translations (also frequently called calques) are examples *par excellence* of replication. Investigating loan translations has had a long history in the field of language contact since Betz's (1949) fine-grained typology of calquing which distinguishes between loan translation, loan rendition, and loan creation according to the degree of literality in the replicated form. While originally the concept has mostly been used for the rendering of complex lexical units from code A as more or less literally translated into code B in studies on loanwords (as in Weinreich's examples of Wisconsin German *Pferds-Rettich* from E. *horse radish* or Florida Spanish *poner a dormir* from E. *to put to sleep*, 1953: 51), contact linguistic research has described the same principle in the replication of grammatical patterns (e.g. Aikhenvald 2006) and even in pathways of grammaticalization (Heine and Kuteva 2005). Furthermore, research has discussed loan translation in relation to other processes of language contact (cf. Jarvis 2009 for loan translation and transfer; Backus and Dorleijn 2009 for loan translation and codeswitching).

As a type of replication, the notion of loan translation (calquing) is not a straightforward category of language contact, particularly when the more or less literal translation of an expression or term from a source language into a recipient language completely draws on linguistic substance and structures of the recipient language. If that is the case, there is no formal linguistic indication that the unit might be contact-induced. Furthermore, if loan translation is not tied to any linguistic markers that can establish a relation between the source and recipient codes, it becomes difficult to distinguish it from any other instances of translation. Strictly speaking, any act of translation would then also be a loan translation. To avoid this problem, some language-systemic and usage-based evidence can be relied upon before classifying units in a specific code as examples of loan translations. On the language-systemic side, clear instances of loan translation occur if the literally translated units combine in a way that reflects their source language structure. At the same time, evidence is increased if the source language structure is a marked or untypical structure in the recipient language. The Italian term *ferrovia*, for example, shows an unusual nominal, right-headed compounding structure, which underlines its potential origin as a loan translation from German *Eisenbahn* (I. *ferro* = G. *Eisen*, 'iron'; I. *via* = G. *Weg*, *Straße* and by extension *Bahn*, 'street, road, track'). In the speech of multilingual people and language learners, loan translations can occur online during language production. Jarvis (2006: 114–115) refers to Ringbom's (2001: 64) examples of the creation *youngman* for *bachelor* following Swedish *ungkarl* and *animaldoctor* for *veterinarian* as a direct translation from Finnish *eläinlääkäri*. Since these forms are one-off creations and do not represent the usual English terms for these concepts, there is simple usage-based evidence that these terms are the product of loan translation. This type of replication can also involve more complex expressions such as idioms and syntactic constructions which can be translated from one language to another one. From a diachronic point of view, if a replication has spread among a shared community code, it has turned into a code-specific unit or construction that is part of the automatic, code-specific patterns of activation in a speaker's mental network.

While calquing, i.e. the replication of La meaning in Lb with the help of linguistic forms of Lb, is the most frequent process of replication, it can also happen that speakers replicate an La form in Lb and give it a totally new (and unrelated) meaning in Lb. This phenomenon has been described as a form of pseudo loan (see Humbley 2015 for an overview). In this case, language users motivate the meaning of the source language form in the recipient language anew but do not copy the meaning of the source language form. Examples of that process are pseudo anglicisms such as *footing* ('jogging') in French and Italian or *handy* ('mobile phone') in German.

As a note to the side, language contact can lead to the creation of hybrid forms that combine language material from two (or more) languages in one unit (also see Zenner, Backus, and Winter-Froemel, this volume). Hybrid forms (i.e. loan blends in Haugen's terminology) can relate to all four language contact phenotypes. They can involve spontaneous codeswitching as in Pennsylvania German *wasewe(r)* ('whatever') or in the hybrid compound *Grundfloor* ('ground floor', Weinreich 1953: 52). As Haugen notes when discussing similar examples as loanblends, "it is conspicuous that in practically every case the substitute closely resembles the foreign term in sound and has a meaning not too remote from it" (1950: 219). This actually underlines that such hybrid forms can be facilitated by transfer/interference processes in online multilingual speech. In loanword research, the question arises whether hybrid compounds are the result of a partial replication (i.e. one constituent of the compound has been translated while the other one maintains its original form as in G. *Haarspray* from E. *hairspray*, Carstensen and Busse 1993: 67) or of the productive use of an already borrowed form in the recipient language (cf. Knospe 2014: 65–68 for discussion). Results in various corpus-based studies on loanwords have shown that hybrid compounds are far more often the result of a productive word formation process in the recipient language than subject to partial replication (see, e.g., Knospe 2014; Onysko 2007; Degani and Onysko 2010).

Phonetic changes in language contact situations are further phenomena that can be related to different contact phenotypes described in the model. Without the necessary space for going into detail, suffice it to mention here that phonetic changes can be described by three contact types in the model: (1) replication if the speaker of an L2 substitutes phonemes according to L1 conventions (and these are fixed in the speaker's speech habits as in the example of L1 accent in L2); (2) transfer/interference if the speaker of the L2 substitutes phonemes according to L1 conventions "on the fly" (i.e. during speech) but they are not stable features that would characterize an accent of the speaker; (3) borrowing if an SL phoneme has been integrated into an RL and has become commonly used in the speaker community.

To sum up, the major phenotypes of language contact described in this section emerge from two different cognitive dispositions of activation in the mental network, which relate to three basic states on a continuum of language modes. At the same time, the major types of language contact phenomena can also be described in language-systemic terms. As a whole, the model provides a cognitive grounding for the range of contact phenomena that surface in language use.

5 Conclusion

In line with the aims of the current volume, this article has attempted to carve out the connection between language contact phenomena and their cognitive motivations, following a cognitive linguistic view of language as activation in a usage-based mental network. To do so, the discussion has drawn on important approaches and terminology in the traditional field of language contact and on insights established in the area of multilingual cognition. The merger of these two domains has inspired a cognitive model of language contact phenotypes and their language-systemic descriptions. The model highlights how different surface instantiations of contact in language use relate to basic cognitive dispositions and to different language modes of multilingual speakers. On the descriptive level of language analysis, the same phenotypes of language contact are separated according to different constellations of how form/meaning units in one specific-code are transmitted into another code. The model offers a comprehensive and integrated approach, which intends to map the whole range of contact phenomena. Future empirical research testing the predictions of the model will allow to further refine our understanding of the essential relation between language contact phenomena and cognition. For cognitive-psycholinguistic research, it will be crucial to create environments that can control for the language mode of multilingual participants. If that empirical challenge can be solved, the relation of language mode to the different contact phenotypes can become more strongly empirically grounded.

Acknowledgments: I would like to thank the editors of the volume for their patience and diligence in handling this paper. Additional thanks go to Eline Zenner and Esme Winter-Froemel for meticulous comments that could sharpen some of the points raised in the article and to an anonymous reviewer for further suggestions. All remaining infelicities and inadequacies are my responsibility.

References

Abutalebi, Jubin & David Green. 2008. Bilingual language production: The neurocognition of language representation and control. *Journal of Neurolinguistics* 20. 242–275.

Aikhenvald, Alexandra Y. 2006. Grammars in contact: A cross-linguistic perspective. In Alexandra Y. Aikhenvald & R. M. W. Dixon (eds.), *Grammars in Contact: A Cross-linguistic Typology*, 1–66. Oxford: Oxford University Press.

Arêas Da Luz Fontes, Ana B. & Ana I. Schwartz. 2010. On a different plane: Cross-language effects on the conceptual representations of within-language homonyms. *Language and Cognitive Processes* 25 (4). 508–532.

Auer, Peter. 1984. *Bilingual Conversation*. Amsterdam & Philadelphia: John Benjamins.

Auer, Peter (ed.). 1998. *Code-Switching in Conversation: Language, Interaction and Identity*. London & New York: Routledge.

Backus, Ad. 1996. *Two in One: Bilingual Speech of Turkish Immigrants in the Netherlands*. Tilbug: Tilburg University Press.

Backus, Ad. 2014. A usage-based approach to borrowability. In Eline Zenner & Gitte Kristiansen (eds.), *New Perspectives on Lexical Borrowing*, 19–40. Berlin & New York: De Gruyter.

Backus, Ad & Margreet Dorleijn. 2009. Loan translations versus code-switching. In Barbara E. Bullock, Almeida Jacqueline Toribio (eds.), *The Cambridge Handbook of Linguistic Code-switching*, 75–93. Cambridge: Cambridge University Press.

Bao, Zhiming. 2015. *The Making of Vernacular Singapore English: System, Transfer, and Filter*. Cambridge: Cambridge University Press.

Betz, Werner. 1949. *Deutsch und Lateinisch: Die Lehnbildungen der althochdeutschen Benediktinerregel*. [German and Latin: The loan formations of the Old High German Regula Benedicti]. Bonn: Bouvier.

Bialystok, Ellen. 2009. Bilingualism: The good, the bad, and the indifferent. *Bilingualism: Language and Cognition* 12 (1). 3–11.

Blom, Jan-Petter & John Gumperz. 1972. Social meaning in linguistic structures: Code-switching in northern Norway. In John Gumperz & Dell Hymes (eds.), *Directions in Sociolinguistics: The Ethnography of Communication*, 407–434. New York: Holt, Rinehart and Winston.

Bullock, Barbara & Almeida Jacqueline Toribio (eds.). 2009. *The Cambridge Handbook of Linguistic Code-Switching*. Cambridge: Cambridge University Press.

Bybee, Joan. 1985. *Morphology: A Study of the Relation between Meaning and Form*. Amsterdam & Philadelphia: John Benjamins.

Bybee, Joan. 2007. *Frequency of Use and the Organization of Language*. Oxford: Oxford University Press.

Bybee, Joan. 2010. *Language, Usage and Cognition*. Cambridge: Cambridge University Press.

Canseco-Gonzalez, Enriqueta, Laurel Brehm, Cameron A. Brick, Sarah Brown-Schmidt, Kara Fischer & Katie Wagner. 2010. Carpet or Cárcel: The effect of age of acquisition and language mode on bilingual lexical access. *Language and Cognitive Processes* 25 (5). 669–705.

Carstensen, Broder & Ulrich Busse. 1993/1994/1996. *Anglizismen Wörterbuch* [Dictionary of Anglicisms]. 3 Vols. Berlin & New York: De Gruyter.

Clyne, Michael. 1987. History of research on language contact. In Ulrich Ammon, Norbert Dittmar & Klaus J. Mattheier (eds.), *Sociolinguistics – Soziolinguistik. Ein internationales Handbuch zur Wissenschaft von Sprache und Gesellschaft*, 1. Halbband, 452–459. Berlin & New York: De Gruyter.

Clyne, Michael. 2003. *Dynamics of Language Contact: English and Immigrant Languages*. Cambridge: Cambridge University Press.

Coetsem, Frans Van. 2000. *A General and Unified Theory of the Transmission Process in Language Contact*. Heidelberg: Winter.

Crowley, Terry. 2004. Bislama: Morphology and syntax. In Bernd Kortmann, Kate Burridge, Rajend Mesthrie, Edgar Schneider & Clive Upton (eds.), *A Handbook of Varieties of English, Vol. 2: Morphology and Syntax*, 682–701. Berlin & New York: De Gruyter.

De Bot, Kees. 1992. A bilingual production model: Levelt's 'Speaking' model adapted. *Applied Linguistics* 13. 1–24.

Degani, Marta & Alexander Onysko. 2010. Hybrid compounding in New Zealand English. *World Englishes* 29 (2). 209–233.

Deuchar, Margaret & Jonathan Strammers. 2016. English-origin verbs in Welsh: Adjudicating between two theoretical approaches. *Languages* 1 (7). 1–16. doi:10.3390/languages1010007.

Dijkstra, Ton & Walter Van Heuven. 2002. The architecture of the bilingual word recognition system: From identification to decision. *Bilingualism: Language and Cognition* 5. 175–197.

Finkbeiner, Matthew, Tamar H. Gollan & Alfonso Caramazza. 2006. Lexical access in bilingual speakers: What's the (hard) problem? *Bilingualism: Language and Cognition* 9. 153–166.

Gardner-Chloros, Penelope. 2009. *Code-Switching*. Cambridge: Cambridge University Press.

Geeraerts, Dirk. 2016. The sociosemiotic commitment. *Cognitive Linguistics* 27 (4). 527–542.

Goldberg, Adele. 2006. *Constructions at Work*. Oxford: Oxford University Press.

Grosjean, François. 2001. The bilingual's language modes. In Janet L. Nicol (ed.), *One Mind, Two Languages: Bilingual Language Processing*, 1–22. Oxford: Blackwell.

Gumperz, John. 1982. *Discourse Strategies*. Cambridge: Cambridge University Press.

Harder, Peter. 2010. *Meaning in Mind and Society. A Functional Contribution to the Social Turn in Cognitive Linguistics*. Berlin & New York: De Gruyter.

Hartsuiker, Robert & Martin Pickering. 2008. Language integration in bilingual sentence production. *Acta Psychologica* 128 (3). 479–489.

Hartsuiker, Robert J. & Sarah Bernolet. 2017. The development of shared syntax in language learning. *Bilingualism: Language and Cognition* 20 (2). 219–234.

Haugen, Einar. 1950. The Analysis of Linguistic Borrowing. *Language* 26. 210–231.

Heine, Bernd & Tania Kuteva. 2005. *Language Contact and Grammatical Change*. Cambridge: Cambridge University Press.

Heine, Bernd & Tania Kuteva. 2008. Constraints on contact-induced linguistic change. *Journal of Language Contact*, Thema 2. 57–90.

Höder, Steffen. 2012. Multilingual constructions: A diasystematic approach to common structures. In Kurt Braunmüller & Christoph Gabriel (eds.), *Multilingual Individuals and Multilingual Societies*, 241–258. Amsterdam & Philadelphia: John Benjamins.

Höder, Steffen. 2014a. Constructing diasystems: Grammatical organisation in bilingual groups. In Tor A. Åfarlí & Brit Maehlum (eds.), *The Sociolinguistics of Grammar*, 137–152. Amsterdam & Philadelphia: John Benjamins.

Höder, Steffen. 2014b. Phonological elements and Diasystematic Construction Grammar. *Constructions and Frames* 6 (2). 202–231.

Höder, Steffen. Forthc. Grammar is community-specific: Background and basic concepts of Diasystematic Construction Grammar. In Hans Boas & Steffen Höder (eds.), *Constructions in Contact. Constructional Perspectives on Contact Phenomena in Germanic Languages* [working title]. Amsterdam & Philadelphia. Benjamins.

Humbley, John. 2015. Allogenisms: The major category of true false loans. In Cristiano Furiassi & Henrik Gottlieb (eds.), *Pseudo English: Studies on False Anglicisms in Europe*, 35–58. Berlin & New York: De Gruyter.

Isurin, Ludmilla, Donald Winford & Kees de Bot (eds.). 2009. *Multidisciplinary Approaches to Code Switching*. Amsterdam & Philadelphia: John Benjamins.

Jacobson, Rodolfo (ed.). 1998. *Codeswitching Worldwide*, Vol. 1. Berlin & New York: De Gruyter.

Jacobson, Rodolfo (ed.). 2001. *Codeswitching Worldwide*, Vol. 2. Berlin & New York: De Gruyter.

Jarvis, Scott 2009. Lexical transfer. In Anita Pavlenko (ed.), *The Bilingual Mental Lexicon: Interdisciplinary Approaches*, 99–124. Clevedon: Multilingual Matters.

Jarvis, Scott & Aneta Pavlenko. 2007. *Crosslinguistic Influence in Language and Cognition*. London & New York: Routledge.

Johanson, Lars. 2002. *Structural Factors in Turkic Language Contacts*. Richmond: Curzon.

Johanson, Lars. 2008. Remodeling grammar: Copying, conventionalization, grammaticalization. In Peter Siemund & Noemi Kintana (eds.), *Language Contact and Contact Languages*, 61–79. Amsterdam & Philadelphia: John Benjamins.

Knospe, Sebastian. 2014. *Entlehnung oder Codeswitching? Sprachmischungen mit dem Englischen im deutschen Printjournalismus* [Borrowing or Codeswitching? Language mixing with English in German print media]. Frankfurt a. Main: Peter Lang.

Kootstra, Gerrit J. & Muysken P. 2017. Cross-linguistic priming in bilinguals: Multidisciplinary perspectives on language processing, acquisition, and change. *Bilingualism: Language and Cognition* 20 (2). 215–218.

Kristiansen, Gitte & René Dirven (eds.). 2008. *Cognitive Sociolinguistics*. Berlin & New York: De Gruyter.

Kroll, Judith F. & Erika Stewart. 1994. Category interference in translation and picture naming: Evidence for asymmetric connections between bilingual memory representations. *Journal of Memory and Language* 33. 149–174.

Kroll, Judith F. & Daan Hermans. 2011. Psycholinguistic perspectives on language processing in bilinguals. In Monika Schmid & Wander Lowie (eds.), *Modeling Bilingualism: From Structure to Chaos*, 15–36. Amsterdam & Philadelphia: John Benjamins.

Kroll, Judith F., Jason W. Gulliver & Eleonora Rossi. 2013. The multilingual lexicon: The cognitive and neural basis of lexical comprehension and production in two or more languages. *Annual Review of Applied Linguistics* 33. 102–127.

Lemhöfer, Kristin, Ton Dijkstra & Marije C. Michel. 2004. Three languages, one ECHO: Cognate effects in trilingual word recognition. *Language and Cognitive Processes* 19 (5). 585–611.

Levelt, W. J. M. 1989. *Speaking: From Intention to Articulation*. Cambridge, MA: The MIT Press.

Lowie, Wander & Marjolijn Verspoor. 2011. The dynamics of multilingualism: Levelt's speaking model revisited. In Monika Schmid & Wander Lowie (eds.), *Modeling Bilingualism: From Structure to Chaos*, 267–288. Amsterdam & Philadelphia: John Benjamins.

Malcolm, Ian. 2004. Australian creoles and Aboriginal English: Morphology and syntax. In Bernd Kortmann, Kate Burridge, Rajend Mesthrie, Edgar Schneider & Clive Upton (eds.), *A Handbook of Varieties of English, Vol. 2: Morphology and Syntax*, 657–681. Berlin & New York: De Gruyter.

Matras, Yaron. 2009. *Language Contact*. Cambridge: Cambridge University Press.

Milroy, Lesley & Pieter Muysken (eds.). 1995. *One Speaker – Two Languages: Cross-Disciplinary Perspectives on Code-Switching*. Cambridge: Cambridge University Press.

Müller, Max. 1861. *Lectures on the Science of Language*. London: Longman, Green, Longman, and Roberts.

Muysken, Pieter. 1981. Half-way between Quechua and Spanish: The case for relexification. In Arnold Highfield & Albert Valdman (eds.), *Historicity and Variation in Creole Studies*, 52–79. Ann Arbor, MI: Karoma.

Muysken, Pieter. 2000. *Bilingual Speech*. Cambridge: Cambridge University Press.

Myers-Scotton, Carol. 1993. *Duelling Languages: Grammatical Structure in Code-Switching*. Oxford: Clarendon Press.

Myers-Scotton, Carol. 2002. *Contact Linguistics: Bilingual Encounters and Grammatical Outcomes*. Oxford: Oxford University Press.

Nicolaï, Robert. 2017. Meanderings around the notion of 'contact' in reference to languages, their dynamics, and to 'WE'. *Journal of Language Contact*, Advance Article, doi: 10.1163/19552629-01002011.

Odlin, Terence. 1989. *Language Transfer: Cross-Linguistic Influence in Language Learning*. Cambridge: Cambridge University Press.

Onysko, Alexander. 2007. *Anglicisms in German: Borrowing, Lexical Productivity and Written Codeswitching*. Berlin & New York: De Gruyter.

Onysko, Alexander. 2016. Modeling world Englishes from the perspective of language contact. *World Englishes* 35 (2). 196–220.
Paradis, Michel. 2004. *A Neurolinguistic Theory of Bilingualism*. Amsterdam & Philadelphia: John Benjamins.
Paul, Hermann. 1886. *Prinzipien der Sprachgeschichte*. Halle: Niemeyer.
Poplack, Shana. 1980. Sometimes I'll start a sentence in Spanish Y TERMINO EN ESPAÑOL: Toward a typology of code-switching. *Linguistics* 18 (7/8). 581–618.
Poplack, Shana. 2012. What does the Nonce Borrowing Hypothesis hypothesize? *Bilingualism: Language and Cognition* 15 (3). 644–648.
Poplack, Shana & Nathalie Dion. 2012. Myths and facts about loanword development. *Language Variation and Change* 24. 279–315.
Poplack, Shana & Marjory Meechan. 1998. How languages fit together in code-mixing. *International Journal of Bilingualism* 2 (2). 127–138.
Price, Cathy, David Green & Roswitha von Studnitz. 1999. Functional imaging study of translation and language switching. *Brain* 122. 2221–2236.
Pütz, Martin, Justyna Robinson & Monika Reif (eds.). 2012. Cognitive Sociolinguistics: Social and cultural variation in cognition and language use. Special issue in *Review of Cognitive Linguistics* 10 (2). Amsterdam & Philadelphia: John Benjamins.
Ringbom, Hakan. 2001. Lexical transfer in L3 production. In Jasone Cenoz, Britta Hufeisen & Ulrike Jessner (eds.), *Cross-linguistic Influence in Third Language Acquisition: Psycholinguistic Perspectives*, 59–68. Clevedon: Multilingual Matters.
Schmid, Hans-Jörg. 2016. Why cognitive linguistics must embrace the pragmatic and social dimensions of language and how it could do so more seriously. *Cognitive Linguistics*, 27 (4). 543–557.
Schuchardt, Hugo. 1884. *Slawo-deutsches und Slawo-italienisches*. Graz: Leuschner and Lubensky.
Smith, Geoff. 2004. Tok Pisin: Morphology and syntax. In Bernd Kortmann, Kate Burridge, Rajend Mesthrie, Edgar Schneider & Clive Upton (eds.), *A Handbook of Varieties of English, Vol. 2: Morphology and Syntax*, 720–741. Berlin & New York: De Gruyter.
Starreveld, Peter A., Annette M. B. De Groot, Baart M. M. Rossmark & Janet G. Van Hell. 2014. Parallel language activation during word processing in bilinguals: Evidence from word production in sentence context. *Bilingualism: Language and Cognition* 17 (2). 258–276.
Strammers, Jonathan & Margaret Deuchar. 2012. Testing the nonce borrowing hypothesis: Counterevidence from English origin verbs in Welsh. *Bilingualism: Language and Cognition* 15 (3). 630–643.
Thomason, Sarah G. 2001. *Language Contact: An Introduction*. Edinburgh: Edinburgh University Press.
Treffers-Daller, Jeanine & Jeanette Sakel. 2012. Why transfer is a key aspect of language use and processing in bilinguals and L2-users. *International Journal of Bilingualism* 16 (1). 3–10.
Weinreich, Uriel. 1953. *Languages in Contact*. The Hague: Mouton.
Whitney, William Dwight. 1881. On mixture in language. *Transactions of the American Philosophical Association* 12. 5–26.
Winford, Donald. 2003. *An Introduction to Contact Linguistics*. Malden, MA: Blackwell Publishing.
Winford, Donald. 2008. Processes of creole formation and related contact-induced language change. *Journal of Language Contact*, Thema 2. 124–145.

Winter-Froemel, Esme. 2011. *Entlehnung in der Kommunikation und im Sprachwandel*. Berlin & Boston: De Gruyter.
Wohlgemuth, Jan. 2009. *A Typology of Verbal Borrowings*. Berlin & New York: De Gruyter.
Zenner, Eline. 2013. *Cognitive Contact Linguistics. The Macro, Meso and Micro Influence of English on Dutch*. Unpublished PhD Thesis, KU Leuven (University of Leuven).
Zenner, Eline, Dirk Speelman & Dirk Geeraerts. 2012. Cognitive Sociolinguistics meets loanword research: Measuring variation in the success of anglicisms in Dutch. *Cognitive Linguistics* 23 (4). 749–792.
Zenner, Eline, Dirk Speelman & Dirk Geeraerts. 2014a. What makes a catchphrase catchy? Possible determinants in the borrowability of English catchphrases in Dutch. In Eline Zenner & Gitte Kristiansen (eds.), *New Perspectives on Lexical Borrowing*, 41–64. Berlin & New York: De Gruyter.
Zenner, Eline, Dirk Speelman & Dirk Geeraerts. 2014b. Core vocabulary, borrowability and entrenchment: A usage-based onomasiological approach. *Diachronica* 31 (1). 74–105.

Anna Verschik
2 English-Estonian code-copying in blogs: Combining a contact linguistic and cognitive approach

Abstract: As suggested by Backus (2012, 2015, usage-based models of contact-induced language change), this paper combines a cognitive approach with the code-copying framework (CCF) developed by Johanson (1992). One of my points of departure is that changes in morphosyntax and lexicon are to be considered in the same terminological framework, as is done by Johanson, because they are subject to the same underlying cognitive mechanism (copying). I will pursue the line of argument suggested by Backus and Verschik (2012) who reconsider traditional borrowing hierarchies and claim that frequency and the type of meaning affect the degree of copying that can be global (lexical borrowing or codeswitching in traditional terminology), selective (structure, pattern) or mixed.

The analysis relies on data from Estonian fashion and life-style blogs (about 150,000 tokens). Belonging to a monological asynchronous genre, blogs provide a window into individual language use, multilingual repertoire, entrenchment of English items and patterns (Backus 2012) and evolution of multilingual speech. As, according to Matras (2009, 2012) and Backus (2012), change in use starts from a multilingual individual, this is why contact linguistics should focus on such individuals in addition to multilingual communities.

I will show that not only semantically specific or transparent items (analytic verbs, compounds) are attractive for copying (in the sense of Johanson 1999). Pragmatic prominence, perceived novelty, metaphoricity and expressive connotation are factors promoting global copying. The data show that the presence of code alternation (stretches in another language, Johanson 1999, Muysken 2000) is better explicable by meaning than by structural factors or macro-sociolinguistic factors, such as typological distance, proficiency in each language, prestige, dominance in use, type of community, etc. (Muysken 2000: 247-249) because English alternations in the blogs are mostly idioms, fixed expressions or syntactically autonomous units with a strong emotional colouring. I assume that the difference between insertions and alternations is not always clear; it is possible that both are brought about by certain types of meaning.

Anna Verschik, Tallinn University

https://doi.org/10.1515/9783110619430-003

Keywords: code-copying, usage-based approach, contact linguistics, Estonian, English

1 Introduction

The focus of the current article is the impact of English on Estonian in light of the Code Copying Framework (CCF) developed by Johanson (1993, 2002, 2006, 2008). Using English-Estonian code-copying data from blogs, I will show that CCF is compatible with cognitive approaches to contact-induced language change, namely, with the usage-based approach advocated by Backus (2012, 2014, 2015).

CCF is a holistic framework that employs the same meta-language for contact phenomena in the lexicon and in morphosyntax (a need for such a framework was explained by Backus 2012: 3-4). CCF is flexible in terminology and accurate at a descriptive level, allowing in this way to have a closer look at phenomena on the interface of lexicon and morphosyntax (Backus and Verschik 2012). I will show how meaning (specificity, expressivity, prominence at the level of discourse), frequency, perceived novelty, metaphoricity, transparency and similarity contribute to copiability (or borrowability) of linguistic items, be it single words, expressions, phrases or alternations. The assumption that type or degree of copying (global, selective and mixed) provides important information (Backus and Verschik 2012; Verschik 2016) will be further developed.

The data comes from 335 entries in Estonian fashion, beauty and lifestyle blogs. The corpus consists of 91,844 words (tokens). As asynchronic monologic genres of computer-mediated communication, blogs provide a window into individual language use. Proponents of usage-based approaches to language contact have emphasized the importance of multilingual individuals as "agents of influence" (Matras 2009: 310-311, 2012; Backus 2012).

The literature on English-Estonian language contacts has been scarce and written in Estonian (Igav 2013; Roosileht 2013; Vaba 2010). A recent exception to this is a study on English code alternations in Estonian blogs (Verschik and Kask, in press) but the focus of that paper is not CCF but rather code alternation and Muysken's (2000) triangular model.

Below, we outline the theoretical background for a cognitive approach, usage-based approach to language contact, presenting the basic points of departure for this paper in more detail. Then the main postulates of CCF will be discussed, with special attention to cognitive components. Next, a brief description of my data will be followed by analysis of code-copying cases, and a discussion of the results.

2 Theoretical background and points of departure

A usage-based approach to language change is not new as such: the need for such an approach was already articulated in the famous work by Weinreich, Labov, and Herzog (1968) where the authors call for the analysis of naturalistic language use as opposed to various formal approaches. As Backus (2014: 91–92) theorizes, the very understanding of language knowledge is different in formal and usage-based linguistics: for the latter, it is not mere knowledge of structures and items, but it is based on the interplay of general cognitive skills (abilities of categorization, generalization, comparison etc.) and communicative needs. Backus (2014: 93) suggests that knowing a certain word or construction means having it stored in one's mind (the cognitive aspect) but storage presupposes experience, that is, the language user knows the word or construction because of previous exposure to it in interaction (the social aspect).

It is not hard to link these observations to issues at play in contact linguistics. Much of the empirical work in contact linguistics is *de facto* usage-based (naturalistic language contact data is collected and analyzed), but articulate attempts for a synthesis between Cognitive Linguistics and contact linguistic research are rather recent (Backus 2012, 2014, 2015). In the similar spirit, Matras (2012) reflects upon connections between linguistic resources and communicative needs and calls this the activity-oriented approach. He argues that a straight correlation between social factors and the change of linguistic structures not always exists. For instance, prestige does not explain why conjunctions are often borrowed in language contact situation (Matras 2012: 18–19). He rather suggests that cognitive factors are at play: in earlier writings (Matras 1998) he explains that, when language use is less restricted by norms, a multilingual can draw on his/her multilingual resources, which helps to relieve the cognitive load.

Based on these previous insights, this paper sets forward a number of theoretical points of departure. These are outlined in the remainder of this section.

a. Cognition and social experience (communication) are linked
Cognition and social experience are linked because cognition affects and shapes language according to communicative needs; in turn, communicative needs, experience and exposure to certain varieties, styles, type of communicative situations affect cognition (i.e., what we acquire and how our language resources and linguistic awareness change in time and space). This usage-based view on competence is shared with much work in Cognitive Linguistics and was adopted by Blommaert and Backus (2011: 7–8) to account for multilingual repertoires. They

mention that linguistic and communicative competence are not separate but one should be conceptualized as the other. This proposition is related to (d).

b. Change as an inherent feature of language

Change is a built-in feature of language (but has not always been prominent in language theorizing, Backus 2012: 6). Formal approaches often view language as a closed homogenous system of stable and invariant components. On the surface, we see change as addition/deletion of an item (new word), structure or combination to a linguistic system. This is not wrong in itself but oftentimes change (also) has cognitive reasons: perception of a gap in the inventory, perception of differences in meaning, style etc. may lead to addition of a new lexical item and deletion of an old one (or division of labour between the two). Johanson (2002: 298) talks about the versatility and ever-changing character of language systems.

Consider the introduction of a new Estonian verb *laikima* 'to like a post, picture or comment in social networks', copied from English *to like*. First of all, a new reality, that of social networks and virtual communication emerges. This reality is being currently conceptualized primarily in English and replicas in other languages (i.e. one can choose Estonian or another language for using Facebook) follow the English original concept and terms. While social networks such as Facebook are available in Estonian, Estonian-speakers nevertheless perceive a conceptual and lexical gap in their linguistic inventory. First, Estonian has a different argument structure: *mulle meeldib* 'I like' means literally 'to me pleases', so when you like a post, you press the button *meeldib* 'pleases' (3SG). But when the focus is on the agent (someone does something), there is no way in Estonian to express it. Second, the verb *meeldima* 'to be to one's liking' has a general meaning, whereas a new lexical item would fit for a quite specific context (internet communication). Therefore, this example illustrates that language change (introduction of a new lexical item) is conditioned by social (need to communicate a new meaning), cognitive (perception of a conceptual gap) and structural (difference in argument structure) factors.

c. Relevance of language contact

Similarly, every language is in contact with other languages and, so to speak, contactlessness is not a default, unmarked state of any language. All sorts of innovations, not only lexical changes, are first introduced by multilingual individuals and, if successful, such innovations may gain currency and become a part of monolingual use so that after some time only specialists in linguistics are aware of the foreign origin of a certain item, pattern or feature. Drawing a parallel to the well-known example by Romaine (1995: 1) that monolingualism is perceived as unmarked and it is hard to imagine a book titled "Monolingualism", one may say that there is ample body of literature on contact linguistics, yet we have to explain that changes through contact are not less important than internal changes. By default, a lot of language theorizing is done with a tacit assumption that "contactlessness" is unmarked and natural, which is particularly true for Cognitive Linguistics.

d. Importance of the individual for Cognitive Contact Linguistics

From the early days of contact linguistics, Weinreich (1953: 71) noted that the locus of language contact is the bilingual's brain. The individual is not just a representative of a linguistic community in a certain sociolinguistic situation but is important in his/her own right. Croft (2000: 35) states that, differently from formal definition of language as "a system of contrasts of signs", a language is a population of utterances in a speech community; grammar is a cognitive phenomenon in the mind of a speaker, whereas grammar is acquired on the basis of exposure of a particular speaker and, therefore, is different in different speakers. In the same spirit, cognitive linguistics is currently paying a lot of attention to the individual (for instance, Dąbrowska 2012).

From a slightly different perspective, Blommaert and Backus (2011: 2) argue that there is great variety in the way and to what extent individuals acquire languages (especially in the reality of superdiversity, growing impact of computer-mediated communication, social networks and mobility) and that linguistic repertoires have a biographical (individual) origin. Thus, a re-orientation of focus towards the individual is welcome.

Continuing this line of thought, Backus (2012: 8) explains that usage is influenced at more particular levels than traditionally community-based factors (language status, dominance, spread of bilingualism and other macro-sociolinguistic aspects of language contacts) and speaker-based factors (socioeconomic class, age, gender, command of languages in question). An innovation (also contact-induced) occurs at first in an individual and may become successful in a micro-community or even in a larger community. If this is not the case, attestation of innovation in an individual is still highly relevant because it provides evidence of what kind of (contact-induced) innovation is possible in principle.

e. Different kind of linguistic awareness in multilinguals

This point has been developed by scholars in bilingualism, for instance, in Cooks' multi-competence model, where multi-competence is defined as "the overall system of a mind or a community that uses more than one language" (Cook 2016: 3). It is claimed that even if a multilingual person is more proficient in one language and less proficient in others, the nature of his/her knowledge of the dominant language differs from such knowledge of a monolingual person. Dewaele

(2016: 403) labels the multi-competence approach as cognitive, i.e. one focusing on mind. I believe many contact linguists would subscribe to the view that multilingual cognition is not a sum of several isolated monolingual cognitive systems. Probably, one of the reasons for difference in the nature of linguistic competence of mono- and multilingual is the option of (conscious or unconscious) comparison between linguistic systems (and different situations experienced in different languages). Comparison is a powerful cognitive instrument that is put at work by the presence of more than one linguistic system. Indeed, if one has only one system, there is nothing to compare to.

Another point is that multilingual awareness (ability to focus on form and sensitivity to how language as such functions) may lead to different treatment of foreign lexical material. Multilinguals do not always need the same mechanisms of adaptation of new items/patterns as monolinguals (see Leisiö 2001 on Finnish nouns in the Russian morphosyntactic frame; Zabrodskaja and Verschik 2014 on Estonian nouns in the Russian morphosyntactic frame). Sometimes there are no monolinguals to compare with as all speakers of a certain variety are multilinguals (and no knowledge of the pre-contact situation either). The degree to which a foreign-origin item is entrenched cannot be measured by the degree of adaptation to the rules of that language (i.e. phonological adaptation, addition of inflectional morphology, etc). In this respect, formal monolingual criteria alone cannot help to distinguish between single word CS and lexical borrowing. Also note that formal criteria cannot be applied to patterns and constructions where no obviously foreign items appear (word for word renditions of fixed expressions, changes in word order and argument structure, etc.).

Speaking of the entrenchment of a foreign origin item or a construction, cognitive-social explanations seem more reasonable than formal ones: the more one is exposed to a certain innovation, the more this innovation becomes a habitual part in individual linguistic repertoire. This innovation may become successful when many language users "discover" it independently and favour it to such a degree that the innovation in question becomes conventionalized at a community level.

f. Lack of strict (cognitive) separation between morphosyntax and lexicon
There is no strict cognitive division between morphosyntax and lexicon (holistic approach to contact-induced language change). This claim may appear extreme at a first glance. For instance, Matras (2012) suggests that replication of foreign origin lexical items (matter replication, or MAT in the terms of Matras and Sakel 2007) is more conscious than replication of other language patterns (pattern replication, or PAT).

Nevertheless, there is evidence that in certain instances of compromise forms emerge in multilingual speech where an insertion of a lexical item affects grammar. This has been discussed by Auer and Muhamedova (2005), Backus

(2005), Clyne (2003) and many others. To give one example of my own, let us consider (1a), Estonian in italics and English in bold.

(1a) *Kiri* **from** *Rimmel*
letter from Rimmel (family name)
'a letter from Rimmel'

Estonian is rich in inflectional morphology (14 cases) and in monolingual Estonian this is rendered as in (1b) by the means of ablative case (ABL):

(1b) *Kiri* *Rimmel-i-lt*
letter Rimmel-STEM-ABL
'a letter from Rimmel'

English does not have case marking and upon the insertion of the English preposition *from* Estonian noun does not receive the ablative marker but instead is treated as if it were an English noun. From a cognitive point of view, this means emergence of a compromise form (English-Estonian prepositional phrase without case marking) and, if the innovation gains currency, a potential candidate for structural change (or at least a parallel variant alongside with the conventional one).

Having presented the theoretical departure points, I am going to turn to a general description of CCF and its cognitive aspects.

3 CCF and its cognitive aspects

Johanson (2002) concentrates mostly on structural and sociolinguistic aspects of language contact but also mentions several concepts that may as well be interpreted from a cognitive linguistic point of view. He believes that, while structural tendencies may also cause linguistic change, extra-linguistic factors, including cognitive ones, are decisive for the actual language change (Johanson 2002: 286). First, I will present the basic concepts of Code-Copying Framework (CCF) and then discuss its cognitive components.

3.1 Basic premises of CCF

Picking up on earlier arguments by Einar Haugen, Johanson (1993: 198-199) claims erroneous metaphors about language contact distort the picture. The most common metaphors are those of borrowing (something taken from another place) and switching (a clear point where a switch turns and a person starts talking in another language). In fact, a "borrowed" linguistic item is not taken away from another language (and does not have to be returned); as for switch, it is not always abrupt and the borders between languages are not always clear. Where there are clear chunks of another language, this is called code alternation (CA). Contact-induced influence in all subsystems of language is considered as copying. It is a mechanism underlying language contacts and refers both to lexical and non-lexical features (meaning, combinability, frequency, etc).

In Johanson (2002) the interaction between varieties (codes) is subdivided into CA and code-copying. I will show that CA is also relevant from a cognitive point of view, although Johanson does not give CA as much attention.

The code from where one copies is called model code. From this items and properties are copied into the basic code. Copying is bi-directional, i.e. both L1 > L2 and L2 > L1, which holds for both sociolinguistically dominant languages and for minority languages. It is important that there is a distinction between sociolinguistic dominance and dominance in the terms of proficiency. Copying L1 > L2 is called imposition and L2 > L1 adoption. Both imposition and adoption happen in the same speaker.

Every item has four kinds of properties: material, semantic, combinational and frequential. All properties of an item may be copied into the basic code, yet the copy is not the same as the original. It "lives its own life" in the basic code. If all properties are copied, it is a global copy (henceforth GC). GC corresponds to borrowing/insertional codeswitching (CS) in conventional terms. Thus, above-mentioned items *laikima* and *from* (1a) are examples of GC.

If only some properties are copied, then we deal with selective copy (SC). This notion corresponds to convergence, structural change, grammatical transfer in other frameworks and to pattern replication in Matras and Sakel (2007). One can copy semantic, combinational, material properties etc. but not all of them. For instance, Estonian *jääge meiega* 'stay with us' is a semantic combinational copy from English *stay with us*. Prior to contact, this phrase was not conventionalized as a semantic whole and literally meant something like 'please, stay with us and don't leave yet'. Now it is used in the same context as the English model (broadcasting, TV talk shows etc). Or consider the spread of use of Estonian inessive form of *ma*-infinitive (*mas*-form like *tulemas* 'coming') modelled on English progressive in contexts where present tense form would be expected (Metslang 2006, Backus and Verschik 2012).

Compounds, analytic verbs, fixed expression, i.e., what can be labelled as multi-word items can produce different degrees of copying. Consider (2) where *töötav* 'working' is Estonian:

(2) **hard**-töötav
    hard-working
    'hard-working'

It would be counterintuitive to analyze *hard* as GC because both parts "hold together" semantically and are conventionalized as a whole. Quite often, the whole meaning is not a mechanical sum of the meanings of separate components. Instances as (2) are called mixed copies (MC). This is a useful descriptive category (more details in Backus and Verschik 2012, on Estonian-Russian MC, see also Verschik 2016). The more items a multi-word item has, the more variation in copying is possible.

Multiword items may exhibit variation in copying. For instance, *outfit-pilt* 'outfit picture' is half-English and half-Estonian, so to say. The two elements, *outfit* and *pilt* 'picture' co-occur often in fashion blogs. Note that English *outfit* does not receive Estonian genitive marking –*i*: one would expect *outfit-i pilt* 'a/the picture of a/the outfit' (genitive + nominative) but having both nouns in nominative is also possible in some contexts. The blog data also contain the GC *outfit picture* or *outfit (photo)shoot* where both components are from English.

Various types of copies will be considered in Section 5; now we move to cognitive aspects of CCF.

3.2 Cognitive aspects of CCF

In my view, the following topics in CCF can be considered as related to cognition: the holistic approach (no strict border between synchronic and diachronic contact processes, no strict border between lexicon and morphosyntax); attractiveness, salience, transparency of linguistic items, cross-linguistic similarity, meaning, habitualization and conventionalization of copies.

I have emphasized elsewhere (Verschik 2008, 2016) that the tradition of separating (1) synchronic and diachronic processes and (2) contact effects in lexicon (borrowing, CS) and morphosyntax (convergence, structural change) may be counterproductive. Similar views have been expressed by Backus (2005, 2012: 5) and Backus and Verschik (2012). According to the usage-based approach (and also cognitive-functional approach developed by Matras 2009), changes start at the individual level and may subsequently spread and become conventionalized, i.e. a part of general use. Thus, changes in speech are not less "serious" than those that have become a part of language.

As for (2), I elaborated on this in Section 2 f. In this connection, recall that counterexamples have been attested for all kind of proposed constraints on CS. The same is true for proposed constraints to contact-induced language change. As Backus (2005) demonstrated, CS often leads to language change; CS (i.e. introduction of other language lexical items) can drag along morphosyntactic properties from that language. In the same vein, Auer and Muhamedova (2005) show how Russian adjective phrases within a Kazakh morphosyntactic frame behave according to Kazakh rules (the adjective is always assigned masculine gender because Turkic languages have no gender category). To put it in Myers-Scotton's (1993) terms, the Embedded Language island (the stretch, i.e., adjective phrase in Russian) is not "well-formed" and does not maintain Embedded Language grammar but is impacted by the Matrix Language (Kazakh) grammar. Similar examples are analysed in Verschik (2015). As an alternative, take example (1a) where the English preposition provokes treating the Estonian noun as an English one, i.e., without case marking.

Johanson (2002: 294) believes that allegedly universal constraints are merely tendencies. I agree with this view. It does not mean that copying is chaotic, but there are no universal constraints and "morphosyntactic conflict" is not an obstacle for copying: so anything can be copied.

Thus, whether we notice and copy/replicate a word or a pattern, the mental operation is basically the same, namely copying. Matras and Sakel (2007) and Matras (2009) have a similar understanding, labelling the mechanism as "replication". For them, global copies and selective copies are matter replication and pattern replication respectively. However, the "half and half" cases (i.e. MC) are not analysed by Matras and Sakel 2007 (see critique in Backus and Verschik 2012). MC are a demonstration of the sameness of the mechanisms of contact-induced language change in lexicon and morphosyntax.

Attractiveness/attractivity is, according to Johanson (2002: 309), an empirically manifested susceptibility to copying. Relatively simple, regular and transparent structures are good candidates for copying. Here Johanson also refers to usage (what is attractive, can be derived from empirical data). Also in a later work (Johanson 2006: 25) he states that transparent, regular, analytical, simple properties are more attractive to copying. It appears that Johanson understands attractivity as a complex of structural characteristics: items have certain structural properties that make them more attractive (Johanson 2002: 286). Let us now examine the cognitive factors that may explain why these properties are attractive.

Salience is a concept used in many fields of linguistics (cognitive linguistics, dialectology, sociolinguistics, SLA). Johanson (2002: 309) understands it as perceptual or cognitive prominence, whereas speakers are aware of salient properties. This concept is less elaborated in CCF, yet its cognitive aspect is obvious from Johanson's definition. I will return to attractiveness and salience in the discussion section.

An understanding that similar structures, items, patterns are easier to copy is not novel as such (see Clyne's 2003 concept of facilitation in transfer, congruent lexicalization in Muysken 2000). Johanson (2002: 293–294, 306) mentions code-internal factors that facilitate copying: similar elements fit better, common ordering principles providing equivalence favour copying. Similarity makes copying easier but is not a necessary prerequisite thereof. It should be added that similarity may be perceived, i.e. it is not necessarily the same for linguists and laypeople. Increased contact and increased copying may lead to changes that increase similarities between two varieties and this facilitates copying (snowball effect).

One may ask whether analyticity, transparency, regularity, etc. are structural characteristics or structural and cognitive at the same time. There is empirical evidence that analytic structures are often copied in many contact situations (compound nouns, analytic verbs, see Verschik 2008, Chapter 4). Probably, this is so because analytic structures have a transparent meaning and are salient (outstanding, cognitively prominent) and thus easily intelligible. Thus, what is traditionally considered as structural properties is closely linked to meaning and perception, which are cognitive qualities.

From a cognitive point of view, meaning is also relevant. Johanson (2002: 306) claims that specific meaning favours copying. This correlates well with Backus' (2001) notion of semantic specificity. Empirically, specific items are prone to global copying (Backus and Verschik 2012).

Johanson (2002: 298–299) introduces concepts of habitualization and conventionalization. Habitualization is probably understood as a stage on the conventionalization continuum rather than as rootedness in an individual's use, as understood by Backus (2012). Johanson notes (2002: 298) that there are diachronic dimensions in the life of a copied element and that what starts as a momentary instance of copying may become frequently used and habitualized in individuals and/or groups and later conventionalized as a new norm. In later work (Johanson 2008: 65), he distinguishes between momentary, habitualized and conventionalized copies, emphasizing that these stages form a continuum. If a copy is not successful, it can become deconventionalized and lost (Johanson 2008: 66). Importantly, the degree of adaptation is not a criterion of habitualization and conventionalization (Johanson 2002: 302).

Above I have formulated a number of principles that together can be part of a theoretical account of contact effects that is grounded in what we know about human cognition. In the remainder of the article I will analyse contact data from Estonian blogs which use a considerable amount of English. The analysis will be descriptively grounded in Johanson's Code Copying Model while my account of the data will make use of the abovementioned principles.

4 Data and informants

As mentioned, my data comes from fashion, beauty and life-style blogs. All bloggers live in Estonia (information available from their profile) and their first language is Estonian (this is clear from the context). I have written in detail about the usefulness of blogs for contact-linguistic research (Verschik 2016, Verschik and Kask, in press). Here I will only briefly name some points.

a. one can observe language use during a certain period of time (some idea about emergence of contact-induced features and their further use/disappearance);
b. being an individual monologic asynchronous genre, it provides insight into individual repertoire and resources (in other words, it is a bottom-up approach that allows looking at entrenchment, cf. Backus 2012);
c. specific topics (gardening, life-style, fashion, handicraft, sports etc) are addressed, allowing us to look closer at specificity (semantic specificity is gradient and relative, Backus and Verschik 2012; i.e. what is specific for a given topic, what is conventionalized beyond given thematic blogs);
d. observing several blogs on the same topic helps to expose the norms of the genre (say, compulsory and optional features of a fashion blogs, like post titles in English).

The data comes from 20 blogs (observed during the period 2013-spring 2016), one of which is kept by two males and the rest by females. This is understandable given that the topics are fashion and beauty. The corpus consists of 91,844 words (335 posts). Only posts that have contact-linguistic effects are saved; every post is saved as a separate file. Data on copies is presented in the next section.

5 CCF in blogs

In this section I will consider copies according to their types: global, selective and mixed copies (respectively GC, SC, MC) and code alternations (CA). I am aware that it is not always easy to tell the difference between CA and insertional GC (in Muysken's 2000 terms, alternational and insertional CS), for instance, a fixed expression may be syntactically autonomous but have an overall figurative meaning and thus be indivisible into separate components.

The overall picture of different types of copies in the corpus (91,844 words) is as follows (Table 1):

Table 1: Number of copies in the corpus.

Types of copies	Number of copies	Notes
GC	536	Content words, including 31 discourse marker and 1 conjunction
SC	11	Semantic copying (expansion of meaning of common internationalisms), word-for-word renditions of idioms; 1 case of argument structure copying
MC	53	Including in-between cases, see more in MC section
CA	540	Including titles that are syntactically autonomous

As it is evident from Table 1, GC and CA constitute the largest part of all copying cases. The prevalence of GC is not surprising: other researchers of English-Estonian code-copying have attested the same (Igav 2013; Roosileht 2013; Vaba 2010).

Mostly, GC are content words, which is, again, not surprising, because they are primary candidates for copying because of their specific (unique or concrete) meaning. In this group there are some discourse markers, traditionally not considered in borrowability hierarchies (van Hout and Muysken 1994; Field 2002: 34–40), yet increasingly important in language contact research (see seminal studies by Salmons 1990; Maschler 1994; Matras 1998, 2012) and recently with the socio-pragmatic turn in Anglicism research (Andersen 2014; Onysko 2009; Peterson and Vaattovaara 2014; Zenner and Van De Mieroop 2017)

Low number of SC has been reported in other studies as well (Roosileht 2013 discussed data most similar to mine) and also in other language pairs (Estonian and Russian, Verschik 2014a), where Estonian is the source of copying. My observations are based on similar kind of data (blogs) and it is entirely possible that for different text types (for instance, non-monological genres of internet communication, oral speech etc) the share of SC may be higher than MC. I will propose a possible explanation to this. The number of MC is not high either but is nevertheless higher than that of SC. MC includes some in-between cases where it is hard to draw a strict border because there is a question to what degree components "belong together" in order to count as a semantic conventionalized whole.

The high number of CA needs explanation. CA is seldom looked into in contact linguistic studies (but is an important topic in pragmatically oriented approaches to multilingual interaction). On the first glance it appears that nothing happens there from the point of view of structural change, for CA are wholesale chunks from a different language. However, recently Demirçay and Backus (2014: 34) pointed out that sometimes there is no clear difference between insertions and alternations (in Muysken's terms). It makes sense that the longer the stretch in a different language is, the safer to count it as CA. In the current article I will not deal with the question of delimitation between CA and insertions (GC in our terms) but rather with cognitive reasons for CA.

Now we start the analysis with GC, SC, MC and then move to CA.

5.1 Global copies

As argued by Backus and Verschik (2012), copying specific meaning goes hand in hand with the copying of an overt form, that is, GC. Content words do have specific meaning, as opposed to general meaning. Most often, we need specific words for communication. Because of their function, i.e. naming things, nouns are by far the most specific in their meaning and are the first candidates for global copying (in fact, nouns occupy the first position in all known borrowability hierarchies, whereas authors differ what category immediately follows, adjectives or verbs).

In my data, GC are mostly nouns, followed by adjectives, discourse markers and occasionally verbs. Adjectives have either a highly specific meaning or high expressivity. As these are thematic blogs, it is expectable that quite a few GC would be terms specific to fashion, beauty and photography. Consider example (3):

(3) *Ma olen viimasel ajal täiesti **highlighter**-i-te lummuses!*
 highlighter-STEM-GEN PL
 'recently I've been completely under the spell of highlighters!'

Specific adjectives, as in (4), may be considered as terms, such as nuanced colour names (*taupe, nude*) or referring to qualities of fabrics and silhouettes (*fluffy, chunky, oversized*) or to wardrobe composition principles (*basic, matching*), as in (5):

(4) *Must ja **nude** sobivad omavahel nagu maasikas ja vahukoor*
 'black and nude fit together like strawberries and wiped cream'

(5) *Fännan CK'i **basic** riideid, nagu näiteks teada-tuntud pesu, T-särgid ja pusad.*
 'I fan CK basic clothes like for example well known underwear, T-shirts and sweaters'

On the structural note, the adjective *basic* does not receive Estonian inflectional morphology, although in Estonian adjectives agree with nouns in case and number (here *riideid* is partitive plural). This has been attested by Verschik and Kask (in press); it is not entirely clear yet why and in what instances English adjectives do not receive Estonian morphological markers. In any case, absence of full morphosyntactic integration is not an indicator of novelty (as opposed to conventionalized copies): a search of the collocation *basic asjad* 'basic things' in Estonian (google.ee) yields 624,000 results (not all are relevant instances, but a majority of the verified examples are). Such Internet searches provide some idea about conventionalization in general use and in different genres of internet texts. I will return to internet search as an auxiliary technique in Section 5.2 on SC.

Emotionally loaded English adjectives are characteristic not only of blogs but of oral speech, too. Although there are no studies to quote, adjectives like *cool, chill, hot, awesome, fancy, scary, creepy* and the adjectivized participle *obsessed* are familiar to anyone who is exposed to Estonian speech of urban youngsters and people in their thirties (i.e., socialized after the restoration of the independence in 1991). See (6) and (7) from the blog data:

(6) *Ja   kui   midagi   **fancy**-m-a-t   otsida*
    and   if   something:PART   fancy-COMP-STEM-PART   Search
    siis   Raimondi-sse
    then   Raimond-ILL
    'and if you are looking for something more fancy, then to Raimond'

(7) *Ma pole ammu millestki nii **obsessed** olnud.*
    'I have not been so obsessed with anything for a long time'

Example (7) is instructive from a structural point of view because Estonian does not have a strict equivalent of the verbs *to obsess* and the participle *obsessed* and the question of argument structure remains open. English has *to be obsessed with* but Estonian shows variation. In (7) the pronoun is in the form of elative: *millest-ki* (anything-EL-NEG), which literally means 'to be obsessed from'. It may be an analogy with Estonian adjectivized participles that require elative, like *häiritud* 'disturbed', *vaevatud* 'exhausted', 'haunted' and many others. It appears that the argument structure *obsessed* + elative has not been completely conventionalized: I searched google.ee for *ära ole obsessed* 'don't be obsessed'(I used an Estonian-English phrase in order to get Estonian-language results) and there are options *obsessed* + elative like in (7) but also *obsessed* + instrumental: *oled obsessed selle... teema-ga* (topic-INSTR) 'you are obsessed with this... topic', which would be a copy of the English construction. Thus, there are potential variants: either

GC as in (7) or a GC that brings along English argument structure and introduces a SC. Again, this demonstrates that syntactic conflict is not an obstacle for copying (see more in Section 5.2) and, from a cognitive point of view, strong emotional loadedness facilitates copying.

Compounds are also subject to global copying: some of them are fixed expressions like *step-by-step* (see (11)), some have components linked in a looser manner, like *cheat day* or *skinny scarf* (imagine variation like *cheat week* or *skinny jeans*):

(8) ... *ja sellise dieedi kõrval on mul iga nädal ka üks* **cheat day**
'... and in addition to this diet I have also one cheat day every week'

(9) **Skinny scarf** *on tegelikult märksa palju praktilisem*
'skinny scarf is actually a lot more practical'

As discussed earlier, Johanson claims that transparent meaning facilitates copying but the question is what type of copying that is. It has been argued that the more components a multi-word item has, the more potential variation there is (Backus and Verschik 2012). It makes sense that items like *cheat day* and *skinny scarf* in (8) and (9) can also yield MC: *cheat päev* ('day') and *skinny sall* ('scarf'). In fact, Google does produce *cheat päev* as the first result. Also Estonian has *skinny teksa(se)d* 'skinny jeans' as a conventionalized unit (google.ee search yields 266,000 results).

Another prominent group of GC comprises discourse particles, known also under different names (discourse words, discourse pragmatic words etc). It is a loose group of words that, according to Maschler (1994) belongs to meta-language as opposed to propositional language. Unlike propositional language, addition/deletion of meta-language elements does not change the sense of an utterance but modifies it, communicating the speaker's attitudes (by the means of words like *cool, no way, sorry* etc) or demonstrating how propositions are connected with each other (by the means of conjunctions). Contact linguistics literature on borrowing/copying of discourse particles is substantial and such copying happens in a wide variety of sociolinguistic situations (see seminal work by Salmons 1990). The much quoted paper by Matras (1998) on utterance modifiers, as he calls this group of words, argues that they come from a pragmatically dominant language (that is, not necessarily sociolinguistically dominant language). According to Matras (1998), bilinguals tend to have one set of utterance modifiers. This set helps to relief the cognitive load of non-monolingual communication. Noteworthy, in some contact situations all kinds of utterance modifiers get copied (Wertheim 2003 on Russian-Tatar contacts), whereas in some modifiers other than conjunctions are copied (or vice versa, see Verschik 2014b on Lithuanian conjunctions in Yiddish).

Although there is no research on English discourse particles (including conjunctions) in Estonian, based on everyday experience it is safe to claim that many English utterance modifiers such as *sorry, whatever, anyway* have become conventionalized in colloquial Estonian and are not specific to blogs. This is in line with the findings in socio-pragmatic research on Anglicisms. With this group of GC, I have only one instance of conjunction copying (recall Table 1):

(10) **although** *see oli synnal*
      'although it was at the birthday party'

Thus, my results are not different from those by Igav (2013), Roosileht (2013) and Vaba (2010). Global copying is facilitated by semantic specificity, prominence at the discourse level, expressivity and analyticity (multi-word items with transparent meaning).

5.2 Selective copies

As it is clear from Table 1, there are very few SC in the corpus (almost 5 times less than MC and almost 49 times less than GC). It may be claimed that a low number of SC is a tendency in blogs (Roosileht 2013) and other types of internet communication (Igav 2013 on Facebook, Vaba 2010 on Skype). This is true not only about English impact on Estonian but also about Estonian impact on Russian in Russian-language blogs (Verschik 2014a).

SC appear as semantic expansions (1 occurrence) and mostly as word-for-word renditions (loan translations in a different terminology, see Backus and Dorleijn 2009) of English idioms and fixed expressions.

Some information concerning the spread and conventionalization of SC can be easily found via internet searches, because, unlike GC, SC by definition contain no foreign stems and morphemes. Such a search gives at least circumstantial evidence, whether a certain SC is just an individual occasion in the data or entrenched in one's idiolect or is being used elsewhere.

Example (11) illustrates the copied meaning of the common internationalism:

(11) *Mu igapäevane soengu**rutiin step-by-step***
      'my everyday hairdo routine step-by-step'

In common Standard Estonian, *rutiin* means mostly 'a (dull) series of repetitive acts' and not just 'repetitive acts, habitual activities' as English *routine*. The new expanded meaning appears in fashion and style blogs because of the conventionalized usage in English in the context of daily procedures, like skin care routine etc. Methodologically, in order to check the spread and conventionalization of selective copying, one may use Google search. It is trickier for GC if the languages in question use the same alphabet (like Estonian and English) because it would be extremely difficult to filter the results. SC do not have overt elements of another language and this is why a search yields less ambiguous results. Google search in Estonian (google.ee) for *rutiin* yields 225,00 hits, of which at least at a first glance most demonstrate the conventional Estonian meaning of the word.

Other cases are copies of idiomatic expressions. Consider *ühel leheküljel* 'on the same page' example (12):

(12)   ... *et te tegelikult olete selle eelmise artikli autoriga selles osas siiski* **ühel leheküljel**
'... that in fact you and the author of that article are on the same page in this respect'

Google search shows that *ühel leheküljel* occurs in its literal meaning, i.e. certain items are or should be placed on the same page of the manuscript etc.

The copying of the idiom *is (not) my cup of tea* is gaining currency in the form *on (ei ole) minu teetass* is an instance of ongoing conventionalization in modern common Estonian.
Consider (13):

(13)   *Täpselt* **minu teetass!**
'my cup of tea exactly!'

The search of *ei ole minu teetass* 'not my cup of tea' and *on minu teetass* 'is my cup of tea' yield 14,400 and 21,500 results respectively. In the negative form, a couple of the first hits demonstrate the copied figurative meaning (*muusikalid pole päris minu teetass* 'musicals are not exactly my cup of tea'); in the affirmative the first results show the literal meaning.

The SC exhibits more than a new figurative meaning. In Estonian, *tee-tass* (tea:GEN- cup) means 'tea cup' and not 'cup of tea'. In order to render the meaning 'cup of tea', it is necessary to use the partitive case and the reversed word order: *tass tee-d* (cup tea-PART) 'cup of tea'.

One case of SC is especially instructive because it shows how GC brings along SC (in other words, another use of a compromise form on the border of lexicon and morphosyntax). In Example (14a), GC of discourse particle *no way* is followed by the Estonian verb in the affirmative, i.e., English argument structure is copied:

(14a) Sest **no way** ma oleks läinud trolli peale inimesega, kes on ilmselgelt millegi mõju all
'because no way I would have taken the trolleybus with a person who is clearly under the influence of some substance'

Ole-ks	läi-nud
be-COND	go-PAST PRT
'would have gone'	

Compare with English in (14b) and monolingual Estonian in (14c) with the expected negative:

(14b) English
No way I would have gone

(14c) Estonian
(Mitte)	mingi-l	juhu-l	ma	ei	ole-ks
no	some-ADES	case-ADES	I	not	be-COND

läi-nud...
go-PAST PRT
'No way I would have gone'

As mentioned, the low number of SC tends to be a general trait. I assume that this has at least partially to do with the text genre: blogs are personal virtual spaces where bloggers consciously or unconsciously implement their personal language policy. If one can criticize public language use, then a blog can be overtly bilingual and not only in the sense that the same entry appears in two languages but in the sense of alternate use of linguistic items from different languages. It is completely possible that the same idioms like *to be on the same page* and *it is (not) my cup of tea* appear as global copies. In fact, we saw in Section 5.1 that fixed expressions are subject to global copying. I assume that the picture would be different in genres that are monolingual at least in theory (newspaper article, digest, translation). There no overt foreign items may appear without a reason but (conventionalized) selective copies may find their way unconsciously.

Thus, the presence of SC probably depends on the genre. They are facilitated with (perceived) material similarity and figurative meaning that fixed expressions have.

5.3 Mixed copies

MC can be a diverse group containing more and less prototypical cases. I have written elsewhere (Verschik 2016) on typology of MC in Estonian-Russian code-copying; in future it would be desirable to move to a general typology of MC. Cases as (2) *hard-töötav* 'hard-working' are prototypical: a compound where the GC part is semantically specific (*hard-working* is more specific than *working*). Johanson (1992: 183) describes similar cases as an illustration to the phenomenon of MC. Some cases may have one element that is similar in two languages (for instance, in closely related languages or in the instance of common internationalisms). Depending on the realization of the common but not identical element, the result can be GC or MC. Also, as discussed in Section 5.1, especially example (9), there can be variation and the same model can yield GC or an MC: *cheat day* or *cheat päev*.

In examples like (9) connection between the elements is more loose than in idioms or fixed expressions. It is a matter of interpretation whether and to what extent the elements 'belong together'. Interpretation is subjective but frequent use facilitates perception of a collocation as a whole. Consider English noun *office* and possible collocations such as *office building*, *office outfit* or *office theme*. In example (15) the blogger writes MC *office-temaatikaga* 'with office theme, office-themed' with a hyphen, which shows that for her these items form a kind of compound:

(15) *Sügisel toimus meil pildistamine Tallinn Dolls'iga, kus kasutasime TD'i* **office**-*temaatikaga riideid ja mantleid.*
'in autumn we had a photo session with Tallinn Dolls where we used office-themed clothes and coats by TD'

Most of MC in my data are similar examples, such as compound nouns *töövaib* (where *töö* 'work' + *vaib* 'vibe' < *vibe*) 'work vibe', *outfit-postitus* 'outfit post', *over-the-knee-saapad* 'over-the-knee-boots', *love-hate suhe* 'love-hate relationship' etc.

MC occur in idioms and figurative expressions as well. Consider the phrase *X is entering/leaving the building* (or in a different tense: *X has left the building*). In (16) it is used in a metaphorical sense in the context of deteriorating health. The blogger demonstrates metalinguistic awareness by separating the English stem *building* and the elative case marker (*building'ust*):

(16) On   minu   tervis   **building**'u-st   lahku-nud
     is   my   health   building'STEM-EL   leave-PAST PRTC
     'my health has left the building'

It is entirely possible to have a GC (or CA, depending on the interpretation) here. Vaba (2010: 65) attests (17) in an ironic context (meaning that someone has already brought some rhubarb to the office in order to make a cake):

(17) rabarber **has entered the building**
     'rhubarb has entered the building'

Thus, MC appear in compounds and collocations (as suggested in various works by Johanson) but also in idioms and fixed expressions. As mentioned in Section 3.2, cognitive-structural transparency of compounds is one of the factors facilitating copying. Another factor appears to be figurativeness or metaphoricity of an expression. We saw it in some instances of SC and in MC. Figurative and/or highly expressive meaning place a role in CA, to be considered in the next section.

5.4 Code alternations

As some recent works demonstrate, morphosyntactically the difference between insertions and alternations (in the terms of Muysken 2000) is not always clear (Demirçay and Backus 2014). Johanson does not say much on CA, as his main concern is copying. In any event it is safe to claim that syntactically independent elements like sentences or combinations thereof are CA. English CA appears to be a permanent feature in Estonian fashion blogs and as a paper focusing on CA in particular is to appear soon (Verschik and Kask, in press), I will not go into much details here but briefly summarize our findings that are relevant for the present article.

Theoretically, CA can be quotations, renditions/paraphrases of direct speech, chunks in another language on a particular topic etc. The data presents a different kind of material. Due to the blog genre, renditions of others' speech are unlikely. Sometimes there are longer stretches of English text in blogs that are explicitly bilingual, i.e., present the same information in English and Estonian.

Another type of CA in blogs are fixed expressions, idioms or phrases that are highly expressive and emotional. Consider fixed expression in (18) and highly emotional phrase in (19):

(18) **Stay tuned**, sest uus postitus tuleb välja juba homme!
     'stay tuned because the new post will appear already tomorrow!'

(19) **So sweet,** *aitäh Sulle!*
'so sweet, thank you!'

CA in my data cannot be explained by factors such as community type, degree of proficiency in L1, typological distance between the languages (analysis of various factors is provided in Verschik and Kask, in press). Yet, meaning does play a role here: Backus and Verschik (2012) have noted that prominence at discourse level (in the case of utterance modifiers) facilitates copying; so it makes sense that figurative meaning, expressivity and the social meaning derived from association with the English-speaking world make an item, including a syntactically independent unit or a longer stretch, highly noticeable at discourse level and thus attractive for copying.

Figurative expressions from another code may appear novel in comparison to what exists in the basic code. Of course, a fluent speaker of another code would realize that the whole meaning of an expression is not a sum of meanings of each component but at the first encounter the novelty of a certain combination makes the expression in question stand out. In the terms of Johanson (2002: 309), figurative expressions are salient (cognitively prominent).

In the next section I will discuss the importance of figurative meaning in more details.

6 Discussion

It was argued above that several characteristics of language items, such as type of meaning (specific, figurative, expressive), perceived transparency and analyticity, and prominence at the discourse level facilitate copying. In what follows I will try to propose a descriptive cognitive-structural model of copying and discuss how the named characteristics affect copying and at what stage each of them comes in. I am taking further cognitive aspects of Johanson's CCF and incorporate them into my model.

6.1 The process of copying

I suggest that the process of copying can be presented in the following way:

(20) Availability > noticing > comparison > establishment of equivalence/gap > copying > (entrenchment, conventionalization)

Let us turn to each concept starting from left to right. Availability of an item or a combination of items means that the item/combination is in use of other speakers around you. Availability presupposes at least some knowledge of a different code, otherwise you cannot make sense of items of this code even if it is used in the environment. Thus, availability means that a feature or a pattern has "to be there" for the user.

At a certain point, a language user notices an item. This is followed by comparison or matching, which can be unconscious. In the process of comparison, one establishes (partial) equivalence (item X in code A corresponds to item Y in code B) or a gap (nothing corresponds in code B to item X in code A). Potentially, there is a choice between an old and a new element (see Onysko and Winter-Froemel 2011; Zenner, Speelman, and Geeraerts 2014).

One may ask what the nature of equivalence is (see description by Heine and Kuteva 2005: 219–233, albeit they put structures centre stage and concentrate on grammar and, to a lesser extent, on meaning but not on lexicon). There are tensions between structuralist accounts and explanation in terms of mental representation/speakers' knowledge/use. This question is not resolved. Neither it is known when a difference is salient enough, to what degree social factors play a role in the matching, etc. Johanson (2013: 102) claims that operation of copying is based on the speakers' subjective assessment of equivalence, that is, of what is felt to be analogous, not necessarily on typological equivalence in any precise linguistic sense. It can be understood as the process of comparison and establishment of equivalence in the process.

Mark Sebba (1998, 2009: 51) has extensively discussed congruence (another term for equivalence) and explains that congruence between categories cannot be viewed in structural terms only; it is a product of both linguistic and social processes (also Hamers and Blanc 2000: 269). We tend to discuss equivalence in structural terms but a language-user is not a structuralist, so linguistic knowledge inside a speaker is different. Thus, under "equivalence" I understand equivalence perceived by the speaker.

Both entrenchment and conventionalization were discussed in Sections 2 and 3.2. In (20) both are placed in brackets because not every occurrence of copying becomes rooted in individual usage (entrenchment) and in a wider usage of a community (conventionalization).

6.2 Factors facilitating copying

There are certain factors that not simply promote copying but rather facilitate noticing and comparison/establishment of equivalence. As shown in (20), noticing and establishment of correspondences precede copying. Some of these factors were discussed in Section 3.2.

At first I will stop at cognitive factors.

(21) Cognitive factors:
- meaning (specificity, expressivity, pragmatic prominence, social meaning)
- frequency
- novelty, metaphoricity

All cognitive factors contribute to salience of linguistic items in another code. Meaning and novelty/metaphoricity can be viewed as factors constituting prototypical attractiveness. This notion should be developed in future research. Although it is difficult to define salience, here I adhere to Johanson's (2002) understanding thereof (salient = cognitively prominent, i.e. attracting cognitive attention). The importance of meaning (specifity, pragmatic prominence, expressivity) has been explained above. Frequency has been discussed in Backus (2012, 2014, 2015). Obviously, it is easy to notice a frequent item or pattern. So both uniqueness and high frequency facilitate copying but different types: specific items are likely to be copied globally and frequent schematic pattern selectively (Backus and Verschik 2012) but we do not really know the reasons yet. Here I will discuss novelty and metaphoricity (both are linked because a figurative expression appears as novel to a speaker).

It sounds logical that we register something new in language use. The same thing, phenomenon or process can be conceptualized differently in different languages. It can be a lexical item for a new concept or a specific term from a certain domain or another grammatical pattern. Also multiword items such as figurative expressions and metaphors may be perceived as novel. Idiomatic expressions in another code appear novel because of their figurative, non-direct meaning. From SLA perspective, Kecskés (2006) says that figurative meaning of an idiom in L1 is unmarked. He describes an interaction from where it follows that the English expression *to be held up* is perceived by native speakers by default as 'to be robbed' and only then 'to meet unexpected obstacles and as a consequences be unable to do things on time'. In other words, the novelty of the metaphor has faded for English-speakers. However, for language users who encounter this expression for the first time, the figurative meaning is strikingly new and expressive (see also Winter-Froemel, this volume). This is not to say that proficient language users understand such items word for word but rather they notice expressivity and a new way to render something. Take the Estonian idiom *süda tilkub verd* 'heart is bleeding from distress, pity, sorrow, etc.' (literally, 'heart is dripping blood'): the novelty has faded for speakers of Estonian and they would not realize they are talking about heart and blood here, while someone who hears the saying for the first time may be surprised by its expressive power. At the same time, an Estonian blogger would find this English expression as fresh and powerful:

(22) *Aga mul lihtsalt pea valutab ja hirmsasti tahaks magada, aga lihtsalt ei õnnestu.* ***I am crying on the inside.***
'but I just have a headache and terribly want to sleep but cannot. I am crying on the inside'

Thus, it is not accidental that bloggers copy fixed expressions and idioms. These can be both phrases or compounds or CA (syntactically independent utterances): recall examples (13) and the section on CA, examples (16), (17).

Other factors facilitating noticing can be labelled structural or structural-cognitive, as mentioned above, because it is about perception, an aspect of cognition:

(23) Structural-cognitive factors:
 – Transparency
 – Similarity

There is evidence that compounds and analytic verbs are likely candidates for all degrees of copying (see Backus and Verschik 2012). I believe that various multi-word items, including idioms, fit under this category as well: the fact that a meaning is expressed with several lexical items makes an item cognitively prominent (i.e. standing out in some way).

It is a matter of perception and, probably, of meta-linguistic awareness, too, what one finds similar across languages: one has to match the given items or patterns across languages and to decide that they are similar. The matter has been discussed in detail by Clyne in his early works on triggering and then summarized under the heading of facilitation in transfer (Clyne 2003: 111). Although English and Estonian are typologically different, there is some common ground there, such as a general tendency for analyticity and compounding in grammar and common internationalisms in lexicon (recall example [11]). Similarity facilitates copying, albeit it is not the only necessary condition for copying to occur. The more copying occurs and the more copies become entrenched/conventionalized, the more similarity there is, which, in turn, creates even more common ground facilitates copying again.

Finally, we have to take into account micro- and macro-sociolinguistic factors that do not affect linguistic matter as such but are driving forces (or ultimate causes) behind language contacts ("why-global" in the terms of Backus 2005: 321). Micro-sociolinguistic factors include individual linguistic repertoire, language awareness, language attitudes, communicative situation, communicative goals, participants, medium or genre (oral, written, CMC). Macro-sociolinguistic factors include such things as status and prestige of languages in question, discourse about languages, attitudes to multilingualism and so on. The descriptive model in full is presented in (24).

(24)

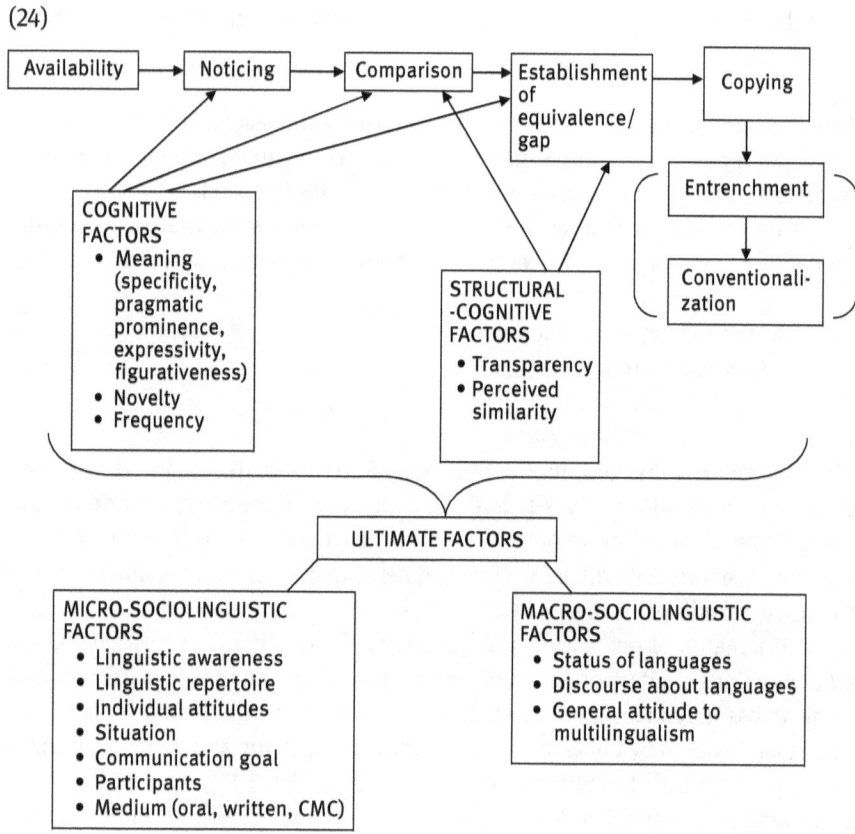

7 Conclusions

My data and analysis show that a usage-based approach to language contact is useful. The cognitive approach is compatible with my data. If establishment of equivalence is subjective and if cognitive factors such as (social) meaning, novelty, expressivity, prominence at discourse level, frequency are at play, then so-called "structural conflict" between given languages cannot prevent copying. Innovative compromise forms show that there is no strict cognitive division between treatment of lexicon and morphosyntax.

CCF, albeit formulated as a structural model, is heavily leaning towards cognitive explanations that have not been explored by Johanson in detail but merely listed (attractiveness, salience etc). Based on earlier studies on entrenchment and specificity by Backus, I took the cognitive aspects of CCF further and proposed a descriptive framework that explains the process of copying. Although there is a basic understanding of what degree of copying occurs in what items (specific > GC, general > SC, multi-word items > all degrees), this part has to be refined in future.

References

Andersen, Gisle. 2014. Pragmatic borrowing. *Journal of Pragmatics* 67. 17–33.
Auer, Peter & Raihan Muhamedova. 2005. 'Embedded language' and 'matrix language' in insertional language mixing: Some problematic cases. *Italian Journal of Linguistics / Rivista di linguistica* 17 (1). 35–54.
Backus, Ad. 2001. The role of semantic specificity in insertional codeswitching: evidence from Dutch-Turkish. In Rodolfo Jacobson (ed.), *Codeswitching Worldwide II*, 125–54. Berlin and New York: Mouton de Gruyter.
Backus, Ad. 2005. Codeswitching and language change: one thing leads to another? *International Journal of Bilingualism* 9 (3–4). 307–340.
Backus, Ad. 2012. A usage-based approach to borrowability. Tilburg Papers in Culture Studies. Paper 27. https://www.tilburguniversity.edu/research/institutes-and-research-groups/babylon/tpcs/download-tpcs-paper-27.pdf.htm (accessed 6 June 2016).
Backus, Ad. 2014. Towards a usage-based account of language change: implications of contact lingusitics to lingusitics theory. In Robert Nicolaï (ed.), *Questioning Language Contact. Limits of Contact, Contact and its Limits*, 91–118. Leiden & Boston: Brill.
Backus, Ad. 2015. A usage-based approach to code-switching: a need to reconcile structure and function. In Gerald Stell & Kofi Yakpo (eds.), *Code-Switching between Structural and Sociolinguistic Perspectives*, 19–37. Berlin: Mouton de Gruyter.
Backus, Ad & Margreet Dorleijn. 2009. Loan translations versus code-switching. In Barbara Bullock & Almeida Jaqueline Toribio (eds.). *The Cambridge Handbook of Linguistic Code-Switching*, 75–93. Cambridge: Cambridge University Press.
Backus, Ad & Anna Verschik. 2012. Copyability of (bound) morphology. In Lars Johanson & Martine Robbeets (eds.) *Copies versus Cognates in Bound Morphology*, 123–149. Leiden: Brill.
Blommaert, Jan. & Ad Backus. 2011. Repertoires revisited: 'Knowing language' in superdiversity. *Working Papers in Urban Language and Literacy* 67, available at: http://www.kcl.ac.uk/innovation/groups/ldc/publications/workingpapers/download.aspx (accessed 10 June 2016).

Clyne, Michael. 2003. *Dynamics of Language Contacts*. Cambridge: CUP.
Cook, Vivian. 2016. Premises of multi-competence. In Vivian Cook & Li Wei (eds.), *The Cambridge Handbook of Linguistic Multi-Competence*, 1–25. Cambridge: Cambridge University Press.
Croft, William. 2000. *Explaining Language Change: an Evolutionary Approach*. Longman: Harlow.
Dąbrowska, Ewa. 2012. Different speakers, different grammars: individual differences in native language attainment. *Linguistic Approaches to Bilingualism* 2 (3). 219–253.
Demirçay, Derya & Ad Backus. 2014. Bilingual constructions. Reassessing the typology of code-switching. *Dutch Journal of Applied Linguistics* 3 (1). 30–44.
Dewaele, Jean-Marc. 2016. In Li Wei & Vivian Cook (eds), *The Cambridge Handbook of Linguistic Multi-competence*, 403–419. Cambridge: Cambridge University Press.
Field, Fredric. 2002. *Linguistic Borrowing in Bilingual Contexts*. Amsterdam: John Benjamins.
Hamers, Josiane F. & Blanc, Michel H. A. (2000). *Bilinguality and Bilingualism* (2nd edn.). Cambridge, UK and New York: Cambridge University Press.
Heine, Bernd & Kuteva, Tania, 2005. *Language Contact and Grammatical Change*. Cambridge: Cambridge University Press.
Igav, Reet. 2013. *Inglise-eesti koodikopeerimine Facebooki vestlustes* [English-Estonian code-copying in Facebook conversations]. Tallinn: Tallinn University Unpublished MA thesis.
Johanson, Lars. 1992. *Strukturelle Faktoren in türkischen Sprachkontakten [Structural factors in language contacts of Turkish]* (Sitzungsberichte der Wissenschaftlichen Gesellschaft an der J. W. Goethe-Universität Frankfurt am Main, 29: 5). Stuttgart: Steiner.
Johanson, Lars. 1993. Code-copying in immigrant Turkish. In Guus Extra & Ludo Verhoeven (eds.), *Immigrant Languages in Europe*, 197–221. Clevedon/Philadelphia/Adelaide: Multilingual Matters.
Johanson, Lars. 1999. The dynamics of code-copying in language encounters. In Bernt Brendemoen, Elizabeth Lanza & Else Ryen (eds.), *Language Encounters across Time and Space*, 37–62. Oslo: Novus forlag.
Johanson, Lars. 2002. Contact-induced change in a code-copying framework. In Mari C. Jones & Edith Esch (eds.), *Language Change. The Interplay of Internal, External and Extra-Linguistic Factors*, 286–313. Berlin, New York: Mouton de Gruyter.
Johanson, Lars. 2006. Turkic language contacts in a typology of code interaction. In Henrik Boeschoten & Lars Johanson (eds.), *Turkic Languages in Contact*, 4–26. Wiesbaden: Harrassowitz.
Johanson, Lars. 2008. Remodelling grammar. Copying, conventionalization, grammaticalization. In Peter Siemund & Noemi Kintana (eds.), *Language Contacts and Contact Languages*, 61–79. Amsterdam, Philadelphia: John Benjamins.
Johanson, Lars. 2013. Isomorphic processes. Grammaticalization and copying of grammatical elements. In Martine Robbeets & Hubert Cuyckens (eds.), *Shared grammaticalization. With special focus on Transeurasian languages*, 101–109. Amsterdam: John Benjamins.
Kecskés, Istvan. 2006. On my mind: thoughts about salience, context and figurative meaning from a second language perspective. *Second Language Research* 22 (2). 1–19.
Leisiö, Larisa. 2001. Integration and gender assignment in Finland Russian. *SKY Journal of Linguistics* 14. 87–119.
Maschler, Yael. 1994. Metalanguaging and discourse markers in bilingual conversation. *Language in Society* 23 (3). 325–366.

Matras, Yaron. 1998. Utterance modifiers and universals of grammatical borrowing. *Linguistics* 36 (2). 281–331.
Matras, Yaron. 2009. *Language Contact*. Cambridge, New York: Cambridge University Press.
Matras, Yaron. 2012. An activity-oriented approach to contact-induced language change. In Claudine Chamoreau & Isabelle Léglise (eds.), *Dynamics of Contact-Induced Language Change*, 17–52. Berlin: Mouton de Gruyter.
Matras, Yaron & Jeannette Sakel. 2007. Investigating the mechanism of pattern replication in language convergence. *Studies in Language* 31, 829–865.
Metslang, Helle. 2006. Predikaat ajastut kogemas [Predicate is experiencing the epoch]. *Keel ja Kirjandus 9*, 1–14.
Mysers-Scotton, Carol. 1993. *Duelling Languages*. Oxford: Oxford University Press.
Muysken, Pieter. 2000. *Bilingual Speech: A Typology of Code-mixing*. Cambridge: Cambridge University Press.
Onysko, Alexander. 2009. Divergence with a cause? The systemic integration of anglicisms in German as an indication of the intensity of language contact. In Falco Pfalzgraf (ed.), *Englischer Sprachkontakt in den Varietäten des Deutschen/English in Contact with Varieties of German*, 53–74. Frankfurt am Main/New York: Peter Lang.
Onysko, Alexander & Esme Winter-Froemmel. 2011. Necessary loans – luxury loans? Exploring the pragmatic dimension of borrowing. *Journal of Pragmatics* 43 (6). 1550–1567.
Peterson, Elisabeth & Johanna Vaattovaara. 2014. Kiitos and pliis: the relationship and borrowed politeness markers in Finnish. *Journal of Politeness Research* 10 (2). 247–269.
Romaine, Suzanne. 1995. *Bilingualism*. Oxford: Blackwells.
Roosileht, Helin. 2013. Inglise-eesti koodikopeerimine *blogides* [English-Estonian code-copying in blogs]. Tallinn: Tallinn University Unpublished MA thesis.
Salmons, Joseph. 1990. Bilingual discourse marking: Code switching, borrowing and convergence in some German-American dialects. *Linguistics* 28 (3). 453–480.
Sebba, Mark. 1998. A congruence approach to the syntax of codeswitching. *International Journal of Bilingualism* 2 (1). 1–19.
Sebba, Mark. 2009. On the notions of congruence and convergence in code-switching. In Barbara E. Bullock & Almeida Jacqueline Toribio (eds.), *Cambridge Handbook of Linguistic Code-Switching*, 40–57. Cambridge: Cambridge University Press.
Van Hout, Roeland & Pieter Muysken. 1994. Modelling lexical borrowability. *Language Variation and Change* 6 (1). 39–62.
Vaba, Marja. 2010. Inglise-eesti koodikopeerimisest Skype'i Tallinna kontori kahe vestlusgrupi näitel [On English-Estonian code-copying on the example of two chat groups at Tallinn Skype office]. Tallinn: Tallinn University Unpublished MA thesis.
Verschik, Anna. 2008. *Emerging Bilingual Speech: From Monolingualism to Code-Copying*. London: Continuum.
Verschik, Anna. 2014a. Estonian-Russian code-copying in Russian-language blogs: language change and a new kind of linguistic awareness. In Virve-Anneli Vihman & Kristiina Praakli (eds.), *Negotiating Linguistic Identity*, 59–87. Oxford: Peter Lang.
Verschik, Anna. 2014b. Conjunctions in early Yiddish-Lithuanian bilingualism: heritage language and contact linguistic perspectives. In Heli Paulasto, Lea Meriläinen, Helka Riionheimo & Maria Kok (eds.), *Language Contacts at the Crossroads of Disciplines*, 33–57. Cambridge: Cambridge Scholars Publishing.
Verschik, Anna. 2015. Towards a typology of phenomena on the interface of lexicon and morphosyntax. Paper presented at Estonian Association of Applied Linguistics Annual

Conference. Institute of Estonian Language and Tallinn University, Tallinn, 23–24 April 2015.

Verschik, Anna. 2016. Mixed copying in blogs: evidence from Estonian- Russian language contacts. *Journal of Language Contact* 9 (1). 186–209.

Verschik, Anna & Helin Kask. To appear. Estonian-English code alternation in fashion blogs: structure, norms and meaning. In Heiko Marten & Sanita Lazdina (eds.), *Book on Multilingualism and Minorities in the Baltic States*. Palgrave.

Weinreich, Uriel. 1953. *Languages in Contact*. New York: Publications of the Linguistic Circle of New York, 1.

Weinreich, Uriel, William Labov & Marvin Herzog. 1968. Empirical foundations for a theory of language change. In Winfred P. Lehmann & Yakov Malkiel (eds.), *Directions for Historical Linguistics: A Symposium*, 95–188. Austin: University of Texas Press.

Wertheim, Suzanne. 2003. *Linguistic Purism, Language Shift and Contact-Induced Change in Tatar*. Ph. D. dissertation, University of California, Berkeley.

Zabrodskaja, Anastassia, & Anna Verschik. 2014. Morphology of Estonian items at the interface of Russian-Estonian language contact data. *Sociolinguistic Studies* 8 (3). 449–474.

Zenner, Eline, Dirk Speelman & Dirk Geeraerts. 2014. Core vocabulary, borrowability and entrenchment: a usage-based onomasiological approach. *Diachonica* 31 (1). 74–105.

Zenner, Eline & Dorien Van De Mieroop. 2017. The social and pragmatic function of English in weak contact situations: Ingroup and outgroup marking in the Dutch reality TV show Expeditie Robinson. *Journal of Pragmatics* 113. 77–88.

Esme Winter-Froemel
3 Reanalysis in language contact: Perceptive ambiguity, salience, and catachrestic reinterpretation

Abstract: Some lexical borrowings show striking divergences with respect to the source language items they originate from, as illustrated by F. *people* 'celebrities' (borrowed from E. *people*), G. *Testimonial* 'person expressing a testimonial' (< E. *testimonial*), and F. / It. *dancing* (< E. *dancing hall / dancing room*). According to previous research, semantic and morphological innovations in the situation of borrowing (going beyond the adaptation of pronunciation, spelling, and morphological features of the loanwords) are rather exceptional cases. The present paper aims at studying similar cases of innovation in order to determine their importance and ask how they can be explained from a usage-based perspective. I will show that semantic and morphological change is much more frequent than generally assumed. Moreover, I will argue that the concept of reanalysis permits us to analyse many of the semantic and morphological innovations in a straightforward way in which reanalysis turns out to be a type of linguistic change central to linguistic borrowing. The reflections will be mainly based on a survey of 500 lexical items borrowed from English into Italian as documented by the etymological dictionary DELI (*Dizionario Etimologico della Lingua Italiana*), but occasionally point to parallel developments in other recipient languages and contact situations as well. Based on Detges' and Waltereit's (2002) approach, I will elaborate a semiotic model of reanalysis which helps us to account for the paradox that the innovations happen without being intended or even noticed by the speakers and hearers. The notion of perceptive ambiguity will be proven to be of key importance to explain this paradox and provide new insights into the restrictions that have been identified in previous research. Additionally, it will be shown that the salience of the concepts and referents involved as well as the semantic and morphological transparency of the linguistic items represent important factors in this explanatory framework. Finally, I will comment on a specific subtype of semantic innovation which can be labelled catachrestic reinterpretation and which is characterised by the fact that the loanwords obtain a new meaning and thereby fill a lexical gap in the recipient language (e.g. It. *policeman* 'police agent in English-speaking countries', E. *sombrero* 'broad-brimmed hat', F. *grappa* 'Italian pomace brandy', F. *flipper* 'pinball, pinball machine').

Esme Winter-Froemel, Universität Trier

Keywords: ambiguity, catachrestic reinterpretation, ellipsis, reanalysis, salience, semantic change, semiotic model

1 Introduction

Lexical borrowings are frequently characterised by adaptations of pronunciation and spelling; similarly, certain integrations into the morphological system of the recipient language (e.g. gender assignment and inflection) can represent inevitable processes in borrowing proper or in later reuses of the loanwords, depending on the recipient language. True morphological or semantic innovations in the situation of borrowing, in contrast, are rather exceptional cases according to previous research. This is also reflected by the fact that borrowing has often been treated as one type of lexical innovation besides semantic change and word formation, which seems to imply that lexical borrowings are characterised by semantic and morphological stability. However, although borrowing represents undoubtedly a very important source for lexical expansion, this traditional view appears to be problematic. This is due to the fact that it suggests that the three options represent alternative approaches. Just as recent research in cognitive linguistic approaches has insisted on the necessity – and potential – of analysing semantic aspects of word formation (see e.g. Onysko and Michel 2010), it seems equally necessary to analyse the semantic and morphological dimension of borrowing and to ask how semantic and morphological changes occurring in situations of borrowing can be explained within usage-based, cognitive linguistic frameworks (see also Zenner and Kristiansen 2014 and Alexander Onysko's reflections on reframing language contact phenomena from a cognitive perspective, this volume). The aim of this paper is to analyse a sample of 500 lexical items imported from English into Italian as documented in the etymological dictionary DELI (*Dizionario Etimologico della Lingua Italiana*) in order to determine the overall importance of semantic and morphological changes in borrowing as well as to provide more insights into restrictions to specific subtypes and pathways of change, and finally, to propose a semiotic framework of semantic reanalysis that allows us to explain the changes from a usage-based perspective.

The paper is structured as follows: After some general remarks on the data and reference sources chosen (section 2.1), I will comment on changes that can be observed in spelling, semantics, and morphology (sections 2.2–2.4). The data provided by DELI offers a rich and easily accessible sample which will be exhaustively analysed, commenting on regular patterns that emerge as well as on unclear cases and methodological problems. In this way, certain limits of purely lexicographic analyses will emerge and the necessity and challenges of reinterpreting the analyses from a usage-based perspective will be shown. I will then argue that reanalysis is a type of linguistic change which is central to linguistic borrowing and which permits us to analyse many of the semantic and morphological changes in a usage-based framework. I will refer to the concept of reanalysis proposed by Detges and Waltereit (2002) and focus on the semiotic conditions under which reanalysis takes place in speaker-hearer interaction. The requirement of referential identity, which is not included in Langacker's definition of reanalysis, but stressed in Detges and Waltereit (2002), will be rephrased in terms of perceptive ambiguity and I will argue that this latter concept gives us a better understanding of why reanalysis can occur at all (section 3). In section 4, the concept of reanalysis will be applied to situations of language contact and borrowing and I will discuss additional factors that come into play and that characterise different contact scenarios (section 4.1). Section 4.2 will show how the changes observed in the data can be explained in the semiotic framework proposed, and point to parallel developments in other languages. The basic results and some perspectives for further research will be presented in section 5.[1]

2 Morphological and semantic innovation in borrowings from English into Italian

2.1 The data: overview, methodological issues, general results

The analyses in this paper are based on a survey of anglicisms, more specifically of loanwords imported from the source language English (SL) into the recipient language Italian (RL), as documented in the Italian etymological dictionary DELI. This choice is motivated by the fact that DELI represents an authoritative source which allows investigating established borrowings according to their etymology and possible pathways of diachronic evolution. Compared to other dictionaries, DELI provides in some cases very detailed information about concrete historical contexts in which loanwords were introduced into Italian. The dictionary also

---

[1] I would like to thank Ad Backus, Ulrich Detges, Alexander Onysko, Eline Zenner and an anonymous reviewer for their very helpful comments. Moreover I would like to thank Martina Bross for the stylistic revision of this paper.

cites previous studies on particular lexical items as well as other lexicographic sources.[2] Thus, it gives a synthesis of previous studies.

Moreover, the use of the 1999 edition of the DELI guarantees that the items analysed are established borrowings, which will be analysed from a certain temporal distance, so that a certain (provisional) closure of the lexical evolutions is ensured. However, as we can generally observe a strong dynamism in the lexicon, and as the English language continues to exert a strong influence on Italian, it has to be admitted that the data analysed cannot be taken to directly correspond with the current state of affairs, i.e. further borrowings of anglicisms or further uses of the anglicisms in new semantic domains may be observed (see e.g. the recent introduction of the expression *Surf and turf / surf 'n' turf* into Italian in the gastronomic domain), and some of the anglicisms analysed here may have fallen into desuetude or may have changed with respect to their usage. It is thus important to stress that the main aim of this paper is not to give an overview of the current use of anglicisms in Italian, but to use a corpus of anglicisms in Italian to chart general pathways of semantic and morphological evolution of borrowings, and more specifically, to investigate and explain restrictions on possible semantic and morphological innovations occurring in situations of borrowing.

From the total of more than 19,000 DELI entries in the CD-ROM edition, 416 entries containing "Vc. ingl" (for "voce inglese" 'English keyword') in the etymological section were retrieved. This search criterion identifies loanwords imported from English with only few false positives, but it has to be admitted that this choice implies a relatively high number of false negatives. This is due to the fact that anglicisms are also identified by other lexicographic marks in DELI. A search for "ingl" in the etymological section yields 1,709 results; however, this criterion was not chosen, as the results also contain many items characterised by other forms of English influence or only by parallel developments in English. This means that the quantitative influence of English is stronger than the number of items included in this survey suggests, but, given the focus of analysis, the data

---

[2] For example, for I. *flipper*, the etymological section of the DELI entry indicates: "in the pinball game [...], the flippers are the small wings that throw back the ball, but in Italian this expression has been extended to the whole game", "in different gadgets of this type, the word *flipper* is precisely written on the small wing that gives the saving shot" ['nel biliardino elettrico (detto in America pinball [sic] game) i flippers sono quelle alette che rilanciano la pallina, ma in italiano questo termine è stato esteso al gioco intero' (Klajn [1972] 105); 'in vari aggeggi di questo tipo la parola *flipper* è appunto scritta sull'aletta che distribuisce la sventola salvatrice' (A. Menarini, 'Le lingue del mondo' XXIV (1959) 246)]. For analyses of borrowings following a usage-based approach, this strong focus on concrete contexts of borrowing / innovation appears to be particularly productive.

can be considered a representative sample, which is defined by a clear criterion and which was exhaustively analysed.

In many cases, DELI lists different RL meanings of the items borrowed. In order to investigate semantic divergences with respect to the SL meanings, the RL items were split up into different lexical units defined as pairs of 1 form and 1 meaning (see Cruse 1986: 49). In this way, 513 lexical units were obtained. Among these, 13 were excluded from further analyses since they are pseudo-anglicisms (*beauty-case, ski-pass*) or lexical units which were considered not to represent loanwords borrowed from English (e.g. calques).[3] The decision to exclude these categories from further analysis is motivated by the fact that, although they represent cases where an English influence can be observed, they arise from different subtypes of lexical innovation.

For the 500 remaining lexical items, their form and meaning was compared to the SL form and meaning with the help of the OED, and semantic and/or structural divergences were registered. The items and their developments will be described by referring to the system developed by Blank and Koch (see e.g. Blank 1997, 2001; Koch 2000, 2001) in order to analyse innovation vs. stability for all types of lexical innovation in a comprehensive framework. According to this system, three basic dimensions of lexical innovation (semantics, morphology, stratification) are distinguished, and the antecedents and successors of a certain process of lexical innovation are compared along these three axes. For the first axis (semantics), in addition to identity (absence of semantic innovation, identical meaning for antecedent and successor, e.g. Latin *manus* → F. *main* 'hand'), Blank and Koch have established seven universal categories of semantic relations that serve to describe the divergences observed. These are contiguity (the meanings of successor and antecedent are linked by contiguity, and the concepts designated belong to a common cognitive frame, e.g. F. *bureau* 'desk' → 'office'), metaphorical similarity (such as illustrated by E. *mouse* 'rodent' → 'pointing device'), taxonomic subordination (the meaning of the successor is more specific than the meaning of the antecedent, e.g. Middle French *viande* 'food, viands' → Modern French *viande* 'meat'), taxonomic superordination (the meaning of the successor is more general than the meaning of the antecedent, e.g. Latin *passer* 'sparrow' → Sp.

---

3 The items excluded are 6 calques (*austero, convertire / convertibile*, and *camera*, which has four different RL meanings and thus corresponds to 4 lexical units), the loanword variant *ghenga*, which coexists with I. *gang* (counted as 2 lexical units because of its different meanings in Italian) and is characterised by a different degree of loanword integration, 2 cases where "ingl" appears in the entry of a form that does not represent a loanword borrowed from English (*piro-* and *cine-*), and *stage* WORK EXPERIENCE, INTERNSHIP, which appears to be a borrowing from French rather than from English.

pájaro 'small bird'), cotaxonomic similarity (the meanings of successor and antecedent are co-hyponyms, e.g. Latin *sorex* 'shrew' → F. *souris* 'mouse'), cotaxonomic contrast (e.g. F. *terrible* 'terrible' → 'wonderful', i.e. the meanings are direct opposites), and conceptual contrast (e.g. Old French *oste* 'guest' → 'hostage'). These options exhaustively describe the semantic relations of source and target items in cases of semantic change, word formation as well as lexical borrowing.

For the second axis (formal innovations / morphology), processes of word formation such as suffixation, composition, conversion, ellipsis, etc. are concerned, while purely phonetic changes are abstained from. We will see that for the purpose of this paper, the category of ellipsis / truncation turns out to be of key importance. Finally, the third axis of stratification concerns the question whether the innovations take place within a certain language ('stratum') or lexical items are imported from another language ('borrowing'). Obviously, it is the latter category which is central to this paper.[4]

Adopting this system, the relations between the SL and the RL items will be described in this following notation format for the remainder of this paper: "[SL item = antecedent] → [RL item = successor]: > semantic relation . structural relation . stratification >", yielding descriptions as given in (1) and (2).[5]

(1) E. *window-shopping* n. 'the action of browsing or looking at goods displayed for sale, esp. in a shop window, without intending to make an immediate purchase, either as a recreational activity or with a view to buying something in the future' (OED) → It. *shopping* s.m. 'id.' (cf. DELI): > identity . ellipsis . borrowing >

(2) E. *flipper* 'small wing in the pinball game throwing back the ball' → It. *flipper* 'pinball game': > contiguity . continuity . borrowing >

Unless there is strong evidence that the semantic or morphological divergences identified by the comparison of the SL and the RL items have been introduced

---

4 Calques such as It. *grattacielo*, in contrast, need to be analysed as analogical innovations characterised by more complex innovation patterns, allotting both the material RL forms from which the new items are created (It. *grattare* SCRAPE + *cielo* SKY) and the foreign models that are imitated by the calques (E. *skyscraper*) (see Winter-Froemel, forthc. a).

5 For the SL and RL items, the parts of speech and, if applicable, grammatical gender, are indicated as given in the reference dictionaries (It. s.m. = masculine noun, s.f. = feminine noun, inv. = invariable, agg. = adjective). Definitions of the meanings of the SL and RL items will be given in single quotation marks ('...') (expressing meanings in the SL or RL lexicon). Small caps, on the other hand, are used to refer to the concepts designated when analysing the ways in which the items are used by the SL and RL speakers in concrete scenarios of communication in sections 3 and 4 of this paper.

within the RL after the importation of the borrowings, I assume that the innovations had taken place in the situation of borrowing proper. Admittedly, this decision can be controversially discussed and an alternative analysis of two subsequent subprocesses of lexical innovation is in many cases possible (first, importation of the loanword into the RL without semantic or morphological change, possibly without the original version of the loanword being lexicographically documented[6], then semantic or morphological change within the RL). Nevertheless, to my view, the stance taken in this paper can be justified, as we are dealing here with a general methodological challenge of analyses of semantic change: studying semantic change generally implies the necessity to reconstruct hypothetical scenarios of innovation because of the general insufficiency of corpus data available, which will normally not permit us to identify the stage of innovation proper, i.e. the first use of the new item. Moreover, from a usage-based perspective, it seems plausible to assume alternative pathways of evolution for the lexical items, so that alternative analyses need not exclude each other. In other words, even if a particular borrowing may first have entered the RL in a SL-truthful form and only have undergone semantic or morphological change in a subsequent step, RL speakers may nevertheless interpret the borrowings in their altered form as having been directly changed in the course of borrowing. We will see that this means that the notion of semantic and morphological transparency is of key importance here, and its importance illustrates the wide implications of a usage-based approach to phenomena of language contact and (lexical) innovation.

Another caveat to be made is that for certain anglicisms an additional influence from French or other European languages can be observed or assumed (see also Klajn 1972: 16–20). In some cases, a French influence is indicated by DELI (e.g. for *stand*, DELI indicates: "*Stand* thus means in English, among its many senses, also stand (in races), and this word is transported 'by anglomania' into new French, and thus, to us" [*Stand* in inglese vale poi, fra i molti sensi, anche tribuna delle corse e tale parola «per anglomania» è trasportata nel nuovo francese, e quindi fra noi"]), but this kind of information is not systematically provided. It represents a potentially far-reaching factor, as many of the borrowings have (quasi-)simultaneously been introduced into several European languages, so that the different RLs may have influenced each other (see e.g. the borrowings of *spider* and *flipper*, both documented in French, German, Italian,

---

[6] It is highly plausible that this constellation is far from being marginal, as dictionaries such as DELI generally register only the most common variants of the items, i.e. the variants that have become conventionalised in the RL.

Portuguese, Spanish, etc.). However, this means that it is in many cases difficult to determine the exact chronology of the borrowings and influences. Again, unless there is evidence for a strong and direct additional influence, this aspect will thus be abstained from here and left to follow-up studies.

The main lexicographic references consulted for the survey are DELI and OED, but occasionally, additional sources were taken into account as well. For example, although the OED defines E. *boogie-woogie* as a music style only, its use for a dance is also well documented in the SL, so that no semantic change was assumed for the borrowing in both meanings. To keep the analyses manageable, however, additional sources were only occasionally consulted; moreover, because of the strong dynamics which is inherent to the lexicon of a language, the possibility of further semantic changes in the SL and in the RL needs to be admitted as a general option (e.g. the items may have developed additional meanings in the RL, which are not taken into account here).

A last preliminary remark is that I will refer to the notions of (semantic / morphological) *innovation* and *change* without elaborating this distinction (for a discussion of the stages of language change, see e.g. Winter-Froemel 2008, 2011, 2012: 152–153). The usage-based focus on scenarios of language contact and borrowing means that (hypothetical) innovation scenarios, understood as concrete discourse events, are studied; at the same time, all of the borrowings analysed have been conventionalised in the RL, so that we are faced with processes of change on the level of the linguistic items as being part of the RL, i.e. as being shared by the speech community. I thus refer to semantic and morphological innovations when concrete communication scenarios are described, and refer to semantic and morphological changes when the SL and the RL items are compared and divergences are observed. Further methodological issues will be discussed in the followings sections on morphological and semantic changes.

As a general result, the survey yields a surprisingly high proportion of anglicisms exhibiting semantic and / or morphological change with respect to their SL equivalents. Among the 500 lexical items analysed, 61 cases of semantic change are documented (12 instances of contiguity, 3 potential cases of metaphorical similarity, 1 instance of taxonomic superordination, and 45 examples of taxonomic subordination). Furthermore, the results show 30 instances of morphological change, among which 27 can be analysed as cases of ellipsis or truncation (see section 2.4 below). This means that semantic and morphological changes in borrowing are far from being an exception, as they concern about 18% of the data analysed. Against these results, it is even more surprising that, at least to my knowledge, no extensive research has been conducted in this domain in cognitive linguistic and usage-based frameworks, especially concerning the semantic changes that occur. In addition, most previous studies only comment on a few striking examples of semantic divergences (e.g. It. *flipper, jolly*), but risk to overlook less conspicuous cases of semantic or morphological changes.

2.2 Changes at the level of spelling

Before analysing the semantic and morphological changes which represent the main focus of this paper, it is interesting to briefly comment on some changes at the level of spelling which can be observed and which involve a semantic / motivational dimension.[7] A first group of changes can be observed for lexical items which originate from proper names and keep the initial capital letter in the SL, but are de-capitalised in the RL: E. *Airedale* → It. *airedale*, E. *Boston* → It. *boston*, E. *Eskimo* → It. *eskimo*, E. *Charleston* → It. *charleston*, E. *Chippendale* → It. *chippendale*, E. *Derby* → It. *derby*, E. *Oxford* 'Oxford cloth' → It. *oxford*, E. *Scotch* → It. *scotch*, E. *Winchester* → It. *winchester* (see also E. *Asdic* → It. *asdic*, which represents a SL acronym). In these cases, the initial capital letter maintains the strong link to the proper name which represents a motivational base for the lexical items. De-capitalisation implies that this motivational relation and semantic transparency is weakened. The resulting RL items could therefore be considered to be unmotivated to the same extent that other loanwords are generally semantically non-transparent in the RL. At the same time, the RL items can be perceived as being marked for the RL speakers due to their structural features (e.g. non-native graphemes and phonemes, graphotactics and phonotactics), so that the RL speakers might process and use these items in a more conscious way, possibly relating the items to the proper names in spite of the divergence with respect to the initial letter, especially if the proper names are internationally diffused.

A de-capitalisation can also be observed for E. *(the) Establishment* → It. *establishment*, and E. *(the) Shake* 'a dance characterised by shaking movements' → It. *shake*. In these cases, the capital letter serves in the SL to mark a special use of the forms (deviating from other more frequent uses of the items); for the RL, this function cannot be applied – but is also not necessary –, as the items exist only in these special uses in the RL.

---

7 To keep the complexity of the analyses manageable, the following remarks are exclusively based on the SL and RL spellings indicated by the OED and the DELI, without taking into account further variants that may exist in both languages.

A second, important group of changes are hyphenations, which represent a frequent phenomenon in borrowings from English into Italian (cf. Klajn 1972: 94–95).[8] Interestingly, we can identify two different pathways leading to hyphenation. On the one hand, there are developments from compound spelling to hyphenation (E. *babysitter* → It. *baby-sitter*, E. *bebop* → It. *be-bop*, E. *bluebell* → It. *blue-bell*, E. *bookmaker* → It. *book-maker*, E. *eyeliner* → It. *eye-liner*, E. *globetrotter* → It. *globe-trotter*, E. *pickup* → It. *pick-up*, E. *popcorn* → It. *pop-corn*). On the other hand, SL items with separate spelling can also be borrowed in a hyphenated form (E. *music hall* → It. *music-hall*, E. *blue jeans* → It. *blue-jeans*, E. *bow window* → It. *bow-window*, E. *call girl* → It. *call-girl*, E. *ferry boat* → It. *ferry-boat*, E. *ice field* → It. *ice-field*, E. *motor scooter* → It. *motor-scooter*, E. *music hall* → It. *music-hall*, E. *plum cake* → It. *plum-cake*, E. *pop art* → It. *pop-art*, E. *stunt man* → It. *stunt-man*, E. *baby doll* → It. *baby-doll*). There are only very few exceptions to the general tendency towards hyphenation (E. *upper cut* → It. *uppercut*, E. *copy-writer* → It. *copywriter*, E. *guard-rail* → It. *guardrail*, E. *two-step* → It. *two step*), so that it can be argued that hyphenation represents the preferred option for borrowings with several root morphemes (usually two, as given in all cases documented in the data).

However, although this feature has been structurally described in previous research, the question remains how it can be explained. A possible answer can be gained from a usage-based approach focusing on the ways in which the RL speakers might perceive the different options. From their perspective, hyphenation can be seen as a good solution, as it indicates the togetherness of the elements functioning as a structural unit, thus offering a benefit compared to separate spelling. But at the same time, hyphenation signals the compositional structure of the items borrowed – possibly facilitating a partial semantic transparency for the RL speakers with respect to highly frequent SL elements (e.g. E. *eye*, *book*, *corn*, *window*, *call*, *girl*) or formally close RL equivalents (E. *blue* – It. *blu*, E. *globe* – It. *globo*, E. *music* – It. *musica*, E. *art* – It. *arte*). It thus breaks the long strings of segments of the SL items into two subsegments of shorter length which can be processed more easily.

---

8 It seems interesting to observe that hyphenation is otherwise rare in Italian. It can be found for some compounds (e.g. *auto-analisi*, *italo-americano*), but stable lexicalised items are generally used without a hyphen (e.g. *autocritica*) (Dardano and Trifone 1995: 698). This can be seen as additional evidence for the usage-based explanation proposed here in order to account for the use of the hyphen in borrowings.

2.3 Semantic changes

When analysing the semantics of borrowings from English into Italian, the importance of specific semantic domains clearly emerges. The most important domain in our data is sports and games, and a considerable amount of anglicisms is represented by technical terms, especially from horse-racing, boxing, football, cycling, boat races, card games, and poker. In many cases, the technical uses are already registered for the SL items, which are borrowed in this specific meaning, so that no semantic change takes place. These items will therefore not be discussed in more detail in this paper. From a purely contrastive perspective, however, some of these items show clear differences with respect to their place in the systems of the SL and the RL: while the RL items may exist only with the particular meaning in which they have been imported, the corresponding SL forms are often polysemous, and the meaning concerned in borrowing is only one specific (and possibly quantitatively marginal) meaning in the SL.[9] This implies that contrarily to the RL items, the SL items are motivated (or can be perceived as being motivated) by other SL lexical items, and while the RL items immediately evoke the specific domain of their technical use, this is not the case for the SL items (see e.g. E. *crawl* vs. It. *crawl* [used only in the meaning 'crawl-stroke'], E. *short* vs. It. *short* [used only for 'short film'], E. *container* vs. It. *container* ['receptacle for the transportation of freight'], E. *dry* vs. It. *dry* [which is only used for alcoholic drinks], etc.).[10]

We could speak here of cases of apparent semantic change. From a usage-based perspective, the items have a different motivational pattern for the speakers of the SL and the RL, but there is no semantic innovation to be observed when they are borrowed. In spite of the shortness of her paper and although she does not refer to the concept of reanalysis, Alexieva (2008) presents very important reflections which are highly relevant to this paper and which are compatible with the approach that will be presented here. She insists on the fact that the traditional view of processes of borrowing suggested by the terms 'borrowing' and 'loanword' is crucially wrong or "illusionary", and that what takes place is not a "transition of words from one language into another" (2008: 47), but "the creation of close lexical copies of the respective foreign words by the 'borrowing'

---

9 This observation can be linked to findings on linguistic codeswitching, where domain effects have been observed, i.e. inserted content words tend to come from specific domains which are typically associated with the other language (see e.g. Backus 2001).

10 In some cases, however, the technical meaning is not registered at all for the SL, whereas the usage and meaning of the item is restricted to a specific context of use in the RL (e.g. sports or a particular sport only). These cases will therefore be included as semantic changes in the form of taxonomic subordinations (see the further discussion in this section).

language itself" (2008: 48), which means that the loss of morphological and semantic transparency emerges as a basic feature of borrowing (as already pointed out by Hope 1971). This also accounts for the fact that terminological meanings (e.g. for borrowings of E. *goal*, and the examples from our data given above) are "primary and hence unmotivated" in the recipient languages, "while those of their English etymons *goal* [... etc.] are secondary, which means that they are motivated" (2008: 49).

It is important to insist on these cases of apparent semantic change, as in previous research of linguistic borrowing, there has sometimes been a confusion between this pattern of reduction of polysemy and genuine semantic change in borrowing. Alexieva proposes to distinguish between 'semantic reduction' and 'semantic narrowing' (2008: 43). The reduction of polysemy can be seen as a general pattern in borrowing,[11] for which a usage-based approach provides a straightforward explanation: as the borrowings occur in concrete scenarios of language contact and innovation, the SL forms are actualised in these concrete usage events in one specific meaning, and it is only this specific meaning which will be transferred into the RL (or undergo semantic change).

The importance of distinguishing between changes taking place in the situation of borrowing proper and changes that can already be observed in the SL prior to borrowing, is also illustrated by the noun *big*, meaning 'important / authoritative / influential person' both in the SL and in the RL (cf. OED, DELI). We can observe a SL ellipsis (originating from E. *big shot*) and a clear difference in frequency and semantic transparency (the English noun *big* is strongly motivated by the corresponding adjective), but we can nevertheless assume a borrowing without semantic innovation. Similar observations can be made for other SL items arising from an ellipsis which, however, already takes place in the SL, so that no change in borrowing needs to be assumed (e.g. E. *koala (bear)*, *(ice) pack*, *reflex (camera)*, *short (film)*, *(Negro) spiritual*, *tandem (bicycle)*, etc., but see also note 25 in section 2.4 below).

Genuine semantic changes in borrowing, in contrast, represent a distinct phenomenon. According to previous research, there are only two possible types of semantic relations occurring in the situation of borrowing proper: taxonomic subordination and contiguity, i.e. semantic change in borrowing is restricted to semantic specialisation / narrowing and metonymy (cf. Winter-Froemel 2014). However, at least to my knowledge, up to now this assumption has not been tested by systematically analysing larger samples of borrowings, and the relative

---

[11] Pulcini (2002: 162) states: "As a rule, the meaning of loanwords is restricted." (see also Klajn 1972: 104).

importance of taxonomic subordination and contiguity is described in various ways: while some approaches stress the importance of the former type of relation (Alexieva 2008: 43; Busse and Görlach 2002: 162; Humbley 2008: 231), Pulcini assumes a key role of contiguity: "[...] the original meaning of the loanword may be changed, especially through metonymic modifications" (Pulcini 2002: 162; see also Klajn 1972: 105: "I veri e propri cambiamenti di significato, per lo più di natura metonomica [...]" [the real semantic changes, most of which are of metonymic nature...]).

Against this background, our survey on 500 lexical items borrowed from English into Italian provides new insights that both confirm and refine previous analyses. First, there is the surprising result that a relatively high number of borrowings exhibit semantic changes that can be assumed to have taken place in the situation of borrowing proper (about 12% of the lexical items analysed, see 2.1). Semantic change in borrowings is thus a phenomenon which is far from being marginal. Moreover, this result appears to be even more striking, as relatively narrow criteria were adopted to define cases of semantic change in borrowing.[12]

As the overview in 2.1 has shown, among the semantic changes observed in the data, taxonomic subordination clearly prevails, followed by contiguity. This finding confirms previous studies which have stressed the importance of these two relations, and it provides an answer to the question of the relative importance of both types of relations: taxonomic subordinations are nearly four times as frequent as metonymic changes (i.e. changes based on contiguity relations), and although this finding needs to be tested for larger data samples and for other SLs and RLs, the clear prevalence of taxonomic subordination can be assumed to hold for other contact scenarios as well (reflections on how this tendency can be explained from a usage-based perspective, focusing on potential scenarios of innovation, will be presented in section 4 of this paper).[13] Moreover, the data shows that beyond these two relations, and contrary to what has been previously assumed in research on linguistic borrowing, there are also a few cases

---

[12] For example, the borrowing of It. *stop* could be explained as arising from the more general SL meaning 'mark or point of punctuation' (OED), but it was not included as a case of semantic change, as the OED also indicates this specific usage ("Short for *full stop* n. 1: (a) as used, spelt out, in a telegram"; OED, s.v. *stop*, n.2). Similarly, the item *freezer* is frequently used in English for a 'machine for freezing' in general, whereas it means in Italian only 'the superior compartment in the refrigerator', but again this sense is also indicated by the OED, so that no semantic change was assumed. Similarly, the items *boom*, *cocktail* and *slang* registered by Klajn (1972: 105–107) among the borrowings accompanied by semantic change were analysed as cases of borrowing with semantic identity here, as the RL meanings are also documented in the SL.

[13] Cf. also the survey on anglicisms in Spanish by Serigos (2016), showing a clear tendency towards semantic specialisation in borrowing.

of innovations following other semantic relations. Due to the high total number of cases of semantic change in borrowing, it will not be possible to comment on all examples in detail, and the following discussion will be limited to examples exhibiting characteristic pathways of evolution; where possible, I will point out cases documented in the data which exhibit similar patterns of evolution.

With respect to semantic innovations based on relations of contiguity, different subtypes of metonymic relations can be found: transitions between several spatially contiguous elements within a frame or from a (salient) element to the frame itself (see (3), (4), (5)), or from concrete objects or persons to more abstract meanings describing the action taking place (see (6)), or the other way round (see (7)).[14]

(3) E. *trotter* 'a horse which trots' (OED) → It. *trotter* s.m. 'ippodromo per le corse al trotto' [hippodrome for trotting races] (DELI)

(4) E. *Eskimo* 'a member of an aboriginal people inhabiting northern Canada, Alaska, Greenland, and eastern Siberia' (OED) → It. *eskimo* s.m. 'ampio giaccone con cappuccio, di tela impermeabile, spec. grigioverde, generalmente foderato di lana' [winter jacket with hood, of waterproof material, especially glaucous, generally lined with wool] (DELI)

(5) E. *welter* 'heavy-weight horseman or pugilist' (OED) → It. *welter* s.m. 'categoria di peso della lotta e del pugilato' [weight class in wrestling and boxing] (DELI)

(6) E. *music hall* n. 'a public hall or theatre used for musical performances' (OED) → It. *music-hall* s.m.inv. 'lo spettacolo stesso' [the performance taking place there] (DELI)

(7) E. *cutting* 'the action of the verb cut' (OED) → It. *cutting* s.m. 'insieme dei frammenti di roccia che si formano nella perforazione dei pozzi petroliferi' [totality of fragments of rock produced during oil drilling] (DELI)

Finally, there are also transitions from a part to the whole (see (8)) or vice versa ((9), (10)).[15] Some previous approaches have included part-whole or whole-part

---

14 For the borrowing of *cutting*, no detailed information on a possible innovation scenario is provided by DELI. Further research is required, as the technical term used in the SL is *drilling*, not *cutting*, and an influence of E. *cutting fluid* could be assumed.
15 For the borrowing of (9), an additional influence of the English expression "The City of London" designating 'the small historic central part of London situated within its ancient boundaries and under the jurisdiction of the Lord Mayor and the City of London Corporation, having

transitions in the category of synecdoche, but from a cognitive semantic point of view they are better described as a special type of metonymic relations, namely meronymic or part-whole relations (see Koch and Winter-Froemel 2009).

(8) E. *flipper* 'part of a pinball machine used to strike the ball' (this meaning is not indicated by the OED, however) → It. *flipper* s.m. 'biliardino elettrico a gettoni' [pinball machine] (DELI)

(9) E. *city* 'a large or important municipality' (OED) → It. *city* s.f. 'centro politico e finanziaro di una metropoli' [political and financial centre of a metropolis] (DELI)

(10) E. *mixer* 'a machine or device for mixing' (OED) → It. *mixer* s.m.inv. 'parte del frullatore' [a part of the mixer] (DELI)

In addition to the examples analysed here, relations of contiguity also play a fundamental role for ellipses occurring in borrowing, as will be shown in section 2.4: For example, comparing the SL and RL meaning of *plaid* (designating the material in the SL and a piece of clothing made of this material in the RL), a semantic relation of contiguity can be traced. However, it is plausible to assume that the borrowing has occurred via ellipsis from E. *plaid-shawl* and not via a direct semantic change of E. *plaid*; nevertheless, the relation of contiguity still plays an important role in this evolution, and provides an additional pathway of potential interlingual motivation of the RL item *plaid*. Moreover, based on these reflections ellipsis can be considered to be a potential pathway also for some of the examples cited above. For instance, the borrowings in (4), (5), (6), and (8) could also have occurred via ellipses of forms like *Eskimo jacket*, *welter class / welterweight class*, *music hall performance* and *flipper machine*. For some of the borrowings, however, an ellipsis does not appear to be a plausible option (e.g. *mixer*), so that contiguity keeps its validity as a defining feature of a basic subtype of semantic innovation in borrowing.

The second and even more important type of semantic divergence identified in previous research is taxonomic subordination. However, there is a general difficulty which can be observed for this subtype of changes and which arises from the closeness and partial compatibility of the SL and the RL meanings. Depending on the ways in which the SL and RL meanings are paraphrased, the RL

---

official city status in its own right' (OED) seems possible; in this case, the example could be analysed as a case of ellipsis and taxonomic superordination ("The City of London" → It. *city* 'the central part of any metropolis').

items may be interpreted as being semantically identical or taxonomically subordinated to the SL items. For example, for It. *performance*, DELI only paraphrases the sports meaning ("nel linguaggio sportivo, ..." [in the language of sports, ...]), although in general use, the use of *performance* is not restricted to this domain. Thus, the identification of taxonomic changes crucially hinges on the lexicographic descriptions and decisions. This difficulty can also be illustrated by the borrowing of *team*. One of its meanings in Italian is described by DELI as a 'group of scientific researchers' ['gruppo di ricercatori scientifici']; for the SL, the OED indicates:

> A group of people, nations, etc., who are associated in a particular action or endeavour. Now chiefly: a group of two or more people who work together in a professional capacity, or who collaborate on a particular task. Also in extended use. (OED, s.v. *team*, 6.a)

Based on these definitions, the following analyses could be envisaged:

(11) E. *team* → It. *team*
   a) 'group of people associated in a particular action' → 'group of people associated in scientific research'
   \> taxonomic subordination . continuity . borrowing \>

   b) 'group of people working together on a professional level' → 'group of people working together on a professional level in scientific research'
   \> taxonomic subordination . continuity . borrowing \>

   c) 'group of people associated in a particular action, e.g. scientific research' → 'group of people associated in scientific research or similar activities'
   \> identity . continuity . borrowing \>

As a general methodological principle, the analyses chosen here closely follow the definitions given in the reference dictionaries. As the OED gives a general meaning for *team*, whereas the DELI gives a more specific definition, this lexical item was included in the category of changes by taxonomic subordination. However, the distinctions are often very subtle, and some of the analyses could therefore be controversially discussed or would have to be analysed differently if additional reference dictionaries with partly diverging definitions were taken into account. Moreover, we are faced again with the general methodological challenge of locating the semantic changes observed: do they occur in the situation of borrowing proper, or may they already have occurred in the SL, or only in the RL after the introduction of the loanword? In many cases the information provided by the dictionaries permits several alternative analyses; as a general rule, the analyses stick closely to the information on the SL and RL meanings provided by our main reference sources.[16]

With these caveats, various observations on taxonomic subordination in borrowing can be made. A very frequent pattern is the restriction to a more specific meaning by restricting the usage of the item borrowed to the context where the borrowing takes place. This tendency is very clear for the terminology of different sports, i.e. items with a more general SL meaning are imported into the RL in specific contexts and are exclusively used in these contexts in the RL. For example, the interjection It. *break*, the nouns *ring* and *swing* ('slap in the face', cf. DELI), and the adjective *groggy* are exclusively used in Italian in the context of boxing; It. *out* is used only in the context of tennis (while this specific use is not registered by the OED); It. *driver* only designates a specific kind of driver, 'the driver in trotting races' (a meaning which is not documented in the OED); It. *racer* only means 'racing boat'; It. *score* is used only in the context of soccer according to DELI. A further interesting case is the borrowing of *mister*, for which DELI indicates two senses, which are both more specific than the SL meaning: 'the winner of a beauty contest' and 'soccer / football trainer', which is a very clear case of taxonomic subordination with respect to the SL meaning. In a partly similar way, the meaning of E. *boy* is restricted to a very specific usage when the item is borrowed into Italian:

(12) E. *boy* n. 'a male child or youth' (OED) → It. *boy* s.m. 'ballerino di uno spettacolo di rivista' [male dancer of a revue performance] (DELI)

Moreover, there are some items which can be used for different sports in the RL, but nevertheless show a semantic specialisation with respect to the SL, where their use is not limited to the domain of sports. To this group belong the items It. *forcing*, *forfeit*, and *leader* 'nello sport, chi è in testa alla classifica' [championship leader] (DELI), as well as *tandem*, used in Italian only for two athletes participating in a competition and closely understanding each other (cf. DELI).

---

16 It also needs to be stressed that the compilation of dictionaries clearly depends on the lexicographic strategies employed by their compilers. Especially when it comes to borrowings, on attitudinal grounds, there could be a tendency for compilers to focus on specialised meanings or hyper-specialise the meanings of borrowings to highlight their usage in a language as mostly technical terms but not as terms that are part of the general lexicon. Data of loanword usage in context might thus show a different semantic scope of a borrowing than described in a dictionary (cf. also current uses of It. *team* in the business context), and it would be desirable to refine the reflections presented here by follow-up studies taking into account authentic usage of the loanwords in context (cf. e.g. the contributions in Zenner and Kristiansen 2014).

Besides the domain of sports, semantic specialisations can also be observed for other domains and contexts: It. *catgut* is used only in medical contexts, whereas it has a more general meaning in the SL ('used for the strings of musical instruments; also as bands in lathes, clocks, etc.'; OED); It. *tester* is used only for the testing of electronic devices etc.; It. *suspense* is only used when talking about literary texts or other genres that create suspense such as films; It. *trend* is used only in the context of economy; It. *peeling* is only used in the context of cosmetics; It. *handling* is only used for the treatment of flight passengers (cf. DELI); It. *specimen* means only 'specimen copy of a book'.[17]

By being restricted to a more specific use, the items borrowed acquire an additional semantic feature; in many cases they are thereby integrated into the conceptual hierarchies of the RL and become hyponyms of other RL items which would represent possible translations for the SL items: It. *killer* means 'contract killer' and is thus taxonomically subordinated to It. *assassino* (or *omicida*), which translates the more general meaning of E. *killer* [+/- acting on contract] (see also It. *break* meaning 'break from work' and being subordinated to It. *pausa*).[18]

In some cases, the semantic feature which is added to the RL meaning is also directly linked to the culture of the SL, as illustrated by It. *policeman* 'police agent in English-speaking countries' (DELI).[19] Another example which equally shows that linguistic change and societal change are intertwined is the item *partner*. For the SL meaning, the OED indicates: "Now increasingly used in legal and contractual contexts to refer to a member of a couple in a long-standing relationship of any kind, so as to give equal recognition to marriage, cohabitation, same-sex relationships, etc." Faced with the need to designate new legally relevant categories of partnership, the RL speakers have also made use of this

---

[17] For this example, alternative analyses would be either an ellipsis from E. *specimen book* 'a book of specimens or samples' [OED], or a semantic change in the RL, where the more general meaning is also attested.

[18] See also Alexieva's comments on the narrowing of meaning that can be observed for borrowings of E. *meeting*, *dog*, and *killer* into different recipient languages: "First, all the recipient languages have their own words for the general concepts expressed by *meeting*, *dog* and *killer* in English. And second, it is the very loss of morphological and semantic motivation that allows the three loans to change the English general meanings into more specific ones" (Alexieva 2008: 49).

[19] In addition, there are many more borrowings documented in the data for which the concept designated is closely related to the SL culture or environment, but which are analysed as cases of semantic identity, as the meaning remains constant in borrowing (e.g. *airedale, boomerang, boston, cent, college, cricket, dominion, fox-trot, hickory, husky, koala, one-step, peck, penny, skunk, squaw, tomahawk, whig, whist, yard*).

expression, attributing a more specific meaning to it, however: It. *partner* s.m. 'l'uomo o la donna d'una coppia non sposata' [the man or woman in an unmarried couple] (DELI).

These evolutions (*killer, policeman, partner*) can be explained as being motivated by the aim to avoid the introduction of a semantic equivalent and to make use of the new lexical item (the item borrowed) to express an additional semantic distinction in the lexicon of the RL. This pattern can be labelled 'catachrestic reinterpretation' (Winter-Froemel 2011: 314, see also Onysko and Winter-Froemel 2011; Winter-Froemel 2014) and will be discussed from the perspective of speaker-hearer interaction in communication in section 4.

In addition, the data confirms the finding of previous studies that SL items can be borrowed several times, the various meanings and semantic domains often being very different from each other. In these cases, it can thus be assumed that the borrowings occur independently from each other.[20] This has already been illustrated by the borrowings of *mister*, which acquires two specific and clearly distinct meanings in the RL. Further examples are It. *speaker* (introduced into Italian in the domain of radio or television, and for 'the speaker giving the information about an ongoing sportive competition (in a stadium etc.)'), and It. *stayer*, which is used in the context of cycling ('the rider who drives behind a motorcycle in a specific type of track cycling [It. *mezzofondo*]', DELI) and in the context of horse-racing, these RL meanings being more specific than the SL meaning 'a person or animal having great 'staying power'' (OED). Another good example is E. *box*, which is borrowed in three different meanings which are each taxonomically subordinated to the SL meaning: 1) 'pit (for pit stops in a car race)', 2) 'small garage (as a building intended to the storage of cars etc.)', 3) 'foldable playpen where young children are put before they can walk' ['recinto pieghevole in cui si pongono i bambini prima che sappiano camminare'] (DELI).

In the survey, further semantic relations beyond contiguity and taxonomic subordination were identified, which are unexpected according to previous research. The relation between the SL and RL meanings of *raid, bar* and *identikit* can be analysed as metaphorical similarity, as the meanings are linked by similarity and belong to clearly distinct semantic (or cognitive) frames (soldiery vs. sports for *raid*, catering vs. furniture for *bar*, crime vs. politics for *identikit*, see (13) to (15) below). Assuming that the metaphorical innovations occurred in the situation of borrowing proper would thus mean that the RL hearer faced with the innovation would have to identify the new item and its meaning by retracing the

---

[20] Cf. the methodological decision made in this survey not to count borrowed forms, but to split them up into different lexical units, if they have more than one meaning in the SL; see section 2.1.

conceptual mapping based on the SL meaning. Although this option cannot be completely ruled out, it appears to be quite difficult to imagine that this pathway was followed, as this would have required a high processing load for the RL hearer. However, the examples cited do not necessarily have to be interpreted as cases of semantic change having occurred in the situation of borrowing proper. A metaphorical change before or after the borrowing appears to be a possible and more plausible analysis: metaphors transferring source meanings from the domain of WAR and VIOLENCE to the domain of SPORTS are frequently used in the SL as well (see e.g. *attack*, *defense*, etc.), so that the conceptual metaphor SPORTS IS WAR explains the use of E. *raid* in the context of sports as a use in discourse, even though this use is not registered by the OED. If the original military meaning of *raid* occurred in Italian besides the sports meaning, we should expect it to be indicated by the DELI; as this is not the case, it appears more probable to assume that the metaphor was already introduced in the SL, from which the item was then borrowed into Italian. For the semantic evolution of *bar*, in contrast, the situation is different, as both meanings ('inn', 'piece of furniture') are documented in Italian. It is thus possible to assume a semantic innovation in the RL after the introduction of the loanword (which however does not exclude parallel semantic innovations in the SL), without having to assume a new subtype of semantic change in the situation of borrowing proper. For *identikit*, DELI indicates that this item has been analysed as an "interesting case of transition of a term from the domain of crime reports to political reports" ("caso interessante di passaggio di un termine dalla cronaca nera a quella politica"). The study by M. Dardano from which this citation is taken ("Il linguaggio dei giornali italiani", 1973, cited in DELI, s.v. *identikit*) indicates that the innovation occurred in the context of journalistic texts and that it can be analysed as a RL innovation which has been coined after the introduction of the loanword in its first meaning.

(13) E. *raid* n. 'a mounted military expedition; a hostile and predatory incursion (originally on horseback); an aggressive foray' (OED) → It. *raid* s.m.inv. 'viaggio lungo e difficoltoso, compiuto come impresa sportiva' [long and difficult journey, conducted as a sportive enterprise] (DELI)

(14) E. *bar* n. 'a barrier or counter, over which drink (or food) is served out to customers, in an inn, hotel, or tavern, and hence, in a coffee-house, at a railway-station, etc.; also, the space behind this barrier, and sometimes the whole apartment containing it' (OED) → It. *bar* s.m. 'mobile per tenervi liquori e bevande' [piece of furniture to keep liquors and drinks] (DELI)

(15) E. *identikit* n. 'a system for assembling a composite picture of a person whom the police wish to interview, from features described by witnesses;

a picture assembled in this way' (OED) → It. *identikit* s.m. 'insieme dei requisiti necessari a fornire l'immagine ideale dell'esponente di una data categoria di persone' [totality of necessary requirements that constitute the ideal image of the representative of a certain category of persons] (DELI)

For the borrowing of *residence*, the semantic relation between the SL and the RL meaning can be described in terms of a taxonomic superordination: while the item is restricted to the context of universities or colleges in the SL, it can be generally applied to buildings comprising furnished apartments in the RL according to the DELI. In this case, it can be assumed that the borrowing was based on SL uses of this item in its original meaning, from where it was reinterpreted in a more general sense.[21] Generalisation in borrowing thus appears to be a possible option, but the fact that *residence* is the only example documented in the data points to a marginal role, especially if compared to the converse development (specialisations). Further research is needed to investigate the importance of generalisations for other contact situations as well.

(16) E. *residence* n. 'in universities and colleges: a building providing accommodation for students' (OED; "Chiefly N. Amer.") → It. *residence* s.m.inv. 'edificio, funzionante come un albergo, costituito di interi appartamenti completamente arredati' [building functioning as a guesthouse, with entire apartments that are completely furnished] (DELI)

2.4 Morphological changes

With respect to the level of morphology, the word class remains identical for most items borrowed from English into Italian. Depending on the word class, we can however observe processes of gender assignment (for nouns), integration into RL inflection patterns for pluralisation, verb and adjective morphology, etc. These processes will not be further considered here, as the focus of analysis is on morphological innovations that pertain to the domain of word formation. Previous research has shown that borrowings are frequently accompanied by ellipsis (cf. also Klajn 1972: 70–72 and Alexieva 2008, who speaks of loan clippings or clipped loanwords). The corpus data confirms the importance of this

---

21 Besides the meaning indicated, the SL form also has the meaning 'a dwelling, a house, esp. an impressive, official, or superior one; a mansion'. However, in this meaning, a residence is usually inhabited by only one family, and a semantic evolution based on the meaning indicated in (16) therefore seems more plausible.

type of innovation, where only one element of a SL compound is kept when the item is borrowed, while the meaning of the SL compound is preserved (see (17)).

(17) E. *window-shopping* 'the action of browsing or looking at goods displayed for sale, esp. in a shop window, without intending to make an immediate purchase, either as a recreational activity or with a view to buying something in the future' (OED) → It. *shopping* 'id.' (cf. DELI)

In order to explain the evolution of It. *shopping*, DELI cites another lexicographic source (G. Rando, *Dizionario degli anglicismi nell'italiano postunitario*, 1987) which explicitly proposes a development via ellipsis ("è prob. ellissi dell'ingl. *window-shopping* «il girare i negozi per guardare la merce, senza fare acquisti»" [is probably an ellipsis from E. *window-shopping* 'to take a stroll through shops in order to look at the offer, without making a purchase']). This explanation gains in plausibility from the fact that the compound is registered by the OED with a meaning that matches the RL item.

For most other cases documented in the data, DELI does not explicitly point to ellipsis in the etymological section of the entries, but an analysis via ellipsis also appears to be highly plausible if we consider the meanings of the RL items.

(18) E. *plaid-shawl* n. (OED s.v. *plaid*: General attrib., as *plaid cloak*, *plaid-shawl*, *plaid trousers*, etc.) → It. *plaid* s.m. 'scialle o coperta di lana con disegni a grandi quadri e a colori vivaci' [shawl or blanket made of wool with a design in big squares and lively colours] (DELI)

(19) E. *dancing-room* n. 'a room for dancing; spec. one for public dancing' (OED) / *dancing-hall* → It. *dancing* s.m. 'sala da ballo' [room / hall for dancing, ballroom] (DELI; cf. also Cypionka 1994: 187–189 on F. *dancing*)

(20) E. *flint-glass* 'a pure lustrous glass, now made from a composition of lead oxide, sand, and alkali; originally made with ground flint or pebble as the siliceous ingredient' (OED) → It. *flint* s.m. 'vetro con notevole contenuto di ossido di piombo, di forte potere dispersivo' [glass with high portion of lead oxide, with strong power of dispersion] (DELI)

(21) E. *holding company* 'a trading company which possesses the whole of, or a controlling interest in, the share capital of one or more other companies' (OED) → It. *holding* s.f. 'società finanziaria che detiene la maggioranza azionaria, e controlla l'attività di un gruppo di imprese' [finance company which holds the majority of the share capital and controls the activities of a group of companies] (DELI)

(22) E. *gentleman-jockey* (OED) / *gentleman-rider* (OED, DELI), *gentleman-driver* (DELI) → It. *gentleman* s.m. 'chi gareggia come dilettante in corse ippiche o automobilistiche' [who competes as an amateur in horse races or motor races] (DELI)

(23) E. *jazz-band* (OED) → It. *jazz* s.m. (DELI: anche ellissi di *jazz-band* [also ellipsis of *jazz-band*])

(24) E. *skeleton bob* / *skeleton sleigh* (OED) → It. *skeleton* s.m. 'slitta monoposto a pattini d'acciaio che sviluppa notevole velocità' [single rider sled with steel runners which develops very high speed] (DELI)

(25) E. *shopping bag* (OED) → It. *shopping* s.m. 'particolare tipo di sacchetti con manici' [a particular kind of bag with handles] (DELI)

(26) E. *drink-party* (OED) → It. *drink* s.m. 'piccola festicciola o riunione in cui si offrono bevande alcooliche' [small party or meeting where alcoholic drinks are served] (DELI)

(27) E. *match race* n. 'a race, esp. a horse race, run according to competition rules' (OED: chiefly U.S.) → It. *match* s.m.inv. 'nell'ippica, corsa nella quale sono impegnati due soli cavalli' [in horseracing, a race in which only two horses compete] (DELI)

(28) E. *stop light* n. 'a light on the rear of a motor vehicle, which is automatically illuminated when the brakes are applied' (OED) → It. *stop* s.m., 'fanalino d'arresto negli autoveicoli' [stop light in automobiles] (DELI)

(29) E. *stop sign* n. 'a sign indicating that traffic should stop' (OED) → It. *stop* s.m., 'obbligo d'arresto per i veicoli segnalato da apposito cartello o da dicitura sulla carreggiata' [obligation for vehicles to stop indicated by an appropriate road sign or a written message on the lane] (DELI)

(30) E. *ring doffer* 'a doffer (in a carding machine) covered with separate circles of filleting' (OED) → It. *ring* s.m.inv. 'filatoio continuo, nel quale il filo riceve la torsione passando attraverso un anello [...]' [spinning machine in which the thread receives its twist passing through a ring] (DELI)

For all of the examples, the SL meanings of the RL items semantically correspond to the modifying element in the meaning of the RL items (see the definitions given), and the semantic relation between the modifying element in the SL and the meaning of the RL item is a relation of contiguity ("shawl or blanket *made of wool*

/ *plaid*", "room / hall *for dancing*", "glass [...] originally *made with ground flint* or pebble", "small party *where [alcoholic] drinks are served*", etc.). It is thus highly plausible to assume that the RL items have developed from the compounds which combine these modifying elements (related to the compound meaning by contiguity) with a head representing the superordinate category (*shawl, room / hall, glass, company, jockey / rider / driver, band, bob / sleigh, bag, party, race, light, sign*).[22] The SL compounds which can be assumed to represent the source of the RL items thereby correspond to a frequent pattern of semantic / cognitive-associative relations, namely combinations of contiguity + taxonomic subordination (see e.g. Koch and Marzo 2007). The compounds are registered by the OED (while the elided forms are not registered by the OED in the respective meaning), which strengthens the assumption that the RL items have developed out of SL compounds.[23]

Moreover, typological aspects may contribute to the frequency of this pattern in the data: compounding is clearly less common in Italian than in English which is why there might be a general tendency to reduce the word if the reference is clear. And as compounds are left-headed in Italian (vs. right-headed in Germanic languages), from the perspective of the RL speakers faced with the semantically non-transparent compound, the element retained could be interpreted as a "pseudo-head" (which, of course, does not correspond to the compound structure in the SL).[24]

For the items cited, the assumption of an ellipsis and of a borrowing from English into Italian thus appears to be highly plausible. However, it has to be admitted that in many cases the lexicographic documentation does not provide sufficient information on the chronology of the two subprocesses of change. Thus, alternatively to the analysis as an ellipsis occurring at the stage of language contact / borrowing proper, we also need to consider the possibility that

---

[22] The evolution of It. *ring* is not entirely clear; E. *ring doffer* only designates a part of the spinning machine, while DELI gives the meaning 'spinning machine [...]' for the item *ring*. This could be explained by several subprocesses of change (which are not clearly documented in the sources consulted) or by a semantic change of E. *ring* taken in isolation.

[23] English *skeleton* can be used as a single noun for the sport, but not as a designation for the sled.

[24] Possible exceptions to the tendency observed (requiring further investigations) are E. *jigsaw puzzle* → It. *puzzle* and E. *crossword puzzle* → It. *puzzle*, where the SL head is retained. For *jigsaw puzzle*, this could be motivated by structural features, as the form *jigsaw* might have been perceived as being difficult by RL speakers due to the non-native graphic elements (<ji>, <w>). For *(crossword) puzzle*, the borrowing might have occurred in contexts where E. *puzzle* is used as a headline for rubrics of crossword puzzles in magazines or journals, or in magazine titles; this would mean that the borrowing could also represent a case of direct semantic change or an ellipsis of other compounds where it represents the modifying element (*puzzle magazine, puzzle selection, puzzle collection*, etc.).

the ellipsis had already occurred in the SL, and the elided form was then borrowed into Italian, or the possibility that the compounds had been borrowed into Italian and the ellipsis took place only in a second step within the RL. Although the elided form is not registered by the OED in the respective meaning, the first option appears to be a plausible pathway for the borrowing of English *holding*, as the elided form can also be traced in the SL. Conversely, e.g. for the items *jazz* and *drink*, the ellipsis could also be a RL-internal evolution. Further investigations would be necessary here, and we are faced with a general methodological challenge that cannot always be dealt with in an uncontroversial way. A possible answer to this problem is to admit alternative analyses, which can be taken as alternative and possibly parallel pathways of evolution, some of which might follow different micro-pathways of evolution (ellipsis in borrowing or ellipsis after borrowing, etc.).[25]

This leads us to a further methodological problem that has to be dealt with: the data available may permit alternative analyses that differ not only with respect to the chronology of subprocesses of innovation and change, but also with respect to the nature of the innovations. If the components of the SL compounds for which an ellipsis in borrowing is assumed continue to exist also independently in the SL, a direct borrowing of the component which is conserved in the RL, accompanied by a semantic change (and in some cases a conversion) is also theoretically possible: E. *plaid* n. 'woolen fabric' → It. *plaid* s.m. 'shawl or blanket made of plaid fabric' (borrowing accompanied by a semantic innovation based on contiguity: > contiguity . continuity . borrowing >), E. *dancing* n. 'the action of *to dance*' → It. *dancing* 'ballroom' (borrowing accompanied by a semantic innovation based on contiguity: > contiguity . continuity . borrowing >), E. *hammerless* adj. 'without a hammer (of a gun)' → It. *hammerless* s.m. 'hammerless gun' (borrowing accompanied by a semantic innovation based on contiguity and a conversion: > contiguity . conversion . borrowing >; see (33) below), etc.

---

[25] Cases in the data where the elided form is already registered by the OED were not counted as cases of morphological change in borrowings (e.g. E. *Oxford* "short for *Oxford cloth*", see also E. *air hostess* → E. *hostess*, E. *caterpillar tractor* → E. *caterpillar*, E. *cocktail party* → E. *cocktail*, E. *corner-kick* → E. *corner*, E. *crawl-stroke* → E. *crawl*, E. *crown glass* → E. *crown*, E. *folk-music* → E. *folk*, E. *full stop* → E. *stop*, E. *hesitation waltz* → E. *hesitation*, E. *husky dog* → E. *husky*, E. *koala bear* → E. *koala*, E. *Negro spiritual* → E. *spiritual*, E. *private detective* → E. *detective*, E. *Scotch whisky* → E. *Scotch*, E. *short film* → E. *short*, E. *tandem bicycle* → E. *tandem*, E. *zip-fastener* → E. *zip*). Admitting alternative pathways of evolution (here, ellipsis occurring in the situation of borrowing proper), however, suggests a more complex picture as well as a possibly even more important role of ellipsis in contexts of borrowing.

These pathways of evolution appear to be less plausible than the scenarios via ellipsis: for the latter, concrete innovation scenarios where the meaning of the SL compound is actualised are immediately identifiable, and the fact that their meaning is then conserved in the RL item implies a less complex innovation scenario, characterised by morphological and stratificational innovation, combined with semantic stability (> identity . ellipsis . borrowing >). Nevertheless, the alternative pathways cannot be completely ruled out, and they might facilitate the diffusion of the borrowed items in the RL. To my view, the importance of such alternative pathways represents an important topic to be studied in further research.

Another interesting case documented in the data is the noun It. *jolly*, where the RL meaning 'joker' clearly deviates from the meaning 'joyous', 'jovial' of the SL form, which, in addition, is only used as an adjective. To explain the changes that have occurred, DELI explicitly refers to ellipsis. More specifically, DELI presents a concrete innovation scenario to explain the use of *jolly* in Italian, namely the use of the expression "The Jolly Joker" in a set of playing cards containing a joker card showing a laughing jester: "dalla scrizione *The Jolly Joker*, che appare sulla carta, dov'è raffigurato 'l'allegro buffone' (lett. 'giocatore')" [from the inscription *The Jolly Joker*, which appears on the playing card where the 'Joyful Jester' (literally, 'player') is represented].

(31) E. "The Jolly Joker" (written on a playing card) → It. *jolly* s.m. 'joker' (cf. DELI)

In this case, in contrast to the examples cited above, the SL item assumed to represent the starting point of the lexical innovation is not documented in the OED, and it is not a lexicalised item of the SL. From a usage-based perspective, however, the context described by DELI to explain the borrowing comes even closer to a genuine explanation, as the scenario described directly points to concrete situations of communication / language contact, where RL speakers are faced with a SL utterance (the inscription on the card).

These reflections can be extended to the other examples as well. Thus, explaining the changes that have occurred implies that we need to transfer the abstract lexicographic descriptions to the level of the actual and individual discourse events, as it is only at this level of concrete events of communication between a speaker and a hearer that explanatory factors can be proposed. This illustrates the importance – but also the implications – of a usage-based approach to language contact and borrowing: single uses of the SL item may be sufficient to trigger innovations in the RL, but identifying these innovation scenarios generally represents a methodological challenge, as the specific uses of the SL item may not always be documented in corpora and in lexicographic sources.

This is also confirmed by It. *blue-bell*, where the RL meaning 'female dancer' clearly deviates from the SL meaning (E. *bluebell* 'Any of several plants of the genus Campanula [...], with delicate blue bell-like flowers [...]', OED). What appears to be a semantic change at first sight can be explained in a (more) straightforward way by assuming an ellipsis (in addition, an intermediate step can be assumed, i.e. a borrowing from English into French from where the item was imported into Italian):

(32) E. "The Bluebell Girls" (a group of female dancers performing at the Lido in Paris between the 1940s to the 1960s) → [Fr. →] It. *blue-bell* 'ballerina' [female dancer] (DELI)[26]

Based on these reflections, it seems appropriate to consider ellipsis as a potential option also for other examples. For the following items, the hypothetical SL compounds are not recorded in the OED, but an ellipsis appears to be highly plausible as well:

(33) It. *hammerless* s.m. 'fucile da caccia a cani interni' [hunting gun with hidden hammer] (DELI): ← E. *hammerless gun* (cf. OED s.v. *hammerless* adj.: "without a hammer, esp. of a gun")

(34) It. *scotch* s.m. 'nome commerciale d'un nastro autoadesivo' [product name of a sticky tape] (cf. DELI: "il nastro adesivo 'È (sic) stato inventato in America da un ex-suonatore di banjo. Venne chiamato "scozzese" per il fatto di restare attaccato a tutto come gli scozzesi ai soldi' (Cort.-Card.)"): ← E. *Scotch tape*

(35) It. *slow* s.m. 'fox-trot a ritmo lento' [foxtrot with slow rhythm] (DELI): ← E. *slow foxtrot*

(36) It. *cargo* s.m. 'aereo da carico' [cargo plane] (DELI): ← E. *cargo plane / cargo aircraft*

(37) It. *topless* s.m.inv. 'indumento, costume femminile, spec. da bagno, che lascia scoperto il petto' [female garment, piece of clothing, especially a swimsuit which leaves the breast uncovered] (DELI): ← E. *topless bathing-suit* (cf. OED, s.v. *topless* adj.: "Designating or pertaining to a garment, esp. a (woman's) bathing-suit or dress, having little or no material above the waist; that does not cover the breasts and upper body")

---

[26] The meaning indicated by the DELI appears too general, however, as the item designates only certain kinds of female dancers (especially revue dancers).

For *scotch* and *topless*, we can imagine scenarios of language contact in advertising language, where the items are written on product packages etc., and where typographical aspects and a reduced syntactic complexity of the utterances may come into play as additional factors facilitating the changes that take place: *Scotch* is originally the name of the company which appears on the packages of different products, and which is normally presented with a different typography (different typeface, different font colour and font size, etc.), so that the ellipsis – and the semantic reinterpretation of the name as a designation for one of the most important products sold by this company – is facilitated.[27] For *topless*, we can imagine contexts of language contact where this form is written on the package of a (topless) bathing-suit, either together with the expression *bathing-suit* or in isolated form, possibly next to a picture of the product, so that the context makes it sufficiently clear that *topless* refers to a bathing-suit. In this case, ellipsis thus equally appears as a plausible scenario to explain the development of this item.

Finally, some borrowings exhibiting morphological changes seem to represent special cases. For reasons of space, I will only comment on It. *looping* and It. *catch* here. It. *looping* s.m. is explained by DELI as originating from the expression E. *looping the loop* ('to perform the feat of circling in a vertical loop, orig. on a specially prepared track [...], later in an aeroplane'; "Orig. a fairground phrase."; OED). It. *catch* s.m. is led back by DELI to E. *catch-as-catch-can* 'the Lancashire style of wrestling' (OED). In these cases, a long and fixed SL expression is reduced by keeping only the first item. Therefore, these examples to a certain extent question the assumption of an ellipsis where the speaker is aware of the morphologically complex structure of the expression and then reduces it. Especially for *looping*, the basic procedure at work rather seems to be a truncation, i.e. the RL speakers just cut off the second part of the SL expression irrespective of its semantics (from the perspective of the semantics of the SL expression, a borrowing of the noun *loop* would be a more straightforward solution, as this item more directly corresponds to the concept the RL item designates).[28] These reflections can be generalised to all of the examples

---

27 Cf. also Cypionka (1994: 193–195), who argues that the French equivalent *scotch* should be analysed as a direct borrowing of the brand name; however, in my view, an ellipsis still seems possible, as it can be assumed that the product packages presented the expression "Scotch tape". At the same time, Cypionka's analysis confirms the innovation scenario (advertising language) assumed here.

28 See also Alexieva commenting on similar cases of structural simplifications: "The deverbal *-ing* forms in Engl. *parking-lot* and *camping-site* cannot absorb the place meanings of their second components, just as the *-ing* form in *holding company* is unable to take on the meaning of 'company', whereas in the respective, structurally simple, loans *parking*, *camping / kemping* and *holding* the element *-ing* is only a characteristic final element with a certain 'English' feel for

discussed above: the question whether the evolutions might be better analysed as truncations crucially hinges on the innovating speakers' capacity to analyse the full forms. It thus appears more reasonable and more adequate to speak of 'ellipsis / truncation' in the context of borrowing.

Moreover, as we have seen, the meanings attributed to the RL items correspond to elements that are present in the concrete context of the hypothetical innovation scenario. The concrete actualised meanings and the salience of the communicative referents which are directly accessible in the situation of borrowing are thus at least as important as the SL meanings of the items (e.g. *looping* and *catch*). This leads us back to the general claim that usage-based explanations of the changes observed need to be traced back to individual discourse events by rooting the explanations in the speaker's and hearer's communicative exchange and their linguistic activity.

Summing up, although some of the morphological changes observed can be described as involving conversions, ellipsis / truncation seems to represent the main pathway for changes in borrowing involving the level of morphology (word formation). A basic principle at work here seems to be the reduction of the structural complexity of the items borrowed. This also matches the observations made with respect to changes in separate spelling or compound spelling vs. hyphenation (see section 2.2). Adopting a usage-based approach to borrowing, the factors explaining the changes need to be identified and formulated in a way which is directly related to the speakers who use and interpret the items.

3 Reanalysis as a general subtype of language change

The discussion in the previous sections has revealed certain patterns of semantic and morphological change, and shown the importance of context in borrowing. What remains to be seen is how the borrowings take place in concrete scenarios of communication. In the remainder of this paper, I will argue that the concept of reanalysis as defined by Detges and Waltereit (2002), together with a discussion of its semiotic foundations and the role of ambiguity in reanalysis, provides a key to a better understanding of the processes involved from a usage-based perspective.

---

non-native speakers of English, but without any morphological meaning. So there is no obstacle to shedding as irrelevant the second element (*-lot, -site, company*) of what must have been felt as a longish opaque word, but still preserving the overall meaning" (Alexieva 2008: 50; in this context she also points to similar developments in *happy ending → happy end, air-conditioning → air-condition, basketball → basket*).

According to Langacker's seminal definition, reanalysis represents "a change in the structure of an expression or class of expressions that does not involve any immediate or intrinsic modification of its surface manifestation" (Langacker 1977: 58). In this sense, reanalysis crucially involves a morphosyntactic dimension, such as morphosyntactic rebracketing and category relabeling. For Detges and Waltereit (2002), in contrast, reanalysis is a primarily semantic mechanism (for another semantic approach to reanalysis, see Eckardt 2006). In their account, the basic feature defining processes of reanalysis is thus not a structural-descriptive one, but their aim is to provide a genuine explanation of processes of reanalysis by investigating the basic principles which guide the innovating speakers and hearers. They stress the proximity of reanalysis and semantic changes based on contiguity which do not involve rebracketing or relabeling (e.g. Latin *focus* 'fireplace' → 'fire', see Detges and Waltereit 2002: 163–166), and consider the latter to be "merely dispensable side-effects" of reanalysis (Detges and Waltereit 2002: 169; for other approaches which also include hearer-induced changes without a morphosyntactic dimension, see e.g. Bauer et al. 2010: 60; Winter-Froemel 2012).

In my view, a broad approach to reanalysis, including changes with and without a morphosyntactic dimension, has the advantage of providing a category for a general subtype of linguistic change that is not yet satisfactorily understood but that can be defined in a precise way within a usage-based paradigm. Following Detges and Waltereit, reanalysis is a hearer-induced change which is determined by strategies of understanding. More specifically, they argue that reanalysis is guided by two constraining factors, which are the principle of reference and the principle of transparency. These principles represent pragmatic strategies followed by the speakers (or, more exactly, by the hearers or listeners[29]). The principle of reference is the default principle, and it can be characterised as "a general semiotic principle concerning the relation between meaning and reference" (Detges and Waltereit 2002: 160). This principle is defined as follows: "Assume that the conventional semantics of the sound chain you hear corresponds to what seems to be meant in the situation" (Detges and Waltereit 2002: 156). The principle of transparency, in turn, acts as a subsidiary principle which implies a certain knowledge of the relevant language; it is defined as follows: "Match the sound chain you hear with other sound chains of the language that you already know" (Detges and Waltereit 2002: 159).

Both principles describe very basic cognitive processes which do not only account for reanalysis, but which are followed whenever hearers interpret

---

29 Detges and Waltereit refer to listeners in their paper. I will use both expressions here, understanding them as synonyms.

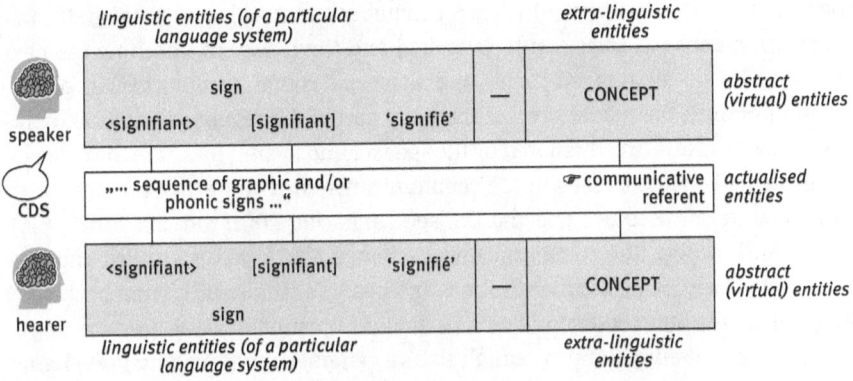

Figure 1: A comprehensive model of communication (Winter-Froemel 2014: 76).

speakers' utterances: the principle of reference accounts for the fundamental semasiological process taking place in understanding, when the hearer is faced with a concrete sound chain and tries to identify its meaning and reference in the particular context. The formulation of the principle of transparency can in turn be understood as relating to the basic principle of taking into account linguistic knowledge when interpreting a concrete utterance, i.e. it refers to abstract knowledge of other linguistic items which are not realised in the utterance and which are paradigmatically related to the utterance.

However, this does not yet sufficiently explain why a certain linguistic structure or item should be reanalysed, and if and how reanalyses are further constrained by additional principles and conditions. More insights into these questions can be gained if we consider the semiotic conditions under which reanalyses take place (see Figure 1, taken from Winter-Froemel 2014: 76). The model builds upon previous semiotic models, most importantly Saussure's *circuit de la parole*, which aims to stress the cyclical nature of communication and to describe the different status of the entities involved in the various subprocesses (in Saussure's terms, physical, physiological, and psychological phenomena / processes, see Saussure [1916] 1960: 28), and Raible's (1983) and Blank's (2001) semiotic models.[30] The model of communication in Figure 1 thus shows the interaction of a speaker and a hearer, realised by the speaker formulating an utterance, i.e. producing a sequence of graphic and / or phonic signs which points to a communicative referent (which can be a concrete object or an abstract notion), and the hearer (or reader) being faced with this utterance and having to interpret it by identifying

---

[30] For a more extensive discussion of these models and the modifications proposed here, see Winter-Froemel (2011: 250–256).

the communicative referent which is presumably intended by the speaker. If communication goes on, roles can be switched and the hearer can become the next speaker. The model thus represents one phase of a communicative exchange.

Importantly, the model stresses that only part of the semiotic entities and processes involved are directly shared by the speaker and hearer; these are the concrete entities which are actualised in the communicative turn and which are integrated into the current discourse space (CDS, see Langacker 2001: 144, 2007: 425–426). Moreover, however, the communicative exchange also involves entities and processes which are located in the speaker's and hearer's minds and cannot be directly accessed by the other communication partner (as illustrated by the grey shading).

The basic feature defining reanalysis as a general subtype of language change is thus the fact that reanalysis arises from a communicative exchange where the hearer correctly identifies the sequence of graphic and phonic signs as well as the communicative referent the speaker intends to designate; nevertheless, s/he assigns a partly different interpretation to the utterance. This description may at first sight seem contradictory. This is due to the fact that the notion of 'interpreting' an utterance can be understood in different ways, which relate to different tasks the hearer has to comply with: s/he has to 1) correctly perceive the sequence of phonic and / or graphic signs, 2) relate this sequence of signs to previous linguistic knowledge (by identifying lexical items, morphosyntactic structures, etc.; interpreting$_1$), and 3) relate the sequence of signs to a presumed referential meaning (by identifying the communicative referent, interpreting$_2$). In successful communication, both interpretations usually match for the speaker and hearer, i.e. the hearer correctly identifies the linguistic items and structures as well as their communicative meanings as intended by the speaker.

However, communication may also be characterised by an incomplete match of the speaker's and hearer's interpretations. A first basic scenario, which will not be commented on in more detail here, are cases when the hearer (or reader) is unable to identify the sequence of phonic and / or graphic signs, e.g. due to background noise. For misunderstandings, in contrast, the hearer correctly perceives the sequence of signs but fails to identify the communicative referent / meaning intended by the speaker, i.e. fails to correctly interpret$_2$ the speaker's utterance (see Figure 2). This may arise from a misidentification of the linguistic items and structures (failure of interpretation$_1$ / semantic misunderstanding). However, misunderstandings can also arise in spite of the hearer understanding the syntax and semantics of the utterance as intended by the speaker (successful interpretation$_1$) if s/he nevertheless fails to identify the adequate communicative meaning (pragmatic misunderstanding, e.g. in cases of irony or indirectness which is not understood; see also Winter-Froemel, forthc. b).

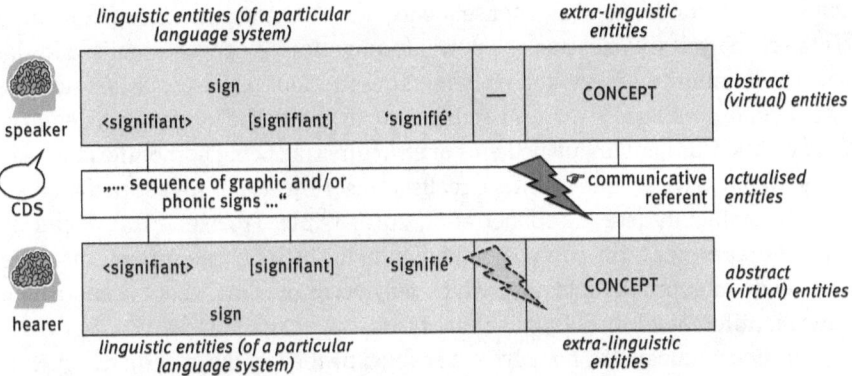

Figure 2: Misunderstanding.

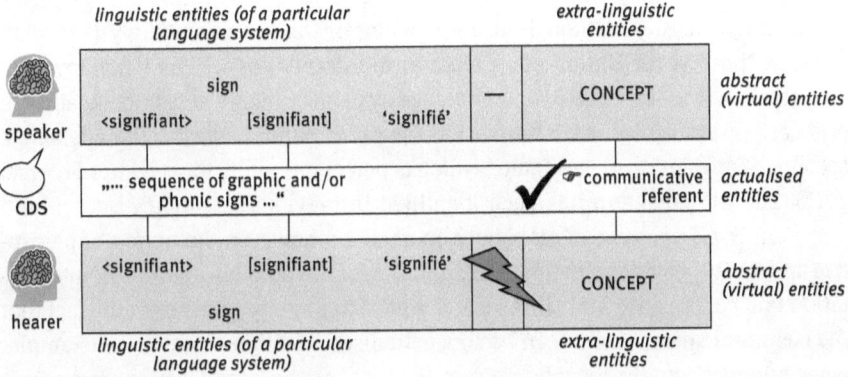

Figure 3: Reanalysis.

Reanalysis, in turn, is characterised by a correct (i.e. matching) identification of the communicative referent (interpretation$_2$), but a (partly) diverging interpretation$_1$ of the utterance by the speaker and hearer, as shown in Figure 3.

The correct identification of reference is thus a basic feature of reanalysis, which is also stressed by Detges and Waltereit (2002): "The requirement of the identity of reference imposes certain constraints on the nature of the semantic relation between the old and the new analysis" (Detges and Waltereit 2002: 168; see also Koch in Bauer et al. 2010: 60, who speaks of a 'pragmatic constancy'). However, from the perspective of the speakers (or more exactly, the hearers), reanalysis cannot primarily be explained by a restriction, but, in a first step, we need to account for the fact that certain interpretative options can be observed at all.

To determine the nature of these options, the notion of ambiguity is helpful. Detges and Waltereit assume that ambiguity is not a precondition for reanalysis, but should be understood as a consequence of reanalysis that occurs if (and only if) the reanalysis diffuses and the new interpretation₁ is conventionalised in the speech community. Detges' and Waltereit's descriptions refer to a specific subtype of ambiguity, which is structural ambiguity existing in the language system, i.e. the fact that different linguistic items or structures (as being part of the language system) may have identical surface realisations. However, if we adopt a broader view of ambiguity (see e.g. Bauer et al. 2010; Winter-Froemel 2013), it can be argued that besides this subtype of ambiguity in the language system, there are also other subtypes of ambiguity, which may occur only in discourse and which concern different levels of linguistic analysis.

In such a framework, reanalysis is enabled by the fact that a certain sequence of signs, uttered in a concrete context of communication to designate a communicative referent, licenses different interpretations: one the one hand, the sequence of signs permits different interpretations₁, i.e. it can be related to different linguistic items and structures. Although at the moment of the hearer's reanalysis (understood as the first realisation of an alternative interpretation₁), the items involved are clearly not ambiguous in the language system, it makes sense to speak here of a case of ambiguity in discourse. On the other hand, however, there is also a second manifestation of ambiguity, which is perceptive ambiguity (Winter-Froemel 2013). The phenomenon has been identified in previous research[31], but without being analysed as a case of ambiguity. In my view, however, the notion of perceptive ambiguity provides a better understanding of the possible margins of interpretation that can be observed. This second type of ambiguity arises from the fact that the communicative referent can be conceptualised in different ways. For example, when talking about the neighbours' dog, the speaker and hearer may categorise this animal as an ANIMAL, a DOG or a POODLE, and assuming that the lexical item uttered by the speaker is unknown to the hearer, s/he may add the item to her / his lexicon by assigning it one of the possible conceptual interpretations mentioned.[32] This is what happens, for example, in overgeneralisations in language acquisition, and, as we will see in section 4, in semantic and morphological changes of borrowings.[33]

Perceptive ambiguity allows us to explain in a straightforward way why reanalysis is limited to taxonomic and metonymic relations, as it is precisely for

---

[31] See the identity of reference put forward by Detges and Waltereit as well as the notion of bridging contexts, which equally stresses the compatibility of different interpretations (Evans and Wilkins 2000).

[32] As we are now dealing with the concepts designated, I switch to the use of small caps.

[33] Of course, depending on the different communication scenarios, there are additional factors which motivate the choice of a certain level of conceptual abstraction; some of these factors (relevant to situations of borrowing) will be discussed in section 4 below.

these relations that the extensions of the linguistic items involved may overlap (cf. Detges and Waltereit 2002: 168). Moreover, this subtype of ambiguity seems to be even more important to reanalysis than the ambiguity of the linguistic items and structures, as the plausibility of the conceptual interpretation may even override the truthfulness of the identification of the surface structure of the speaker's utterance. This can be illustrated by cases of folk-etymological change such as given in (38), which are analysed as cases of "transparency-based reanalysis" by Detges and Waltereit (2002: 160). Another important group of reanalyses involving non-identical surface structures are cases of boundary loss (see (39), taken from Detges and Waltereit 2002, and (40)); interestingly, these latter changes do not increase the motivatedness of the items (as in (38)), but lead to lexical items which are processed in an unanalysed form and are therefore *less* transparent (the overall meaning of the items remaining constant). This shows that ease of processing is a further factor of key importance to reanalysis.[34]

(38) Portuguese *vagabundo* 'vagabond' → *vagamundo* (*vaga* + *mundo*, 'who strolls around the world')

(39) English [cup$_N$board$_N$]$_N$ [kʌpbɔːd] → cupboard$_N$ [kʌbbəd]

(40) German [Schub$_N$laden$_N$]$_N$ [ʃuːplaːdə] → Schubladen [ʃʊplaːdə]

4 Reanalysis in borrowing as an explanatory process

4.1 Specificities of reanalysis in interlingual settings

Based on these general reflections on reanalysis, it remains to be seen how this concept can be applied to the domain of linguistic borrowing. Comparing reanalysis in language contact situations to other manifestations of reanalysis, we

---

[34] It should be noted, however, that the cases cited – which have all been included in the category of reanalysis in previous research – do not respect the defining feature of having identical surface structures. This issue thus requires further discussion, potential options being either the exclusion of the phenomena concerned from the domain of reanalysis, or a modification of the standard definition of reanalysis in order to include cases with only imperfect identity of the surface structures (this option would of course provide the possibility of introducing further distinctions of subtypes of reanalysis).

can immediately observe that the different subtypes of reanalysis involve different communicative settings, most importantly the fact that in language contact, several linguistic systems interact and that the speakers' and hearers' competence with respect to these languages may differ. Moreover, we have already seen that in many cases words are borrowed in specific contexts (e.g. in a particular sport) and communicative practices (or discourse traditions or text types, e.g. newspaper reports about sports matches etc.), so that the group of innovating speakers / hearers is relatively homogeneous (with respect to shared interests, shared background knowledge, etc.). This characteristic is not particular to borrowing, however (see the high number of recent studies investigating the importance of discourse traditions in internal language change, e.g. Pusch, Kabatek, and Raible 2005; Winter-Froemel et al. 2015; Kabatek 2016), and there are also borrowings which are used in a broad variety of situations by different speakers (see e.g. uses of the anglicism *stop* in Italian on road signs or as an interjection meaning 'stop it, enough!').

Beyond the parameters mentioned, situations of language contact may involve many more and very different communicative settings. Basic parameters identified by previous research to characterise situations of language contact (see e.g. Thomason and Kaufman 1988, Winter-Froemel 2011: 214–224) are the intensity of contact, the degree of bilingualism, prestige (the relative prestige of the languages in contact with respect to each other), speaker attitudes, structural similarity and genealogical relatedness of the contact languages. For example, the discussion of orthographic changes in loanwords in section 2.2 has confirmed that semantic transparency / intransparency is an important aspect in borrowing and that hyphenation can be seen as a means to facilitate the processing and memorisation of the SL items introduced into the RL. Therefore, for genealogically related languages, there may be an interlingual transparency of the lexical items acting as an additional factor that influences the ways in which the borrowings are realised and semantic and / or morphological changes are introduced.

In addition to the relations between the SL and the RL, some contact settings also involve an influence of further contact languages: in some instances, there are chains of borrowings, and the items are introduced via a third language (see e.g. the borrowing of *yak* from Tibetan into English, from where it is introduced into Italian, or Dutch *jaght(e)* → English *yacht* → Italian *yacht*, etc.; cf. OED, DELI). In other cases, items from a particular SL can be introduced into several RLs which might then mutually influence each other. This latter aspect is important for the anglicisms in Italian studied here, as the international diffusion of the anglicisms facilitates their introduction and diffusion in Italian.

Moreover, it has been shown that the modalities of borrowing strongly depend on the features of the linguistic items involved, e.g. with respect to parts of speech / morpheme type, frequency and semantic domain. Factors which should be added to this list are the linguistic context in which the SL items are realised, and the discourse tradition in which the language contact takes place, and which may be characterised by specific features such as e.g. reduced syntactic complexity. In addition, there are specific contact scenarios which favour semantic and morphosyntactic reanalysis. Previous research on reanalysis has clearly shown that processes of creolisation facilitate reanalyses (see the numerous examples of agglutinations and deglutinations cited in the research literature on pidgins and creoles). This can be straightforwardly explained by the reduced SL knowledge of the hearers and by the fact that the creole languages arise from pidgins, i.e. from simplified languages where the utterances exchanged are usually strongly embedded in a social and pragmatic context (see also reduced syntactic complexity in foreigner talk as well as syntactically reduced utterances in advertising texts as discussed with respect to the borrowing of It. *topless* in section 2.4). It can be assumed that foreigner talk utterances (exhibiting a "reduced" SL grammar) potentially facilitate certain forms of reanalysis, and it would seem interesting to investigate in more detail the role of foreigner talk in scenarios of borrowing.[35]

The potential role of the different parameters and contact settings can also be illustrated for semantic changes which arise from the choice of a level of categorisation in the RL which differs from the SL. Detges and Waltereit discuss this aspect in the context of their presentation of the principle of reference:

> What level of categorization is relevant for the listener's interpretation depends of course on the situation. In the unmarked case the listener will choose the basic level interpretation DOG, in other types of situations he might select the superordinate level categorization MAMMAL or, on the contrary, a subordinate level categorization like BADGER DOG or DACHSHUND. The principle of reference makes no prediction about levels of categorial abstraction. (Detges and Waltereit 2002: 156)

Further factors come into play here. For example, borrowings from a SL with high prestige frequently undergo taxonomic subordination by integrating an additional feature of exclusivity into their meaning; borrowings designating a concept for which there is already a RL item available may be reinterpreted in a more specific meaning and designate a new concept in the RL (catachrestic reinterpretation, e.g. Sp. *sombrero* HAT → E. *sombrero* BROAD-BRIMMED HAT). For reanalysis in creolisation contexts, in turn, it can be expected that the new RL items will mainly be basic level terms, if there is no other basic level term available, as it seems in a first

---

[35] An additional methodological issue concerning reanalysis in creolisation processes arises from the fact that in contrast to other scenarios of contact between a SL and a RL, there exists no "RL" (cf. Winter-Froemel 2011: 225).

step paramount for the speakers to have linguistic items on this level with which they can adequately operate in many communicative exchanges. These reflections also permit us to explain why processes of taxonomic superordination appear to be very marginal (or nearly inexistent) in borrowing (see the data discussed in section 2.3): choosing the superordinate level of categorisation appears to be an implausible choice, if there is already a RL basic level term and a superordinate level term available, whereas the subordinate level exhibits a dynamic potential by allowing the speakers to integrate cognitively salient subcategories and distinguishing features into the meaning of new lexical items.

For reasons of space, the different parameters cannot be discussed in more detail here, and the remarks in 4.2 will focus on one specific setting of language contact, which is the contact between English and Italian.

4.2 Explaining the changes observed

For anglicisms in Italian, English can generally be analysed as an international prestige language, so that cultural prestige is a factor motivating the introduction of anglicisms to designate concepts for which there are already native Italian items available. This may lead to an additional pragmatic value being integrated into the meaning of the items borrowed. This type of 'connotational (or pragmatic) specialisations' is typically observed for loanwords that have a semantic (near-) equivalent in the RL and that have therefore been labelled as "luxury borrowings" in previous research. We can discard this strongly judgmental concept but nevertheless characterise the borrowings identified by this criterion as a group of items which are relatively marked choices having a stronger communicative effect and typically generating additional pragmatic implicatures of markedness (e.g. prestigiousness). This could be illustrated by It. *stop* compared to It. *basta*, It. *business* compared to It. *affare*, or It. *businessman* compared to It. *uomo d'affare*. However, the semantic meaning indicated by the lexicographic sources consulted for the RL is identical to the SL meaning, and these examples were thus analysed as cases of semantic identity in the present survey (for a more detailed analysis of the pragmatic effects occurring in borrowings, see Winter-Froemel 2011: 295–319; Onysko and Winter-Froemel 2011; Winter-Froemel 2014).

Besides these pragmatic changes, there are also specialisations which affect the semantic meaning of the items borrowed, i.e. borrowings where an additional semantic feature is integrated into the meaning of the RL item, so that it has a more specific meaning, and the RL meaning is taxonomically subordinated to the SL meaning. We have already observed in section 2.3 that this pattern of change concerns a relatively high number of borrowings, and we can identify in the data various subpatterns: in some cases, the items borrowed designate concepts which are closely related to the SL environment, and the semantic feature added in borrowing concerns precisely the fact that the item designates a concept which belongs to the SL culture. This pattern can be illustrated by *policeman*, designating in the RL a POLICEMAN IN ENGLISH-SPEAKING COUNTRIES (cf. DELI).

The semantic specialisation occurring here leads to a divergence with respect to the SL meaning; at the same time, it introduces an additional semantic distinction (here, between police agents from English-speaking countries vs. from other countries) into the RL by designating a new concept. This can be analysed as a case of catachrestic reinterpretation, i.e. as a reinterpretation leading to a new lexical item which fills a lexical gap (Winter-Froemel 2011; Onysko and Winter-Froemel 2011; Winter-Froemel 2014), preventing the item borrowed becoming a synonym for an existing (native) RL items (e.g. It. *poliziotto*). Other examples that illustrate this pattern are F. *grappa* (borrowed from It. *grappa* POMACE BRANDY and designating only POMACE BRANDY PRODUCED IN ITALY), or It. / F. / E. *sombrero* / G. *Sombrero* designating a BROAD-BRIMMED (MEXICAN) HAT, whereas the SL item Sp. *sombrero* designates the taxonomically superordinated concept HAT (see also the examples cited in section 2.3).

In a second group of cases, the concept designated by the anglicism belongs to a specific domain for which English is perceived as the "expert language". In this case, again, taxonomic subordinations may occur, if the item borrowed has a more general (non-terminological) meaning in the SL, but is restricted to the specific domain concerned in the course of borrowing (see e.g. the specialisations observed for the domains of sports and games, the textile industry, the automobile industry, etc.). This can be illustrated by the examples of It. *catgut* (restricted to the medical domain exclusively in the RL), *boy* (restricted to male dancers in revue performances), *break*, *forfeit*, *driver*, etc. (which are all restricted to uses in the domain of sports). It should be added, however, that this group of specialisations can overlap with the first one; a key aspect which is central to both of them is the prestige of the SL and the SL culture.

A further aspect which appears to be central to these semantic changes is the (relative) cognitive salience of the concepts involved: it is highly plausible that the additional feature introduced in borrowing – and thus the more specific concept chosen by the RL hearer – is more salient for the RL hearer than for the SL speaker, i.e. the foreign origin or the specific domain in which the item is used matters to a higher degree to the RL hearer.

In order to explain how the semantic specialisations can be introduced in speaker-hearer interaction, we can come back to the example of E. *leader* and apply the semiotic model presented above, so that the following scenario of language contact can be proposed: an SL speaker uses the item *leader* in the context of sports in its conventional SL meaning to refer to a championship leader; in interpreting the utterance, however, the RL hearer understands the item as referring to the more specific concept of a CHAMPIONSHIP LEADER. In the concrete situation of communication, no problem arises at all, and we can assume that the speaker and hearer are not even aware of the divergence of their interpretations, as both interpretations are perfectly compatible with the communicative referent under discussion (see Figure 4).

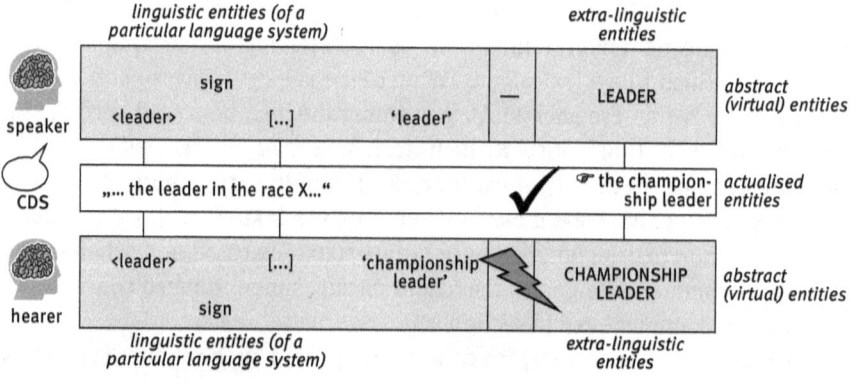

Figure 4: Reanalysis of E. *leader* (taxonomic subordination).

Turning towards the second basic type of semantic divergence in borrowing, i.e. to divergences based on contiguity, it has already been pointed out in section 2.3 that various subtypes of contiguity relations can be distinguished: spatial contiguities, contiguity between the action performed and the participants / objects involved, part-whole or whole-part contiguities, etc. In a general way, the notion of salience proves to be very important for metonymic changes as well, as the RL concept needs to be an equally salient concept in the concrete situation. Figure 5 shows how the semiotic model can be applied to the metonymic shift occurring in the borrowing of E. *music(-)hall*: in a hypothetical scenario of language contact where the reanalysis occurs, the SL speaker uses the item in a context where both the locality and the performance given there are salient concepts belonging to the general frame of ENTERTAINMENT; the RL hearer may reinterpret the item as designating the performance given. This pattern of explanation can also be transferred to metonymic changes occurring in other SL and RL language pairs and showing similar patterns of evolution, e.g. the semantic change that can be observed for E. *testimonial* borrowed into German *Testimonial* and designating also the PERSON EXPRESSING A TESTIMONIAL (this meaning is not indicated by the *Duden*, but is clearly attested in the Internet).

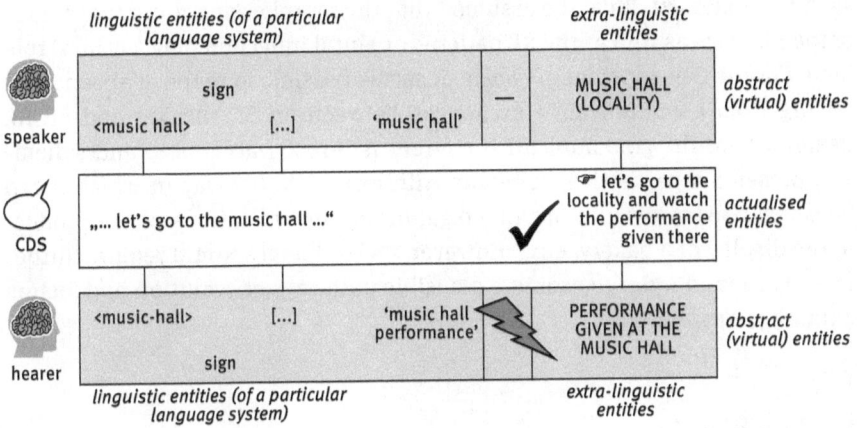

Figure 5: Reanalysis of E. *music hall* (contiguity).

For both scenarios, it can be assumed that the items diffuse in the RL, being reused in similar contexts in their new RL meaning. However, additional aspects influencing the innovations' success, stability and subsequent diffusion in the RL would need to be investigated in further research (compare e.g. Zenner, Speelman, and Geeraerts 2013).

The cases of ellipsis / truncation observed in the data, in contrast, cannot be explained by reanalysis, as the requirement of identical (or nearly identical) surface forms is clearly not respected. The RL items show clear formal divergences compared to the SL forms. What is important here is ease of processing; at the same time, in spite of the morphological change, the requirement of referential identity is met: in the (hypothetical) innovation scenarios where the ellipsis / truncation occurs, the communicative referent remains identical. What is crucially different for the SL speaker and the RL hearer, however, is the semantic transparency of the item concerned. This shows that although ellipsis / truncation in borrowing represents a phenomenon to be separated from reanalysis, some of the basic principles that guide reanalysis in borrowing are also active and influence the ways in which the innovations are realised.

Still another subtype of morphological changes that can occur in borrowing are changes in grammatical number. For the anglicisms studied in this survey, no changes of this type are documented, but they can be observed e.g. for borrowings from Italian into French or German, which are often characterised by reinterpretations of the SL plural forms (It. *spaghetti*, *tagliatelle*, etc.) as singulars (see RL plurals such as French *spaghettis*, *tagliatelles*, etc.; cf. also the reanalysis of E. *cookies* as a singular when the item is introduced into French as "un cookies"[36]). It can be assumed that the morphosemantic transparency of the SL items as well as the RL patterns of plural inflection play a central role here. For the development of *cookie*, it seems possible to propose a reanalysis arising from communicative exchanges between an SL speaker and an RL hearer where the communicative referent is directly accessible and salient, and presents a perceptive ambiguity with respect to the way in which it can be categorised (we could imagine e.g. written denominations of the product in the display of a bakery, etc.). However, these changes would require further investigation in order to examine plausible pathways of evolution and factors guiding the evolutions.

5 Conclusion

Our analysis of 500 lexical items borrowed from English into Italian has revealed the importance of semantic and morphological changes in borrowing. In line with previous studies, taxonomic subordinations and metonymic changes were identified as the most important types of semantic changes. With respect to the open question of the relative frequency of these two options, taxonomic subordinations were shown to clearly prevail. Moreover, it was shown that in addition to these semantic relations, other subtypes of change can occasionally be observed. While for metaphorical changes it appears more plausible to assume that they occurred in the SL before borrowing or in the RL after borrowing, cases of taxonomic superordination represent a viable, albeit rather exceptional option. Their marginal status can be accounted for by the fact that there is usually already an alternative RL item available to designate the superordinate concept[37] and that one frequent pattern in borrowing is catachrestic reinterpretation, i.e. the new item is reinterpreted in a more specific meaning, permitting to express an additional semantic distinction in the RL; this latter tendency thus strongly favours taxonomic subordinations in borrowing.

---

36 This form is not lexicographically documented, e.g. it is not indicated by the PR, but it can be observed in everyday usage.

37 In addition to the relation between the source concept and the target concept, their absolute status represents an important factor as well: it could generally be assumed that taxonomic superordinations from subordinate level concepts to basic level concepts are cognitively easier than superordinations from basic level concepts to superordinate level concepts. Moreover, these descriptions would need to be refined by taking into account the specific settings of concrete situations of language contact.

In order to account for the changes observed, I have argued for a usage-based approach to borrowing. I have proposed an explanatory framework which is built on Detges' and Waltereit's (2002) semantically based conception of reanalysis and focuses on the (hypothetical) semiotic scenarios of speaker-hearer interaction in which the new items are introduced. I have argued that the notion of perceptive ambiguity helps us to explain the restrictions that can be observed: from a cognitive point of view, taxonomic subordinations (and superordinations) can arise from scenarios where the communicative referent presents a perceptive ambiguity with respect to the level of abstraction chosen. More specifically, in contexts of borrowing there is a tendency to integrate contextual features (i.e. features of the concrete situational context in which the borrowing occurs) into the lexical meaning, and a frequent pattern is thus the specialisation to certain semantic domains. In other cases, the taxonomic specialisations can be motivated by the introduction of a new concept alongside the new expression (catachrestic reinterpretation); and the two aspects can also be combined. The metonymic changes, in turn, can be led back to scenarios permitting metonymic figure-ground shifts. This confirms the key importance of the constancy of reference; at the same time, we have seen that the cognitive salience and the morphological and semantic transparency of the lexical items equally play an important role.

Moreover, we have seen that for many instances which at first sight appear as metonymic changes, an analysis of ellipsis or truncation is more plausible. For the morphological changes, ellipsis / truncation is by far the most important pattern to be observed, and this can be explained as a reduction of the formal complexity of the plurimorphemic SL expressions which are usually not transparent in the RL. The semantic (in)transparency of the items borrowed thus represents another important aspect. This is equally confirmed by the changes in spelling, especially the strong tendency towards hyphenation, which emerges as an alternative to ellipsis / truncation: it visually splits up the long SL items into compositional units built up from smaller units that can be processed more easily. Although the hyphenations cannot be interpreted as cases of reanalysis, they nevertheless show the importance of the motivational dimension of borrowings, and the active role of the (RL) speakers, as put forward by usage-based approaches. At the different levels of linguistic structure, we can thus observe how the RL speakers' usage of the items borrowed partly reshapes the items, adapting them to their communicative and cognitive processing needs and routines. In my view, this illustrates the benefits of usage-based approaches to borrowing and the possibility of gaining new insights into the phenomena observed. In this way, the present contribution ties in with the cognitive reframing of language contact phenomena proposed in the introduction to this volume. At the same time, various perspectives for future research have been identified, most importantly the identification of subtypes of reanalysis in linguistic borrowing, depending on structural, cognitive and contextual aspects as well as on the social dimension of the contact settings. I hope to have convincingly argued that taking seriously a usage-based approach to language contact and borrowing (and language change in general) sets very high standards on what can be considered to be a valid explanation for processes of change. We thus need to continue to discuss also the question of how the methodological challenges that have to be met can be dealt with in an adequate way.

References

Alexieva, Nevena. 2008. How and why are Anglicisms often lexically different from their English etymons? In Roswitha Fischer & Hanna Puławczewska (eds.), *Anglicisms in Europe: Linguistic Diversity in a Global Context*, 42–51. Cambridge: Cambridge Scholars Publishing.

Backus, Ad. 2001. The role of semantic specificity in insertional codeswitching: Evidence from Dutch-Turkish. In Rodolfo Jacobson (ed.), *Codeswitching Worldwide II* (Trends in Linguistics, Studies and Monographs 126), 125–154. Berlin & New York: Mouton De Gruyter.

Bauer, Matthias, Joachim Knape, Peter Koch & Susanne Winkler. 2010. Dimensionen der Ambiguität. *Zeitschrift für Linguistik und Literaturwissenschaft* 158. 7–75.

Blank, Andreas. 1997. *Prinzipien des lexikalischen Bedeutungswandels am Beispiel der romanischen Sprachen* (Beihefte zur Zeitschrift für romanische Philologie 285). Tübingen: Niemeyer.

Blank, Andreas. 2001. *Einführung in die lexikalische Semantik*. Tübingen: Niemeyer.

Busse, Ulrich & Manfred Görlach. 2002. German. In Manfred Görlach (ed.), *English in Europe*, 13–36. Oxford: Oxford University Press.

Cruse, D. Alan. 1986. *Lexical Semantics*. Cambridge: Cambridge University Press.

Cypionka, Marion. 1994. *Französische «Pseudoanglizismen»: Lehnformationen zwischen Entlehnung, Wortbildung, Form- und Bedeutungswandel*. Tübingen: Narr.

Dardano, Maurizio & Pietro Trifone. 1995 (3rd edn.). *Grammatica italiana. Con nozioni di linguistica*. Bologna: Zanichelli.

DELI = Cortelazzo, Manlio & Paolo Zolli. 1999 (2nd edn.). *Il nuovo etimologico. DELI – Dizionario Etimologico della Lingua Italiana*. Bologna: Zanichelli.

Detges, Ulrich & Richard Waltereit. 2002. Grammaticalization vs. Reanalysis: A Semantic-Pragmatic Account of Functional Change in Grammar. *Zeitschrift für Sprachwissenschaft* 21. 151–195.

Duden. *Deutsches Universalwörterbuch*. 2007 (6th edn.). Mannheim: Bibliographisches Institut.

Eckardt, Regine. 2006. *Meaning Change in Grammaticalization. An Enquiry Into Semantic Reanalysis*. Oxford: Oxford University Press.

Evans, Nicholas & David Wilkins. 2000. In the mind's ear: Semantic extensions of perception verbs in Australian languages. *Language* 76. 546–592.

Hope, T. E. 1971. *Lexical Borrowing in the Romance Languages. A Critical Study of Italianisms in French and Gallicisms in Italian from 1100 to 1900*. 2 vols. Oxford: Basil Blackwell.

Humbley, John. 2008. [Review] Jansen, Silke (2005), Sprachliches Lehngut im world wide web [...]. *Neologica* 2. 228–233.

Kabatek, Johannes (ed.). 2016. *Lingüística de corpus y lingüística histórica iberorrománica*. Berlin & Boston: De Gruyter.

Klajn, Ivan. 1972. *Influssi inglesi nella lingua italiana*. Firenze: Olschki.

Koch, Peter. 2000. Pour une approche cognitive du changement sémantique lexical: aspect onomasiologique. In Jacques François (ed.), *Théories contemporaines du changement sémantique* (Mémoires de la Société de Linguistique de Paris, N.S. 9), 75–95. Leuven: Peeters.

Koch, Peter. 2001. Lexical typology from a cognitive and linguistic point of view. In Martin Haspelmath, Ekkehard König, Wulf Oesterreicher & Wolfgang Raible (eds.), *Language Typology and Language Universals. An International Handbook*, Vol. 2, 1142–1178. Berlin & New York: Mouton De Gruyter.

Koch, Peter & Daniela Marzo. 2007. A two-dimensional approach to the study of motivation in lexical typology and its first application to French high-frequency vocabulary. *Studies in Language* 31(2). 259–291.

Koch, Peter & Esme Winter-Froemel. 2009. Synekdoche. In Gert Ueding (ed.), *Historisches Wörterbuch der Rhetorik*, Vol. 9, 356–366. Tübingen: Niemeyer.

Langacker, Ronald W. 1977. Syntactic reanalysis. In Charles N. Li (ed.), *Mechanisms of syntactic change*, 57–139. Austin: University of Texas Press.

Langacker, Ronald W. 2001. Discourse in Cognitive Grammar. *Cognitive Linguistics* 12(2). 143–188.

Langacker, Ronald W. 2007. Cognitive Grammar. In Dirk Geeraerts & Hubert Cuyckens (eds.), *The Oxford Handbook of Cognitive Linguistics*, 421–462. Oxford: Oxford University Press.

OED = *Oxford English Dictionary*. 2007. Oxford: Oxford University Press. http://www.oed.com (accessed 15 September 2017).

Onysko, Alexander. This volume. Reconceptualizing language contact phenomena as cognitive processes. In Eline Zenner, Ad Backus & Esme Winter-Froemel (eds.), *Cognitive Contact Linguistics. Placing Usage, Meaning and Mind at the Core of Contact-Induced Variation and Change*, 23–50. Berlin & Boston: De Gruyter Mouton.

Onysko, Alexander & Sascha Michel (eds.). 2010. *Cognitive Perspectives on Word Formation*. (Trends in Linguistics, Studies and Monographs, 221). Berlin & New York: Mouton De Gruyter.

Onysko, Alexander & Esme Winter-Froemel. 2011. Necessary loans – luxury loans? Exploring the pragmatic dimension of borrowing. *Journal of Pragmatics* 43(6). 1550–1567.

PR = *Le Petit Robert de la Langue Française. Version numérique du Petit Robert / Dictionnaire alphabétique et analogique de la langue française*, Nouvelle édition (version 4.2) – millésime 2016. http://pr.bvdep.com (accessed 15 September 2017).

Pulcini, Virginia. 2002. Italian. In Manfred Görlach (ed.), *English in Europe*, 151–167. Oxford: Oxford University Press.

Pusch, Claus D., Johannes Kabatek & Wolfgang Raible (eds.). 2005. *Romanistische Korpuslinguistik II. Romance Corpus Linguistics II. Korpora und diachrone Sprachwissenschaft. Corpora and Diachronic Linguistics*. Tübingen: Narr.

Raible, Wolfgang. 1983. Zur Einleitung. In Helmut Stimm & Wolfgang Raible (eds.), *Zur Semantik des Französischen. Beiträge zum Regensburger Romanistentag 1981* (= Beihefte zur Zeitschrift für französische Sprache und Literatur 9), 1–24. Wiesbaden: Steiner.

Saussure, Ferdinand de. 1960 [1916]. *Cours de linguistique générale. Publié par Charles Bally et Albert Sechehaye*. Paris: Payot.

Serigos, Jacqueline. 2016. Using distributional semantics in loanword research: A concept-based approach to quantifying semantic specificity of Anglicisms in Spanish. *International Journal of Bilingualism*, 1–20. https://doi.org/10.1177/1367006916635836 (accessed 04 February 2018).

Thomason, Sarah Grey & Terrence Kaufman. 1988. *Language Contact, Creolization, and Genetic Linguistics*. Berkeley, Los Angeles & London: University of California Press.

Winter-Froemel, Esme. 2008. Towards a comprehensive view of language change. Three recent evolutionary approaches. In Ulrich Detges & Richard Waltereit (eds.), *The Paradox of Grammatical Change. Perspectives from Romance* (= Current Issues in Linguistic Theory 293), 215–250. Amsterdam & Philadelphia: Benjamins.

Winter-Froemel, Esme. 2011. *Entlehnung in der Kommunikation und im Sprachwandel. Theorie und Analysen zum Französischen* (Beihefte zur Zeitschrift für romanische Philologie 360). Berlin & Boston: De Gruyter.

Winter-Froemel, Esme. 2012. Ambiguitätsphänomene im Umfeld des Verbs in der Diachronie der romanischen Sprachen. *Romanistisches Jahrbuch* 63. 139–171.

Winter-Froemel, Esme. 2013. Ambiguität im Sprachgebrauch und im Sprachwandel: Parameter der Analyse diskurs- und systembezogener Fakten. *Zeitschrift für französische Sprache und Literatur* 123(2). 130–170.

Winter-Froemel, Esme. 2014. Formal variance and semantic changes in borrowing: Integrating semasiology and onomasiology. In Eline Zenner & Gitte Kristiansen (eds.), *New Perspectives on Lexical Borrowing* (Language Contact and Bilingualism 7), 65–100. Berlin: Mouton De Gruyter.

Winter-Froemel, Esme. Forthcoming a. Trois dimensions de la diachronie lexicale: sémantique, forme, stratification. In Christiane Marchello-Nizia, Bernard Combettes, Sophie Prévost & Tobias Scheer (eds.), *Grande Grammaire Historique du Français* (GGHF). Berlin & Boston: De Gruyter Mouton.

Winter-Froemel, Esme. Forthcoming b. Ambigüité et marges de l'interprétation en synchronie et en diachronie lexicales: entre innovation et mésinterprétation. In Guy Achard-Bayle, Maximilien Guérin & Marina Krylynschin (eds.), *Les actes du colloque organisé par l'ASL en décembre 2015*. Limoges: Lambert-Lucas.

Winter-Froemel, Esme, Araceli López Serena, Álvaro Octavio de Toledo y Huerta & Barbara Frank-Job (eds.). 2015. *Diskurstraditionelles und Einzelsprachliches im Sprachwandel / Tradicionalidad discursiva e idiomaticidad en los procesos de cambio lingüístico*. Tübingen: Narr.

Zenner, Eline & Gitte Kristiansen (eds.). 2014. *New Perspectives on Lexical Borrowing* (Language Contact and Bilingualism 7). Berlin: Mouton De Gruyter.

Zenner, Eline, Dirk Speelman & Dirk Geeraerts. 2013. Cognitive Sociolinguistics meets loanword research: Measuring variation in the success of anglicisms in Dutch. In Laura A. Janda (ed.), *Cognitive Linguistics: The Quantitative Turn*, 251–294. Berlin: Mouton De Gruyter.

Stefania Marzo, Eline Zenner and Dorien Van de Mieroop
4 When third-wave sociolinguistics and prototype analysis meet: The social meaning of sibilant palatalization in a Flemish Urban Vernacular

Abstract: This paper reveals how the study of contact-induced variation and change can benefit from a cross-fertilization between a third wave perspective on the social meaning of variation and a prototype-theoretical representation of meaning.

As a case study we analyze the use of palatalized and non-palatalized /s/ in a corpus of self-recorded speech of speakers living in Flemish Limburg. Sibilant palatalization is one of the distinctive features of what is often called *Citétaal*, a contemporary urban vernacular that is spreading in the region.

We hypothesize that the social meaning of sibilant palatalization results from a combination of social and interactional categories at play in variant selection and that this combination adopts a prototype structure, characterized by salient and less salient categories and by fuzzy boundaries between the categories. This prototype-based representation of social meaning not only has the potential to add to our understanding of the social meaning of variation, it also furthers the incipient social turn in Cognitive Linguistic research, as we will analyze the social meaning of specific linguistic variants (*viz.* palatalized and non-palatalized /s/), rather than of whole sets of varieties and lects as was done so far.

Keywords: prototype theory, third wave sociolinguistics, social meaning, urban vernaculars

1 Introduction

This paper explores the possibilities that follow from cross-fertilizing a third wave perspective on the social meaning of variation and a prototype-theoretical representation of meaning. We argue that a sociolinguistic representation of social meaning has quite some commonalities with a prototype-based representation of meaning. At the same time, both perspectives can benefit from being brought

---

Stefania Marzo, Eline Zenner and Dorien Van de Mieroop, KU Leuven

https://doi.org/10.1515/9783110619430-005

closer together: we will show how the sociolinguistic methods for studying social meaning offer a strong empirical basis for cognitive linguistic representations and that, in turn, a prototype representation of social meaning will reveal a series of conceptual characteristics that remain latent in sociolinguistic analyses.

Although the study of meaning has always been pivotal in Cognitive Linguistic theory, its interest in the *social* meaning of language has only grown systematically since the advent of Cognitive Sociolinguistics (see e.g. Kristiansen and Dirven 2008, Geeraerts et al. 2010). This paper wishes to contribute to this social turn in Cognitive Linguistics by investigating how sociolinguistic theories and methods can provide new insights and empirical input for a Cognitive (Socio) Linguistic representation of the social meaning of variation, focusing particularly on contact-induced variation and change. When combining these perspectives, two important challenges will however need to be addressed.

In terms of the sociolinguistic theories and methods followed, we adopt a third wave sociolinguistic approach. The third wave perspective defines social meaning as a speaker's expression of its identity through stylistic practices (see Eckert 2012), entailing that at least two perspectives need to be taken into account when aiming for a comprehensive account: a quantitative variationist method that derives the social meaning potential of variation from the correlation between linguistic features (e.g. –ing/-in variation) and social categories (e.g. gender), and an interactional method that defines variation as the 'practice' of constructing social meaning in discourse.

The second challenge concerns our aim to ground these sociolinguistic perspectives on social meaning in a Cognitive Linguistic framework of meaning. This particularly entails that we need to reflect on the relationship between what we consider an empirical definition of social meaning, based on external, objectively verifiable parameters (generally used by sociolinguists) and a more cognitive definition of (social) meaning as a mental representation (used by cognitive linguists).

In this chapter, we hypothesize that the social meaning of variation results from a combination of social and interactional categories at play in variant selection and that this combination adopts a prototype structure, characterized by salient and less salient categories and by fuzzy boundaries between the categories (Geeraerts, Grondelaers, and Bakema 1994). This prototype-based representation of social meaning not only has the potential to add to our understanding of the social meaning of variation, it also furthers the incipient social turn in Cognitive Linguistic research, where prototype structures are already relied on for the representation of lects and varieties. We will try to push this social turn further by applying prototype theory to the social meaning indexed by specific linguistic variants rather than to whole sets of varieties and lects. Additionally, we reveal the opportunities of this approach for the study of contact-induced variation and change.

As a case in point we look at /s/ palatalization in a contact variety called Citétaal, a contemporary urban vernacular that is spreading in the easternmost province of Flanders (Limburg). Our analysis relies on data drawn from the use of palatalized and non-palatalized /s/ in a corpus of self-recorded speech. This empirical background will be further presented in Section 2, which also presents the methodological guidelines of our study of this particular urban vernacular, and succinctly presents the social turn in prototype theory. Section 3 then presents the corpus and the variables used in our investigation. Section 4 proceeds with an initial quantitative scrutiny of sibilant palatalization in *Citétaal*, based on a number of variationist parameters, which will be complemented by a qualitative discursive analysis in Section 5 and a multifactorial regression analysis (random forest and conditional inference tree) in Section 6, where discursive and variationist parameters are brought together. Based on the results of this combined approach to the study of /s/ palatalisation, in Section 7 we reflect on the possibilities of representing the social meaning of this feature while discussing the opportunities offered by Cognitive Linguistics for future discussion on the social meaning of variation. We specifically represent our results in a prototype structure characterized by family resemblance. In the last section, we discuss in more detail which crucial next steps need to be taken to further corroborate the applicability of this proof of concept.

2 Laying the groundwork

Before we proceed to a description of the data and variables used for our study of the social meaning of sibilant palatalization, it is necessary to introduce the three cornerstones of this contribution in some more detail: (1) from a theoretical perspective, we briefly describe the social turn in prototype theory; (2) from an empirical perspective, we introduce Citétaal as Flemish Contemporary Urban Vernacular; (3) from a methodological perspective, we highlight the importance of a mixed-method approach in the study of the social meaning of markers of Contemporary Urban Vernaculars.

2.1 Towards a prototypical structure of social meaning

Prototype research (first applied by Eleanor Rosch for charting the psychological principles behind information processing, see Mervis and Rosch 1981) has long been part and parcel of the Cognitive Linguistic enterprise (see Polzenhagen and Xia 2015 for a well-focused overview, and see section 7 below). Starting with semantic descriptions of lexical categories (Geeraerts, Gondelaers, and Bakema 1994) and later turning to acoustic descriptions of phonological categories (Mompéan 2004, Kristiansen 2008) or prototype analyses of grammatical structures (Ramoulin-Brunberg 1994), researchers demonstrated the importance of key concepts of prototype theory, such as family resemblance, flexibility and salience for language categorization and processing. Although these studies took the cultural embedding of prototypes into account to some degree, only minimal attention was paid to socio-lectal variation. Socio-lectal components were included in prototype analysis only when the interest in the lectal component of language started to grow with the advent of Cognitive Sociolinguistics (Kristiansen and Dirven 2008, Geeraerts et al. 2010). Typically, researchers have verified how prototype structures for linguistic categories differ between lects (e.g. Grondelaers and Geeraerts 2003, see also Polzenhagen and Xia 2015) or how varieties are built up by prototypically organized linguistic variants (e.g. Pustka 2009, Altendorf 2016). In this paper, we aim to push this interest in the social component further by switching the perspective and upgrading the social dimension to the centre of the Cognitive Linguistics analysis. Instead of charting socio-lectal variation in the prototype structure of linguistic categories, we aim to describe the prototypical structure of the social meaning indexed by linguistic variants. Specifically, we will focus on the social meaning structure of sibilant palatalization in Citétaal.

2.2 Citétaal

We use the term *Citétaal* as an umbrella term for Contemporary Urban Vernaculars (CUVs) observed among adolescents and young adults in the former ghettoized areas (*cités*) in the easternmost region of Flanders (Belgian Limburg). These vernaculars emerged in small mining neighborhoods of the city of Genk and are now used and diffused by local youngsters with heritage background in the broader area of Limburg. The term *cité* in Citétaal refers to the former mining neighbourhoods, where these ways of speaking emerged and have been diffused, probably since the 1970s (Marzo and Ceuleers 2011). The cités were the ghettoized mining areas built especially to accommodate the first wave of migrant workers from Southern Europe. Continuous first-hand language contact between Dutch and the present heritage languages ensued over an extended period. This, in turn, led to the emergence of a contact variety (Dutch with features from other present minority languages), which served as input for the next generations. Citétaal now generally refers to the linguistic practices of (native and non-native Flemish) youngsters in and beyond the cité-neighbourhoods who use, diffuse and further elaborate the linguistic resources of the previous generations (Svendsen and Marzo 2015).

The most salient feature of the Citétaal repertoire is the palato-alveolarization of /s/ followed by a consonant, e.g. in words as *stijl* 'style', that are then pronounced as [ʃtɛil] instead of [stɛil]). Other recurrent features are the generalization of the definite article *de* instead of the neutre *het* (*de meisje*, 'the girl') and the generalized use of non-neuter gender in the demonstrative pronoun paradigm (*die meisje*, 'that girl'). Both the palato-alveolarization and the loss of grammatical gender also occur in Netherlandic CUVs (see Mourigh 2017 for sibilant palatalization and Cornips 2008 for grammatical gender).

Our paper focuses on /s/ palatalization. The reason for this is that /s/ palatalization has become a "stereotype" in Labov's terms (Labov 1972): it is a variable that has been subject to considerable metapragmatic discussion (Marzo and Ceuleers 2011) and that has acquired a social value that language users are typically aware of (Johnstone et al. 2006; Eckert 2008). The broad diffusion of /s/ palatalization results, among others, from its use in social media, in local hip hop scenes and in fiction series. It is now spreading in and across other Flemish provinces, but according to attitude research, it is still associated with urban speech styles of youngsters in the larger Limburg area (Marzo 2016). Stereotype features of this kind are particularly interesting for our multi-methodological analysis, because speakers are more likely to consciously exploit them as discursive strategies in interaction.

2.3 An integrated mixed-method approach

As speakers typically rely on CUVs for social profiling of all sorts, scholars have been trying to fathom the CUVs' indexical meaning potential. Roughly speaking, variationist scholars generally explain the shifts to CUV features by correlating linguistic (e.g. frequency of use of a given CUV-variant, such as palatalized /s/, versus standard use) and macro-social (e.g. ethnic background, gender) categories (Van Meel, Hinskens and, Van Hout 2016). Discourse-oriented scholars pay more attention to the way speakers use CUV-resources to actively (re-)create social meaning in discourse: they study *in-situ* meaning creation through ethnographic (interactional or discursive) and micro-sociolinguistic methods, explaining the use of CUV features as a tool that speakers can freely deploy in identity construction (e.g. Rampton 2011).

In line with other authors (Quist 2008; Svendsen 2015) and with third wave sociolinguistic and Cognitive Sociolinguistic views on social meaning, we argue that an integrative approach is needed in which a macro-social perspective is combined with a fine-grained micro-social analysis. Only through such a combined approach can we offer an encompassing insight into the social meaning of urban vernaculars.

3 Data and methods

We draw on a corpus of 20 hours of manually transcribed spontaneous interactions that took place in the easternmost province of Limburg. The conversations were recorded by youngsters in two interactional settings, viz. at home and during leisure time with peers. While the youngsters responsible for the recordings are actively participating in most interactions, there are also recordings of interactions between their parents or between other adults (e.g. siblings, family friends).

The 20 hours of high-quality audio recordings were transcribed using the Chat conventions of the Childes project (MacWhinney 2000). Fragments that were analyzed in more detail in the discursive analyses (section 5) were additionally transcribed using the Jeffersonian system. All statistical analyses were conducted in R.

Our analysis zooms in on those utterances that contain standard [s] and palatalized [ʃ]. Instances of standard [s] are only considered in sequences of [s] + consonant, as palatalization only occurs in this specific phonetic context. Although the original corpus contains 34 speakers, our analysis for this paper is based on those 20 speakers with more than 10 observations of /s/. Table 1 lists all information about these speakers together with the total number of utterances for the speakers, the number of standard and palatalized /s/ (respectively ST and PAL in the tables), and the proportion of palatalized /s/.

As Table 1 reveals, our speakers are relatively homogenously distributed over four dimensions: gender (12 female and 8 male speakers), age (10 adolescents – 4 informants and 6 friends of the informants – 2 young adults – the older siblings of the informants – and 8 adults, who are the parents of the informants), migration background (13 speakers are of Italian descent and 7 speakers are native-born Flemish), and role of the speaker (4 informants or main speakers, 6 peers, 2 older siblings and 8 parents). Once we start crossing the dimensions, the distributions are however no longer perfectly balanced. For example, among the group of adolescents, there are 4 boys, and among them 2 have immigrant roots and 2 are native born Flemish speakers), and 6 girls, of whom only 1 speaker is a native born Flemish speaker. Such asymmetries in the dataset will be further discussed and remediated in Section 6, where we will bring the discussed parameters together in an encompassing multifactorial analysis.

Table 1: Overview of the dataset with the four dimensions and proportions of palatalizations.

Alias	Gender	Migration background	Age	Role	PAL	ST Dutch	% PAL
Seppe	MALE	native-born	adolescent	informant	8	29	0.216
Cindy	FEM	native-born	adolescent	peer	1	10	0.910
Anja	FEM	native-born	young adult	sibling	4	7	0.364
Francesco	MALE	migrant background	adolescent	informant	77	94	0.450
Finn	MALE	native-born	adolescent	peer	18	36	0.333
Sabrina	FEM	migrant background	young adult	sibling	0	64	0.000
Marie	FEM	native-born	adult	parent	5	67	0.690
Mark	MALE	native-born	adult	parent	0	86	0.000
Paolo	MALE	migrant background	adolescent	informant	33	61	0.351
Moira	FEM	migrant background	adolescent	peer	39	74	0.345
Antonella	FEM	migrant background	adult	parent	6	73	0.760
Franco	MALE	migrant background	adult	parent	8	37	0.178
Sofia	FEM	migrant background	adolescent	peer	9	61	0.129
Cinzia	FEM	migrant background	adolescent	peer	8	27	0.229
Anita	FEM	native-born	adult	parent	3	15	0.167
Alberto	MALE	migrant background	adult	parent	3	14	0.176
Chiara	FEM	migrant background	adolescent	informant	34	98	0.258
Alessia	FEM	migrant background	adolescent	peer	8	24	0.250
Mauro	MALE	migrant background	adult	sibling	6	7	0.462
Maria	FEM	migrant background	adult	parent	4	41	0.890

In all, our data contain 1199 observations of /s/ + consonant, 925 (or 77%) of which are Standard Dutch and 274 (or 23%) are palatalized. Although there is a clear preference for the standard variant, it is particularly interesting to study the linguistic, social and interactional circumstances that explain the 23% palatalized /s/ in our corpus.

4 Linguistic and variationist parameters

This section starts off with a brief discussion of the impact of three quantifiable linguistic features (phonetic context, priming, and part of speech of the observed occurrence). Next, we will consider a few variationist parameters (age, gender, migration background and role of speaker). In this first stage, the data are analyzed using Chi-square tests for significance (with Bonferroni correction) and Cramer's V tests to measure effect size. The latter test captures the strength of association between two nominal variables, expressed in a value between zero and one that can be interpreted in a way that is similar to Pearson's correlation for numerical data, such that zero means "no association" and one means "complete association".

To complement these typically variationist analyses, section 5 will study the variation between standard and palatalized /s/ through a discourse analytical lens. Both variationist and discursive perspectives will serve as a final input of an encompassing regression tree, which reveals the relative impact of the discussed variables on the choice of the palatalized /s/ (Section 7).

4.1 Linguistic features

Three linguistic features have been examined. First of all, we analyze whether priming can explain the alternation between standard and palatalized /s/. Although different types of priming can be studied (e.g. one can look at the prime in the entire discourse of all the interlocutors or at the prime in the utterance of the speaker himself), we here look at the standard (ST) or palatalized (CT) sibilant that was used most recently in the five previous utterances in the conversation by any of the interlocutors, as this concerns the most straightforwardly coded type of autocorrelation we can attest in the data. Future research will of course need to study the effect of other types of priming. As a second linguistic parameter, we verify the effect of the phonetic context in which the palatalized /s/ occurs. We have coded for two phonetic contexts: /s/ followed by a single consonant (as in *stijl* [steil]) and /s/ followed by [x] (as in *school* [sxo:l]. Finally, we analyze the impact of the part of speech of the palatalized /s/ word, contrasting palatalization in nouns (N), verbs (V) and adjectives/adverbs (ADJ/ADV).

Table 2: Linguistic features

PRIMING	PAL	ST	Proportion PAL	
Noprime	237	650	0.267	Chisquare < 0.0001
ST-prime	6	272	0.022	Cramer's V 0.371
CT-prime	31	3	0.912	
PHONETIC CONTEXT	**PAL**	**ST**	**Proportion PAL**	
S+cons	134	781	0.146	Chisquare < 0.0001
S+X	140	144	0.493	Cramer's V 0.349
POS	**PAL**	**ST**	**Proportion PAL**	
N	98	396	0.198	Chisquare < 0.0001
V	70	334	0.173	Cramer's V 0.172
ADJ/ADV	106	195	0.352	

Table 2 reveals a strong priming effect. The pattern is significant (p < 0.0001) and Cramer's V reveals a fair association (0.316). This means that speakers palatalize significantly more when a palatalized /s/ occurs in the preceding five utterances and use it significantly less when a standard prime was used. Palatalization also increases in the [sx] clusters, with, once again, a fair association value (0.349). Finally, palatalization is significantly more frequent in adverbs and adjectives, although Cramer's V detects only a weak association (0.172).

4.2 Macro-social variables

We have also examined the effect of four macro-social variables, viz. gender (male/female), ethnicity (migrant background/native born speaker), age (adolescent/young adult/adult) and role of the speaker (informant/peer/family member). The selection of these parameters is based on existing literature on the use and diffusion of CUV among youngsters. According to various studies (for an overview, see Nortier and Svendsen 2015), CUVs generally emerge in areas shaped by migration (Rampton 2011) and they are directly linked to the local youngsters' heritage languages. Moreover, as these vernaculars are highly stigmatized in different European countries (Svendsen 2015), they are spoken predominantly in youngsters' in-group interactions and less in interactions with adults or persons with authority (e.g. teachers). Also, an important number of investigations have shown that male youngsters are the most frequent users of CUVs (e.g. Cheshire et al. 2011). Of course, exceptions can be noted, whereby female youngsters seemed to be more innovative concerning the use and spread of these vernaculars (Svendsen and Røyneland 2008).

In our dataset, the effect of these variables on /s/ palatalization is however not clear at all. Although males are using more palatalization (with a significant effect), Cramer's V reveals only a weak correlation between gender and palatalization. The same is true for ethnicity: speakers with a migration background use significantly more palatalized /s/, but the association is again very weak. The association is somewhat stronger for age and for role of the speaker, and we have significantly higher use of palatalization among the informants (with a proportion of 0.350) in our datasets who are still adolescents (with a proportion of 0.314). All details are shown in Table 3.

Table 3: Macro-social variables.

Gender	PAL	ST	Proportion PAL	
Female	121	561	0.177	Chisquare < 0.0001
Male	153	364	0.296	Cramer's V 0.138
Ethnicity	**PAL**	**ST**	**Proportion PAL**	
Migrant background	235	675	0.258	Chisquare < 0.001
Native-born speaker	39	250	0.135	Cramer's V 0.123
Age	**PAL**	**ST**	**Proportion PAL**	
Adolescent	235	514	0.314	Chisquare < 0.0001
Young adult	4	71	0.053	Cramer's V 0.268
Adult	35	340	0.093	
Role	**PAL**	**ST**	**Proportion PAL**	
Informant	152	282	0.350	Chisquare < 0.0001
Peer	83	232	0.263	Cramer's V 0.274
Family	39	411	0.087	

Although we need to take into account the relatively limited number of speakers in our database, it appears that a purely variationist analysis of /s/ palatalization does not provide us with a sufficient explanation for the alternation between palatalized and non-palatized /s/ in our corpus. To allow a better understanding of the attested variation, we switch to a discursive perspective in the next section, complementing our first results with a qualitative and in-depth exploration of the interactions containing /s/ sibilants. These discursive analyses will demonstrate that the alternation between palatalized and non-palatalized /s/ strongly depends on the type of discursive context in which /s/ occurs, and on the loading of the utterance. These insights will be translated in two new variables that can be integrated in a final quantitative model.

5 From discursive analyses to discursive variables

Given the relative infrequency of palatalization in the corpus, we now focus on the question why some users, who, according to our expectations, use less Citétaal features, palatalize their /s/ in some specific instances. Put differently, we focus on interactions which typically should have a (even) lower-than-average palatalization rate which do however contain palatalization. In particular, we will focus on three speakers in a few inter-peer interactions, viz.
- Seppe, a youngster who is not expected to be a core user of Citétaal due to his Flemish roots.
- Chiara, a youngster with Italian roots who is situated outside the prototypical core due to her gender.
- Maria, a middle-aged adult with Italian roots, who it situated outside the prototypical core due to fact that she is not a youngster, nor a man. As Maria is an adult, the inter-peer interaction in which she participates is situated outside the prototypical core as it does not involve youngsters.

On the basis of our discursive analyses, we have identified two such commonalities: s-palatalizations occur frequently among these atypical speakers in (1) commenting negatively on others or oneself and (2) telling sensational stories. We now discuss these two types successively.

5.1 Commenting negatively on others or oneself

In the subset of our data under scrutiny, the interlocutors often utter negative comments which occur in both serious and jocular contexts. These comments may target the speakers themselves, or they may address co-present or absent others. During such commenting activities – which include the comment as well as its follow-up – speakers frequently palatalize their s-sounds. We now discuss a few examples selected from the various types of commenting activities.

In a first fragment, we zoom in on Seppe who is watching a TV-show together with his sister Anja. In particular, Seppe is commenting on the looks of a Flemish fashionista celebrity on TV. The palatalized sound occurs in the word that is in boldface[1]:

---

[1] The fragments were transcribed using transcription conventions that are based on the Jeffersonian transcription system. One important exception, however, is that boldface is used here for indicating the words in which the /s/ is palatalized.

Fragment 1 – Seppe

```
1    SEP    hh. £die lijkt op dinge (.) van da sjpelleke£ @@
2           ((celebrity's name)) die lijkt=op
3    (1.1)
4    SEP    .h flappybird [@@@
5    ANJ                  [@@@
6    (.)
7    SEP    .hh £op di[e vogel£ @@@
8    ANJ              [°flappybird ja:::°

1    SEP    hh. £she looks like thingy (.) of that little game£ @@
2           ((celebrity's name)) she looks=like
3    (1.1)
4    SEP    .h flappybird [@@@
5    ANJ                  [@@@
6    (.)
7    SEP    .hh £like th[at bird£ @@@
8    ANJ               [° flappybird ye:::s°
```

In this fragment the negative comment is uttered in a jocular frame, which is clear from the start of the interaction due to the smiley voice that Seppe almost consistently uses in this fragment. Within this frame, the palatalization (of the word *spelleke*, 'little game') is uttered in the introduction to the comment. There are many such jocular commenting activities in this interaction, which happens parallel with the TV-show, and in many of these, palatalizatons occur. In another example, we see Seppe commenting on a guitar player's bad hairstyle: "mè die man die [...] op die gitaar **sjpeel**- die zijn kapper is dood denk ik" ('mè that man who [...] **plays** on that guitar, his hairdresser died I think'). Again, in this jocular phrase, he palatalizes the onset consonant of 'spelen' (to play) in the lead-up to the actual jocular comment.

Besides in comments that target absent others, palatalization also occurs in jocular commenting activities that focus on co-present others. To illustrate this, we focus on Chiara (CHI), whose behavior is being challenged in a jocular way by one of her friends Alessia (ALE):

Fragment 2 – Chiara

```
1    ALE    ↑WA (.) doet gij nu?
2    CHI    mijn handsjchoene [aandoen
3    ALE                      [wilt ge michael jackson
```

4		nadoen of wa?
5	CAT	[↑<u>AUW</u>
6		[(((mimicking Michael Jackson))
7	?	( )
8	ALE	nee doe 'ns (.) who's tha::t
9	CHI	who's ba::d

1	ALE	↑WHAT (.) are you doing now?
2	CHI	putting on my **glo**[ves
3	ALE	[do you want to imitate
4		michael jackson or what?
5	CAT	[↑<u>AUW</u>
6		[(((mimicking Michael Jackson))
7	?	( )
8	ALE	no do it once (.) who's tha::t
9	CHI	who's ba::d

In this extract, Alessia's question in line 1 is clearly not a request for information, since both the marked prosody (the initial loud volume and the pause) and the visual input of Chiara's action are sufficient to understand what the latter is doing. Yet, Chiara treats Alessia's utterance as a request for information, and provides her with a mock informative response in which the word *handsjchoenen* 'gloves' is palatalized. In overlap, Alessia utters a challenge of Chiara's behavior by framing it as an attempt to imitate Michael Jackson. Catherine (CAT) immediately jumps in by loudly mimicking Michael Jackson's signature sound (*auw*, line 5) after which Alessia prompts Chiara to imitate the chorus line of Michael Jackson's song *Bad*. Interestingly, though Alessia mimicks the lengthened sound of the chorus line, she utters the wrong word (*tha::t*, line 8), and while complying with the request in line 9, Chiara executes an embedded correction (Jefferson 1983), as such preventing any potential face loss for Alessia which might have occurred in case of an exposed correction. This choice for an embedded correction further underscores the fact that the initial challenge does not pose a real face threat to Chiara, since, otherwise, one might have expected that she, in turn, would have challenged Alessia's pronunciation mistake. So again, the negative comment – and its response in which palatalization occurs – is situated in a jocular frame.

However, the jocular nature of the comment is not a prerequisite for palatalization, as we see in the following serious negative comment uttered by Maria, who challenges her husband's (Enrico, ENR) lack of adherence to the rules they agreed on regarding their respective cars.

Fragment 3 – Maria

1	ENR	dan moet ge luisteren als ik iets zeg (.)
2		ge doet da maar op [juist als de vorige keer]
3	MAR	[ge moet van de mijne] (.)
4		GIJ moet van de mijne ↑af↓ blijven (.)
5		da heb ik u nog al ↑ge↓ zegd (.)
6		al zes jaar lang zeg ik u ↓ da
7	ENR	([ )
8	MAR	[nee en die van u want die heeft een **sjch↓onere**
1	ENR	*then you have to listen when I say something (.)*
2		*you just spend that [just like the last time]*
3	MAR	*[you have to off mine] (.)*
4		*YOU have to stay away from ↑mi↓ne (.)*
5		*I have told you that ↑al↓ ready (.)*
6		*already for six years I tell you ↓that*
7	ENR	([ )
8	MAR	*[no and yours because he has a more **beautiful** ↓one*

In this fragment, negative comments on co-present others are ubiquitous, as the two interlocutors blame each other for not listening (line 1, line 5–6) and for not abiding to the rules of spending money (line 2) or handling each other's cars (line 4). The overlaps (lines 3 and 8), the marked falling turn-final intonation (lines 4–6 and line 8) as well as the loud voice that Maria is using (lines 4–6, line 8) all paralinguistically mark the interaction as a discussion. This is further supported linguistically by the fact that in every turn, the addressee is directly linked to an accusation – hence the presence of second person pronominal forms in each line of this fragment – and that these accusations have a preferred turn shape. At the end of the discussion, Maria responds to an unintelligible turn by her husband (line 7), which, in turn, does not make the exact meaning of her utterance clear either. Yet, it is clear that her response is another challenge, as the turn-initial negative particle ('no', line 8) indicates. In this final turn, we observe the occurrence of a palatalization, this time thus situated in a non-jocular commenting activity.

Finally, besides negative comments vis-à-vis absent third parties or vis-à-vis each other, there are also many cases of negative self-evaluations in which palatalizations occur. This can be seen in the following short extract, in which Chiara has forgotten to bring her own sandwiches to school and, due to her diet, she refuses to order food from the school canteen. She thus watches her friend Alessia eat and comments as follows:

Fragment 4 – Chiara

1	CHI	>ah da's zo kut da' k geen boterhamme meege**pa**kt heb<
2		ik ben da zo vergeten
3	ALE	ja ik zou u een koe- een euh koek wille meegeven ma-
4	(4.7)	
5	CHI	°ik ben zo **sjtom** ↓eh°

1	CHI	>*ah that's so crappy that I didn't **ta**ke any sandwiches*<
2		*I just forgot*
3	ALE	*yes I would like to give you a bis- a erm biscuit but-*
4	(4.7)	
5	CHI	°*I'm so **stupid** ↓eh*°

After Chiara utters her frustration with her own forgetfulness (line 1–2), Alessia expresses her empathy by hypothetically wanting to help her friend out by giving her one of her own biscuits. By means of the 'but' at the end of line 3, this first part takes the form of a preliminary turn constructional unit (Lerner 1991) in a contrastive pattern ("I would like to do that but I can't because..."). So this second part of the turn would normally contain an account concerning the infeasibility of the biscuit-remedy. Yet, Alessia breaks off her turn and no account is uttered for her lack of helpfulness. A long pause follows in which this broken-off turn is sort of hanging in the air, after which Chiara self-selects with another expression of her own frustration. This takes the form of a self-deprecating comment uttered with an s-palatalization. The falling intonation as well as the low speaking volume all indicate that Chiara now resigns herself to the situation of being hungry for the rest of the day.

Thus, irrespective of the commenting target (be it another person, co-present or not, or oneself) or the jocular or serious nature of the commenting activity, these negative commenting activities form contexts in which palatalizations occur frequently. These may either occur in the negative comments themselves, as well as in the turns surrounding the comments, thus demonstrating that it is the commenting activity as a whole – rather than the evaluations – that elicit the occurrence of this Citétaal feature.

5.2 Telling sensational stories

In mundane interactions, competition amongst interlocutors to obtain the floor is often high, and this is especially the case in the youngsters' inter-peer interactions in our corpus. However, telling stories requires extensive floor-holding rights for the narrator and so the story in question had better largely surpass the lower boundary of tellability (Labov 2006; Norrick 2005) in order to justify such an extensive monopolization of the floor. Hence it is not surprising that there are quite a few stories with sensational content in our dataset.

Due to the length of the stories and space limitations, we only show excerpts from stories here. First, we present the complicating action and resolution (Labov and Waletzky 1966) of a narrative of vicarious experience that Chiara tells her friend. The story focuses on a robbery that occurred in her favorite chip shop, owned by a man whom she refers to by his last name (pseudonymized Valotos). The 'he' in the initial line of the fragment refers to the anonymous robber:

Fragment 5 – Chiara

1	CHI	en die heeft daarna gewoon alles m-
2		heel die kassa die die dag heeft verdiend
3		heeft die gewoon allemaal ( ) (.) uitgehaald
4		die heeft <u>hem</u> een **sjlag** op z'n kop ge ↑geven (.)
5		en euhm (.) .h ja d'erna zo een paar weken daarna
6		was Valotos was die terug opengegaan (.)
7		en waren we geweest en
8		had die echt zo hier zo'n **sjchaafwonde** echt
9		ma ja Valotos is kaal ↑eh=
10	ALE	=ja
11	CHI	dus zag echt zo hier die die ↑<u>bult</u> en zo eh
12		waar dat die die op **gesjlagen** had en zo he

1	CHI	*and he then just t- the lot*
2		*the whole cash register that he earned that day*
3		*he just took it all ( ) (.) out*
4		*he gave <u>him</u> a **whack** on his ↑head (.)*
5		*and erm (.) .h yes later on a few weeks later*
6		*had Valotos had he opened again (.)*
7		*and we went there*
8		*and he had really here such a **graze** really*
9		*but yes Valotos is bald ↑eh=*
10	ALE	*=yes*
11	CHI	*so you really saw here that that ↑<u>bump</u> and all eh*
12		*where that he had **whacked** him and all hey*

In this excerpt, we see the end of the complicating action that culminates in the blow the chip shop owner receives to his head (line 4). Chiara's story then moves into the resolution phase, shifting the time frame to 'a few weeks later' (line 5), in which she had eye-witness access (line 7) to the physically visual result of this blow. This is discussed extensively (line 8 and 11–12) and the level of detail is accounted for by the victim's baldness which allows for an unimpeded view of his head-wounds. So these wounds are topicalized both in the story climax and the resolution phase, and they receive emphasis through the elaborated discussion and through prosodic stress (pitch rises in *head*, line 4, and *bump*, line 11). Throughout this excerpt, we can observe the repeated use of s-palatalizations in keywords in this story (*sjlag* 'whack', line 4, *sjchaafwonde* 'graze', line 8, *gesjlagen* 'whacked', line 12).

Palatalizations are observable in various youngsters' storytelling activities in our dataset, but, as in the fragment above, these tend to occur in the local context immediately surrounding the story climax. Another case in point is a story Seppe (SEP) tells his sister about an aggressive dog. This example also demonstrates that the switch to palatalization is hardly ever a total shift:

Fragment 6 – Seppe

1	SEP	gisteren (.) iemand van ((organisatie)) die kwam
2		de sleutels halen van de speelplein he (.) .h en euhm
3		die belt aan die hond die ontploft gewoon he
4		ik was gek aan 't worde he
5		t was tien uur 's ochtends
6		ik was nog gans moe o[p mijn ( )
7	ANJ	[ja::
8	(.)	
9	SEP	.hh he:he:
10		maar=die kom gewoon de sleutel hale he
11		ma nee die hond die **sjtond** bijna op h'r op h'r rug

1	SEP	*yesterday (.) someone from ((organisation)) she came*
2		*to fetch the keys of the playground hey (.) .h and erm*
3		*she rings the bell that dog he just explodes hey*
4		*I was going mad hey*
5		*it was ten o' clock in the morning*
6		*I was still very tired t[o my ( )*
7	ANJ	*[yes::s*
8	(.)	

9	SEP	.hh he:he:
10		*but=she just comes to fetch the key hey*
11		*but no that dog that almost **stood** on her on her back*

In this story, we only see one out of three forms that is palatalized, but, importantly, it is in the repetition of the story climax that we observe the palatalization (*sjtond* 'stood', line 11), while the non-palatalized forms (*sleutel* 'key') are uttered in the orientation phase (line 2) or in a repetition of this orientation phase that serves as an account for the innocent nature of the visitor's action (line 10). So this segment of Seppe's story is a further illustration of the tendency described above, viz. that palatalizations are mainly used in the most sensational parts of the story.

5.3 Defining discursive variables

As palatalization tends to occur when speakers are commenting negatively and telling the climaxes of sensational stories, the question is now what these contexts have in common on a more abstract level and how we can translate this into quantifiable variables. When comparing the examples presented above, we can conclude that all these local contexts are characterized by strong and intensified language use. This is visible on various levels. Firstly, on a content level, contrasts are often established, either between evaluations of speakers (e.g. the discussion of Maria and her husband in fragment 3) or within a story (e.g. the peaceful action of fetching a key versus the aggressive reaction of the dog in the final example). Secondly, prosodically, these fragments are marked by pitch rises and falls, as well as by a louder speaking volume (see especially fragments 2 and 3). And finally, particularly in the stories, palatalization tends to occur in the most dramatic parts of these interactions and their indexical value is thus to add even more emphasis to these utterances.

Resulting, in order to quantify and test these discursive explorations, all utterances with standard or palatalized /s/ in the initial database (including all 1199 utterances) were coded for two new variables: context of the interaction (general, storytelling or commenting) and loading of the interaction (viz. neutral loading or emotionally – positively or negatively-loaded interaction). As shown in Table 4, the discursive insights acquired above are validated through quantitative analyses for the entire database: the palatalized /s/ occurs more frequently when speakers comment negatively on others or themselves and in emotionally-loaded interactions. The differences are significant and the correlation between the two variables is moderate.

Table 4: Discursive variables.

Context of interaction	PAL	ST	Proportion PAL	
General	162	736	0.180	Chisquare < 0.0001
Storytelling	44	125	0.260	Cramer's V 0.261
Comments	68	64	0.515	
load	PAL	ST	Proportion PAL	
Neutral	164	762	0.177	Chisquare < 0.0001
Emotional	110	163	0.403	Cramer's V 0.226

As a final step in our process, after having identified a group of factors that explain the choice in favour of palatalized and non-palatalized /s/, we need to bring the different (linguistic, macro-social and discursive) variables together. Relying on regression trees, we below wish to reveal which of these factors is significant when simultaneously considering the effect of all predictors in the calculations.

6 Bringing the perspectives together

Given that our dataset is built on individual speakers' preferences in the use of palatalization, the best option for a multi-factorial statistical analysis for this study would be a mixed-effect logistic regression, as it takes into account potential speaker-level variation (Speelman, Heylen and Geeraerts 2018). However, due to the combination of data sparseness on different levels and an uneven distribution of independent variables ('multicollinearity', see section 3.2), a mixed-effect regression model will not provide robust, reliable results.

As shown in Tagliamonte and Baayen (2012), the best solution in this case is to construct random forests and conditional inference trees. Random forests provide information about the importance of predictors, even in the case of unbalanced designs with high multicollinearity. Like logistic models, random forests seek to predict, based on a set of predictors, which of the alternatives [s] or [ʃ] is most probable. However, whereas traditional logistic models estimate the effect of predictors with various simplifying assumptions, which makes them again problematic in case of data sparseness, random forests work through the data and establish whether a variable is a useful predictor. Also, as we aim to reflect on how the social meaning of variation can be represented in a prototype structure, we need a model that selects the strongest and, hence, most representative factors predicting the variation. The output of a random forest is a visual representation comparable to typical visualizations of regression models, viz. a dotplot showing the relative importance of the different predictors included in a model. What is not revealed is the precise effects attested for the different predictors.

For this, we turn to conditional inference trees. These trees visualize how multiple predictors operate together. They provide estimates of the likelihood of the value of the response variable (in our case palatalized vs. non palatalized /s/) on the basis of a series of binary questions about the values of predictor variables (age, ethnicity, context, etc.). For instance, for the variable ETHNICITY it considers whether splitting the data into migrant background and no migrant background implies the creation of one set of data points where palatalized /s/ occurs more often and another dataset where standard /s/ is used more often. As such, this algorithm works through all predictors, splitting the data into binary subsets in consecutive runs until further splitting is no longer justified (in other words, until no statistically significant patterns remain). The result of these binary splits is visualized in a conditional inference tree.

For the analyses of our dataset, we made use of the implementation of Random forests and inference trees available in the PARTY and PARTYKIT packages in R. We imported all the nine parameters discussed in the descriptive sections, viz. the three linguistic variables, the four social-demographic factors and the two discursive variables.

The random forest selected seven factors that predict the use of sibilant palatalization in Citétaal. The results are visualized in the variable importance plot in Figure 1.

A variable importance plot shows how important each parameter is when data are being classified. The predictor variables are plotted on the y-axis, the

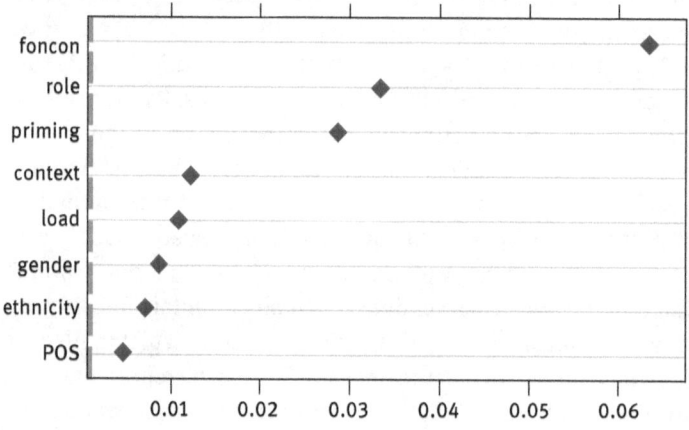

Figure 1: Random forest.

x-axis displays the mean decrease in node impurity. This mean decrease in node impurity is a measure of how each variable contributes to the purity on each node in a tree. Interestingly, the strongest predictors are not socio-demographic factors, but rather linguistic and interactional factors. As such, phonetic context (phoncon) most strongly predicts the use of palatalized /s/, followed by role as the second most important predictor and priming as the third most important predictor. Other important predictors are, in order of importance, context of interaction (context), load, gender, ethnicity and POS (part of speech).

The conditional inference tree as it is visualized in Figure 2[2] highlights the complex interaction that characterizes our dataset. The tree specifically shows that some predictors are relevant only in particular subsets of data, and that other predictors have a different effect depending on the subset under scrutiny. For instance, gender (which is selected only at the bottom of the three, and which is slightly significant) is relevant only for s (not sch) in general and neutral discursive contexts, where no priming occurs. This means that only in those discursive contexts, the men in our dataset palatalize significantly more than the women.

Priming, however, seems to be relevant for the whole dataset, and outwins the other predictors in importance, which is visible in the fact that the first binary split in the tree is made for "CTprime" vs. "noprime"/"STprime. It also returns as an important variable in other subsets, for example in peer and family interactions, where a further split is made between "noprime" and "STprime".

The output generated by the random forest and conditional inference tree analysis offers not only an inclusive account of the linguistic, social and interactional motivations for /s/ palatalization. It also highlights the extremely complex interaction of these motivations. For example, it shows how social factors as gender or ethnicity which seemed to explain variation in the first descriptions become almost marginal when factoring in other predictors.

Despite the rich conclusions to be drawn from the conditional inference tree, the visualization is however impaired in the sense that it – in a typical variationist fashion – reduces the empirical reality to branched structures of binary splits. The way people mentally represent social meaning most likely works in quite a different fashion. In the next two paragraphs we compare the prototype theoretical representation of (social) meaning with the tree shown here, and we try to determine how they can be combined in a way that captures the strengths of both.

---

[2] This model obtained a classification accuracy of 85% (which is fairly good compared to a baseline of 77%), with a C-value of 0.881, which is also good, compared to a customary threshold of 0.8.

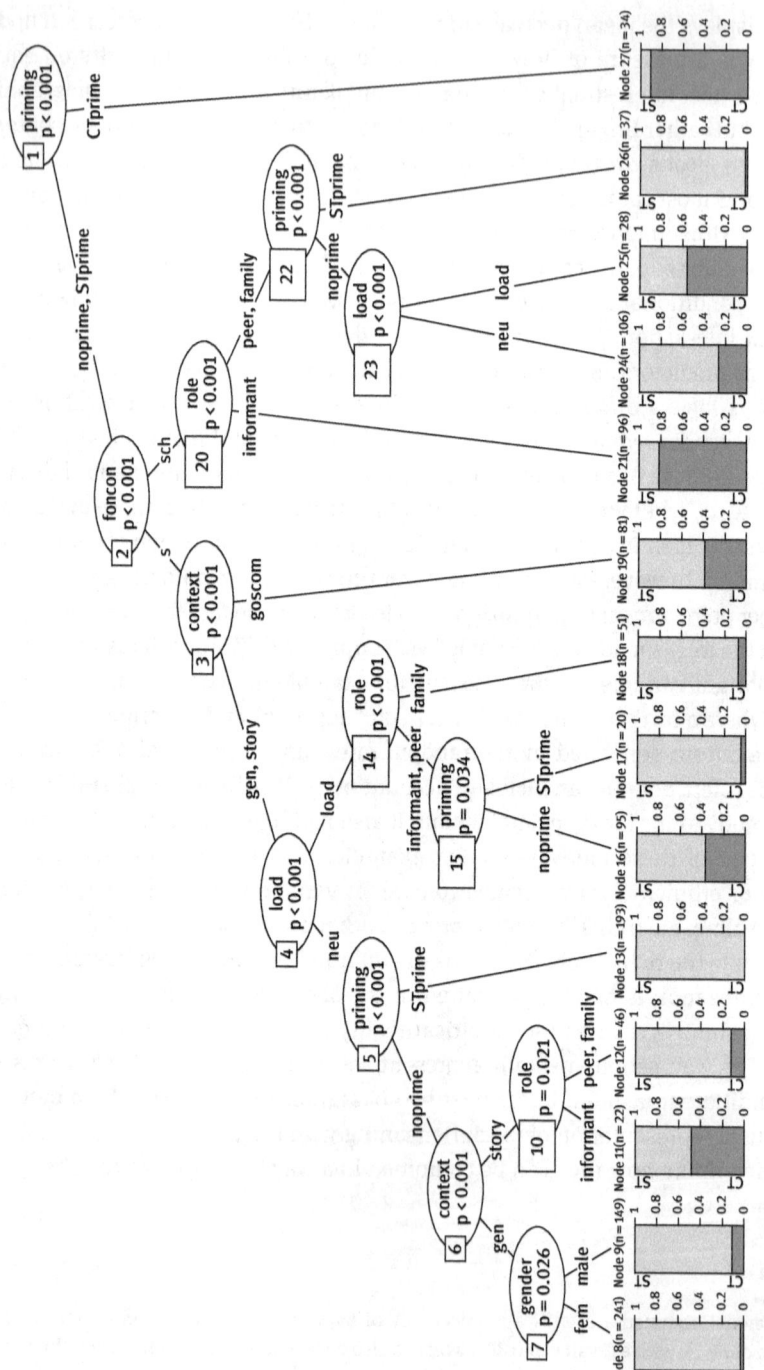

Figure 2: Conditional inference tree.

7 Towards a prototype model of social meaning

Comparing the conditional inference tree to prototype-based classifications of meaning in Cognitive Linguistics, we see several common denominators. Before discussing these, we briefly revisit the main principles of prototype theory through the renowned BIRD category (see Figure 3), as shown in Geeraerts, Grondelaers, and Bakema 's work (1994).

The core principles underlying prototype theory are graded membership, a family resemblance structure and salience. This means that the different descriptive features that define a category (in the figure indicated by the letters a to g) cluster in different combinations and in different degrees of overlap, and that no single set of attributes can exclusively define one category. Natural consequences of this family resemblance structure are that the boundaries between categories are blurred (making it hard to delineate where one category ends and the next begins) and that not all members are equally typical, or representative, of a category. Representative members, then, are to be found in areas of the category that overlap the most. Applied to our example, psycholinguistic experiments for instance revealed that the more descriptive features a certain bird possesses, the more it is considered as a representative member of the category BIRD. This means that the robin, which is centred in the area of maximal overlap of descriptive features, is considered a far more (proto)typical instance of the category BIRD than the kiwi.

Crucial for prototype theory is also that the descriptive features that can be used to describe the category BIRD are not manifested in each and every bird. Where some birds fly, have feathers and are not domesticated (such as robins), others might also have feathers and wings but are not able to fly (such as ostriches). Still other birds, like kiwis, do not have wings and cannot fly but come in the traditional S-shape that other birds such as penguins lack. Finally, according to prototype theory, no set of sufficient and necessary criteria can be produced that neatly delineates the category BIRD from other categories. Even the two common features "being born from eggs" and "having a beak or bill" are together not sufficient. The duck-billed platypus, a mammal that possesses both characteristics, provides a rare, but crucial, counterexample.

Comparing the prototype structure to our variable importance plot and inference tree, we see a few similarities. First of all, our random forest and inference tree have selected a set of features or parameters that, together, define the most 'typical' social meaning of /s/ palatalization. These are, in other words, the most typical, or representative, circumstances for a speaker to palatalize /s/. According to the parameters selected in our tree, the prototypical social meaning of /s/ is found by combining all typical triggers of palatalization: being one of our informants, using words with consonant cluster [sx], being primed in a previous utterance, commenting on other or yourself, interacting in emotionally loaded interactions, and being male. Parameters that did not reach significance in the tree, but that played a role in the exploratory analyses, reveal two other – weaker – components of the prototypical social meaning of s-palatalization: having a migrant background and using adverbs of adjectives. The most representative interaction in our dataset would then be a setting where a speaker who combines all these parameters, as for example Francesco, uses /s/ in a primed context, with consonant clusters [sx] and in emotionally-loaded comments. A second similarity between Figure 2 and Figure 3 is that not all factors selected by the random forest and inference tree are equally typical or carry the same weight (or *salience*). Some of them are less typical, namely ethnicity and gender, as they have low scores. A third crucial similarity is that the factors that can be used to describe the social meaning of /s/ palatalization are not manifested in each and every speaker or in each and every context. Some speakers are adults, and therefore not located in the centre of the prototype structure, but are still palatalizing more than other adults, because they interact in emotionally-loaded story climaxes, as for example Marie. These speakers are not prototypical users of /s/ palatalization, but are situated between the centre and the extreme periphery. And finally, as in the case of the category BIRD, the social meaning of /s/ palatalization cannot be defined by a set of sufficient and necessary criteria. The variable importance plot is not the only and unique set of parameters. Other parameters

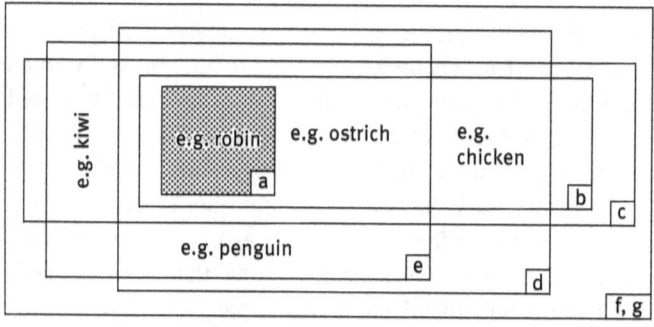

a. "Being able to fly"
b. "Having feathers"
c. "Being S-shaped"
d. "Having wings"
e. "Not domesticated"
f. "Being born from eggs"
g. "Having a beak or bill"

Figure 3: The prototypical structure of the category BIRD (see Geeraerts, Grondelaers and Bakema 1994).

can still be added and investigated, can evolve and change. What is provided here is a set of features that explain a considerable amount of variation in this corpus, but surely other features can still be integrated. If we transform our logistic regression output into a prototype structure, we obtain the following figure (see Figure 4).

Although this prototype structure is based on social feature comparison, and not on semantic feature comparison as in the bird example, essentially, we see the same prototypical cores (with maximal overlap) and peripheries (with less overlap). At the core of the structure, where there is a maximal overlap of the features, we find the typical, or most representative, users of CUVs (as, for example, Francesco) in the typical, most representative contexts of CUVs, (when, for example, commenting on others). As we move away from the core towards the periphery, we find less representative users, as, for example, female adolescents from migrant descent (as Chiara), or at the very periphery, native Flemish female adults in non-emotional contexts.

Now, it is time to deal with the two main concerns of this paper, which are (1) the question whether a third wave sociolinguistic definition of social meaning can offer empirical input for a Cognitive Linguistic analysis of the social meaning of variation and (2) the question which implications follow for the definition of social meaning. As for the first question, by measuring the interaction of social, linguistic and discursive parameters on the alternation between standard and palatalized /s/, we have shown how a third wave sociolinguistic analysis of the social meaning of /s/ palatalization –- can offer a thorough empirical basis for a prototype structure. The combination of these two perspectives and the representation of the social meaning as a prototype structure has several advantages. Firstly, the prototype structure visually illustrates more clearly how the linguistic, social and interactional triggers for palatalization are intertwined, and as such, how blurred the boundaries between them are. Related to this first advantage is the fact that it exemplifies how variationist and discursive perspectives cannot be separated if we want to fully understand why speakers shift to /s/ palatalization. Reformulated in terms of one of the most prototypical example cited for prototype theory in lexical semantics, it would be like explaining the constitutive features of all the possible birds, by separating features as "having wings" or "being born from eggs". Finally, the advantage of using a prototype is that it illustrates more clearly how the explanatory power of a model does not imply any claims of causality. Indeed, what matters is not whether it is the interactional context that elicits palatalizations and male youngsters just happen to use more emotionally loaded interactions in their interpeer interactions (which would make the context the decisive factor), or whether it is the other way around. The model just stipulates that the combination of these factors results in a prototypical context for palatalization.

Regarding the implications for a prototype representation of social meaning, we need to reflect on the bridge that needs to be built between the social and the empirical definition of social meaning, on the one hand, and the cognitive or mental representation of meaning, on the other. Although the representation of the results in Figure 2 in the prototype fashion of Figure 4 is appealing, we must not forget that our third wave perspective on social meaning is based solely on the study of linguistic production: our results present an analysis of the alternation between two variants. The initial scope of prototype structures was however meant for representing the *mental* categorization of categories, which is not some we can make claims on. Therefore, integrating our empirically tested parameters that define the social meaning of variation in language production into a prototype structure will need to be corroborated by research exploring the cognitive dimension of this empirical basis. Further research is needed to test to what extent the prototype structure based on social parameters is effectively represented in the mind of speakers, who *perceive* production of the alternating variables against their own social background. To this end, this study, which mainly serves as a proof of concept, needs to be complemented by experimental

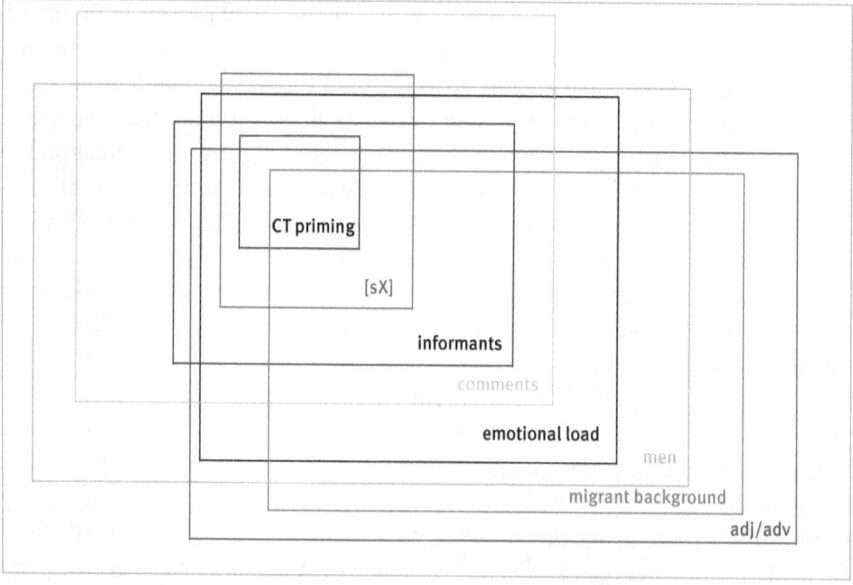

Figure 4: Prototypical structure for /s/ palatalization based on social, linguistic and discursive factors (the QR-code links to a color version of the plot).

research that tries to uncover the mental representation of what we refer to here as the 'empirical reality' or, at least, the reality that is represented through our third wave analyses of variation.

8 Conclusion and perspectives

This paper promotes a bridge from a sociolinguistic analysis of social meaning to a prototype-theoretical representation of meaning. In particular, we have shown that the social meaning of variation – materializing through a combination of social and interactional categories – adopts a prototype structure, characterized by salient and less salient categories, by a family resemblance structure and fuzzy boundaries between these categories. Our analysis has demonstrated that the prototype representation of social meaning adds to our knowledge and understanding of the social meaning of variation, as it highlights the overlap between different parameters, as well as the fuzziness between the categories. In turn, we believe that this paper reveals new avenues, showing how a third-wave perspective on social meaning of variation, thoroughly analyzed through an integration of quantitative variationist and qualitative discursive methods, can offer a strong empirical basis for a usage-based version of a prototype analysis of meaning.

As such, this paper has carefully attempted to take the social turn in prototype-theoretical Cognitive Linguistic research one step further. Although similar initiatives have been already taken by other scholars (e.g. Grondelaers and Geeraerts 2003, Polzenhagen and Xia 2015), our goal was to truly promote the social aspect to the centre of the cognitive linguistics analysis: instead of charting socio-lectal variation in the prototype structure of linguistic categories (see e.g. Altendorf 2016), we have described the prototypical structure of the social meaning indexed by linguistic variants.

Still, what is presented here is no more than a proof of concept and we are aware that quite a bit of work remains to be done. Firstly, the model will most likely benefit from the addition of other features, and, in particular, by features related to the linguistic context in which palatalization occurs, such as the phonological context (e.g. palatalization occurs more frequently in the consonant combination [sX] as in *school*, than in other consonant combinations, as in *staan*). Also, our first analyses indicate that there might be an effect of shibboleth words (palatalization appears more frequently in specific words as *school* or *stijl*). Secondly, as for this proof of concept, since we have focused on the family resemblance between the features, follow-up research will need to clarify other features characterizing prototype structures (e.g. salience, fuzzy boundaries). For example, we will need to measure the effective weight of each feature so that the cells can be designed according to their weight.

Finally, a third fundamental step will need to be taken when we want to arrive at a better understanding of the social meaning of CUVs : a prototype will have to be built for linguistic variants other than s-palatalization, by applying the same cyclical process of variationist and discursive analyses. A comparison of these prototypes will serve to shed light on the theoretical debate regarding the status of CUVs in the speakers' repertoire (e.g. Van Meel, Hinskens and, Van Hout 2016). Variationists often consider CUVs as dialects *sui generis*, as a more or less coherent collection of co-occurring features, whereas interactionists conceive CUVs as a fluid style or collection of feature pools from which speakers freely select. Comparing prototypes for different features and integrating them in one prototype for *Citétaal* provides a novel contribution to this complex question. Moreover, the comparison of the prototypes for different variants will offer new empirical ground for the definition of CUVs as styles of speaking (Keim 2006), for which scholars have already carefully suggested that they have a prototype organization, with fluid and fuzzy boundaries (Hinskens 2011: 124). For now, it suffices to stress the promising opportunities that we see in imbuing third wave sociolinguistics with a prototype-oriented analysis.

References

Altendorf, Ulrike. 2016. Caught between Aristotle and Miss Marple.... A proposal for a perceptual prototype approach to 'Estuary English'. *Complutense Journal of English Linguistics* 24, 129–152.
Cheshire, Jenny, Paul Kerswill, Sue Fox & Eivind Torgersen. 2011. Contact, the feature pool and the speech community: The emergence of Multicultural London English. *Journal of Sociolinguistics* 15(2), 151–196.
Eckert, Penny. 2008. Variation and the indexical field. *Journal of Sociolinguistics* 12. 453–476.
Eckert, Penny. 2012. Three waves of variation study: The emergence of meaning in the study of sociolinguistic variation. *Annual Review of Anthropology* 41. 87–100.
Geeraerts, Dirk, Stefan Grondelaers & Peter Bakema. 1994. *The Structure of Lexical Variation*. Meaning, Naming, and Context. Berlin & New York: Mouton de Gruyter
Geeraerts, Dirk, Gitte Kristiansen & Yves Peirsman (eds). 2010. *Advances in Cognitive Sociolinguistics*. Berlin & New York: Mouton de Gruyter.
Grondelaers, Stefan & Dirk Geeraerts. 2003. Towards a pragmatic model of cognitive onomasiology. In Hubert Cuyckens, René Dirven & John Taylor (eds.), *Cognitive Approaches to Lexical Semantics*, 67–92. Berlin & New York: Mouton de Gruyter.

Hinskens, Frans. 2011. Emerging Morrocan and Turkish varieties of Dutch. Ethnolects or ethnic styles? Friederike Kern & Margret Selting (eds.), *Ethnic Styles of Speaking in European Metropolitan Areas*, 101–129. Amsterdam: John Benjamins.

Johnstone, Barbara, Jennifer Andrus & Andrew Danielson. 2006. Mobility, indexicality, and the enregisterment of 'Pittsburghese'. *Journal of English Linguistics* 32 (4). 77–104.

Keim, Inken. 2006. Interaktionale Soziolinguistik und kommunikative, soziale stylistk. *Sociotlinguistica* 20. 70–91.

Kristiansen, Gitte & René Dirven (eds.). 2008. *Cognitive Sociolinguistics. Language Variation, Cultural Models, Social Systems*. New York & Berlin: Mouton de Gruyter

Kristiansen, Gitte. 2008. Style-shifting and shifting styles: A socio-cognitive approach to lectal variation. In Gitte Kristiansen & René Dirven (eds.), *Cognitive Sociolinguistics: Language Variation, Cultural Models, Social Systems*, 45–88. Berlin & New York: Mouton de Gruyter.

Jefferson, Gail. 1983. On exposed and embedded correction in conversation. *Studium Linguistik* 14. 58–68.

Labov, William. 2006. Narrative pre-construction. *Narrative Inquiry* 16(1). 37–45.

Labov, William & Joshua Waletzky. 1966. Narrative analysis: oral versions of personal experience. In June Helm, *Essays on the Verbal and Visual Arts*, 12–44. Seattle: Universiy of Washington Press.

Labov, William. 1972. *Sociolinguistic Patterns*. Philadelphia: University of Pennsylvania Press.

Lerner, Gene H. 1991. On the syntax of sentences-in-progress. *Language in Society* 20. 441–58.

Marzo, Stefania & Ey Ceuleers. 2011. The use of Citétaal among adolescents in Limburg: the role of space appropriation in language variation and change. *Journal of Multilingual and Multicultural Development* 32(5). 451–464.

Marzo, Stefania. 2016. Exploring the social meaning of contemporary urban vernaculars: perceptions and attitudes about Citélanguage in Flanders. *International Journal of Bilingualism* 20(5). 501–521.

Mervis, Carolyn B. & Eleanor Rosch. 1981. Categorization of natural objects. *Annual Review of Psychology* 32. 89–115.

Mompéan, José A. 2004. Category overlap and neutralization: The importance of speakers' classifications in phonology. *Cognitive Linguistics* 15(4). 429–469.

Mourigh, Khalid. 2017. Stance-taking through sibilant palatalisation in Gouda Moroccan Dutch. *Nederlandse Taalkunde* 22(3). 421–446.

Norrick, Neal R. 2005. The dark side of tellability. *Narrative Inquiry* 15(2). 323–343.

Nortier, Jacomine & Bente A. Svendsen (eds.). 2015. *Language, Youth and Identity in the 21st Century*. Cambridge: Cambridge University Press.

Polzenhagen, Frans & Xiaoyan Xia. 2015. Language, culture and prototypicality. In Farzad Sharifian (ed.), *Routledge Handbook of Language and Culture*, 253–269. New York: Routledge.

Pustka, Elissa. 2009. A prototype-theoretical model of Southern French. In Kate Beeching, Nigel Armstrong & Françoise Gadet (eds.), *Sociolinguistic Variation in Contemporary French*, 77–94. Amsterdam & Philadelphia: John Benjamins.

Quist, Pia. 2008. Sociolinguistic approaches to multiethnolect: Language variety and stylistic practice. *International Journal of Bilingualism* 12(1-2). 43–61.

Ramoulin-Brunberg, Helena. 1994. Prototype categories and variation studies. In Francisco Fernández, Miguel Fuster Márquez & Juan Jose Calvo (eds.), *English Historical Linguistics 1992*, 297–304. New York: John Benjamins.

Rampton, Ben. 2011. From 'Multi-ethnic adolescent heteroglossia' to 'Contemporary urban vernaculars. *Language & Communication* 31. 76–294.

Speelman, Dirk, Kris Heylen & Dirk Geeraerts (eds.). 2018. *Mixed-Effects Regression Models in Linguistics* (Quantitative Methods in the Humanities and Social Sciences). New York: Springer.

Svendsen, Bente A. & Uun Røyneland. 2008. Multiethnolectal facts and functions in Oslo, Norway. *International Journal of Bilingualism* 12(1-2). 62–83.

Svendsen, Bente A. 2015. Language, youth and identity in the 21st century: content and continuation. In Jacomine Nortier & B.A. Svendsen (eds.), *Language, Youth and Identity in the 21st Century*, 3–23. Cambridge: CUP.

Svendsen, Bente A. & Stefania Marzo. 2015. A 'new' speech style is born. The omnipresence of structure and agency in the life of semiotic registers in heterogeneous urban spaces. *European Journal of Applied Linguistics* 3(1). 47–85.

Tagliamonte, Sali A. & Harald R. Baayen. 2012. Models, forests and trees of York English: Was/were variation as a case study for statistical practice. *Language Variation and Change* 24(2). 135–178.

Van Meel, Linda, Frans Hinskens & Roeland van Hout. 2016. Co-variation and varieties in modern Dutch ethnolects. *Lingua* 172–173. 72–86.

Part II: **Associating concepts: Metaphors and cultural models in contact**

Stephen Lucek

5 Notions of CONTAINMENT and SUPPORT in Irish English: Implications of language contact on the cognition of space

Abstract: Over the past 40 years, a number of studies of Irish English have demonstrated the substrate influence of Irish on Irish English. Significant amongst these are the work of, inter alia, Harris (1984), Filppula (1999), and Hickey (2007), all of which treat Irish English as a contact variety of English (and perhaps the oldest such variety). While this line of research has focused on various aspects of language, there is still room to explore the cognitive aspects of language variation in Ireland. This chapter aims to explore the substrate influence of Irish on Irish English as it pertains to the conceptualization of CONTAINMENT and SUPPORT. Using Conceptual Metaphor Theory, the relationship between a structure and the road where that structure is located is shown to vary between the road providing a surface for the structure ("on the road") and the road containing the structure ("in the road"), both of which are found in other studies of Irish English, but thus far, not from the viewpoint of a contact phenomenon that has the capacity to vary between the different conceptualizations. In this chapter, the way in which the Irish language deals with these conceptualizations is described as a distinction of permanency, which leads to the substrate influence on Irish English speakers, who apply this same distinction in describing the conceptualizations in English. The chapter concludes with suggestions for future research.

Keywords: cognition of spatial scenes, Irish English, language contact, substrate influence, conceptual metaphor theory

1 Introduction

Researchers seeking a connection between abstract language and concrete language have examined how metaphor can bridge this gap. A central focus

---

Note: I would like to thank Hans-Georg Wolf, Anna Finzel, Colin Flynn, Jeffrey Kallen, an anonymous reviewer, and the editors of this volume for comments on earlier drafts.

Stephen Lucek, University College Dublin

of Conceptual Metaphor Theory (CMT) research is how metaphors vary and what the reasons for these variations are. In particular, Kövecses (2005) takes a broad look at the place of metaphor in culture, arguing for two levels of metaphor: cross-cultural and within-culture variation. In cross-cultural variation, there is both a "generic-level metaphor and a specific-level one" (2006: 158), which is where universality and variation can co-exist. Specific level metaphors are examples of the generic level, as the following examples illustrate:

(1) THE ANGRY PERSON IS A PRESSURIZED CONTAINER (Kövecses 2006: 157)
(2) ANGER IS IN THE BELLY (Japanese (see Matsui (1995))
(3) ANGER IS A FLUID (Chinese (see Ning Yu 1998))
(4) ANGER IS IN THE HEART (Zulu (see Taylor and Mbense 1998))

While example (1) is taken to be the generic-level metaphor, cultural realizations of this metaphor in (2)–(4) can differ in "what kind of container is used, how the pressure arises, whether the container is heated or not, what kind of substance fills the container (liquid, substance, or objects), what consequences the explosion has" (Kövecses 2006: 157). What is remarkable about these different metaphors is that they routinely exist simultaneously and congruently within different languages. The difference between these metaphors is easily recognizable, but "[w]here they differ is in the specific cultural content that they bring to the metaphor" (2006: 158). Thus, the cultural influence of how we conceptualize anger in these examples is evident at the level of cross-linguistic comparison.

The current paper asks what kinds of conceptualizations are available for Irish English speakers. In particular, the current paper examines how CONTAINMENT and SUPPORT are conceptualized in Irish English, and how much of this can be explained through understanding similar concepts in Irish. CONTAINMENT and SUPPORT conceptualizations that were gathered through questionnaire and interview data are analyzed for the conceptual metaphors at work and explained through long-term contact between English and Irish. The chapter starts with general concepts of language contact and cross-linguistic comparisons of spatial language, before a broad consideration of the conceptual landscape of metaphor variation can be put forward. I then frame Irish English as a contact variety (the oldest contact variety of English other than British English itself), before describing the respective CONTAINMENT and SUPPORT conceptualizations in Irish, English, and Irish English. I then present the results of an empirical study and analyze how CMT can be used to account for variation in the responses to the study. I conclude with recommendations for the future.

2 Background

At issue in this volume is Cognitive Contact Linguistics, a new subdiscipline that takes a conceptual approach to identifying the effects of language contact. Cognitive Linguistics and Contact Linguistics have not always been considered together as complementary disciplines, though this has changed in the past 10 years, as a byproduct of "the increasing use of corpus data in Cognitive Linguistics, as this has brought the empirical base of the two approaches close together" (Backus 2014: 102; see also Zenner 2013). In the following sections, we will see the theoretical approaches to language contact and usage-based aspects of CMT at hand in the current study.

2.1 Language contact

In language contact theory, Lehiste (1988) notes that a major factor in contact involves grammatical interference, where "elements of language B enter language A and are gradually integrated, or when a speaker of language A starts to speak language B and carries over elements of A into B" (Lehiste 1988: 13). In the current paper, we can consider Irish as language A and English as language B. The result of this contact is nearly ubiquitous in situations like that of Irish English, as "change does not often take forms that are qualitatively and quantitatively different from what takes place in monolingual settings" (Backus 2014: 99). The English that developed in Ireland could not have developed in the same manner, had it not been for the influence of the Irish language.

To this end, Filppula's (1999) assumption is that in areas where the Irish language remained for longer, or, indeed, is still quite active (in his data, counties Clare and Kerry on the West coast of Ireland), that the substrate influence would be stronger than in areas where Irish died out earlier (counties Dublin and Wicklow on the East coast). Elsewhere, Odlin (2009) acknowledges that the after perfect has its roots in the substrate influence on the contact between Irish and English, but stresses that "its survival in recent generations in Ireland reflects transmission in an essentially monolingual setting" (Odlin 2009: 51). Siemund (2004) on the other hand notes that in contexts where we cannot be certain that there is substrate influence or superstrate influence through dialect contact, it would be prudent to "take a broader perspective and see where the phenomena […] find their place from a European, if not even wider, cross-linguistic perspective" (Siemund 2004: 413). We will begin by describing CONTAINMENT and SUPPORT in Dutch and Finnish before discussing in more detail English CONTAINMENT and SUPPORT conceptualizations.

2.2 Notions of CONTAINMENT and SUPPORT

Studies of spatial relations have addressed cross-linguistic variation in CONTAINMENT and SUPPORT conceptualizations. Bowerman (1996) looks at Dutch and Finnish from the point of view of seven English prepositional concepts that represent CONTAINMENT and SUPPORT in English. While the CONTAINMENT concepts are not affected, Dutch presents a more complex system for dealing with SUPPORT than English. Like English, Finnish also uses just two prepositions to express CONTAINMENT and SUPPORT, but makes a distinction between internal (*in, into, out of*) and external (*on, onto, off*) concepts using relative distance to differentiate.

There is also a growing body of research of exactly how CONTAINMENT and SUPPORT are conceptualized in English. Garrod, Ferrier, and Campbell (1999) introduce a functional geometry to CONTAINMENT and SUPPORT concepts. Here, the concavity of the GROUND is fundamental to the differentiation between *in* and *on*. This is necessary because the simple constructions of *in* and *on* are insufficient as, "their wide range of usage seems to confound any straightforward treatment of their meaning" (1999: 168). The degree to which an object can be contained and how much contact it must make is problematic in the literature (e.g. Herskovits 1986), leading to the proposition of a hybrid concept of CONTAINMENT:

> [S]ituations where there is a clear geometry of enclosure indicate containment irrespective of control, but for situations where the geometry is marginal, we require evidence of location control before perceiving containment. (Garrod, Ferrier, and Campbell 1999: 186)

SUPPORT is less fully developed in their paper, suggesting in their conclusions that, "precisely where a pear lies relative to a bowl is not so crucial for determining whether it is *in* the bowl or not" (Garrod, Ferrier, and Campbell 1999: 188). Further to these extra-geometric considerations, Coventry and Prat-Sala (2001) use the manipulation of FIGURE and GROUND in an attempt to define how much influence the relata in a conceptualization have on the nature of CONTAINMENT and SUPPORT concepts. In their experiments, it became apparent that the likelihood that a located object (*cup*) will remain SUPPORTed by the SUPPORTing object (*saucer*) if the SUPPORTing object is moved is crucial to SUPPORT conceptualization. SUPPORT and location do the job of defining the boundaries around *on* and *in*. Feist and Gentner (2003) turn our attention to cross-linguistic studies of CONTAINMENT and SUPPORT. Not just geometry, but also animacy and function affect the conceptualization of spatial scenes and influence when CONTAINMENT ends and SUPPORT begins. A great number of factors are active in spatial conceptualizations which complicate "the seemingly simple task of localizing objects" (Feist and Gentner 2003: 5).

Taking a comprehensive look at spatial language from different parts of the world, Levinson and Wilkins (2006) offer differing manners of CONTAINMENT and SUPPORT conceptualizations. Van Staden, Bowerman, and Verhelst (2006) describe the Dutch relationship noted above between adherence (expressed with *op*) and attachment (expressed with *aan*) where English would only use *on*. The Dutch system seems entirely facile compared with that of Yélî Dnye which has "two forms dedicated to containment [...] three forms that cover attachment notions, and no less than six forms that cover the semantic space subsumed by English *on* or *above*, i.e. the concepts of surface support or vertical superposition" (Levinson 2006: 167). While functional geometry helps us understand the concepts of CONTAINMENT and SUPPORT, we need another analytical tool for understanding how physical space is connected to abstract concepts.

2.3 Conceptual metaphor theory

The focus in CMT is not so much on the finer points of FIGURE and GROUND contexts, as in the preceding section, but rather on the ways in which non-physical scenes are processed by humans. There is an experiential basis for all metaphors, whether they are universal or culture-specific. If two cultures disagree on what is up – e.g. whether or not MORE IS UP and RATIONAL IS UP exist in their metaphorical toolkit – then variation exists, because "verticality enters our experience in many different ways and so gives rise to many different metaphors" (Lakoff and Johnson 2003: 19). Thus, experiential truths activate metaphors in a language (or variety of a language) that are not always common to all speakers of that language.

Lakoff and Johnson have applied CMT to event structure which is "metaphorical in significant, ineliminable ways" (Lakoff and Johnson 1999: 171). There are two primary metaphors at play in basic event structure: CAUSES ARE FORCES and CHANGES ARE MOVEMENTS. The difference between these two metaphors can be understood as "one conceptualizes events in terms of locations, the other, in terms of objects" (1999: 179).

This idea of variation in metaphor is further developed by Kövecses (2005, 2006), who identifies universal and contextual metaphors as types of metaphor: metaphors that are common to most cultures and metaphors that are culture-specific. Kövecses suggests that universality in metaphor use exists "because cultures can be viewed, in part, as shared metaphorical understandings of the world and because conventional metaphorical language and metaphorically constituted physical reality have relative time stability" (2005: 284). Variation happens because "the environment, the social-cultural context, and the communicative situation of groups of people or individuals provide these groups and individuals with experiences that are specific to them" (2005: 286).

One metaphor that Kövecses (2006) identified as culture-specific is LOVE IS A JOURNEY that is common in English, but does not parse in Hungarian. This is an area where, "[l]arger cultural themes, or topics, that have the potential to distinguish different cultures manifest themselves and recur in many of [these] examples" (2006: 175). In the current context, contact with Irish will be taken as a cultural theme that sets Irish English apart from other varieties of English. Indeed, one of the major aspects of Irish English that makes it different from other territories where English is the first language – what we might term Inner Circle varieties – is the legacy of the Irish language and the effects it has had on the English spoken here. This will be discussed further in the sections that follow.

Considering the extensive work on variation in cross-cultural comparisons of spatial language (Levinson and Wilkins 2006), then the source domain of physical space can provide variation at the level of metaphor in cross-cultural studies, as well as inter-cultural studies. Gibbs (2011) notes that while a conceptual metaphor can exist in more than one language, "specific linguistic manifestations of these metaphors can reveal subtle differences in the cultural-ideological background in which conceptual metaphors function" (2011: 538). Specifically, this type of culture-specific variation can be seen in how RELATIONSHIP and DEATH are conceptualized in three Formosan languages (Lee 2011). These languages make heavy use of euphemisms for RELATIONSHIPS and DEATH where universality is due to the neural-bodily basis of some metaphors, while variation is due to cognitive processing, and socio-cultural experience is found amongst metaphors in these three related languages. Death is a natural part of life, albeit the final part. Similarly, Galal (2014) looks at DEATH as a euphemism in Arabic and finds that at the universal level, body-based metaphors are common in both Arabic and English, while more cultural metaphors are capable of showing variation between the languages.

More recently, in (Lucek 2017), Irish English speakers who were originally from Dublin were shown to prefer the container metaphor of towns and cities (e.g. "go in to town", "come out from town"). This is particularly noticeable in opposition to other town/city conceptualizations that are used by the rural Irish English speakers who use the vertical axis to conceptualize towns and cities (e.g. "go up to town", "go down to town"). The underlying metaphors (PLACES OF IMPORTANCE ARE UP, TOWN IS DOWN) control not just the place that is *in/out/up/down*, but also any motion in the direction or away from that place. Thus, a native of a town, who hasn't left that place for any significant periods of time might know that "I remember one day I was minding him whilst me mother was *down* the town" (Lucek 2017: 114) because TOWN IS DOWN. While the physical landscape (up/down) of a town might become quite obvious to a new arrival to that town early on, it is much more difficult for that new arrival to apply more conceptual ups and downs to different relata. It is perhaps for this reason that the container conceptualization of a town is easier to apply for new arrivals to an area, as the container binary relationship carries no additional conceptual baggage as PLACES OF IMPORTANCE or THE FUTURE do for the vertical axis.

3 The case of Irish and Irish English prepositions

Given what we know about English prepositions and about the work that has been done on cross-linguistic studies of CONTAINMENT and SUPPORT concepts, let us take a look at how Irish approaches these notions. The prepositions *ar* and *in* are used by Irish speakers to express CONTAINMENT and SUPPORT, and will be discussed separately before explaining some specific conceptualizations.

3.1 *Ar*

In Irish, the preposition *ar* does the job of most SUPPORT conceptualizations. Like most Irish prepositions, *ar* has temporal uses as well, as seen in the examples below.

(5) *Ar   An   gcéad-sholas*
    On   DET   first light
    'At first light.'
    (Cussen 1920: 1)

(6) *Ar   a h-aon déag*
    On   eleven (time)
    'At eleven o'clock.'
    (Cussen 1920: 1)

As a locative marker, *ar* performs both deictic and CONTAINMENT functions, as seen in the example below.

(7) Ar   an   áit   seo   do   rugadh mé
    On   the   place this from   WAS BORN
    'I was born in this place.'
    (Cussen 1920: 1)

(8) Bhí   gealbhan   ar   an tor
    WAS   sparrow   on   bush
    'A sparrow was in a bush.'
    (modified from Cussen 1920: 1)

Ar also performs some possessive duties, as seen below. The SUPPORT functions are evident in the combinatory form *orm/ort/air/uirthi* where possession is expressed.

(9) Tá   tart   uirthi
    IS   thirst   on-3SG.FEM
    'She is thirsty.'

(10) Tá   slaghdán   orm
     IS   head cold   on-1SG
     'I have a head cold.'

We can also see *ar* examples that denote SUPPORT and attachment, as seen in the examples below.

(11) Siúlann an   madra   ar   cheithre   chos
     WALK   the   dog   on   four   Legs
     'The dog walks on four legs.'

(12) An   pictiúr   a bhí   ar crochadh   ar   an   mballa
     the   picture   which was   HANGING   on   DET   wall
     'The picture which was hanging on the wall.'

3.2 *In*

CONTAINMENT tends to be accomplished with the preposition *in*. The temporal uses are quite similar to those of *ar*, as seen in the examples below.

(13) I   gcionn   na   bliana
    In   beginning   of   year
    'At the start of the year.'
    (Cussen 1920: 59)

(14) I   meán   aois
    In   middle   Age
    'Middle-aged'
    (Cussen 1920: 59)

While the above uses are highly idiomatic, locative conceptualizations of *in* are more robust in Irish, denoting deixis, as seen in the following example.

(15) Bhí   sé   ina   n-imeall
    WAS   he   in+3PL.POSS   border
    'He was on their border.'
    (Cussen 1920: 59)

(16) Tá   an   t-úll   sa   bhabhla
    IS   the   apple   in+the   bowl
    'The apple is in the bowl.'

3.3 Media

Irish has some special cases when it comes to the consumption of media. Take for example the following:

(17) Tá   siad   ag féachaint   ar   an   teilifís
    ARE   they   watching   on   the   television
    'They are watching television.'

In English, we have no such need for a preposition in this case, but rather take for granted that they are casting their gaze upon a television. More abstract notions such the relationship between a newspaper and a news story introduce the need for a marker of this relationship; in this case, a preposition does the job. In Irish, the following can be said:

(18) *Bhí   an   scéal   ar   an   nuachtán   áitiúil*
    WAS the story   on   the newspaper local
    ?'The story was on the local paper.'
    'The story was in the local paper.'

Here, in most varieties of English, it would be common to see the use of the preposition *in* rather than *on*. The challenge here is to understand if a newspaper is a surface for ink (the literal meaning) or a collection of stories (the abstract meaning). This suggests that there may be more variation in how some objects are conceptualized: either as surfaces or as containers. This will be further explored below.

3.4 Locations

Similarly, in Irish, there is some variation in how locations are conceptualized. The relationship between roads and objects that are associated with roads is not always straightforward, as seen below:

(19) *Tá   cor   sa   bhóthar*
    IS   curve in+the   road
    'There is a curve in the road.'

(20) *Tá   cuid   mhaith uchtóg   ar   an   mbóthar*
    ARE   share good   bumps   on   the road
    'There are a good number of bumps on the road.'

(21) *Tá   gabhal   sa   bhóthar*
    IS   fork   in+the   road
    'There is a fork in the road.'

(22) *Chuir siad   dolaí   ar   an   mbóthar*
    PUT   they   tolls   on   the road
    'They put tolls on the road.'

In some situations, Irish prefers a conceptualization of a road and an object associated with that road to be conceived in different manners. These are part/whole and surface differentiations, but perhaps not in the manner that would be expected. One feature of the concept of a road is that is has a sense of permanency; to take the curve out of the road, we would have to radically change the road. Similarly, a fork in a road cannot be removed, thus it must be permanent. Conversely, bumps are not an original feature of a road, nor are, presumably, tolls that are placed on a road. These are temporary or newer features of the road, and as such are conceptualized as a surface relationship, whereas the permanent features are essential to the road, and are thus part/whole conceptualizations. Thus, the Irish language provides ways of expressing concepts involving CONTAINMENT and SUPPORT that might not be reflected in English.

3.5 Irish English

In the extant literature, Ireland is seen as "one of the best research sites to study certain types of language change [...] the shift here being the near-extinction of Irish as a community language and the concomitant adoption of English" (Odlin 1997: 1). English was first brought to Ireland in its very early forms in the 13th century. Although the language shift in Ireland was reinforced by strict laws on monolingual English use (see Kallen 1994: 152), bilingualism was maintained in the 19th century. English spread throughout the country mainly by means of adult acquisition at work (Odlin 1997: 6). Odlin points to substrate Irish influence in Irish English as a sign that "large numbers of Irish speakers were involved in [labour] migrations" (Odlin 1997: 11). The linguistic situation in Ireland is considered from a historical pidginization process in Odlin (1997), where simplification evidence is shown in the use of the present simple in place of present perfect, as seen in the example below.

(23) *I been an editor for years.*
    'I have been an editor for years.'

However, the presence of a common feature of Irish English, the 'after perfect'– sometimes known as the 'hot news' perfect (Harris 1993: 181; see also Filppula 1999: 109) – offers evidence of a non-simplified structure (though Kallen 1991 disputes the direct influence of Irish in this regard). Examples of this use in Irish English and a parsed example of Irish are seen below.

(24) *I'm after eating my dinner.*
'I have eaten my dinner.'

(25) Tá   sí   tréis   an   bád   a dhíol
BE   she   after   the   boat   selling
'She has just sold the boat.'
Lit. 'She's after selling the boat.'
(Harris 1993: 181)

This element of substrate influence "is a case of where concepts from second language acquisition must be invoked to explain what proved hard for Irish speakers to master" (Odlin 1997: 25). Harris (1993) prefers to identify Irish English in the Republic of Ireland as a contact jargon, "that is, in circumstances where an indigenous population, either in whole or in part, gives up its native language in favour of that of a colonial power" (1993: 180). In these situations, "the vocabulary of an 'external' language is grafted on to the grammar and pronunciation patterns of an indigenous language" (1993: 180).

3.5.1 Prepositions

The use of prepositions in Irish English is "where the effects of Irish influence are very much in evidence" (Harris 1993: 171). Further to this point, Hickey describes "features which are broadly typical of Irish English and which speakers of Irish to this day are exposed to and which they adopt" (Hickey 2007: 170). These features include specific prepositional uses that are found in Irish English (though not always exclusive to Ireland) that are in some way remarkable. This is a vast topic and the prepositional area cannot be sufficiently addressed in this section. I will focus on two prepositions here, *in* and *on*.

3.5.2 *In*

Previous research into the Irish English uses of *in* has focused on two main topics: location and existence. The primary use of the local *in* is used to describe concrete places, but can also fulfill deictic functions of existence, as seen in the examples below:

(26) *There was acres and miles of land just for to live in it.*
(Filppula 1999: 227)

(27) There used to be a hotel in it.
      (Hickey 2007: 247)

It is commonly held that these related uses are rooted in the Irish prepositional pronoun *ann*, as in the example below.

(28) Tá   trí   sheomra codlata   ann
      IS   three   bedrooms   in-3SG
      'There are three bedrooms there.'

These examples are exclusive of the typical CONTAINMENT uses of *in*.

3.5.3 *On*

A more diverse set of uses exists for *on* in Irish English. Well-known examples include the Dative of Disadvantage, which has direct influence from Irish, as seen in the example below.

(29) Do bhuail   Seumas   mo ghadhar   orm
      STRUCK   James   my dog   on-1SG
      'James struck my dog on me.'
      (Filppula 1999: 220)

This is not to be confused with the use of *on* that relates to possession, as seen in the examples below.

(30) Stiofán   atá   orm
      Stephen   that+is   on-1SG
      'My name is Stephen.'

(31) But I can't think of the name that was on him.
      (Filppula 1999: 221)

This is, again, not to be confused with Irish expressions of inanimate possession, as seen in the examples below.

(32) Tá   brón   orm
      IS   sorrow   on-1SG
      'I am sorry.'

(33) *And this blacksmith was runnin' too, and begor, the breath was gettin' short on him.*
(Filppula 1999: 220)

A final use of *on* that is of particular importance to the current study is in the context "where *on* replaces the [Standard English] *in*" (Filppula 1999: 223), as seen in the example below.

(34) *I was just reading it on the paper here.*
(Filppula 1999: 223)

This is described as local in Henry (1957: 147–148) and as locational by Moylan (1996: 343–344), but will be interpreted from a different point of view in the current article. While the Henry and Moylan examples are locational in nature, the Filppula example calls into question the nature of a newspaper, whether it is a surface for ink or a collection of stories. This is attested to exist in some English varieties of English that fit a different construction than local. We will visit this construction below.

4 Methodology

The goal of this paper is to examine how CONTAINMENT and SUPPORT are conceptualized in Irish English and what impact contact with Irish has affected the English spoken in Ireland. In designing the methods for this study, the strengths and weaknesses of both sociolinguistic research and Cognitive Linguistics were carefully considered. While variationist sociolinguistics was, indeed, appealing, studies that have focused on variation in English, and, particularly in this context, *within* the Irish English variety, have generally delineated geographical boundaries based on vowel length (see Harris 1993) and the supraregional, aspirational social class in-grouping of modern urban Irish English (see Hickey 2007). Conceptual variation has not been a consideration in studies of variation in Irish English, thus making the current paper (and related papers) important in discussing the contact effects on variation in Irish English and, indeed, other contact varieties of English.

Similarly, cross-linguistic treatments of spatial language (see, inter alia, Levinson and Wilkins 2006) have taken a canonical view towards English notions of CONTAINMENT and SUPPORT. Recently, CMT research has been open to the idea of variation both between cultures, but also within cultures, which leads to the theoretical justification for the current study.

4.1 Design

The study consists of a semi-structured sociolinguistic interview, followed by a questionnaire that the participants returned to the Centre for Linguistic and Communication Sciences at Trinity College Dublin.

The interview was conducted as a local history project, where the participants were asked about their early memories of the area where they live and, if it was different, the area where they were born and grew up. The focus of this interview was to gather spatial language in general, a bottom-up construction of conceptual categories.

The well-known sociolinguistic interview is intended to gather spontaneous, unguarded speech and has not changed significantly since Labov (1966). Considerations for the current study were taken from Tagliamonte (2006).

The textual questions on the questionnaire focused on testing the hypotheses of previous research on Irish English (Henry 1957; Moylan 1996; Filppula 1999). Novel images were drawn for testing on a population of Irish English speakers. The inspiration for these images originates in the image series used for, inter alia, Bowerman 1996 (see appendix to Levinson and Wilkins 2006 for the full set of images) as well as those used in Coventry and Prat-Sala (2001), for more focused CONTAINMENT/SUPPORT testing. Some sample texts and images are shown below.

4.2 Participants

The participant pool was assembled using the snowball effect, with the initial interviews conducted with members of the Navan Writing Circle, the Navan Historical Society and the Johnstown Residents Association. While advertisements for participants were distributed throughout the town, only one participant came to the study in this way. In total, 20 participants were interviewed and 19 of them returned the questionnaire. More detailed information about the participants in contained in Table 1, below.

Table 1: Biographical information of the participants.

ID	AGE	SEX	BIRTHPLACE	RESIDENCE	WORKPLACE
P001	64	M	Navan	Navan	Navan
P002	58	F	Tipperary	Navan	Navan
P003	69	M	Bohermeen	Bohermeen	Navan
P004	62	F	Dublin	Navan	Navan
P005	80	M	Roscommon	Ardsallagh	Ardsallagh

(continued)

Table 1 (continued)

ID	AGE	SEX	BIRTHPLACE	RESIDENCE	WORKPLACE
P006	70	M	Navan	Navan	Navan
P007	41	F	Galway	Trim	Navan
P008	71	M	Johnstown	Johnstown	Kells
P009	59	F	Clare	Johnstown	Dublin
P010	33	F	Dublin	Johnstown	Dublin
P011	34	F	Dublin	Johnstown	Dublin
P012	44	M	Dublin	Johnstown	Dublin
P013	40	F	Kildalkey	Johnstown	Unemployed
P014	67	M	Horseleap	Walterstown	Navan
P015	40	M	Dublin	Carnaross	Navan
P016	75	M	Navan	Navan	Navan
P017	38	M	Dublin	Johnstown	Unemployed
P018	75	M	Navan	Navan	Various
P019	50	M	Leitrim	Johnstown	Dublin
P020	36	F	Dunmoe	Dunmoe	Navan

4.3 Sample texts and images

As an obvious outsider (the American accent of the interviewer was sometimes emphasized for effect), I was able to ask questions of genuine ignorance and curiosity. For example, in asking where a ballroom was formerly located, I was able to invite participants to give spatial conceptualizations of location as well as motion and wayfinding, as they were asked how to get there now. Through this method of ignorance, locative *in* and *on* could be evaluated in a natural setting. In a more formal setting, on the questionnaire, the following image was presented with a completion task attached to it.

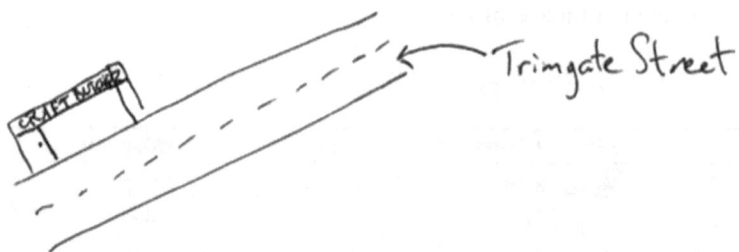

The craft butcher's shop is _____ Trimgate Street.

Figure 1: Test of participants' CONTAINMENT & SUPPORT conceptualizations related to roads (Lucek 2015: 360).

While verb choice is not controlled for here, the prepositional completion was quite telling amongst the participants (see below). I also wanted to test the traditional bounds of CONTAINMENT and SUPPORT as described by Bowerman (1996) and Coventry and Prat-Sala (1999), amongst others. The following images were designed to test these aspects.

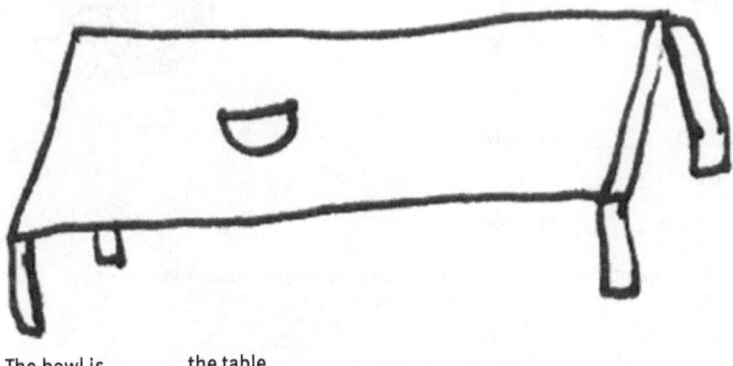

The bowl is _____ the table.

Figure 2: Test of participants' SURFACE conceptualizations related to tables (Lucek 2015: 359).

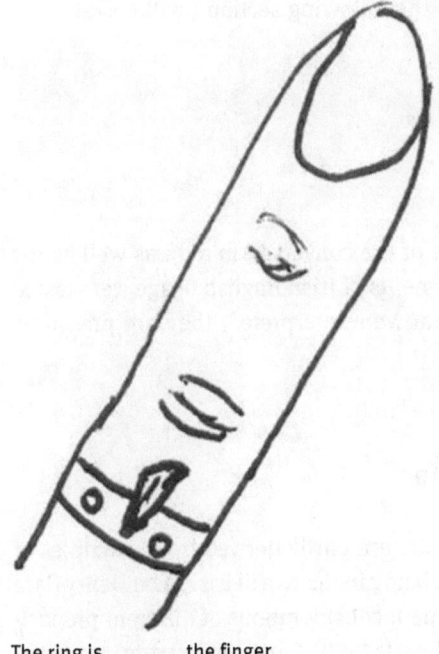

The ring is _____ the finger.

Figure 3: Test of participants' ENCIRCLEMENT conceptualizations related to rings (Lucek 2015: 360).

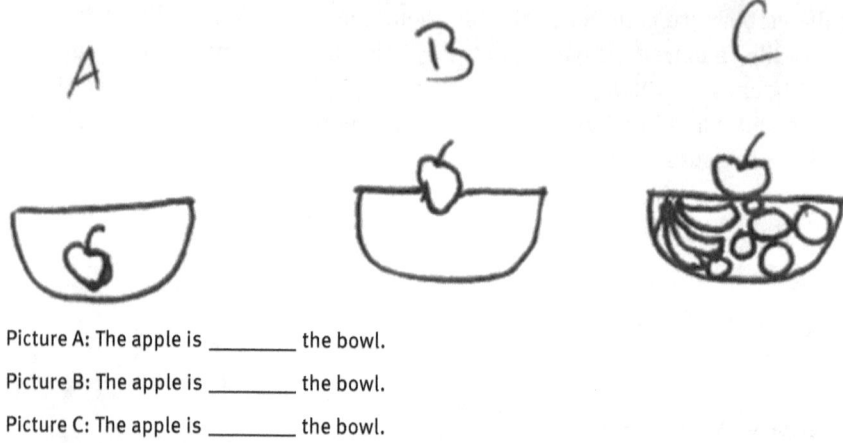

Picture A: The apple is _____ the bowl.
Picture B: The apple is _____ the bowl.
Picture C: The apple is _____ the bowl.

Figure 4: Test of participants' CONTAINMENT & SUPPORT conceptualizations related to fruit (Lucek 2015: 359).

A variable that was not specifically tested for, the media *in* and *on* conceptualization occurred spontaneously in these data. This aspect of cognition is only evaluated through the conversation data. In the following section I will describe the results and analysis.

5 Results

This section will show indicative results of the conversation data as well as the questionnaire data. Some traditional elements of Irish English usage were tested and as a way of showing how these data were interpreted, they are presented below.

5.1 Indicative questionnaire data

The questions in part 1 of the questionnaire are partly derived from examples of preposition uses noted in Henry (1957) as being indicative of Irish. The Henry data has been used as the impetus for subsequent considerations of different preposition use in Irish English (see, inter alia, Filppula 1999). Participants were instructed to fill in the blank with the word or words that best complete the sentence.

5.1.1 Question 1: You've broken my watch _____ me

Table 2: Test participants' application of Dative of Disadvantage (Lucek 2015: 162).

P001	P002	P003	P004	P005	P006	P007	P008	P009	P010
on	for	on	on (but it is not a sentence I'd use)	on	on	on	on	on	on
P011	P012	P013	P014	P015	P016	P017	P018	P019	P020
on	on	on	on	compensate	on	on	on	N/A	on

This question seeks to evaluate the use of the Dative of Disadvantage in the Navan dataset. All but two participants chose to complete this sentence with *on*, which supports the existence of the Dative of Disadvantage in Irish English. One participant chose to complete the sentence with 'compensate', while one other participant completed the sentence with 'for'.

5.1.2 Question 12: Francis has a lot of weight _____ him

Table 3: Test participants' application of physical attribute possession (Lucek 2015: 168).

P001	P002	P003	P004	P005	P006	P007	P008	P009	P010
on	on	on	on	on	upon	on	on	on	on
P011	P012	P013	P014	P015	P016	P017	P018	P019	P020
on	on	on	on	on	on	on	on	N/A	gone from

This question sought to elicit a possession of physical attribute conceptualization. All but one participant completed this sentence with *on*. The outlier was an opposite conceptualization, 'gone from', indicating weight loss rather than a state of possessing a good deal of weight. This would be the expected response not only in Irish English, but indeed, most varieties of English and provides an indication that there are some aspects of possession that are common to most, if not all, speakers of English.

5.1.3 Question 19: What name is _____ that child?

Table 4: Test participants' application of Irish emotional possession (Lucek 2015: 172).

P001	P002	P003	P004	P005	P006	P007	P008	P009	P010
on	given to	suitable for	on	James	given to	on	on	the name of	on
P011	P012	P013	P014	P015	P016	P017	P018	P019	P020
on	giving to	on	on	given to	called	on	on	N/A	on

This question looks to evaluate the participants' application of the Irish language construction *Stiofan atá orm* "My name is Stephen" (lit. *Stephen is on me*). Eleven participants chose to complete with *on*, while four participants completed with 'given to', which would be the expected completion. Other responses include 'suitable for', 'called', and 'the name of'.

5.1.4 Bowerman (1996) and Coventry and Prat-Sala (2001) tests

Table 5: Results of participants' application of Bowerman 1996 & Coventry and Prat-Sala 2001 (Lucek 2015: 319).

Stimulus	Expected Completion	Actual Completion
Image Set 5: The apple is _____ the bowl.	In; On; On (Coventry & Prat-Sala 2001)	In; In; In (1 of 19 participants)
		In; In; On (1/19)
		In; On; On (7/19)
		In; On; Out (1/19)
		In; On; Over (5/19)
		In; On top of; In (1/19)
		In; Over; In (1/19)
		In; Over; On (1/19)
		Down; On; Over (1/19)
Image Set 6: The bowl is _____ the table.	On (Bowerman 1996b.)	**On (19/19)**
Image Set 7: The ring is _____ the finger.	On (Bowerman 1996a.)	**On (18/19)**
		Around (1/19)

In Image Set 5, the participants are being tested on their ability to differentiate between *in* and *on* scenes, using the common stimulus of a bowl of fruit, inspired by Coventry and Prat-Sala (2001) and subsequent research that uses this as its basis. In the first image, the conceptualization of CONTAINMENT is being elicited: the apple is alone in the bowl of fruit. In the second image, a seemingly impossible scenario is proposed: the apple that is balanced on the edge of a bowl of fruit. In the third image, a SUPPORT conceptualization is shown: the apple is balanced on top of a variety of fruit in a bowl. The participants gave a wide range of completions for these images, but the only two sets of completions that are used more than once are the expected sequence and a sequence that varies in only the final element. This result shows that these particular expectations of CONTAINMENT and SUPPORT are upheld in these data.

Finally, in Image Sets 6 and 7, the participants were being tested on their SUPPORT and encirclement conceptualizations of *on*, respectively. This is another area where there was nearly unanimous completion with the expected completions, with the sole deviation from the also acceptable 'around' completion of Image Set 7.

5.2 Roads conceptualization results

The Irish surface/container conceptualization alternation for roads occurred spontaneously in the conversation data.

(35) a. *Peter Finnegan's **in** Ludlow Street. (P003)*
b. *When I parked it here **in** Railway Street, where... where... ehm... where the carpet... whaddyacallit? Kelly's, is it? (P005)*
c. *And actually, we used to even put that on the paths **in** the street. (P006)*
d. *So there seems to be a very high cost to rent a property either **in** the main street or in the shopping centre. (P007)*
e. *Setting up business now **in** the main streets you'd nearly want your head examined, you know? (P008)*
f. *And it went through a bit of land that was owned by the VEC **in** Abbey Road. (P014)*
g. *Because I used to work here **in** Abbey Road and where this road joins here, you would say go out the Dublin Road. (P015)*
h. *No, **in** Ludlow Street in Navan. (P016)*
i. *Used to live **in** a little road called Portmarnock Grove. (P017)*
j. *Oh, it's certainly hurt the shops **in** Trimgate Street there alright. (P018)*
k. *As has happened **in** St Patrick's Terrace, which is just, if you're coming up the Boreen Keel and you go past that little playground. (P020)*

However, in these interview data, there are also a number of *on* conceptualizations. Looking at the examples of *on* spatial locators, some differentiation can be seen:

(36) a. *You had a gate there **on** Trimgate Street, that's one. (P008)*
b. *I would never have... it's probably... I'm more aware of it now since they opened the new retail park out there and because of that, because there are two retail parks, there's one **on** the Kells Road and one on the way out to Tara Mines. (P009)*
c. *It was originally in the Red Cross Centre which is a tiny little one-room community centre **on** Academy Road. (P011)*
d. *No, there none **on** the Naas Road. (P015)*

In the *in* examples, the participants are conceptualizing a pub (35a), a carpark (35b), a path (35c), a shop (35d), (35e), (35j), a school (35f), an office building (35g), and a home or homes (35h), (35i), (35k). Regarding the *on* conceptualizations, the participants are talking about a gate (36a), a retail park (36b), a community centre (36c), and a toll plaza (36d). The *in* conceptualizations are all permanent fixtures of the road: individual structures that cannot come and go, but are integral to the road. The *on* conceptualizations can refer to structures that are no longer in use (a disused gate into the town) and a relatively new structure (a toll plaza). We can see from the context that the community center (36b) was not always the community center, while the new retail park (36c) is by its nature a new feature of the road.

5.2.1 Questionnaire data (Image Set 8: The craft butcher's shop is _____ Trimgate Street.)

In designing the questionnaire, testing how the participants would conceptualize the relationships between roads and a shop seemed a logical visual enterprise. The participants' completions are listed below.

Table 6: Results of participants' CONTAINMENT & SUPPORT conceptualizations related to roads (Lucek 2015: 178).

P001	P002	P003	P004	P005	P006	P007	P008	P009	P010
in	on	on	on	on	in	in	on	located on	on
P011	P012	P013	P014	P015	P016	P017	P018	P019	P020
on	on	on	on	on	in	on	on	N/A	on the right hand side of

Fourteen of the participants completed with *on*, including one participant who completed with a more specific 'located on'. Four participants (P001, P006, P007 & P016) completed with *in*.

5.3 Media conceptualizations results

Similar to the roads conceptualization, the relationship between an article and the newspaper in which the article appears also occurred spontaneously in the interview data. While it is slightly more common to find the *in* conceptualization, as seen in (37a)–(37c), the *on* conceptualizations (37d)–(37f) are still found in these data, as seen below.

(37) a. *It was published **in** the Meath Chronicle. (P001)*
   b. *And it even said it **in** the paper, the Drogheda Argus, there was no Meath Chronicle yet, the Drogheda Argus said that the writing was on the wall for Pierce O'Mahoney. (P008)*
   c. *There was a picture of me **in** the paper playing rugby. (P016)*
   d. *And as I said to myself when I seen it on the radio and read it **on** the paper, 'what the hell are the police doing to allow him to sit in a courtroom, in front of a judge, and when sentence was being passed on him, he sat there, listening to the radio, didn't pass a remark'. (P005)*
   e. *I guess it was **on** the... I can't remember it. Oh, the Sunday Express. (P005)*
   f. *Then it appeared **on** the paper something I said about it. (P014)*

As in the Irish data, *in* conceptualizations above can be identified as a part/whole relationship while the *on* conceptualizations suggest a surface relationship.

6 Analysis

As noted above, the Irish language has a differentiation between objects or features of a road that are integral to the road itself and objects or features that are more temporary or new. This pattern is repeated in these data, using *in* for integral features (older structures) and using *on* for temporary elements of the road (newer structures). If we read these *in* data as an expression of metaphor, we can understand them as:

ROADS ARE CONTAINERS
Target domain: locations   Source domain: containers
Locations can be contained by borders.
Structures are part of a road.
"Jim lives outside of town."
"The butcher shop is in Trimgate Street."

This can be contrasted by the *on* reading:

ROADS ARE SURFACES
Target domain: locations   Source domain: surfaces
Locations are surfaces.
New structures are not integral to a road.
"This buggy is designed for off-roading."
"There are tolls on that road."

These metaphors may seem unnecessary to many English speakers, but the variation exists in Irish and as a result of contact, the differentiation between permanent and temporary/new exists in Irish English. In Irish, the butcher shop example becomes:

(38) The butcher shop   is in *Trimgate Street*
     An siopa búistéara   tá i Sráid Gheata Bhaille Átha Triom
     'Tá an siopa búistéara i Sráid Ghealta Bhaille Átha Triom.'[1]

We can also see how the tolls on the road example works:

(39) There are   tolls   on   that road
     TÁ   dolaí ar   sin   an mbóthar
     'Tá dolaí ar an mbóthar sin.'

Similarly, we have a media metaphor that functions along the same lines as the surface roads metaphor:

NEWSPAPERS ARE SURFACES
Target domain: newspapers   Source domain: surfaces
Newspapers are surfaces for ink.
Articles are printed on the surface of newspapers.
"There was an article on the newspaper last week."
"Then it appeared on the paper."

NEWSPAPERS ARE CONTAINERS
Target domain: newspapers   Source domain: containers
Newspapers are collections of articles.
Articles exist within the borders of a newspaper.
"I saw that in the paper last week."
"Then it appeared in the paper."

Only one of these metaphors is possible in Irish:

(40) *Bhí*   *an*   *scéal*   *ar*   *an*   *nuachtán*   *áitiúil*
     WAS   the   story   on   the   paper   local
     'The story was on the local paper.'

---

[1] The construction An siopa *búistéara* tá **ar Shráid** *Gheata Bhaile Átha Troim* may also be acceptable and is perhaps a further influence on Irish of an English construction.

(41) *Bhí   an   scéal   sa   nuachtán   áitiúil
    *WAS   DET   story   in-DET   paper   local
    *'The story was in the local paper.'

If we take Kövecses' (2005) position that variation in metaphor is an expression of cultural values, then the more Irish the metaphor, the more likely it is to be viewed as a marker of Irish English identity. That both Irish and non-Irish forms (this is an over-simplification, but pertinent within the context of the current discussion) exist simultaneously offers Irish English speakers the choice to ally themselves with more Irish metaphors and less Irish metaphors.

This option is not available for the roads conceptualizations. Rather, the expression of Irish culture here is the alternation between old and new structures.

7 Conclusions

The contact influences of Irish on Irish English can be seen in the prepositional usage and complex locative and media conceptualizations in these data. Elements of ON usage in our data match those described by Henry (1957), although they are more closely aligned to what Filppula (1999) has found. Moreover, the tests described in Bowerman (1996) are also confirmed as part of the Irish English experience of CONTAINMENT and SUPPORT. Where these data find their place in Cognitive Contact Linguistics is through the analysis of the locative and media data using CMT.

Future research should continue to evaluate variation at the level of conceptualization. This line of research can certainly focus at varieties of English. From the perspective of metaphor research, further tests to measure the acceptability rates and perceptions of use/users of these types of metaphors in Irish English can also provide valuable insights. This would include a larger sample that mixes generations as well as urban/rural backgrounds. Moreover, evaluating contact variation through a conceptual lens like Conceptual Metaphor Theory allows us to view these not as simple substitutions in varieties of a language, but rather as variation at the level of conceptualization: these are the speakers' experiential truths, roads and newspapers mean different things to different speakers. If we reject objective truths and work from the point of view of building conceptual systems from the bottom-up, then a usage-based model of conceptual variation can start to take shape. In this way, conceptual variation can be further investigated in contact varieties of a language, providing fertile ground for Cognitive Contact Linguistics to bear fruit.

References

Backus, Ad. 2014. Towards a usage-based account of language change: implications of contact linguistics for linguistic theory. In Robert Nicolaï (ed.), *Questioning Language Contact: Limits of Contact, Contact as its Limits*, 91–118. Leiden, NL: Brill.

Bowerman, Melissa. 1996. The origins of children's spatial semantic categories: Cognitive versus linguistic determinants. In John J. Gumperz & Stephen C. Levinson (eds.), *Rethinking Linguistic Relativity*, 145–176. Cambridge: Cambridge University Press.

Coventry, Kenny R. & Merce Prat-Sala. 2001. Object-specific function, geometry and the comprehension of "in" and "on". *European Journal of Cognitive Psychology* 13. 509–528.

Cussen, Gerard Mannes. 1920. *A Study of the Irish Prepositions: Founded on the Best Folklore and Literary Sources*. Dublin: Browne and Nolan ltd.

Feist, Michele I. & Dedre Gentner. 2003. Factors involved in the use of in and on. *Proceedings of the Twenty-fifth Annual Meeting of the Cognitive Science Society*.

Filppula, Markku. 1999. *The Grammar of Irish English: Language in Hibernian style*. London: Routledge.

Galal, Mohamed M. 2014. Death euphemism in English and Arabic: A Conceptual Metaphorization approach. *International Journal of Linguistics* 6(1). 153–170.

Garrod, Simon, Gillian Ferrier & Siobhan Campbell. 1999. In and on: Investigating the functional geometry of spatial prepositions. *Cognition* 72. 167–189.

Gibbs, Raymond W. 2011. Evaluating Conceptual Metaphor Theory. *Discourse Processes* 48. 529–562.

Harris, John. 1993. The grammar of Irish English. In James Milroy & Lesley Milroy (eds.), *Real English: The Grammar of English Dialects in the British Isles*, 139–186. London: Routledge.

Henry, Patrick L. 1957. *An Anglo-Irish Dialect of North Roscommon*. Dublin: University College, Dublin.

Herskovits, Annette. 1986. *Language and Spatial Cognition: An Interdisciplinary Study of the Prepositions in English*. Cambridge: Cambridge University Press.

Hickey, R. 2007. *Irish English: History and Present-day Forms*. Cambridge: Cambridge University Press.

Kallen, Jeffrey L. 1991. Sociolinguistic variation and methodology: after as a Dublin variable. In Jenny Cheshire (ed.), *English around the World: Sociolinguistic Perspectives*, 61–74. Cambridge: Cambridge University Press.

Kallen, Jeffrey L. 1994. English in Ireland. In Robert Burchfield (ed.), *The Cambridge History of the English Language*, Vol. 5, 148–196. Cambridge: Cambridge University Press.

Kövecses, Zoltán. 2005. *Metaphor in Culture: Universality and Variation*. Cambridge: Cambridge University Press.

Kövecses, Zoltán. 2006. *Language, Mind, and Culture: A Practical Introduction*. Oxford: Oxford University Press.

Labov, William. 1966. *The Social Stratification of English in New York City*. Washington, D.C.: Center for Applied Linguistics.

Lakoff, George & Mark Johnson. 1999. *Philosophy in the Flesh: The Embodied Mind and its Challenge to Western Thought*. New York: Basic Books.

Lakoff, George & Mark Johnson. 2003. *Metaphors we Live by*, 2nd edn. Chicago: University of Chicago Press.

Lee, Amy P. 2011. Metaphorical euphemisms of RELATIONSHIP and DEATH in Kavalan, Paiwan, & Seediq. *Oceanic Linguistics* 50(2). 351–379.

Lehiste, Ilse. 1988. *Lectures on Language Contact*. Cambridge: MIT Press.

Levinson, Stephen C. 2006. The language of space in Yélî Dnye. In Stephen C. Levinson & David P. Wilkins (eds.), *Grammars of Space*, 157–205. Cambridge: Cambridge University Press.

Levinson, Stephen C. & David P. Wilkins (eds.). 2006. *Grammars of Space*. Cambridge: Cambridge University Press.

Lucek, Stephen. 2015. *Talking about Space: The Spatial Reference System of Irish English*. Unpublished PhD Thesis, Trinity College Dublin.

Lucek, Stephen. 2017. UPtown and DOWNtown: the INs and OUTs of how Navan residents conceptualise the town where they live. *English Language Research* 2, 106–125.

Matsui, Keiko. 1995. Metaphors of anger in Japanese. In John R. Taylor & Robert E. MacLaury (eds.), *Language and the Cognitive Construal of the World*. Berlin: Mouton de Gruyter.

Moylan, Séamas. 1996. *The Language of Kilkenny: Lexicon, Semantics, Structures*. Dublin: Geography Publications.

Odlin, Terence. 1997. Hiberno-English: pidgin, creole, or neither. *CLCS Occasional Paper No. 49*. Dublin: Centre for Language and Communication Sciences, Trinity College Dublin.

Odlin, Terene. 2009. Methods and inferences in the study of substrate influence. In Markku Filpulla, Juhani Klemola & Heli Paulasto (eds.), *Vernacular Universals and Language Contacts: Evidence from Varieties of English and Beyond*, 265–279. London: Routledge.

Siemund, Peter. 2004. Substrate, superstrate and universals: Perfect constructions in Irish English. In Bernd Kortmann (ed.), *Dialectology meets Typology: Dialect grammar from a Cross-linguistic Perspective*, 401–434. Berlin: Mouton de Gruyter.

Tagliamonte, Sali A. 2006. *Analysing Sociolinguistic Variation*. Cambridge: Cambridge University Press.

Taylor, John R. & Thandi G. Mbense. 1998. Red dogs and rotten mealies: How Zulus talk about anger. In Angeliki Athanasiadou & Elżbieta Tabakowska (eds.), *Speaking of Emotions: Conceptualization and Expression*, 191–226. Berlin: Mouton de Gruyter.

Van Staden, Miriam, Melissa Bowerman & Mariet Verhelst. 2006. Some properties of spatial descriptions in Dutch. In Stephen C. Levinson & David P. Wilkins (eds.), *Grammars of Space*, 475–511. Cambridge: Cambridge University Press.

Yu, Ning. 1998. *The Contemporary Theory of Metaphor in Chinese: A Perspective from Chinese*. Amsterdam: John Benjamins.

Zenner, Eline. 2013. *Cognitive Contact Linguistics. The Macro, Meso and Micro Influence of English on Dutch*. Unpublished PhD Thesis, KU Leuven.

Anna Finzel and Hans-Georg Wolf
6 Conceptual metaphors as contact phenomena? The influence of local concepts on source and target domain

Abstract: This chapter suggests that conceptual metaphors in World Englishes constitute contact phenomena, albeit more covert ones than code-switching or lexical borrowing, for example. Since "the most fundamental values in a culture will be coherent with the metaphorical structure of the most fundamental concepts in the culture" (Lakoff and Johnson 1980: 22), metaphors in World Englishes within multilingual settings must be shaped through contact with local and culturally salient concepts. Examining metaphors in the light of Cognitive Contact Linguistics thus means turning towards the concepts through which speakers understand the world, because these concepts underlie and influence the meaning of linguistic forms.

A few studies inspired by Cognitive Linguistics have already confirmed this point. For example, Schmid et al. (2008: 93) find that "[s]witching to and fro between languages as they move through their daily lives, [Nigerian English] speakers have to juggle ideas and concepts from totally different historical and cultural contexts". In an attribute-listing task, the authors identified concepts connected to lexemes in Nigerian English and established that these diverge from the concepts in American English (also see Ibriszimov et al. 2005; Ibriszimov and Zulyadaini 2009). Hence, so-called blended concepts have emerged in World Englishes, which – as they contribute to the meaning making of conceptual metaphors – have an impact on the metaphors themselves. These blended concepts consist of two or more input concepts that derive from both local and foreign concepts, the latter implemented through colonisation and/ or globalisation.

In this chapter, three metaphors described in Finzel and Wolf (2017) – A WOMAN IS A WITCH, A WOMAN IS AN OBJECT AND THE PROPERTY OF A MAN and HOMOSEXUALITY IS A DISEASE – are analysed in more detail with respect to the source and target concepts involved. They are cross-checked with the help of an online survey among speakers of British, Indian and Nigerian English that features an association task, an item-linking task and a perceived-strength-of-connection task. All the tasks focus on the source concept WITCH and the target

---

Anna Finzel and Hans-Georg Wolf, University of Potsdam

https://doi.org/10.1515/9783110619430-007

concepts WOMAN and HOMOSEXUALITY. The results shed light on the questions of whether the concepts under scrutiny are blended concepts in Indian and Nigerian English, to what extent word forms in World Englishes have been culturally adapted to local contexts and whether other social factors also play a role.

Keywords: conceptual metaphors, gender metaphors, World Englishes, blended concepts, Cognitive Sociolinguistics, online survey

1 Introduction

Over the past decades, contact linguistics has had a strong focus on contact phenomena such as code-switching or lexical borrowing, in which the impact of contact can easily be observed on the linguistic surface. The first of these phenomena is illustrated in example (1), which demonstrates an instance of code-switching between English and Yoruba, and the second one in example (2), which features lexical borrowing from Hindi into English.

(1) "... I hit him! Ha-ya that was a good one, right on his face... *Ole! E fi'gbati fun yeye!* [Thief! Give the bastard some slaps!]." (Bamiro 2006: 28)

(2) In an industry where the dance director is God and *chalu* [cunning] music adds up to instant popularity of a film, 'Astitva' comes as a breath of fresh air. (Sedlatschek 2009: 57)

However, contact does not only take place on the surface, but also on the conceptual level. Traditional Contact Linguistics had long neglected the conceptual system as a locus of contact. At the same time, even though Cognitive Linguistics by its very nature focused on the conceptual system, it did not pay much attention to the role of linguistic or cultural contact. However, in recent years, some approaches have explicitly turned towards the consolidation of Contact Linguistics and Cognitive Linguistics, which is grasped by the notion of Cognitive Contact Linguistics, as described in Zenner (2013). With respect to lexical borrowing she suggests to expand the scope and to turn away from a "focus on single words and to include a wider, onomasiological perspective in which attention is paid to the concept expressed by the loanword and to alternative (receptor language) lexicalisations for that concept" (Zenner 2013: 30).

The 'concept' is one of the central notions in Cognitive Linguistics and is understood as an abstract mental representation of a linguistic symbol (see Evans and Green 2006: 7). Though not clearly delineated in Cognitive Linguistics,[1] in a Langackerian sense, a concept is part of a conceptual domain which "covers a range of types of cognitive entities, from mental experiences, to representational spaces, concepts, or conceptual complexes" (Cienki 2007: 182). Although the important role of culture with regard to concepts was mentioned early by Lakoff and Johnson (1980: 22) when they stated that "the most fundamental values in a culture will be coherent with the metaphorical structure of the most fundamental concepts in the culture", it has only recently become a major concern in Cognitive Linguistics and cognate disciplines. This interest in particular has pushed forward two branches of Cognitive Linguistics, namely Cultural Linguistics and Cognitive Sociolinguistics. Both subfields highlight that "[c]ulture [...] is not an external category in linguistic investigations [but] an integral dimension of it" (Wolf and Polzenhagen 2009: 19). It is assumed that the concepts individual speakers employ derive from a shared knowledge of a particular speech community (cf. Sharifian 2015). The focus on speech communities makes the varieties of English a more than rich source for observing contact at the conceptual level. Although the same linguistic forms exist across varieties (the so-called 'common core'), their meaning may differ from variety to variety (or from speech community to speech community), since speakers tend to incorporate ideas from the local context into their conceptual set-up (also see Kövecses 2005).

This idea was shown to be true in an interesting study by Schmid et al. (2008) in which the authors address so-called 'blended concepts' which emerge in linguistic and cultural contact situations. Such blended concepts incorporate ideas from several concepts. For instance, in contact situations where English is the L2, English lexemes are likely to develop a meaning that deviates from the meaning of the same word in a native variety. In their study, an attribute-listing task was conducted with Nigerian English speakers who "[s]witching to and fro between languages [...] have to juggle ideas and concepts from totally different historical and cultural contexts" (Schmid et al. 2008: 93). Nevertheless, the conceptual 'blendedness' comes in different degrees: While the concept CAP in Nigerian English has more similarities with the concept in Hausa as opposed to the concept in American English, there are no considerable differences with regard to AIRPLANE between Nigerian English and American English (cf. Schmid et al. 2008: 96–98). In the task, the concepts that are associated with some lexemes in Nigerian English were tested by having the informants list attributes that they associate with certain words. The authors found that in the context

---

1 However, in Cognitive Linguistics and also Cultural Linguistics, the broader and more dynamic notion of 'conceptualisation' is preferred, "defined as any kind of mental experience" (Langacker 2007: 431; also see Sharifian 2015: 477).

of Northern Nigeria, most of the concepts attributed to the tested lexemes in Nigerian English are influenced by concepts from Hausa culture. For example, English *cap* and Hausa *hula* – a local traditional headgear – are given as direct translations in dictionaries. However, the results of the study showed that the concept that Nigerian English speakers associate with *cap* seems to be a conceptual blend between the concept associated with *hula* in Hausa and the concept associated with *cap* in American English, which includes references to a baseball cap. Hence, Schmid et al. (2008) conclude that Nigerian English speakers have a blended concept of CAP in mind. Concrete questions that occur with blended concepts include, for instance, the independence of a blended concept from its input concepts and the type of information that the input concepts contribute as well as the degree to which lexemes in L2 varieties of English are conceptually adapted to the local context.

The question that we particularly address in this paper is whether the concepts associated with three English words – *witch*, *woman* and *homosexuality* – differ across British English, Indian English and Nigerian English. Our findings will show that this is the case in general, although some similarities do exist. In the discussion, we will offer some explanations for the most striking results that emerge due to cultural context. Furthermore, we suggest that conceptual metaphors possibly are contact phenomena in which the result of contact is not as obvious as when compared to phenomena like code-switching or lexical borrowing, because contact is effective at the level of the source and / or target concept and not at the level of the lexicon. These concepts are shared by a majority of speakers of the same speech community, as they derive from culture-specific ways to construe reality. In World Englishes settings, where for most speakers English is an L2 variety, it is therefore likely that metaphorical expressions in English draw their meaning from blended concepts and hence evoke different mappings. Cross-cultural metaphor variation could thus be an indicator of contact-induced variation.

2 Methodology

2.1 Examined concepts

For this paper, an online survey that focused on three particular concepts was conducted: WITCH, WOMAN and HOMOSEXUALITY. These concepts are involved as either source domain (WITCH) or target domain (WOMAN, HOMOSEXUALITY) in three conceptual metaphors that were found in a corpus of British, Indian and Nigerian films. For the construction of the tasks that we conducted, we strongly relied on Finzel and Wolf (2017). The metaphors are described in detail there, so we will only give a brief overview of them here.

Firstly, the metaphor A WOMAN IS A WITCH was instantiated in a British as well as in a Nigerian film. After a closer analysis of the mappings, it was shown that the metaphor was based on two very different cultural models of WITCHCRAFT in the two films respectively. On the one hand, the metaphor in the British film drew its meaning from a European model of WITCHCRAFT, going back to medieval and early modern notions in which witches ride on broomsticks and have a pact with Satan. As was suggested, this model is 'frozen' as witchcraft is not an everyday issue in the Western context and hence does not undergo change. On the other hand, the metaphor in the Nigerian film was based on the West African model of WITCHCRAFT (which is also described in Wolf and Polzenhagen 2009), in which witches are considered to be part of the community and in which witchcraft may be seen as the reason for unfortunate events. Hence, witchcraft in the West African context is a very salient and dynamic issue. These differences were the reason to examine the concept WITCH in British English and Nigerian English speakers more closely.

Secondly, the metaphor A WOMAN IS AN OBJECT AND THE PROPERTY OF A MAN appeared in an Indian film that deals with the topic of honour killings. The model that justifies the murder in the film is ZAN–ZAR–ZAMEEN, also a well-known idiom in India and Pakistan. It means 'women, gold, land', referring to the three possessions of a man for which he may kill in order to protect them. This model is still the cause of a considerable number of homicides in India (cf. Marwah 2014). The concept WOMAN was therefore also part of the survey to see whether such conceptualisations would play a role for Indian English speakers.

Thirdly, an Indian film dealing with homosexuality, which is still a taboo topic in Indian society, contributed the metaphor HOMOSEXUALITY IS A DISEASE. We therefore decided to include the concept HOMOSEXUALITY in our survey in order to see whether Indian English speakers would actually relate to ideas about DISEASE when confronted with it. The concept in the Indian culture(s) (as an overarching generalisation) is likely to be influenced through contact with British rule, as homosexuality was not illegal in India until 1860, when the colonisers introduced laws that prohibited homosexual acts (cf. Hunt 2011); Section 377 of the Indian Penal Code, which criminalises homosexuality, is still in effect (Wikipedia 2017). Prior to British rule, homosexuality was socially more accepted (e.g., it is even mentioned in the Kama Sutra).

At the same time, it was illegal in Britain and also treated as a disease up until the end of the 20th century. On that basis, we assumed that the concept of HOMOSEXUALITY among Indian English speakers is influenced by conceptualisations related to DISEASE.

Moreover, it has to be mentioned that although in our survey the inclusion of the concept WITCH was predominantly targeted towards British and Nigerian English speakers and WOMAN and HOMOSEXUALITY towards Indian English speakers, these concepts were tested with all participants, since we did not want to miss any interesting contrasts. We were particularly concerned with the question to what extent the local context has impacted on the concepts. If there was a difference between speakers of British, Indian and Nigerian English, i.e. if the concepts were locally adapted, then metaphors involving such concepts could also be seen as contact phenomena.

2.2 Survey

The current survey of speakers of British, Indian, and Nigerian English which examined the three concepts WITCH, WOMAN, and HOMOSEXUALITY was conducted online and featured three types of tasks. The survey questions were arranged according to concept (and not according to task), so that participants first saw the three tasks related to WITCH, then the three related to WOMAN and finally the three related to HOMOSEXUALITY. This served to keep conceptual interference to a minimum. Nevertheless, it is still possible that when presented with the second and third concepts, the informants had already established mental links with the concept(s) previously evoked.

An association task was modelled after Schmid et al. (2008) method (which in turn was itself an application of Rosch 1975). Participants were asked to list all attributes that they associate with the given concept. They were provided with a free-text field in which they could type in the association as a keyword or short sentence. After a text field was filled, a new one opened so as to not restrict participants in their number of answers.

After this, the informants saw an item-linking task, in which they were given a set of keywords for each concept. They were then asked to select the seven keywords they most associated with the given concept and also to rank them. In contrast to the association task, where free associations were possible, we pre-selected the keywords with a focus on the assumptions mentioned under 2.1. This procedure will be described in more detail in section 3.

The third task that was applied measured the perceived strength of connection. The keywords that the participants already knew from the item-linking task were listed and people were asked to indicate the strength of the link between the concept in question and the keyword. For this, they were offered to tick one of the following options: 'no link', 'weak link', 'medium link' and 'strong link' displayed next to the keyword.[2] The perceived-strength-of-connection task and the item-linking task were designed after similar tasks that Wolf and Polzenhagen (2009) had applied.

In total, there were nine experimental questions (three concepts and three task types), followed by a couple of questions on demographic data described below.

2.3 Informants

The link to the survey was circulated by contacting university staff in Great Britain, India and Nigeria, through personal contacts and also via the *International Gender and Language Association* mailing list. We explicitly requested our colleagues to forward the link to students, acquaintances and family. In total, we retrieved 48 usable questionnaires, 22 from the UK, 9 from India and 17 from Nigeria.[3]

Since some informants showed a higher degree of mobility inasmuch as they had moved to another country in the course of their lives, it is possible that conceptualisations from these new cultures have blended in. This especially concerns eight informants from the UK, possibly brought about by the EU common market. For British English, we therefore not only looked at the overall numbers, but also at variety-internal differences between 'resident' and 'mobile' speakers, i.e., speakers who have lived abroad for a longer period of time.

We also gathered information about other social variables for a more fine-grained analysis. Since the participants were relatively homogenous in terms of age[4] and level of education[5], these variables will not be considered further. Also, due to inconsistencies in the informants' self-assessment[6] and owing to the

---

[2] The four-point scale was chosen as representing the four most basic currents of opinion. A broader diversity of options might have confused, if not discouraged the participants.
[3] Due to the rather limited numbers, especially of Indian participants, these results are also limited in their generalisability.
[4] Most of the participants were between 25 and 40, and a smaller number between 41 and 65. These age groups were created due to assumed similar living standards caused by milestones such as graduation and career phases.
[5] With the exception of four people, everyone had at least a Bachelor's degree, which is probably due to the manner the link to the survey was spread. Especially in India and Nigeria, it seems impossible to reach less educated parts of society via an online survey. This was also mentioned by an Indian participant. Thus, further fieldwork *in situ* will be required in order to check the validity of the data.
[6] As the participants were allowed to insert a free-text assessment of their ethnicity, the instructions were not quite clear. For instance, some Indian informants wrote down 'Indian', whereas others stated their religion ('Indian Christian'), and some indicated their regional belonging ('Indo-Aryan'). Free text does not seem to be a useful method for assessing ethnicity.

dimensions of this study, ethnicity must be left out here, although it would surely be an interesting variable to include.

All in all, Indian and Nigerian participants were mostly male, while the majority of the UK participants was female. Owing to the gender-oriented topic of the examined concepts, we will also highlight possibly gender-induced conspicuousness in the responses. It is noteworthy that one person identified with a non-binary gender categorisation[7], which was unfortunately not large enough a number to open up a new gender category when cross-checking whether there were any variety-internal gender differences. Future studies could address this important issue.

With regard to the status of the respective varieties, English was the L1 of all British informants. For all but two[8] Nigerian informants, it was the L2 that followed particularly Yoruba and Igbo as L1s. The picture is more diverse for the Indian informants, who learnt English as an L1 as well as an L2 or L3. Besides a number of local languages, all but one also spoke Hindi fluently or at native speaker level.

3 Results

In what follows, we are going to present the results from the online survey for each of the three examined concepts. We will point out the findings and take these up again in the discussion.

As described above, for each concept three tasks were conducted: (1) The association task, in which informants gave keywords and short sentences that they associated with the concept; (2) the item-linking task, where pre-determined keywords were to be ranked according to which ones describe the given concept best; and (3) the perceived-strength-of-connection task, in which the same keywords as in (2) were displayed and these had to be judged with regard to their strength of connection to the concept. The keywords used for the item-linking task and perceived-strength-of-connection task partly referred to the metaphors analysed in Finzel and Wolf (2017; see section 2.1) in that they drew on the particular cultural models that were to be tested. Furthermore, additional keywords were added in order to both distract from the conceptualisation that was actually tested and also to widen the scope of the conceptualisations under scrutiny. These additional keywords are indicated below.

---

[7] In the *gender* field of the survey's sociodemographic section, the options 'female', 'male', 'other' and 'prefer not to answer' were given in order to avoid forcing a gender binarity.
[8] For these two, English was also the L1.

3.1 The concept WITCH

In Finzel and Wolf (2017), the metaphor A WOMAN IS A WITCH was used in the British film *Jane Eyre* (2011) and the Nigerian film *Half of a Yellow Sun* (2013), but its mappings vastly differed. In the British film the concept WITCH was based on a European model, while it expressed the West African model in the Nigerian film. Hence, the inclusion of this concept in the survey was aimed in particular at British English and Nigerian English speakers in order to determine to what extent the two models contribute to the meaning making processes with regard to the related concept.

Table 1 shows the results from the association task, in which the informants wrote down free associations that they had when thinking of *witch*. The associations were summarised in slightly more general categories.[9] If one compares the answers from the British English and Nigerian English speakers, it becomes obvious that the former primarily relate to the outer appearance of a witch (dressed in black, a prominent nose, a green face, long hair) and a number of attributes, such as a broomstick, a hat, a cauldron and a cat. Other mentions suggest that a witch is mostly seen as a fictitious character, for example from a film or a fairy tale, or as a potential costume for Halloween. There were also some references to actual witch-hunts that took place in the UK. Moreover, although a witch is regarded as scary, it is also acknowledged that it might be a creature that is misunderstood; this probably refers to historical accounts of innocent women being accused of witchcraft during the Early Modern period. There are also a few similarities with the Nigerian English concept of WITCH. The speakers of both varieties agree that a witch has supernatural, possibly evil power, is ill-natured and is a woman. In terms of hybrid concepts, the gender association 'female' is particularly interesting. At least in some African languages, terms denoting persons with supernatural powers are gender-neutral (see Wolf and Polzenhagen 2009: 128); the influence of the meaning of the term *witch* in English most likely has had an influence on the nature of the concept in Nigerian English. On the other hand, apart from the belief that a witch is ugly, the Nigerian English concept draws less on the outer appearance. Instead, it emphasises *how* a witch functions (in the spiritual realm, through a pact with Satan or with the help of covens or rituals) and what this entails (being possessed and ungodly). Most associations, however, stress that a witch is preeminently harmful to other people, for instance through sucking blood, causing accidents or as a misfortune carrier. Incidentally, the associations of the Indian English speakers rather resemble the ones of the British English speakers.

---

[9] This summary was done by the first author through qualitative analysis. For instance, the mentions 'crooked nose', 'point nose' and 'a big nose' were all summarised under the category *prominent (ugly) nose*. Unique and therefore possibly idiosyncratic mentions are not displayed in the table.

Table 1: Results from the association task for the concept WITCH. The weight value indicates the likeliness of each informant to mention the given association (weight = frequency : N/100). Table design adapted from Schmid et al. (2008).

WITCH

British English (N = 22)			Indian English (N = 9)			Nigerian English (N = 17)		
association	freq.	weight	association	freq.	weight	association	freq.	weight
broomstick	9	0.41	fictitious character	5	0.56	harmful	13	0.77
fictitious character	9	0.41	with supernatural (evil) power	3	0.33	with supernatural (evil) power	7	0.41
hat	9	0.41	woman	3	0.33	ill-natured	7	0.41
with supernatural (evil)			misunderstood	2	0.22	woman	6	0.35
power	8	0.36	old	2	0.22	spirit(ual) / supernatural	5	0.29
woman	7	0.32				diabolic / in pact with Satan	4	0.24
prefers black clothing	5	0.23				ugly	2	0.12
prominent (ugly) nose	4	0.18				coven / ritual	2	0.12
witch-hunt	4	0.18				possessed	2	0.12
scary	4	0.18				ungodly	2	0.12
(black) cat	3	0.14						
cauldron	3	0.14						
Halloween	3	0.14						
(long, black) hair	2	0.09						
green face	2	0.09						
ill-natured	2	0.09						
misunderstood	2	0.09						

In the item-linking task, the respondents were given a number of keywords and asked to rank them in regard to which ones best describe a witch. There were in total 19 keywords, six of them particularly addressing the European model of WITCHCRAFT (*broomstick, concoction, outsider of society, Satan, sinner, stake*), seven of them the West African model (*educated, family, infertility, medicine, member of society, unmarried, voodoo*) and six of them as rather universal additional keywords (*evil, female, good, human, male, scary*).[10]

It turned out that in all three varieties the items *female, evil* and *scary* rank among the top seven (cf. Table 2). While again British English and Indian English share a couple of features pertaining to the European model (*broomstick, concoction* and *outsider of society*), the Nigerian English ranking integrates Western beliefs about witchcraft (*Satan* and *sinner*), while at the same time includes characteristics from the West African model (a witch as a *member of society* using *voodoo*). Although not shown in Table 2 due to its overall ranking, it needs to be mentioned that *infertility* was among the top ranks for both female Indian English and female Nigerian English speakers.

Table 2: Results from the item-linking task for the concept WITCH. *Evil* and *outsider of society*, as well as *outsider of society* and *good* obtained the same rank.

Rank ↓	British English	Indian English	Nigerian English
1	female	female	evil
2	broomstick	broomstick	scary
3	human	evil	Satan
4	concoction	concoction	female
5	evil	scary	sinner
6	outsider of society	Satan	member of society
7	scary	outsider of society	voodoo
		good	

In the perceived-strength-of-connection task, the participants saw the same keywords and were asked to indicate how strongly they connected each given keyword to *witch*. This provided us with mean values of the perceived strength of connection for every keyword with *witch*. These values are displayed in Figure 1 in which 1.0 denotes no connection and 4.0 a strong connection, with 3.0 marking a medium link and thus separating weak from strong.

---

10 The majority of keywords were taken from the analysis in Finzel and Wolf (2017), where they were, for instance, mappings of the metaphors in question. Further keywords that seemed interesting within the context of the research questions addressed in this paper complemented the list.

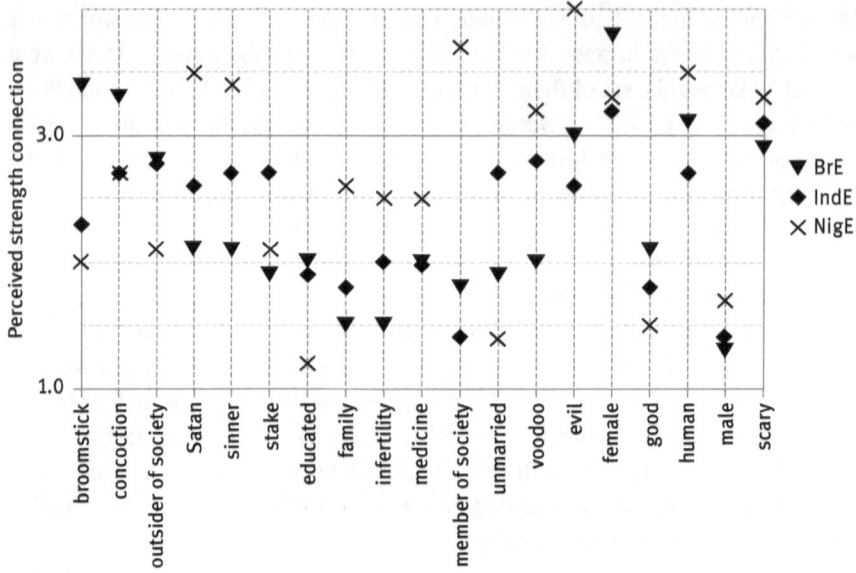

Figure 1: Results from the perceived-strength-of-connection task for the concept WITCH.

Although the first six keywords are taken from the European model of WITCH-CRAFT, British English speakers perceive only two of them as strongly connected (*broomstick* and *concoction*), while Nigerian English speakers also rate two of them above the 3.0 line (*Satan* and *sinner*). The next seven words draw on the West African model and the difference here is somewhat more explicit, because the British English rating does not exceed the border between strong and weak, whereas the keywords *member of society* and *voodoo* are strongly linked with *witch* for Nigerian English speakers. The last group of words is overall perceived as having a relatively strong link by all speakers, with exception of *good* and *male* that seem to have no relevant link. Another interesting observation can be made in respect of *infertility*. Having a mean value of 2.5 in Nigerian English, it scored only 2.2 among male speakers, whereas in contrast female speakers rated it with 3.3.

3.2 The concept WOMAN

The second part of the survey specifically targeted the concept WOMAN. This part was based on the occurrence of the metaphor A WOMAN IS AN OBJECT AND THE PROPERTY OF A MAN in the Indian film *Land Gold Women* (2011), analysed in Finzel and Wolf (2017) and hence tested the degree to which OBJECT was a salient domain in connection to WOMAN.

As becomes clear from Table 3, the answers to the association task did not exhibit any notable conceptualisation of woman as object or property. The majority of associations of the Indian English speakers are based on a more affective, traditional image of women, as indicated by the categories *beauty / pleasant appearance*, *family*, *motherhood*, *loving / caring*, *emotional* and *nurturing*. This tendency also applies to British English and Nigerian English speakers. In contrast, the categories *strong* and *equality* hint to an awareness of female emancipation among the Indian English speakers in the present survey.

In the item-linking task there were again twenty predetermined keywords that the participants saw and were supposed to rank. Eight of them were taken from the model of ZAN–ZAR–ZAMEEN as described in section 2.1 (*family, honour, land, object, possession, precious, protection, sacrifice*), six of them (as additional keywords) referred to ideas related to female independence and autonomy (*autonomy, career, education, freedom, strength, work*), and the remaining six (also as additional keywords) to rather passive, traditional or stereotypical roles (*bearer of sin, beauty, marriage, victim, weakness, widow*). Table 4 shows that although Indian English speakers actually rank three words pertaining to ZAN–ZAR–ZAMEEN high (though admittedly, *family* is a rather general item), there are also three words from the independence / autonomy category in the charts. As opposed to this, Nigerian English speakers appear to have the most conservative view on women, with only *strength* indicating a more autonomous role of women. Remarkably, *honour* is ranked high in Nigerian English as well. It is striking that *beauty* seems to be an important feature of women for all informants, suggesting a universal characteristic, at least for the three cultures in question, as well as the sociodemographic groups to which the survey was limited.

Again, the same keywords were given in the perceived-strength-of-connection task in which the strength of connection to *woman* had to be indicated for each keyword. Figure 2 shows the results with the value 3.0 again signalling the boundary between strong and weak link. It is interesting to note that Indian English speakers generally perceive a stronger connection for the ZAN–ZAR–ZAMEEN keyword group, apart from *land* and *object*. It also has to be noted, though, that both items received relatively high ratings from the female participants, which were then downscaled by the male ratings (for *land*, 3.0 versus 1.3; for *object*, 3.7 versus 1.7). Nigerian English speakers as well show a tendency of rating some the words from this group high, albeit to a lesser degree. The second word group appertaining to the field of independence and autonomy is overall perceived as having a strong connection to *woman*, with Indian English having the highest ratings and Nigerian English the lowest. In the last word group, it is especially *beauty* and *marriage* that are rated high and therefore stand out.

Table 3: Results from the association task for the concept WOMAN. The weight value indicates the likeliness of each informant to mention the given association (weight = frequency : N/100). Table design adapted from Schmid et al. (2008).

			WOMAN					
British English (N = 22)			Indian English (N = 9)			Nigerian English (N = 17)		
association	freq.	weight	association	freq.	weight	association	freq.	weight
is a female person	8	0.36	strong	3	0.33	beauty / pleasant appearance	4	0.24
family	7	0.32	beauty / pleasant appearance	3	0.33	is a female person	4	0.24
partner	7	0.32	family	2	0.22	witch(craft)	4	0.24
strong	7	0.32	partner	2	0.22	love	3	0.18
motherhood	6	0.27	motherhood	2	0.22	family	2	0.12
beauty / pleasant appearance	5	0.23	loving / caring	2	0.22	loving / caring	2	0.12
clothing and makeup	5	0.23	emotional	2	0.22	emotional	2	0.12
body	4	0.18	nurturing	2	0.22	role in society	2	0.12
different from man	3	0.14	equality	2	0.22	weak	2	0.12
loving / caring	3	0.14				help mate	2	0.12
educated / intelligent	2	0.09						
emotional	2	0.09						
fertility	2	0.09						
human being	2	0.09						
nurturing	2	0.09						

Table 4: Results from the item-linking task for the concept WOMAN. *Strength* and *precious* obtained the same rank.

Rank ↓	British English	Indian English	Nigerian English
1	family	beauty	beauty
2	beauty	strength	marriage
3	strength	honour	family
4	education	sacrifice	strength
5	marriage	family	precious
6	autonomy	education	weakness
7	career	work	honour

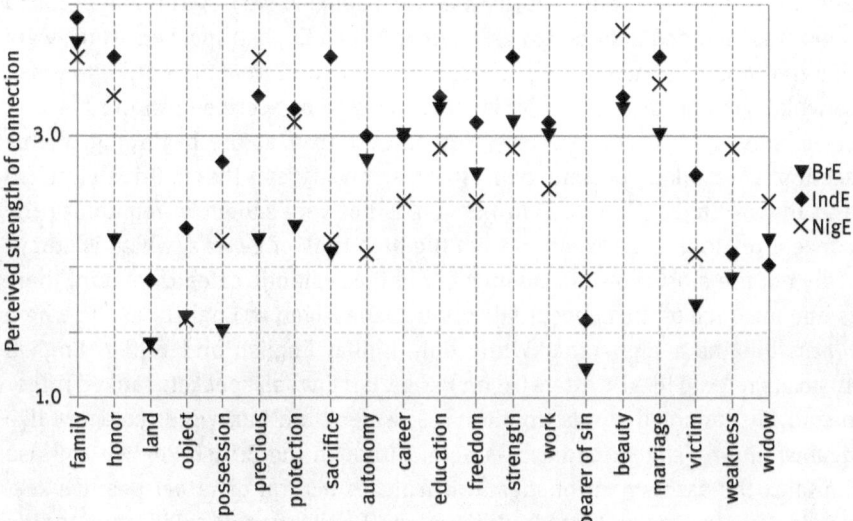

Figure 2: Results from the perceived-strength-of-connection task for the concept WOMAN.

3.3 The concept HOMOSEXUALITY

The inclusion of the concept HOMOSEXUALITY was driven by the occurrence of the metaphor HOMOSEXUALITY IS A DISEASE in the Indian film *Memories in March* (2010), as described in Finzel and Wolf (2017). The aim was to see whether this conceptualisation actually existed among Indian English speakers, and also whether it would be prevalent in British English or Nigerian English.

As is shown in Table 5, there were very few associations pertaining to the domain of DISEASE in the association task, with the exception of two mentions from Nigerian English speakers. Instead, the answers of Indian English and also British English informants represented the concept HOMOSEXUALITY with rather positive connotations. Apparently, it is perceived more negatively in Nigerian English.

The 23 keywords[11] given in the item-linking task contained seven words from the domain of HEALTH and DISEASE (*acquired, cure, doctor, genetic, health, illness, mind*), which were obviously intended to check the salience of the conceptualisation HOMOSEXUALITY IS A DISEASE. Five words tested the assessment of homosexuality (*against nature, destiny, normal, special, stigma*), three words were related to legal matters (*law, marriage, rights*) and five evoked buzzwords and stereotypes (*emotion, excess, lifestyle, rainbow, sex*). Additionally, *Kama Sutra* was included in order to see whether Indian English speakers were aware of a tradition of homosexual practices, and *man* and *woman* in order to grasp to which gender homosexuality is more likely to be ascribed. All but the first seven served as additional keywords as described at the beginning of this section. The ranking presented in Table 6 again suggests that in British English and Indian English the domain DISEASE is not very salient in relation to the concept HOMOSEXUALITY, apart from the high rank of *genetic*, which is admittedly not the most prototypical member of the semantic category. Again, there is one instance of the conceptualisation in the Nigerian English results where *illness* obtains a high rank. While only Indian English and British English speakers refer to legal matters (*rights*), Nigerian English speakers ranked rather negatively connoted words from the assessment and buzzwords category like *against nature*, *stigma* and *excess* high. Although the British English list also contains the assessment of *stigma*, it features neutral or rather positive keywords such as *normal*, *lifestyle* and *rainbow*. Similar can be said for the Indian English ranks with *emotion* on top.

Finally, the same keywords were again used for the perceived-strength-of-connection task. As the findings in Figure 3 indicate, the health and disease word group was all in all not judged as being very close to *homosexuality*. The trends from the item-linking task are visible in the perceived-strength-of-connection task as well, in which the British English and Indian English ratings are in favour of more neutral or positive keywords (e.g., *normal, rights*) and rather negatively connoted words have higher values among Nigerian English speakers (*against nature, excess*). *Sex* is apparently strongly connected to *homosexuality*

---

[11] There were actually 29 keywords in the survey, but six of them did not return very intriguing results, so they were left out here for the sake of brevity.

Table 5: Results from the association task for the concept HOMOSEXUALITY. The weight value indicates the likeliness of each informant to mention the given association (weight = frequency: N/100). Table design adapted from Schmid et al. (2008).

HOMOSEXUALITY								
British English (N = 22)			**Indian English (N = 9)**			**Nigerian English (N = 17)**		
association	freq.	weight	association	freq.	weight	association	freq.	weight
involving men	9	0.41	same-sex / same-gender relationship	2	0.22	revolting / something bad	7	0.41
same-sex / same-gender	8	0.36	equality / fight for rights	2	0.22	same-sex / same-gender relationship	5	0.29
relationship	7	0.32	normal	2	0.22	sin	5	0.29
equality / fight for rights	6	0.27	acceptable	2	0.22	abnormal	4	0.24
positive character traits	5	0.23				involving men	3	0.18
friend(ship) / family	3	0.14				unhealthy / insane	2	0.12
camp	3	0.14						
normal	2	0.09						
acceptable	2	0.09						
coming out	2	0.09						
feminine	2	0.09						
love / happiness	2	0.09						
sexuality is fluent	2	0.09						
involving women	2	0.09						

Table 6: Results from the item-linking task for the concept HOMOSEXUALITY. *Man* and *rainbow* obtained the same rank.

Rank ↓	British English	Indian English	Nigerian English
1	rights	emotion	against nature
2	normal	rights	sex
3	genetic	lifestyle	stigma
4	lifestyle	destiny	illness
5	stigma	genetic	man
6	man	sex	lifestyle
7	rainbow	rainbow	excess

in all varieties, as is *man*, whereas only in Indian English *woman* is perceived as having a stronger link. *Kama Sutra* turned out to have an overall weaker link, even though Indian English speakers most connect it to the given concept. Within the results from Indian English, there are greater gender differences for *emotion* and *lifestyle*, which have higher values for male participants (for *emotion*, 3.5 versus 2.3; for *lifestyle*, 3.5 versus 2.3), as opposed to *stigma* that is rather favoured by female participants (3.7 versus 2.2).

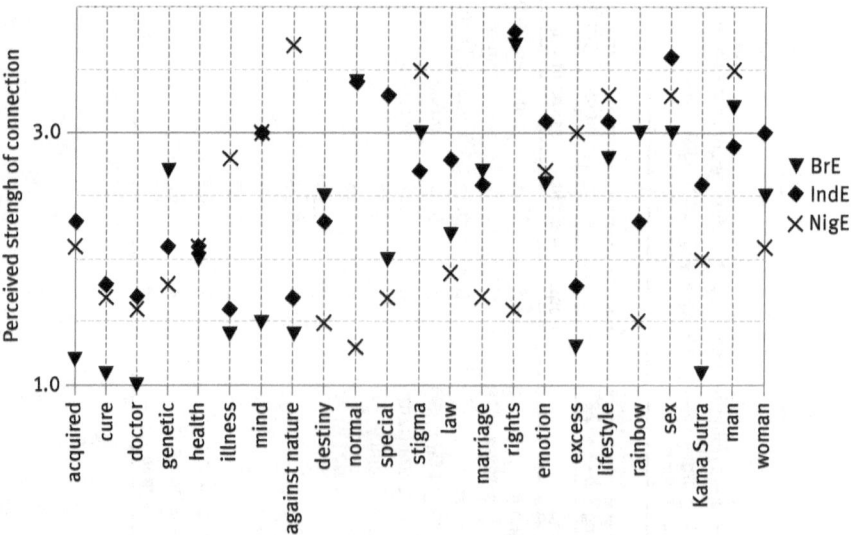

Figure 3: Results from the perceived-strength-of-connection task for the concept HOMOSEXUALITY.

4 Discussion

Our results suggest that there are in fact considerable differences with regard to the concept WITCH between British and Nigerian English. In particular, the association task showed that British informants mostly relate to the European model of WITCHCRAFT, with lots of references to fairy tales, the media or Halloween. The majority of associations involve features of outer appearance in that the stereotypical witch is supposed to have a green face, a prominent nose and long hair, while also in possession of a broomstick, a hat, a cat and a cauldron. This concept is surely influenced by popular fiction like, for instance, *The Wizard of Oz*.

In opposition, in Nigerian English the concept does not entail such associations. Instead, the focus is more on the harmfulness of a witch, i.e. what kind of damage is inflicted on other people or the social order and how, as well as on the reasoning that a witch has these supernatural powers because of a diabolic collaboration with Satan. The results from the item-linking task and perceived-strength-of-connection task confirm these tendencies, but are somewhat less definitive, as not all keywords from the European model were ranked high or perceived as strongly connected by the British respondents. The same holds true for the West African model and the Nigerian English informants. The presentation of other keywords in the task nevertheless might have delivered different results.

In contrast, the concept reflected in the answers of the Indian English speakers in the survey turns out to be closer to the British than the Nigerian one. This is not *per se* surprising, but the lack of distinctive characteristics suggests that witchcraft is not a very relevant issue in India, because otherwise there would be hints to a more culture-specific concept.

All in all, our assumption of an influence of local cultural models on concepts in varieties of English was mainly confirmed. The Nigerian concept lacks most of the features the British concept has, pointing to a completely different understanding of *witch* in the respective varieties of English. It was not confirmed that solely the European model would encompass Christian beliefs; while in our study the concept WITCH in British English lacks religious implications, the Nigerian English concept clearly incorporates them, as indicated by the salience of *Satan* and *sinner*. This goes in hand with what was suggested by Geschiere (1997), namely that the African model of witchcraft is a somewhat hybrid one that has been influenced by Western notions. So obviously, although the Nigerian concept is for the most part formed by the local context, Christian religion also plays a part,[12] while the British concept has lost its religious connotations.

---

[12] In this context, it is worth pointing to rapid rise and spread of Pentecostal churches in Nigeria as an important social and economic factor in the country (see, e.g., Diara and Onah 2014). For

Comments (3) and (4) below, which were left by Nigerian informants[13] at the end of the survey, corroborate this assumption and also allow one to assume that in Nigerian English, the concept WITCH has evolved into a distinct concept deviating from the one connected to *witch* in the native British English variety (lexical and spelling mistakes were not corrected):

(3) Witchcraftcy is any act against the word of God no matter how little it seems. The Bible says stubbornness is like witchcraft. A person who wants to have his / her way resolves to doing so many things which could range from manipulation, intimidation or possession. All these are witchcraft strategies. Women are mostly involved in witchcraftcy because of their subtleness but it does not mean men are not involved.

(4) The witch in Igbo culture is always portrayed as an old woman. She is seen as a malevolent spirit. The spirit of the witch can be transferred to an innocent person through gifts offered by the witch. When this happens, it is said that the person has been initiated.

With regard to the concept WOMAN, we were particularly interested in whether the model of ZAN–ZAR–ZAMEEN would play a role for Indian English speakers. This could not be confirmed through the association task, as there were no such associations. The same applies to the British and the Nigerian English concept. In the item-linking task, it was remarkable that *honour* ranked high in Indian English and Nigerian English. In the perceived-strength-of-connection task, some keywords related to ZAN–ZAR–ZAMEEN, namely *family*, *precious*, *protection* and *honour* stood out in Indian English (the first three also in Nigerian English) and also *possession* was perceived as strongly connected to *woman* – surely the most palpable indicator of the influence of the model. Furthermore, the values of the female Indian participants were high for *land* and *object* as well. In sum, there is evidence that the model of ZAN–ZAR–ZAMEEN has an impact on the Indian English concept to a certain extent. It might be the case that the impact is larger when including more speakers with a lower educational background.

In general, there are some differences between the varieties: The British English and Indian English concept of WOMAN are similar, as they both entail

---

a further discussion of the relation between Christianity and witchcraft in West African contexts and specifically the role of Pentecostalism, see Wolf and Polzenhagen (2009: 108–109).

[13] The Nigerian informants left most insightful comments at the end of the survey. Although the Indian and British participants also commented, they were less concerned with cultural notes than with explanations on their answers.

ideas about female autonomy and self-determination.[14] On the other hand, the Indian English concept is dichotomous inasmuch as it also hints to a more traditional view on women. This is also the case with the Nigerian concept, which overall appears to reflect the most conservative view on women. Considering the following comment from a Nigerian participant, this is not surprising:

(5) The woman in Igbo culture is traditionally seen as a beautiful object to be possessed by man. She lacks total independence. Every girl of marriageable age is expected by tradition to be married. Unmarried girls are not respected. The woman cannot possess landed property.

This comment also explains the closeness of the Nigerian concept to the Indian one, although in light of comment (5), it is remarkable that not more connections from WOMAN to PROPERTY were drawn.

Another question we addressed was whether Indian English speakers would relate to DISEASE when assessing their concept of HOMOSEXUALITY, on the assumption that the imposition of British rule might have had an impact on the concept in India. Nevertheless, our findings entail that HOMOSEXUALITY is not prominently conceptualised as DISEASE in Indian English, and neither in British English. Although in both varieties, *genetic* was among the top ranks in the association task, it is probably one of the less unequivocal keywords. The same can be said about the perceived-strength-of-connection task, in which only *mind* from the domain of HEALTH and DISEASE received a high value among Indian English speakers. Thus, the concept is apparently not as negatively connoted as one might expect, given the legislation regarding homosexuality in India.

In turn, there seems to be a link to DISEASE in Nigerian English. In all three tasks, one can find references and connections to such ideas, as well as a generally negative assessment. This might be caused by prohibitive laws and practices in Nigeria – though one wonders why that would not be the case in India (see above) – that disapprove of homosexuality, a fact that is also contemplated by four informants in the comments section of the survey:

(6) You should understand that Homosexuality is an offence punishable by law in Nigeria. [...] You must also not that the country is largely religious, and none of the recognised religions here preach, permit or even tolerate homosexuality.

---

14 Ironically, it is a former Canadian porn star of Indian descent – Sunny Leone – who is considered the figure head of women's growing emancipation in India today (see Singh Sawhney 2017).

(7) The Igbo Culture abhors homosexuality. It is an abominable act and offenders are banished from the land. The Igbo people do not believe that homosexuality is a medical condition.

(8) Homosexual is outrightly evil.

(9) I don't want to even talk about homosexuality because it is the fulfillment of the scriptures "as it was in the days of Sodom and Gomorha so shall it be" men have forsaken natural affection to run after strange flesh.

In the light of our results, (7) is surprising as it actually supposes that the link to health and disease does not exist. A comparison of the answers in terms of ethnicity sheds slightly more light on the matter, since four of the six Igbo informants (including the Ikwerre subgroup) perceived no or only a weak link between *illness* and *homosexuality*, which was also the case for the Urhobo participant. On the contrary, the connection was perceived as medium or strong by four out of six Yoruba respondents, and also by both Edo participants. It could be a fruitful endeavour to examine these ethnic differences more closely.

Lastly, it is interesting to see that Indian English speakers perceive a hint of a connection to *Kama Sutra*, which could indicate that they are aware of homosexual practices being mentioned in the Kama Sutra, and thus pertaining to an Indian model that is or used to be more tolerant towards homosexuality.

Overall, variety-internal differences between resident and mobile informants were not that substantial in our study. Similar can be said about gender-induced variation, although there were a few differences between men and women. However, the differences in our findings seem to be mostly caused by variation between the three varieties. All of this goes hand in hand with the assumption that it is especially the cultural contact situation which shapes the concepts speakers of World Englishes have.

Although this study differs from Schmid et al. (2008) in that it does not account for locally competing concepts (e.g., the concepts of the same speakers in Nigerian English as well as in Hausa, compared to the concepts of American English speakers), it still permits a couple of conclusions concerning the notion of the blended concept. Firstly, the concepts examined in this paper partly differ across the three varieties in question. While for WITCH and HOMOSEXUALITY, the British and Indian English concept have similarities as opposed to the Nigerian English concept, the Indian English concept of WOMAN appears to be in between the concept in the other two varieties. This prompts the presumption that – in cases where they differ from those in British English as a native variety – the concepts in Indian and Nigerian English might be blended concepts. Secondly, it seems justified to believe that diverging cultural models greatly contribute to the concepts, so that the fewer commonalities two English-speaking cultures have, the more culturally relevant concepts associated with English words differ.[15] All this implies that the local cultural context has a large impact on the concepts of speakers of L2-varieties of English in the form of incorporating elements from local cultural models.

The question addressed in the title of this chapter, if the notion of 'linguistic contact phenomena' can be expanded to include conceptual metaphors, has been dealt with implicitly so far. Above, on the basis of three form-meaning pairings, we have demonstrated how cultural variance is born out conceptually through cultural contact. Since conceptual metaphors are per definition the mapping of a conceptual source domain onto a conceptual target concept, it follows that variation in the conceptual structure of a domain will automatically affect the meaning of a conceptual metaphor that involves any such domain. This holds true for both source and target domain. For example, differences in the source domain WITCH in the conceptual metaphor A WOMAN IS A WITCH – which (not only) exists in British English and Nigerian English – lead to different conceptual mappings, as specified and elaborated in Finzel and Wolf (2017). Equally, cultural variation in the conceptual target domain will also affect the conceptual mappings (cf. Kövecses 2005: 118–121). In this context, it is worth remembering Lakoff (1994: 55), who states "that image-schema structure inherent in the target domain cannot be violated, and that inherent target domain structure limits the possibilities for mappings automatically". Hence, the aforesaid only allows the conclusion that conceptual metaphors squarely fall within the category of linguistic contact phenomena.

5 Conclusion

In this chapter, we aimed to demonstrate how the concepts WITCH, WOMAN and HOMOSEXUALITY are very much influenced by culture-specific norms, laws and history and, as an entailment, how this influence in turn affects conceptual metaphors realised in different varieties of English. Our study draws attention to the importance of closely investigating the individual concepts that are involved in

---

15 The question is whether all concepts are culturally implicated. If one follows Kachru (1983: 9) that second language varieties of English are "used in entirely different semiotic and cultural systems", it seems that they are. Answering this question, however, requires further, substantial empirical verification.

metaphorical mappings for a deeper and more fine-grained understanding of cultural variation in English and other pluricentric languages. Furthermore, we hope to have made a point of understanding conceptual metaphors as potential contact phenomena, in which the result of contact lies beneath the linguistic surface, that is, at the conceptual level. Following this approach is not only of theoretical relevance as regards the application of Cognitive Linguistics to contact linguistics as a sociolinguistic field of enquiry, but also of significance for intercultural understanding. The methodological tools applied in our survey seem to be useful for examining conceptual variation across varieties situated in different cultural contexts.

References

Bamiro, Edmund O. 2006. The politics of code-switching: English vs. Nigerian languages. *World Englishes* 25(1). 23–35.

Cienki, Alan. 2007. Frames, idealized cognitive models, and domains. In Dirk Geeraerts & Hubert Cuyckens (eds.), *The Oxford Handbook of Cognitive Linguistics*, 170–187. Oxford & New York: Oxford University Press.

Diara, Benjamin C. D. & Nkechinyere G. Onah. 2014. The phenomenal growth of pentecostalism in the contemporary Nigerian society: A challenge to mainline churches. *Mediterranean Journal of Social Sciences* 5(6). 395–402.

Evans, Vyvyan & Melanie Green. 2006. *Cognitive Linguistics: An introduction*. Edinburgh: Edinburgh University Press.

Finzel, Anna & Hans-Georg Wolf. 2017. Cultural conceptualizations of gender and homosexuality in BrE, IndE, and NigE. *Cognitive Linguistic Studies* 4(1). 110–130.

Geschiere, Peter. 1997. *The Modernity of Witchcraft. Politics and the Occult in Postcolonial Africa*. Charlottesville, VA: University Press of Virginia.

Hunt, Stephen J. 2011. Conservative Hindu reactions to non-heterosexual rights in India. *International Journal of Sociology and Anthropology* 3(9). 318–327.

Ibriszimov, Dymitr, Hans-Jörg Schmid & Balarabe Zulyadaini. 2005. "My clothes are my home" or what do we really mean? A Hausa example. In Catherine Baroin, Gisela Seidensticker-Brikay & Kyari Tijani (eds.), *Man and the Lake. Proceedings of the XIIth Mega-Chad conference*, 185–195. Maiduguri: Centre for Trans-Saharan-Studies.

Ibriszimov, Dymitr & Balarabe Zulyadaini. 2009. I think what you think. An evaluation of L1 and L2 Hausa cognitive structures. In Eva Rothmaler (ed.), *Topics in Chadic Linguistics V. Papers from the 4th BICCL*, 95–103. Köln: Rüdiger Köppe Verlag.

Kachru, Braj B. 1983. Introduction: The other side of English. In Braj B. Kachru (ed.), *The Other Tongue: English Across Cultures*, 1–12. Oxford: Pergamon.

Kövecses, Zoltán. 2005. *Metaphor in Culture. Universality and Variation*. Cambridge: Cambridge University Press.

Lakoff, George. 1994. What is a conceptual system? In Willis F. Overton & David S. Palermo (eds.), *The Nature and Ontogenesis of Meaning*, 41–90. Hillsdale: Erlbaum.

Lakoff, George & Mark Johnson. 1980. *Metaphors we Live by*. Chicago: University of Chicago Press.

Langacker, Ronald W. 2007. Cognitive Grammar. In Dirk Geeraerts & Hubert Cuyckens (eds.), *The Oxford Handbook of Cognitive Linguistics*, 421–462. Oxford & New York: Oxford University Press.

Marwah, Sonal. 2014. Mapping murder: Homicide patterns and trends in India. An analysis from 2000–2010. *Journal of South Asian Studies* 2(2). 145–163.

Rosch, Eleanor. 1975. Cognitive representations of semantic categories. *Journal of Experimental Psychology* 104. 193–233.

Schmid, Hans-Jörg, Dymitr Ibriszimov, Karina Kopatsch & Peter Gottschligg. 2008. Conceptual blending in language, cognition, and culture. Towards a methodology for the linguistic study of syncretic concepts. In Afeosemime Unuose Adogame, Magnus Echtler & Ulf Vierke (eds.), *Unpacking the new: Critical Perspectives on Cultural Syncretization in Africa and Beyond*, 93–124. Zürich & Berlin: LIT.

Sedlatschek, Andreas. 2009. *Contemporary Indian English: Variation and Change*. Amsterdam & Philadelphia: John Benjamins.

Sharifian, Farzad. 2015. Cultural linguistics. In Farzad Sharifian (ed.), *The Routledge Handbook of Language and Culture*, 473–492. London & New York: Routledge.

Singh Sawhney, Isha. 2017. Sunny Leone is the new face of women's liberation. *The Sunday Guardian*. http://www.sunday-guardian.com/young-restless/sunny-leone-is-the-new-face-of-womens-liberation (accessed 17 January 2017).

Wikipedia. 2017. Section 377 of the Indian Penal Code. https://en.wikipedia.org/wiki/Section_377_of_the_Indian_Penal_Code (accessed 17 January 2017).

Wolf, Hans-Georg & Frank Polzenhagen. 2009. *World Englishes: A Cognitive Sociolinguistic Approach*. Berlin: Walter de Gruyter.

Zenner, Eline. 2013. *Cognitive Contact Linguistics: The Macro, Meso and Micro Influence of English on Dutch*. Dissertation. KU Leuven.

Stefano De Pascale, Stefania Marzo and Dirk Speelman
7 Cultural models in contact: Revealing attitudes toward regional varieties of Italian with Vector Space Models

Abstract: Cognitive linguists have been traditionally interested in uncovering the conceptual representation of cultural knowledge. For that endeavor, the semantic analysis of linguistic usage has become of prime importance in order to reveal metaphorical and associative schemas that as a whole are structured in so-called cultural models. Such models have been suggested for all sorts of events and institutions in the social world, among them also phenomena related to linguistic variation. However, it is less clear, first, how precisely cultural models arise in language contact situations and, second, how data-driven computational-semantic techniques can be employed for analyzing those models. As a case in point, we investigated the cultural conceptualization of regional Italian varieties. These varieties can be considered the result of recent contact between Standard Italian and one of the many local Italo-Romance dialects of Italy. The analysis of the cultural models draws on free association data gathered from 213 university students from all over Italy and further processed making use of Vector Space Models in order to extract semantic domains. Our results show that associations of semantic domains with varieties in contact situations differ across student groups and contact areas, so emphasizing the variability of cultural models. Furthermore, our quantitative approach has proven to be methodologically promising for capturing both expected and novel associative patterns in such very large datasets.

Keywords: cultural models; regional Italian varieties; cognitive sociolinguistics; distributional semantics; vector space model; standardization; meaning of variation

1 Introduction

The growing appeal of Cognitive Contact Linguistics (henceforth CCL), as evidenced by the variety of contributions to this volume, has predominantly spurred investigations into more "tangible" contact phenomena at the level of the linguistic system, such as concept-based approaches to borrowing and Construction Grammatical

---

Stefano De Pascale, Stefania Marzo, Dirk Speelman, KU Leuven

https://doi.org/10.1515/9783110619430-008

accounts of codeswitching (see Zenner and Kristiansen 2013). However, studies that have examined the perceptual side of contact phenomena and contact varieties, which involves alternative cognitive frames and evaluative judgments, remain sparse in CCL. In the framework of Cognitive Sociolinguistics (henceforth CogSoc, see Geeraerts and Kristiansen 2015: 376), this line of inquiry, focusing on the so-called *meaning of variation*, has for instance studied metaphor in cultural conceptualizations of intralinguistic variation (Berthele 2010). This chapter aims to explore precisely how CogSoc in general, and *cultural models theory* in particular, can contribute to shed light on the *meaning of contact-induced variation*.

In the words of Holland and Quinn (1987: 4), we understand cultural models as structured wholes of "culturally constituted understandings of the social world [that] point up not only the degree to which people impose order on their world but also the degree to which such orderings are shared by the joint participants in this world".[1] As such, the idea of cultural models provides us with an especially promising framework to study the social meaning of contact-induced change: it allows us to explore the connection between our folk conceptualization of language varieties as real-world entities and the linguistic structure of those varieties.

As a case in point, this chapter intends to report on the kind of conceptual domains Italian university students tap into to carve up and organize their perceptions of the Italian language area, which is marked by the convergence of local Italo-Romance dialects and Standard Italian that was caused by long-standing contact between both. This convergence has given rise to regional contact varieties of Italian (*italiani regionali*, Telmon 1993) through processes of dialect leveling (on the geographic, horizontal dimension) and standardization or Italianization (on the social, vertical dimension).

Apart from the above-stated descriptive objective, two other key issues will be addressed by this study. On a theoretical level, we argue that a meaning-centered and usage-based approach to the study of cultural models offers considerable advantages over traditional social-psychological analyses and language ideology studies in critical discourse analysis. More concretely, we approach the task of revealing cultural models by extracting semantic fields from a broad

---

[1] From that publication onwards, these models have also been called, almost interchangeably, "folk models" or "(idealized) cognitive models (ICMs)" among others, but we follow the practice of using the term "cultural models" for two reasons: first, it avoids the false dichotomy between "folk" and "expert" models, by underscoring the interconnectedness of distributed knowledge in whole communities (Keesing 1987); second, the "cultural" stresses the context-dependent, variable and changing nature of these representations (Strauss and Quinn 1997) complementary to the universal "cognitive" mechanisms that underlie these models. Furthermore, there is an explicit warning against making far-reaching claims about "Culture-with-capital-C".

sample of semi-experimentally elicited data, c.q. descriptions and evaluations collected through a free association survey administered to Italian students. On a methodological level, we tackle the problem of performing semantic analyses on large databases of free associations with the use of a computational-semantic technique called Vector Space Models.

The structure of the chapter is defined as follows. The next paragraph, Section 2, will make clear what the benefits are of such a meaning-centered, usage-based approach – basically an application of Cognitive Linguistics' tenets – when studying how people categorize their linguistic environment. Section 3 presents the background of our case study, namely the emergence of regional contact varieties in Italy. Section 4 presents the computational-semantic method we used to reveal those cultural models, after which we present the result of the survey in Section 5 and discuss them in Section 6.

2 Attitudes and ideology in Cognitive Linguistics: The cultural models synthesis

The way in which people (and communities) categorize and evaluate their surrounding linguistic environment has been the object of study of at least two other subdisciplines besides Cognitive Linguistics. In the remainder of this section we briefly review the advantages of Cognitive Linguistics, particularly contrasting their cultural models approach with studies on the social psychology of language (Giles and Rakić 2014) and Critical Discourse Analysis (CDA, Fairclough, Mulderrig, and Wodak 2011).[2]

2.1 Attitudes and ideology in social psychology and critical discourse analysis

Traditionally, the focus of research on the social psychology of language has been on language attitudes, viz. the social evaluation of language varieties by correlating them with personal characteristics. Robust psychometrical findings on language attitudes and replicable experimental designs have accumulated within this framework. However, criticism has recently been increasing concerning the lack of methodological

---

[2] In fact, a third line of research could be mentioned here, namely, Perceptual Dialectology (Preston 2005), which has found fertile ground particularly in Italian dialectology (Canobbio and Iannàccaro 2000; Cini and Regis 2002; contributions in Krefeld and Pustka 2010).

innovation and experimental designs tailored for linguistics (Rosseel, Speelman, and Geeraerts 2015). More fundamentally, the application of social-psychological designs to the study of language ideology and attitudes has itself been questioned, as the methods are designed to measure out of context evaluations of language, which goes against the very nature of sociolinguistics (Soukup 2013).

This emphasis on language in context is also a basic tenet in CDA. Language ideologies are displayed in daily language use and are influenced by a myriad of contextual factors that can be uncovered by careful (semantic) analysis of the concepts at stake in the construction of specific ideologies. The objectivity of such analyses has however been questioned, the main claim being that they merely confirm the linguist's preconceptions (Schegloff 1997). Further critique concerns the weakness of CDA's theoretical underpinnings and the fuzziness of its terminology (Widdowson 1995).

2.2 The cultural models synthesis: Quantifying semantics

The way cultural models theory describes the organization of cultural knowledge seems to combine the benefits of social psychology and CDA: theoretically-informed semantic analyses employing quantitative corpus-based techniques are used to uncover meaning-in-use.

This crucial importance of meaning for the description of folk belief systems dates back to the cognitive revolution of the 1950s (D'Andrade 1995). Given cognitive anthropology's increasing reliance on semantic theory, the discipline followed developments in semantic theory itself, which started to adhere to experientialism, emphasizing the encyclopedic nature of meaning-as-conceptualization (the so-called *recontextualising trend*, cf. Geeraerts 2015). As such, cognitive anthropology and linguistics started to share an analytical toolbox that included notions as prototypes (Rosch 1978), schemata or frames (Fillmore 1977), and conceptual metaphors (Lakoff and Johnson 1980). For cognitive anthropology these new theoretical tools served the purpose of describing shared systems of cultural meaning, later named cultural models (Holland and Quinn 1987), but also known as Idealized Cognitive Models (ICMs, Lakoff 1987) in the later Cognitive Linguistics literature.

This recontextualising trend in semantics involved an increased awareness of the sociocultural embedding and usage-based nature of language. Turning to linguistic usage means envisaging language as concrete, quantifiable data and acknowledging its heterogeneity at the level of the community. Whereas the study of cultural models in cognitive anthropology had already been investigated with robust empirical methods for a long time (e.g.: cluster analysis in Boster, Berlin, and O'Neill 1986; triad tests in Romney and D'Andrade 1964), within the Cognitive Linguistics community, empirical assessments or experimental work on ICMs only became common in the last decade (e.g.: Cienki 2005; Berthele 2010), through the advent of Cognitive Sociolinguistics.

The true innovative contribution of Cognitive Sociolinguistics to cultural models theory is visible, in our opinion, in two areas. Theoretically, the discipline has brought into the picture the relevance of focusing on cultural conceptualization of speakers' *linguistic* environment, the so-called meaning of variation: "[cultural] models about the way in which language varieties are distributed over a language community and about the way in which such distribution should be evaluated" (Geeraerts 2003, p. 26). Methodologically, it has popularized data-driven approaches for the study of the variation of meaning, which are more commonly subsumed under the heading of distributional semantics. Here the meaning of words is extracted from corpora and constructed as numerical vectors, potentially reaching a representation of whole sections of the lexicon as a semantic space.

The main aim of this study is to investigate the benefits of such a distributional semantics approach for research on cultural models. Cognitive Linguistics has promoted the lexicon, rather than syntax, as the default level of analysis to investigate the structure of our linguistic knowledge. It might thus be fruitful to reveal the organization of the words we use instead of inspecting lists of individual keywords when we aim to disclose the structure of our beliefs and stereotypes. In other words, an approach that favors an aggregate perspective on word usage and semantic relations and that as such is able to extract relevant semantic fields, is probably best fit to bring us closer to the endeavor described in the previous paragraphs (for similar applications, see Grondelaers and Speelman 2016; Peirsman, Heylen, and Geeraerts 2010). On the other hand, corpus-based research on ideology, mainly carried out in CDA, has predominantly been conducted in the form of concordance lists and collocation analyses (Baker and McEnery 2005) and recurring themes and groupings are usually inferred by the researchers.

3 Case study: The Italian "dialect-standard" continuum

3.1 Language contact between Italo-Romance dialects and Standard Italian

The language area under investigation in this paper is the Italian peninsula, characterized by multiple contact situations on the so-called "dialect-standard" continuum. In particular, our study focuses on four contact situations that have arisen in the four (main) regions of Italy, each of which is characterized by the presence of an Italo-Romance dialect and a (supra) regional variety: Lombardy (Milan) in the north, Tuscany (Florence) and Latium (Rome) in the center, and Campania (Naples) in the south. Before we present these contact settings in more detail, let us first clarify our understanding of the notion "dialect" and the peculiarities of the language contact that has taken place in Italy.

As concerns the term "dialect", we follow Coseriu (1973) as an alternative to the more widespread Anglo-Saxon dialectological terminology, making a distinction between primary, secondary and tertiary dialects (although this classification is also contested; see Krefeld 2011). In this perspective, the Italo-Romance dialects (e.g: Piedmontese, Neapolitan, Sicilian), to which also Tusco-Florentine belongs, are called primary dialects: these are geographical sister varieties of the one dialect (i.e. Tusco-Florentine) that has historically been elevated to standard language. In the remainder of the paper we will also refer to them as local dialects.

Although the debate is quite recent (see Cerruti 2011), there are legitimate reasons to claim that contact-induced variation and change is at play in the Italian language. First, regarding spatial contiguity, the contact between Standard Italian and the Italo-Romance dialects has taken place in the same linguistic space, i.e. the peninsula at the foot of the Alps. Second, with respect to linguistic relatedness, both Standard Italian and the Italo-Romance dialects descend from the vulgar Latin spoken in the first centuries of the Common Era. However, only the Tusco-Florentine dialect of modern Tuscany became codified as the standard language in the 16th century, while all other dialects were relegated to informal domains of use.[3] The consequence of this is that Standard Italian was a native variety for only a minority of residents of the peninsula and could only function as the written language of the elite. The local dialects were then presumably the code in which the vast illiterate majority of the population satisfied its everyday communicative needs. Put differently, until the first half of the 20th century, Italy showed stable diglossia (Cerruti, Crocco, and Marzo 2017).[4] A third aspect of the Italian contact situation is related to the intensity of the contact between the two poles of the dialect-standard continuum. Estimates of the number of speakers of Standard Italian after the Unification in 1861 do not exceed 10% (Castellani 1982). Only after the drastic socioeconomic transformation of the fifties and sixties did Italy achieve a "critical mass" of italophones

---

[3] The local dialects of larger urban centres that fell outside of the sphere of direct linguistic influence of Tusco-Florentine (most notably Venice and Naples) were later able to acquire some local prestige through their use in literary works (Krefeld 1988).
[4] It should be noted here that we use the term in the extended definition of Ferguson's original proposal, so as to comprise the configuration of different linguistic systems rather than just different varieties of one language (see the discussion in Berruto (1995: 191–211)).

so as to trigger internal differentiation of the standard (Sobrero 1988). Italy has no longer been characterized by diglossia since the 1970's, but by *diaglossia* (Auer 2005) or the equivalent *dilalia* (Berruto 1995): the prestigious variety has gained access to the informal contexts that were previously restricted to the low variety, c.q. the local dialects. The consequence is the emergence of hybrid, geographically marked varieties, located on a continuum between standard and dialect.

From a Coserian perspective, these varieties would be called tertiary dialects: these are geographical varieties that have emerged by areal differentiation of the standard language after its initial diffusion (e.g: Northern Italian, Neapolitan Italian). We will refer to them as regional varieties or regional accents. In conclusion, we will define these regional varieties as varieties of Standard Italian originated through the dialectal substratum of the speaker's area (for larger overviews and recent research on those varieties, see Cardinaletti and Munaro 2009; Cerruti 2009; De Blasi 2014; Fusco and Marcato 2001).

3.2 Regional varieties of Italian: Structure, attitudes and research questions

A diversity of historical developments has also yielded clear differences in the reception of the standard language in the different regions (Telmon 1993). The outcomes of these different histories are illustrated in Figure 1, which attempts to visualize the structural distance of the regional varieties with respect to the two poles in the dialect-standard continuum.

First, while the central regions Tuscany and Latium were standardized soon after Standard Italian had come into existence, the northern and southern areas of Italy only caught up with standardization in the 20th century. Consequently, at present the structural distance between the central local dialects and the central regional varieties is smaller than the distance between the respective lects in northern and southern Italy. It is even argued that the central base dialects can be equated with heavy-accented, informal regional varieties of Standard Italian (Berruto, 1995: 248). The result of this first wave of standardization is illustrated in Figure 1, in the cones representing the linguistic repertoire of Tuscany and Latium. The distance separating the local dialects (i.e. the lower strata) and the regional varieties (i.e. the intermediate strata) has shrunk, and by consequence the intralinguistic variability in the lowest strata has diminished. Second, the aforementioned socio-economic transformation of the mid-20th century also led to a second wave of standardization: the industrial and more prosperous North created the conditions for increased standardization, while reception of Standard Italian slowed down in the southern regions, which is also represented in Figure 1. The distance between the highest

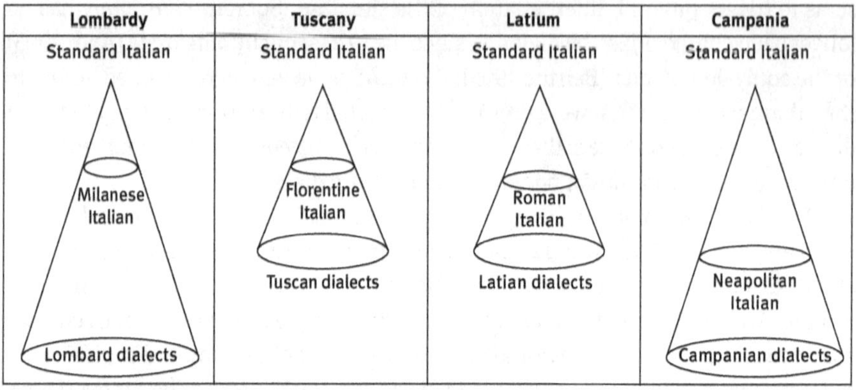

Lombardy	Tuscany	Latium	Campania
Standard Italian	Standard Italian	Standard Italian	Standard Italian
Milanese Italian	Florentine Italian	Roman Italian	Neapolitan Italian
Lombard dialects	Tuscan dialects	Latian dialects	Campanian dialects

Figure 1: Stratificational structure of linguistic repertoire in four Italian regions.

stratum (i.e. Standard Italian) and the Naples-based regional variety is much larger than the stratificational distance between Standard Italian and Milanese Italian. Although the overall stratificational distance of the linguistic repertoire in the central regions of Tuscany and Latium remains the smallest, this second wave of standardization has had less impact in those regions and did not elevate their regional varieties significantly towards the standard variety (for similar discussions and representations, see Auer [2005] and Cerruti and Regis [2014]).

The central question of this paper does not concern the actual linguistic distance between these lects, but the attitudes and ideological stances towards them. Some scholarly attention was devoted to this topic during the eighties, with empirical inquiries by Baroni (1983), Galli de' Paratesi (1984) and Volkart-Rey (1990). These studies mostly focus on the four main regional varieties, following an old division first proposed by De Mauro (1970) between Milanese Italian, Florentine Italian, Roman Italian and southern (Neapolitan) Italian. The criteria adopted for this partition are mainly sociological, since the areas covered by the labels do not cover the whole nation and certainly do not correspond to the administrative regions of Italy. They represent instead the four most important urbanized centers that attract the adjacent communities by virtue of their historical cultural-linguistic, economic or political influence (in accordance with an urban hierarchy model of supraregionalization, see Britain 2004). As mentioned in the first paragraph of this section, we will continue using that quadripartite division, given its sociological relevance.

The most interesting of these older studies for our present purposes concerns Galli de' Paratesi's (1984) framing of the different ideological conceptualizations of the regional varieties. In a discourse-analytic investigation of a collection of evaluations and other keywords, she concluded that Milanese Italian represents social values that are typically associated with a dominant and culturally elitist group, such as distinction, efficiency and artificiality, either positively or negatively. On the basis of these findings she postulates the plausible candidacy of Milan and the north as the future center for standardization. The Florentine variety triggers associations regarding normativity, while Roman Italian and the southern variety share the image of the picaro, both interpreted negatively ("lack of education", "arrogant") and positively ("spontaneous", "lively"). Moreover, the southern regional dialect suffers from outspoken discriminatory attitudes and has always been placed at the bottom of hypothetical prestige scales (see also De Mauro 1970). In an attempt to update Galli de' Paratesi's findings thirty years later, De Pascale, Marzo, and Speelman (2017) conducted a verbal guise experiment among southern Italian participants and revealed a decreasing negative attitude towards Milanese accented Italian and an increasing negative attitude towards their own variety of reference, i.e. Neapolitan accented Italian.

The question remains how working with a cultural models approach can lead to new findings about the ideological stances towards the regional varieties of Italian. As a steppingstone to the research questions of this paper, we now present a schematization (Figure 2) of how we believe cultural models of language contact to emerge. On the one hand, we have a language variety A, in our case Standard Italian, which is associated with a certain number of semantic fields, which can be positive and/or negative. On the other hand there is another language variety B, a local dialect, that is represented with different semantic fields. The first research question pertains to the conceptualization of the contact variety AB, i.e. the regional accent: to what extent, in terms of association strength, do the semantic fields associated with the original varieties in contact A and B differently contribute to the cultural model of the contact variety AB? The second question involves the abovementioned comparative perspective: to what extent are the cultural models of each of the four regional contact situation (with varieties A, B and AB) shared by different groups of participants? The third question relates to the standardization debate: can the previous findings tell us something about the ongoing processes of standard language change in Italy?

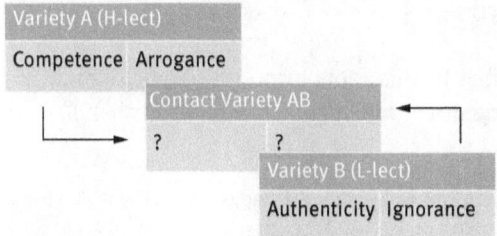

Figure 2: Cultural models in contact.

4 Methods and data: Extracting semantic fields from free association data

In this section we will go through the methodological workflow at the basis of our cultural models study. First, we briefly introduce the way we collected the primary data, i.e. evaluative adjectives, that form the building blocks of the semantic fields. Second, we will introduce the computational-semantic technique that allowed us to model the semantics of those free association data. Then we describe how we applied cluster techniques to extract clusters of related adjectives and present those clusters. Finally, we will discuss the associations between the lects in the Italian repertoire and the extracted semantic fields, relying on correspondence analysis.

4.1 Carrying out a free association task for collecting evaluative adjectives

The primary data for our study was collected through a free association survey that was sent online to different universities across the peninsula. Specifically we asked them to provide us with the first three adjectives that came to mind to describe each of the 9 varieties in the Italian language area (local dialects and regional accents in Lombardy, Tuscany, Latium and Campania, plus Standard Italian). We stressed that there were no wrong answers and that participants had to respond as spontaneously and quickly as possible. We also included short audio fragments of the varieties under scrutiny to avoid misunderstanding regarding the identification of the labeled varieties.[5] In total, we collected completed surveys from 213 university students (58 from the Center of Italy, 86 from the North and 69 from the South), which resulted in a database of 5628 adjective tokens distributed over 935 adjective types.

4.2 Semantic Vector Space Models: Calculation of semantic similarity between words

The statistical modelling of meaning has its roots in post-Bloomfieldian structuralism (Harris 1954) and the British corpus-linguistic school (Firth 1957). At

---

[5] The glottonyms for the local dialects were formed by adding the adjective for the region to *un dialetto* (e.g.: *un dialetto lombardo*, a Lombard dialect) and the ones of the regional accents by the construction *l'italiano parlato a* [city name] (e.g.: *l'italiano parlato a Firenze*, Italian spoken in Florence).

the core of this paradigm, distributional semantics, is the assumption that the meaning of a word can be induced from its co-occurring words in the linguistic context (the distributional hypothesis; Lenci 2008). A corollary of this hypothesis is that words that have similar contexts tend to be semantically related. In computational semantics, the technical implementation of this hypothesis are called Vector Space Models (henceforth VSMs), which have now become the *de facto* standard in statistical natural language processing for the modeling of meaning. Given its usage-based inclination, Cognitive Linguistics has recently embraced the methodological virtues of VSMs as an attractive solution for extracting semantic information from corpora (Geeraerts 2010).

The creation of VSMs is largely bottom-up and automatic. Since it is out of the scope of this chapter to provide an extensive technical discussion on how such VSM parameters are set, we will only explain the conceptual steps involved.

Since meaning depends on context, a first step is to decide what counts as contextual unit. We prefer to work with *bag-of-words models*, that start from a corpus of texts and consider a predefined number of content words in a window left and right around each corpus instance of a certain target word, irrespective of their syntactic relation. The reason is that bag-of-words models perform well on the retrieval of looser semantic relations between words. In order to discover the relevant semantic fields –those that laymen employ to talk about language variation– we need the type of model that can bring to light which words are related, perhaps only broadly, and not just sets of synonymous words (Peirsman and Geeraerts 2009).

Let's have a look at the following constructed examples, to make the discussion more concrete:

(1) ... but then she laughed, a low **melodious** sound that once more fired his senses ...

(2) ... the translator produced a **melodious** sound not unlike a clarinet quartet ...

(3) ... assign each group a different voice with a distinct **rhythmic** profile ...

(4) ... I can still hear the **rhythmic**, continuous sound of a dog barking outside ...

(5) ... the amplified sound of **chanting** Buddhist monks rose up the slope ...

(6) ... listening to the sound of her childish voice **chanting** the alphabet ...

(7) ... those tribes have lost much of their land to support this **agricultural** production ...

(8) ... particularly to the allocation of land for **agricultural**, open space and forest use ...

For this example, we would like to create a model that clusters together target adjectives as *melodious, rhythmic* and *chanting*, which –albeit non-synonymous– all index the domain of MUSIC. Such a model should also be able to exclude a totally unrelated word like *agricultural* from this cluster. Therefore we use the context words left and right of these target adjectives. In our examples these context words are *sound, laughed, clarinet, land, production* etc. In the actual study the target words are the evaluative adjective collected in the free association survey.

The second step involves the statistical implementation of the context words of a target adjective. This is done by taking into account the total frequency with which each context word appears within a certain window around the adjective in the whole corpus of reference (cfr. infra). The semantic information is formalized in vectors, hence the name of Vector Space Models. Table 1 brings together the vectors for the target adjectives of our previous constructed examples, constructing a term-by-context-word matrix that allows us to observe the distributional behavior of several words simultaneously.

The number of context words can be thought of as the number of dimensions that form the so-called distributional or semantic space, in which the position of the target words is determined by the co-ordinates in the vectors. In reality the matrix will have thousands of context words as dimensions, and the cells will have large co-occurrence frequencies, but it is clear from Table 1 that words like *rhythmic* and *chanting* have more context words in common (*sound* and *voice*) than *agricultural* (which has none, in fact). To obtain the frequency information for the vectors of our study, we choose the itWaC corpus ("Italian Web as Corpus" M. Baroni, Bernardini, Ferraresi, and Zanchetta 2009), which is the largest annotated collection of Italian web texts (1.5 billion words).

Table 1: Term-by-document matrix: rows = target words, columns = context words, cells = co-occurrence frequency.

ADJECTIVES	CONTEXT WORDS						
	sound	*laughed*	*clarinet*	*voice*	*land*	*production*	...
melodious	2	1	1	0	0	0	...
rhythmic	1	0	0	1	0	0	...
chanting	2	0	0	1	0	0	...
agricultural	0	0	0	0	2	1	...
...	...	...	...	...	...	...	...

After creating a vector for every adjective, the vectors are compared pairwise and their degree of similarity are assessed with the cosine similarity index. After obtaining the pairwise similarity indices between all adjectives, which generates a symmetric term-by-term matrix, we applied some statistical corrections to allow better performance in the next step. Table 2 reproduces an example of this type of term-by-term matrix, based on the (scarse, but realistic) frequencies found in Table 1.

Table 2: Symmetric term-by-term matrix (cells = cosine distance between target adjectives, ranging from 0 (no similarity) to 1 (identity)).

ADJECTIVES	melodious	rhythmic	chanting	agricultural	...
melodious	1	0.58	0.73	0	...
rhythmic	0.58	1	0.95	0	...
chanting	0.73	0.95	1	0	...
agricultural	0	0	0	1	...
...	...	...	...	...	...

4.3 Cluster analysis: Identification of semantic fields

The next stage of the process involves revealing the semantic fields that our participants draw from when asked to describe and evaluate language varieties, as a means to uncover the underlying cultural models. A non-hierarchical cluster analysis (k-medoids clustering, Divjak and Fieller 2015) with 15 clusters was conducted on the term-by-term matrix. The choice for 15 clusters is a matter of judgment that weighs up different criteria: the length of the adjectives list, the type/token ratios of these adjectives, the final visualization of the association patterns between semantic fields and lects, the interpretability of the clusters, etc. The labeling of the clusters with some sort of neutral cover term (*archisememe*) to capture the semantic field is the only task up to now that requires the interpretative intervention of the researcher. In practice, it is quite hard to find a sufficiently neutral superordinate term for those semantic fields that contain a majority of strongly positive or negative adjectives. We can therefore identify a first dimension of affective involvement, that distinguishes semantic fields on a continuum that goes from neutral to strongly emotional (with either negative or positive valence). A second dimension that can be discerned is one related to roughly two groups of referents to which the fields apply. In this respect there are fields that contain adjectives used for the characteristics of animate objects, i.e. "speakers". On the other hand, we have the group of fields that cluster adjectives related to inanimate object, i.e. "varieties", and that tend to coincide with material or external properties of those

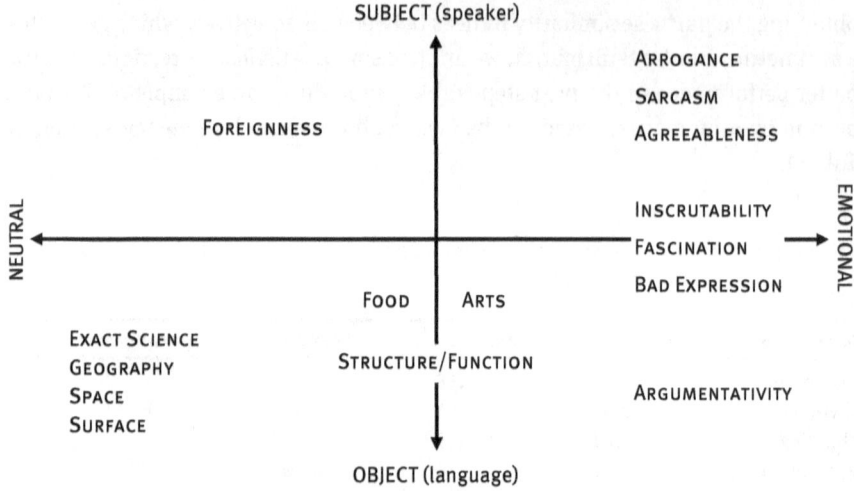

Figure 3: Diagram of semantic domains (labeled with archisememes): from left to right the domains are ordered along growing "emotional involvement" (from neutral to positive); from the bottom to the top they are ordered along reference to person characteristics (from object-oriented to subject-oriented).

objects. Figure 3 situates the 15 semantic domains, with their respective labels, along these two dimensions.[6]

An appendix at the end of this chapter provides all the adjectives for each of the archisememes visualized in Figure 3. We will now run through the different fields with short summarizing descriptions of their meaning. In the bottom-left corner one finds four domains that contain adjectives describing objective aspects of languages. The first of the four is called Exact Science and clusters adjectives typical of exact science writings, which largely denote schematic representation (e.g.: *dynamic, static, linear*). The second group receives the generic label Space because it tends to group adjectives whose common denominator is their description of spatial configuration (e.g.: *vertical, anterior, upward*). The third field in this group is labeled Geography and brings together many adjectives referring to the

---

6 As is evident from the diagram there is no even distribution of the semantic domains along the two axes, and, in fact, some correlations might exist between the "subject-emotional" and "object-neutral" end. Thus although it might be the case that some "subject-related" domains are "subjective" (in the sense of "influenced by emotions"), it would still be reductive to conflate these dimensions. In any case, those two dimensions need to be taken as loose heuristics, not based on quantitative but interpretative analysis, rather than as stable and foundational aspects of our semantic space.

diffusion and areal coverage of objects (c.q. language varieties, e.g.: *provincial, national, local*). Finally, there is the semantic domain called SURFACE which collects most adjectives that have to do with the external appearance of physical objects, such as color (e.g.: *dark, grey, opaque*) and shape (e.g.: *smooth, thick, round*).

The location of the next four semantic fields is harder to determine. The central adjectives of the field labeled FOREIGNNESS evoke a general notion of "distance", with references to foreign nationalities (e.g.: *Spanish, Portuguese, French*) or to high social function (e.g.: *imperial, papal, distinguished*). This field arguably leans more towards the subject-related end of the continuum. While it was rather easy to identify archisememes for the semantic domains of FOOD (e.g.: *sliced, uncooked, fresh*) and ARTS (e.g.: *musical, theatrical, cinematographical*), it proved a more difficult task to find one for the semantic domain eventually labeled STRUCTURE/FUNCTION. This field clusters together many adjectives with a more or less overt normative judgment (e.g.: *correct, adequate, necessary*), but also words describing structural properties (e.g.: *simplified, selective, articulated*). Overall, this seems to be the semantic domain most closely associated with aspects typical of standard languages, and will therefore be of particular relevance in our discussion.

The remainder of the semantic domains are clearly concentrated in the emotional end of the continuum, given the high polarity of their adjectives. Most of the time those fields contain a majority of adjectives on one end of the polarity scale, and they target personal characteristics. So we have a negative, speaker-related field such as ARROGANCE (e.g.: *presumptuous, hypocritical, arrogant*), a less stigmatizing domain SARCASM (e.g.: *caricatural, sarcastic, mocking*), although with negative connotations, and a general positive field of AGREEABLENESS (e.g.: *tender, gentle, sincere*). Next there are three semantic fields that can be situated somewhere between the subject- and object-related perceptions. This is the case for the field INSCRUTABILITY which groups items evoking darkness, lack of control and unfathomable depths (e.g.: *tragic, profound, obscure*). Another negative field is the one named BAD EXPRESSION that clusters together all description of unmannered and unpleasant ways of expressing yourself vocally (e.g.: *screamed, yelled, mumbled*). The third field has a clear positive valence and is labeled FASCINATION (e.g.: *fascinating, romantic, imaginative*). The fifteenth field ARGUMENTATIVITY, in the bottom-right quarter of the figure, collects words that might be considered to describe and/or to be used in arguments and debates, to judge, often negatively, others' opinions and rhetoric (e.g.: *unacceptable, understandable, unsustainable*). In a certain sense, it is a semantic field that seems complementary in terms of valence to the STRUCTURE/FUNCTION field. A caveat to this assessment is that the cluster is composed by both positive and negative adjectives.

4.4 Correspondence analysis: Visualizing the semantic fields and the Italian lects

Correspondence analysis is an exploratory technique that helps to visualize correlations between sets of categorical data (Glynn 2015). In our case, it takes as input the frequencies of each semantic field (more precisely, the frequencies of the adjectives within a particular field per Italian lect).[7] This contingency table (15 rows by 9 columns, see Appendix) is then reduced to a two-dimensional plot from which can infer three types of relations: between the different varieties, between the different semantic fields and between the varieties and the semantic fields. Additionally, we want to explore the influence of region of birth of the participants, in order to investigate the variability in cultural models. We decided to further split each column (that is, each variety) in three, so that frequencies of the semantic fields per variety would be differentiated along the macro-region of the respondent: the North, the Centre (which includes Tuscan and Latian participants) and the South. This triplication of the contingency table unfortunately causes a loss of accuracy in two-dimensional visualization, but we will compensate for this by working with a three-dimensional reduction: the variance explained and faithfully represented by our analysis in just two dimensions amounts to only 52.7%. Working with a three-dimensional solution increases that variance by 15%, which proves that it is necessary to take into account such a third dimension. The three contingency tables can be found in Appendices 2a to 2c.

5 Results

We will now present the results of the correspondence analysis, by focusing on the four linguistic contact areas under investigation: Lombardy (Milan), Tuscany (Florence), Latium (Rome) and Campania (Naples). The plots will be analyzed from two perspectives: first, we will focus on the distances between the lects, so as to determine which lects are conceptually more similar or different overall and how this conceptualization varies per group of participants.

---

[7] Not unimportantly: before summing the raw frequency of the adjectives, we weighted these frequencies by means of the silhouette width of the respective adjective within the cluster. Loosely speaking, silhouette widths are estimates of the classification accuracy of the adjectives in a certain cluster (Rousseeuw 1987). The rationale is that adjectives with high silhouette widths are more defining of the meaning of the whole cluster (they are closer to the ideal center) and should have a greater impact than adjectives with low silhouette widths, which indicate peripheral adjectives.

Second, we will focus on which particular semantic fields play a role in causing these distances. Each biplot shows the lects in black bold font and the semantic fields in lightgrey italic font (The QR-codes point to the same figures in color). Lects starting with *DIA* refer to local dialects, while those starting with *ITA* indicate the regional accents (except for the label ITASTA, which stands for Standard Italian). The small letters at the end of the labels represent the region of birth of the student participants: *n* for northern Italy, *c* for the center of Italy and *s* for the south of the peninsula. As a case in point, the position of DIALOM.s in the plot corresponds to the overall conceptualization of the local dialect of Lombardy by university students from the south, which is an "averaged" representation that takes into account associations with all the semantic fields and the other lects.

Let us first observe the correspondence plot for the lects of the Lombard contact area (see Figure 4a/4b). First of all, a fact that will remain constant throughout the plots is the position of Standard Italian, on the left edge of the plot. Two factors contribute to the isolation, or better, to the conceptual distinctiveness of the standard language: the absence of variability in conceptualization between student groups (confirmed by the third dimension, see Figure 4b) and the strong association with a single semantic field, not surprisingly the STRUCTURE/ FUNCTION field, whose adjectives have a strong normative and functional orientation. From the reverse perspective it can be argued that the STRUCTURE/

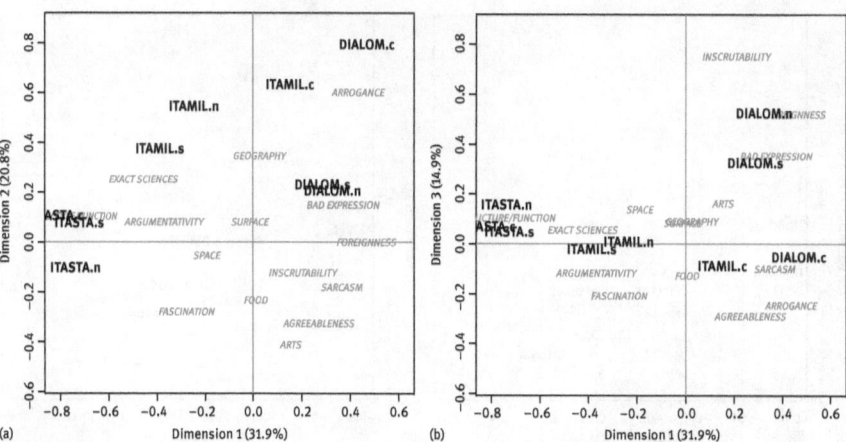

Figure 4a/4b: Correspondence biplots of Lombard contact area [DIALOM = Lombard dialect; ITAMIL = Milanese variety] (4a: plot of the 1st and 2nd dimensions, 4b: plot of the 1st and 3rd dimension).

FUNCTION field is very infrequently associated with the other lects. The situation is different for the Milan-based regional accent and local dialect. Here we see a split between, on the one hand, the northern and southern participants, and, on the other hand, the central participants. If we interpret the horizontal dimension as a diglossic spectrum, then we could say that the first group situates the regional variety conceptually closer to the standard, while the central participants consider it closer to the local dialect end. The horizontal dimension also seems to differentiate the neutral semantic fields at the left side, from the more affectively charged fields. Northern and southern students associate the regional variety to EXACT SCIENCE and to a lesser extent to ARGUMENTATIVITY, two language-related fields, while it is more difficult to pin down a semantic field that central students strongly associated with the regional accent. We see the same split with the associations of the local dialect. The former groups both highlight perceptions of unpleasant and raw sounds of the local dialect (BAD EXPRESSION), whereas the central group finds the speaker of local dialects particularly arrogant (ARROGANCE). These interpretations are also confirmed after the inclusion of the third dimension.

In contrast with the Lombard case, the Tuscan regional variety and local dialect exclusively occupy the bottom half of the plot (see Figure 5a). At least three other differences can be observed with respect to the previous visualization. First, the overall conceptual-semantic distance between all the Tuscan lects (DIATOS, ITATOS) is much smaller than in the case of the respective Lombard

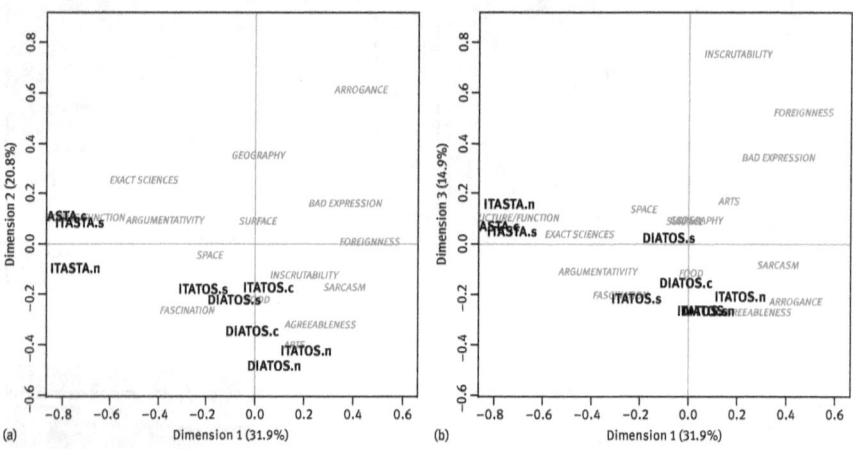

Figure 5a/5b: Correspondence biplots of the Tuscan contact area [DIATOS = Tuscan dialect; ITAFIR = Florentine variety].

lects (DIALOM, ITAMIL). Second, there is no obvious cline from standard to regional accent to dialect as in the previous configuration, but the lects cluster together, with the regional varieties surrounding the local dialects. Third, groups of respondents rather than groups of lects seem to be set apart in the plot, suggesting that perceptions vary most overtly across participants for the Tuscan area as a whole. Taking into account the third dimension (see Figure 5b) we can see that northern participants consider Tuscan Italian speakers gentle, warm and sincere (AGREEABLENESS) and associate them with arts and high-brow culture (ARTS). The group of central students makes a curious association of the regional variety – nota bene one of the reference varieties for this group – with the FOOD-field (for instance with adjectives such as *dolce*). That Tuscan Italian (and the Tuscan dialect in large part too) seems conceptualized with a metaphorical mapping of an edible product could be derived from a possible initial association of its speakers with cosy cooking settings and, in general, homey and familial atmospheres. Finally, in their appreciation of Tuscan Italian, the southern speakers lean most towards the standard language end of the horizontal continuum and tend to associate the regional accent with the positive field of FASCINATION and the rather neutral domain of SPACE.

Turning to Figure 6a/6b, we see that all but one of the lects of the Latian contact area are located in the top-right quadrant, from the perspective of the first and second dimensions (Figure 6a). Although the pattern that horizontally distinguishes more from less "Italianized" varieties is restored, there do not seem

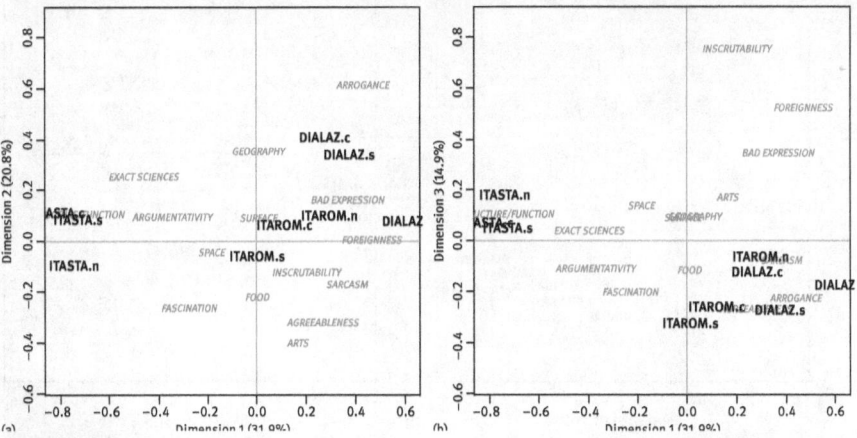

Figure 6a/6b: Correspondence biplots of the Latian contact area [DIALAZ = Latian dialect; ITAROM = Roman variety].

to be tight associations between lects and semantic fields. This absence becomes even more evident when one looks at the contribution of the third dimension (see Figure 6b), which does not confirm the associations seen using the first two dimensions. Some caution is thus in order in the interpretation of the Latian contact area. A general observation is that local dialects of Latium are situated in the same quadrants as negative semantic fields, such as BAD EXPRESSION and especially ARROGANCE, and a neutral field like FOREIGNNESS. A plot mapping the first and third dimension (Figure 6b) downgrades the association with BAD EXPRESSION but upgrades the one with SARCASM, a field containing many adjectives indexing an energetic, teasing and mischievous personality. As far as the regional accents are concerned, the conceptualizations of the different student groups are distributed along the horizontal dimension so that southern students lean more towards the neutral end of the continuum than the central ones, and the latter more than the northern participants (more precisely: the conceptualization of the regional accents by the students does not lean towards the affectively charged negative fields, like their local Latian dialect conceptualizations).

Finally we arrive at the correspondence plot for the Campanian contact area (Figure 7a/7b). This time the lects gravitate more in towards the bottom-right quadrant of the plot, which generally contains semantic fields with many positive adjectives. Apart from the horizontal cline that we discovered in the previous plots (except for Tuscany), Figure 7a also shows that conceptual-semantic distances

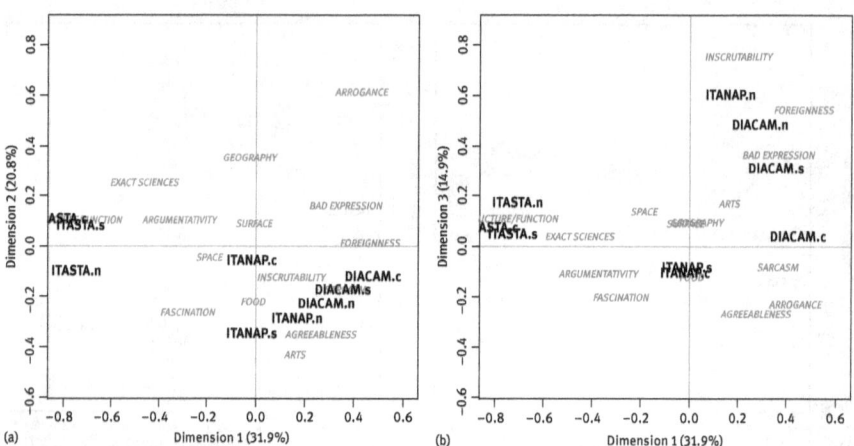

Figure 7a/7b: Correspondence biplots of the Campanian contact area [DIACAM = Campanian dialect; ITANAP = Neapolitan variety].

between the local dialects and Neapolitan-accented Italian are different across groups of students. Whereas the central and southern ones clearly distinguish between those two levels, the northern students have a roughly similar conceptualization of them. This participant-related distinction becomes even clearer when one takes into account the third dimension (in Figure 7b), in which the labels ITANAP.c and ITANAP.s almost overlap at a large distance from the ITANAP.n, which is in turn very close to the DIACAM.n label. Regarding the semantic fields employed, it is difficult to discover very strong associations with particular fields, although invoking the third dimension of the correspondence plot (Figure 7b) reveals that the students from central and southern regions associate the regional variety with terms related to food and cooking (FOOD). Participants from northern Italy consider Neapolitan Italian speakers agreeable people (AGREEABLENESS). But what is really confirmed by the third dimension is the strong association with the field of INSCRUTABILITY, the only really negative field in that group: the Neapolitan accent and its speaker are therefore considered mysterious and obscure. The conceptualizations of the local Campanian dialect cluster around the field of SARCASM, although looking at the combined perspective of the first and third dimensions does not confirm this association for the three respondent groups. According to that alternative visualization, northern students tend to stress the social distance and non-Italian nature of this lect (FOREIGNNESS) and the southern ones mostly employ the field of BAD EXPRESSION.

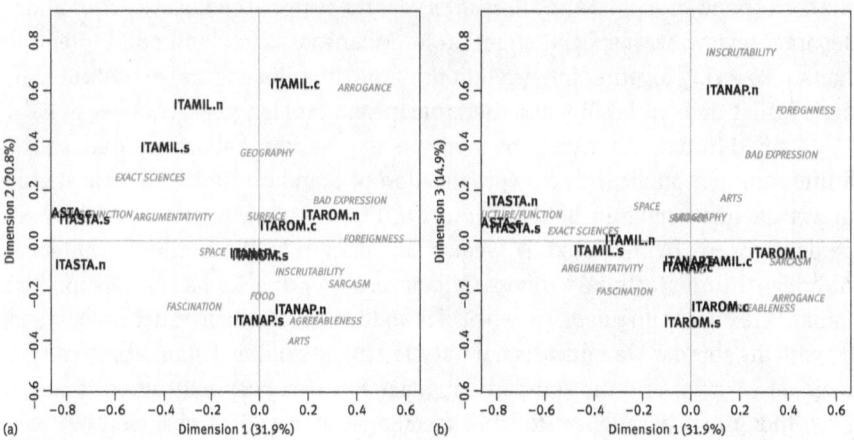

Figure 8a/8b: Correspondence biplots of the regional (contact) varieties.

To conclude, Figures 8a/8b show the correspondence biplots that bring together all regional varieties under scrutiny, which allows us to better grasp how varieties of one language can be attributed very different associations due to the substratum language and/or stereotypes about the area in which they are spoken. Three areas can be distinguished in Figure 8a: the first one clusters perceptions of Standard Italian, the second sets apart Milanese Italian (albeit with some variability between the participant groups) and the third one contains all the other southern and central regional varieties. Furthermore, the Neapolitan and Florentine varieties roughly occupy the same space as the non-negative semantic fields, such as FOOD, ARTS, AGREEABLENESS, FASCINATION and SARCASM. The only exception in this group is the position of the conceptualization of Neapolitan Italian by the northern students, which only becomes manifest if one adds a third dimension (Figure 8b). In that case, the variety stands totally isolated and gets associated with the fields INSCRUTABILITY and FOREIGNNESS. The Roman variety is situated at the periphery of this bottom cluster and tends to lean more towards the fields that are either negative or at least not positive (BAD EXPRESSION, SPACE and SURFACE).

6 Discussion

In the following paragraphs, we first summarize the overall structure revealed by the correspondence plots and afterwards pass the regional contact varieties under separate review, with special attention for Milanese, Neapolitan and Florentine Italian. We bring together interpretations of the different cultural models at play, and discuss their variability and their role in standard language changes in Italy.

A small initial note should be made about Standard Italian: our data shows a uniform, monothematic conceptualization of Standard Italian, in that it only draws on one semantic field (STRUCTURE/FUNCTION, which is shared by all student groups (with a slightly weaker association in the northern students). Although the four regional varieties (Milanese, Florentine, Roman and Neapolitan Italian) are clearly linguistic varieties of Standard Italian, their structural similarity with the standard language is not reflected in the smaller distance between the regional varieties and the standard language in the conceptual-semantic space. Even though no parallelism for this specific relation can be observed between structural properties and cultural models, it is still possible to come up with a sensible interpretation for the distribution of the lects in the horizontal dimension. This dimension distinguishes the various strata of the contact continuum, with Standard Italian in isolation at the left, the regional varieties in the middle and the local dialects at the right of the plot. The only exception to this pattern are the lects of Tuscany, which are clustered together. This sort of interpretation is harder to apply for the distribution of the semantic fields, as they seem not to be organized along a cline, but rather grouped into areas of the plot: the object- or language-related fields are in the top right quadrant (except for FOOD), the positive fields are situated in the bottom of the plot and the more one climbs to the top right quadrant, the more the fields become negative, with ARROGANCE as the most stigmatizing stereotype.

If we superimpose the space defined by the lects onto the space defined by the semantic fields, some interesting co-occurrence patterns emerge. Starting with the Lombard contact area, it is striking that conceptualizations strictly separate central participants from the northern and southern students. While northern and southern students hold distinct cultural models of local dialect and variety, but evaluate both on object-related or linguistic grounds (EXACT SCIENCES, ARGUMENTATIVITY), the central students express a negative person-related attitude towards the residents of Lombardy (ARROGANCE), regardless of whether they speak the Lombard dialect or the Milanese variety. The region's economic power and its rising role as the most standardized region poses a threat to the monopoly that the central regions, and especially its capitals Florence and Rome, have enjoyed in the standard language debate for centuries (even constituting the so-called "linguistic axis" during fascist era). The cultural models that Roman and Florentine speakers have of that area might indicate a more defensive attitude resulting from growing linguistic insecurity. Conversely, the association with neutral fields among non-central speakers suggests that Milanese Italian is losing geographic and social markedness among the northern and especially southern speakers and is thus assuming a more standard-like cultural model. We believe, however, that different motivations for this non-negative attitude have played a role for both groups: for northerners the increased self-awareness of the prestige of their own regional variety, and for southerners the absence of a significant linguistic heritage that needs to be safeguarded from the threat posed by the northern regional variety, combined with a delayed standardization in the south (see section 3). Further evidence for the Milanese variety's fading ties with its regional homeland compared to the other varieties might also be deduced from the relatively high density of semantic fields associations for the central and southern varieties compared to the quadrants where Milanese Italian is situated. If we interpret this as a lack of a focused and rich cultural model, then this might also be caused by the fact that the variety is not perceived as a distinct entity (i.e. a lack of cognitive salience). However, more experimental studies will be needed to disentangle both aspects (recognition and evaluation) more effectively.

It is surprising to see conceptual-semantic contiguity between the regional varieties in Tuscany and those in Campania, two regions with a very different (linguistic) history. The lects of both contact areas occupy the space defined mainly by the semantic fields FOOD, FASCINATION and AGREEABLENESS, with just one exception, that is, the northern students' conceptualization of Neapolitan Italian. This last particular pattern is similar to what we saw with the divergent behavior of our central participants with respect to Milanese Italian. Both the local Neapolitan dialect and the regional variety are associated with FOREIGNNESS and to a lesser extent INSCRUTABILITY. In other words, northern speakers do not hold different cultural models for different lects of the continuum, but they hold one for the cultural/contact area as a whole. In addition, the associations are overall more negative than those given by other participants in the survey. These findings seem to be indicative of the large linguistic and cultural differences that have divided Italian society through its geographic middle. The prevalent negative stereotype held by northerners about southern Italy and Italians is confirmed through our analysis: the difficulty to comprehend that cultural area is reflected in the struggle to consider and accept that area as a constitutive part of the Italian language area. That such resentment and mistrust are not shared by participants of the central regions, is probably also because they did not experience mass immigration, and the consequent issues, from southern Italy as the northern regions did in the course of the century. The proximity of a positive field such as AGREEABLENESS to the Neapolitan variety's northern conceptualization, is, in our opinion, more a sign of the condescending attitude that generally prevails when talking about southern Italy.

Finally, we return to the position of the Florentine regional variety within a conceptual-semantic space made up by non-negative fields, with two very positive peaks (FASCINATION and AGREEABLENESS). The first of the two fields gets associated with the Florentine variety especially by the southern students, which might reflect the traditional prestige and respect that the Florence-based pronunciation still enjoys in that section of the population, being the "best speech". Northern participants tend to draw from the field of ARTS to conceptualize the variety, and so highlight the historical role that Florence played as cultural center. The sort of conceptualization that emerges here is one that could rightly fit into the category "old prestige" (Kristiansen 2009): it focuses much more on the aesthetic, moral and historical superiority of standard language use, linked to a class of well-educated high-profile speakers than that it is guided by considerations of situational appropriateness and/or attributions of valuable contemporary personal traits (for instance, dynamism and relaxation). It is a prestige with dwindling power that crystallizes out the variety in question to the level of a historical monument. It is therefore not a coincidence that we do not find the Florentine-based variety in the top-left quadrant.

7 Conclusion

In this contribution we have shown how the main theoretical tenets and the methodological standards of Cognitive Linguistics can contribute to uncovering the cultural conceptualization that speakers hold towards a linguistic landscape marked by contact-induced variation. Specifically, we illustrated this potential by means of a case study of the Italian language area. Thanks to a free association survey we were able to collect descriptions and evaluations from a diverse and large sample of Italian students, that we have further clustered in semantic fields. Associating the semantic fields with the lects under scrutiny (standard language, regional accents and local dialects) allowed us to see which lects share similar conceptualizations and whether the supposed stratificational distances between lects within the continuum of a certain area find a counterpart in the conceptual-semantic distances between those same lects.

Let's summarize the findings emerged in the discussion section. The distribution of the lects in the conceptual-semantic space is evident on the horizontal dimension of the plots, which distinguishes the different strata in the standard-dialect continuum: from left to right Standard Italian, regional accents and local dialects, with the sole exception of Tuscany. This seems to confirm that cultural models of the Italian lects primarily pattern along linguistic strata, and only in the second place according to region. Regarding the individual regional varieties, Milanese Italian seems the only lect coming close to the conceptualization of Standard Italian, a fact that strengthens the perceived loss of geographic and social markedness of that regional accent. This observation is, however, only shared by northern and southern students, whereas central students locate Milanese Italian close to negative semantic domains. Neapolitan Italian and Florentine Italian share a region of the semantic space populated by positive semantic fields, except for the northern students' cultural model of Neapolitan Italian, which is made out of negative associations, just like their cultural model of the local Campanian dialect. This is seen as an indication that northern participants hold a negative attitude over the southern region as a whole, without making a distinction on a linguistic level. Finally, Florentine Italian seems to be considered the variety associated with old prestige values, its conceptualization highlighting historic and moral superiority rather than more modern prestige values, such as appropriateness and dynamism.

On a more general level, this work tried to bring together and put into practice the fundamental ideas underlying Cognitive (Contact) Linguistics for a study on cultural models of people's linguistic environment. We have approached the task of uncovering cultural models as a form of semantic analysis, by extracting semantic fields from free association data. We have taken the usage-based claim seriously by both relying on a collection of semi-elicited survey data and on advanced computational-semantic analysis of that data with the use of Vector Space Models. Finally, we have adopted a community-level and comparative perspective, by looking at how cultural conceptualizations of a particular contact situation are (heterogeneously) represented and distributed across different student groups across geographical areas in Italy.

Bibliography

Auer, Peter. 2005. Europe's sociolinguistic unity, or: A typology of European dialect/standard constellations. In Nicole Delbecque, Johan Van der Auwera, & Dirk Geeraerts (Eds.), *Perspectives on Variation: Sociolinguistic, Historical, Comparative*, 7–42. Berlin: Mouton de Gruyter.

Baker, Paul & Tony McEnery. 2005. A corpus-based approach to discourses of refugees and asylum seekers in UN and newspaper texts. *Journal of Language & Politics* 4(2). 197–226.

Baroni, Marco, Silvia Bernardini, Adriano Ferraresi, & Eros Zanchetta. 2009. The WaCky Wide Web: A collection of very large linguistically processed Web-crawled corpora. *Journal of Language Resources and Evaluation* 43(3). 209–226.

Baroni, Maria Rosa. (1983). *Il linguaggio trasparente. Indagini psicolinguistica su chi parla e chi ascolta*. Bologna: Il Mulino.

Berruto, Gaetano. 1995. *Fondamenti di sociolinguistica*. Bari: Laterza.

Berthele, Raphael. 2010. Investigations into the folk's mental models of linguistic varieties. In Dirk Geeraerts, Gitte Kristiansen & Yves Peirsman (eds.), *Advances in Cognitive Sociolinguistics*, 265–290. Berlin, Boston: De Gruyter Mouton.

Boster, James, Brent Berlin & John O'Neill, J. 1986. The correspondence of Jivaroan to Scientific Ornithology. *American Anthropologist* 88(3). 569–583.

Britain, David. 2004. Geolinguistics - Diffusion of Language. In Ulrich Ammon, Norbert Dittmar, Klaus J. Mattheier, & Peter Trudgill (eds.), *Sociolinguistics/Soziolinguistik* (1), 34–48. Berlin: Walter de Gruyter.

Canobbio, Susanna, & Gabriele Iannàccaro. (eds.). 2000. *Contributo per una bibliografia sulla dialettologia percezionale*. Alessandria: Edizioni dell'Orso.

Cardinaletti, Ann, & Nicola Munaro. (eds.). 2009. *Italiano, italiani regionali e dialetti*. Milano: Franco Angeli.

Castellani, Arrigo Ettore. 1982. Quanti erano gli italofoni nel 1861? *Studi Linguistici Italiani* 1. 3–26.

Cerruti, Massimo. 2009. *Strutture dell'italiano regionale. Morfosintassi di una varietà diatopica in prospettiva sociolinguistica*. Frankfurt am Main: Peter Lang.

Cerruti, Massimo. 2011. Regional varieties of Italian in the linguistic repertoire. *International Journal of the Sociology of Language* 210. 9–28.

Cerruti, Massimo, Claudia Crocco & Stefania Marzo (eds.). 2017. *Towards a New Standard: Theoretical and Empirical Studies on the Restandardization of Italian*. Berlin/New York: De Gruyter Mouton.

Cerruti, Massimo & Riccardo Regis. 2014. Standardization patterns and dialect/standard convergence: A northwestern Italian perspective. *Language in Society* 43. 83–111.

Cienki, Alan. 2005. Metaphor in the "Strict Father" and "Nurturant Parent" cognitive models: Theoretical issues raised in an empirical study. *Cognitive Linguistics 16*. 279–312.

Cini, Monica & Riccardo Regis (eds). 2002. *Che cosa ne pensa oggi Chiaffredo Roux? Percorsi della dialettologia percezionale all'alba del nuovo millennio*. Alessandria: Edizioni dell'Orso.

Coseriu, Eugenio. 1973. *Lezioni di linguistica generale*. Torino: Boringhieri.

D'Andrade, Roy G. 1995. *The Development of Cognitive Anthropology*. Cambridge, UK: Cambridge University Press.

De Blasi, Nicola. 2014. *Geografia e storia dell'italiano regionale*. Bologna: Il Mulino.

De Mauro, Tullio. 1970. *Storia linguistica dell'Italia unita* (2nd [1963]). Bari: Laterza.

De Pascale, Stefano, Stefania Marzo & Dirk Speelman. 2017. Evaluating regional variation in Italian: Towards a change in standard language ideology. In Massimo Cerruti, Claudia Crocco & Stefania Marzo (eds.), *Towards a New Standard: Theoretical and Empirical Studies on the Restandardization of Italian* 6, 18. Berlin: Mouton De Gruyter.

Divjak, Dagmar & Nick Fieller. 2015. Cluster analysis: Finding structure in linguistic data. In Justyna A. Robinson & Dylan Glynn (eds.), *Corpus Methods for Semantics: Quantitative Studies in Polysemy and Synonymy* 43, 405–441. Amsterdam: Benjamins.

Fairclough, Norman, Jane Mulderrig & Ruth Wodak. (2011). Critical Discourse Analysis. In Teun A. van Dijk (ed.), *Discouse Studies. A Multidisciplinary Introduction*, 357–378. London: Sage.

Fillmore, Charles J. 1977. Scenes-and-frames semantics. In Antonio Zampolli (ed.), *Linguistic Structures Processing*. North Holland Publishing.

Firth, John Rupert. 1957. *Paper in Linguistics 1934-1951*. Oxford: Oxford University Press.

Fusco, Fabiana & Carla Marcato (eds.). 2001. L'italiano e le regioni. Udine: Forum.

Galli de' Paratesi, Nora. 1984. *Lingua toscana in bocca ambrosiana. Tendenze verso l'italiano standard: un'inchiesta sociolinguistica*. Bologna: Il Mulino.

Geeraerts, Dirk. 2003. Cultural models of linguistic standardization. In René Dirven, Roslyn Frank & Martin Pütz (eds.), *Cognitive Models in Language and Thought. Ideology, Metaphors and Meanings* 24, 25–68. Berlin: Mouton de Gruyter.

Geeraerts, Dirk. 2010. *Theories of Lexical Semantics*. Oxford: Oxford University Press.

Geeraerts, Dirk. 2015. From structure to context. Modern linguistics from a distance. In *Μελέτες για την Ελληνική Γλώσσα. Studies in Greek Linguistics. Proceedings of the Annual Meeting of the Department of Linquistics, School of Philology, Faculty of Philosophy, Aristotle University of Thessaloniki*, 35–51. Thessaloniki: Aristotle University of Thessaloniki.

Geeraerts, Dirk & Gitte Kristiansen. 2015. Variationist linguistics. In Ewa Dabrowska & Dagmar Divjak (eds.), *Handbook of Cognitive Linguistics* 39, 336–389. Berlin: De Gruyter Mouton.

Giles, Howard & Tamara Rakić. 2014. Language attitudes: Social determinants and consequences of language variation. In Thomas M. Holtgraves (ed.), *The Oxford Handbook of Language and Social Psychology*, 11–26. Oxford: Oxford University Press.

Glynn, Dylan. 2015. Correspondance analysis: Exploring data and identifying patterns. Justyna A. Robinson & Dylan Glynn (eds.), *Corpus Methods for Semantics: Quantitative Studies in Polysemy and Synonymy* 43, 133–179. Amsterdam: Benjamins.

Grondelaers, Stefan & Dirk Speelman. 2016. A quantitative analysis of qualitative free response data. In Jocelyne Daems, Eline Zenner, Kris Heylen, Dirk Speelman & Hubert Cuyckens (eds.), *Change of Paradigms - New Paradoxes. Recontextualizing Language and Linguistics*, 361–384. Berlin, Boston: De Gruyter Mouton.

Harris, Zellig. 1954. Distributional Structure. *Word* 10(2/3). 146–162.

Holland, Dorothy & Naomi Quinn (eds.). 1987. *Cultural Models in Language and Thought*. Cambridge: Cambridge University Press.

Keesing, Roger. M. 1987. Models, "folk" and "cultural." In Dorothy Holland & Naomi Quinn (eds.), *Cultural Models in Language and Thought*, 369–393. Cambridge: Cambridge University Press.

Krefeld, Thomas. 1988. Periodisierung / Periodizzazione. In Günter Holtus, Michael Metzeltin & Christian Schmitt (eds.), *Lexikon der Romanistischen Linguistik. Italienisch, Korsisch, Sardisch*, 748–762. Berlin, Boston: De Gruyter.

Krefeld, Thomas. 2011. «Primäre», «sekundäre», «tertiäre» Dialekte – und die Geschichte des italienischen Sprachraums. In Anja Overbeck, Wolfgang Schweickard, & Harald Völker (eds.), *Lexikon, Varietät, Philologie. Romanistische Studien. Günter Holtus zum 65. Geburtstag*, 137–148). Berlin, Boston: De Gruyter.

Krefeld, Thomas & Elissa Pustka (eds.). 2010. *Perzeptive Varietätenlinguistik*. Frankfurt am Main: Peter Lang.

Kristiansen, Tore. 2009. The macro-level social meanings of late-modern Danish accents. *Acta Linguistica Hafniensia 41*. 167–192.

Lakoff, George. 1987. *Women, Fire and Dangerous Things. What Categories Reveal about the Mind*. Chicago: The University of Chicago Press.

Lakoff, George & Mark Johnson. 1980. *Metaphors We Live By*. Chicago: Chicago University Press.

Lenci, Alessandro. 2008. Distributional semantics in linguistic and cognitive research. *Italian Journal of Linguistics* 20(1). 1–31.

Peirsman, Yves & Dirk Geeraerts. 2009. Predicting strong associations on the basis of corpus data. In *Proceedings of the 12th Conference of the European Chapter of the Association for Computational Linguistics (EACL-2009)*, 648–656. Athens.

Peirsman, Yves, Kris Heylen & Dirk Geeraerts. 2010. Applying word space models to sociolinguistics. Religion names before and after 9/11. In Dirk Geeraerts, Gitte Kristiansen & Yves Peirsman (eds.), *Advances in Cognitive Sociolinguistics*, 111–138. Berlin, Boston: De Gruyter Mouton.

Preston, Dennis R. (2005). Perceptual dialectology. In Ulrich Ammon, Norbert Dittmar, Klaus J. Mattheier, & Peter Trudgill (eds.), *Sociolinguistics/Soziolinguistik* 2, 1683–1696. Berlin: Walter de Gruyter.

Romney, A. Kimball & Roy Goodwin D'Andrade. 1964. Cognitive aspects of English kin terms. *American Anthropologist* 68(3). 146–170.

Rosch, Eleanor. 1978. Principles of categorization. In Eleanor Rosch & Barbara Bloom Lloyd (eds.), *Cognition and Categorization*, 27–48. Hillsdale, NJ: Lawrence Erlbaum Associates.

Rosseel, Laura, Dirk Speelman & Dirk Geeraerts. 2015. Can social psychological attitude measures be used to study language attitudes? A case study exploring the Personalized Implicit Association Test. In *Proceedings of the 6th Conference on Quantitative Investigations in Theoretical Linguistics*. Tübingen.

Rousseeuw, Peter J. 1987. Silhouettes: A graphical aid to the interpretation and validation of cluster analysis. *Journal of Computational and Applied Mathematics* 20. 53–65.

Schegloff, Emanuel A. 1997. Whose Text? Whose Context? *Discourse & Society* 8(2). 165–187.

Sobrero, Alberto A. (1988). Italienisch: Regionale Varianten. Italiano regionale. In Günter Holtus, Michael Metzeltin & Christian Schmitt (eds.), *Lexikon der Romanistischen Linguistik* 4, 732–748. Tübingen: Niemeyer.

Soukup, Barbara. 2013. The measurement of language attitudes - a reappraisal from a constructionist perspective. In Tore Kristiansen & Stefan Grondelaers (eds.), *Language (de)standardisation in Late Modern Europe: Experimental Studies*, 251–266. Oslo: Novus Press.

Strauss, Claudia & Naomi Quinn. 1997. *A Cognitive Theory of Cultural Meaning*. Cambridge, UK: Cambridge University Press.

Telmon, Tullio. 1993. Varietà regionali. In Alberto A. Sobrero (ed.), *Introduzione all'italiano contemporaneo* 2, 93–149. Roma-Bari: Laterza.

Volkart-Rey, Ramón. 1990. *Atteggiamenti linguistici e stratificazione sociale. La percezione dello status sociale attraverso la pronuncia*. Roma: Bonacci.

Widdowson, Henry G. 1995. Discourse analysis: a critical view. *Language and Literature* 4(3). 157–172.

Zenner, Eline & Gitte Kristiansen. (2013). Introduction: Onomasiological, methodological and phraseological perspectives on lexical borrowing. In Eline Zenner & Gitte Kristiansen (eds.), *New Perspectives on Lexical Borrowing. Onomasiological, Methodological and Phraseological Innovations*, 1–18. Berlin, Boston: De Gruyter.

Appendix 1: Adjectives with positive silhouette width per cluster/semantic domain.

C1: Structure/Function (N=71)

[1] "corretto"	"adeguato"	"specifico"	"semplificato"	"oggettivo"
[6] "selettivo"	"articolato"	"necessario"	"definito"	"puntuale"
[11] "diverso"	"particolare"	"differenziato"	"individuabile"	"circoscritto"
[16] "omogeneo"	"concreto"	"estensivo"	"preciso"	"diversificato"
[21] "consulenziale"	"pratico"	"dizione"	"univoco"	"appropriato"
[26] "fondamentale"	"settoriale"	"formale"	"didattico"	"limitato"
[31] "tecnico"	"efficace"	"determinato"	"specialistico"	"imperativo"
[36] "dettagliato"	"contenuto"	"esplicativo"	"pianificato"	"orientato"
[41] "peculiare"	"basilare"	"elaborato"	"proporzionato"	"incompleto"
[46] "discriminatorio"	"esaustivo"	"standardizzato"	"lavorativo"	"abbreviato"
[51] "dislessico"	"atipico"	"inquadrato"	"descrittivo"	"distinto"
[56] "economico"	"assimilato"	"materiale"	"professionale"	"fruibile"
[61] "controllato"	"psicopatologia"	"immediato"	"ristretto"	"regolamentato"
[66] "confidenziale"	"sovraregionale"	"diretto"	"regolare"	"istituzionale"
[71] "familiare"				

C2: Fascination (N=64)

[1] "affascinante"	"romantico"	"fascinoso"	"spettacolare"	"fantasioso"
[7] "intrigante"	"inimitabile"	"fiabesco"	"fantastico"	"accattivante"
[13] "sobrio"	"sensuale"	"chic"	"bucolico"	"inusuale"
[19] "raffinato"	"esuberante"	"decadente"	"austero"	"ingegnoso"
[25] "arioso"	"ritratto"	"piacevole"	"inconfondibile"	"trendy"
[31] "curato"	"armonioso"	"stupendo"	"eccelso"	"pomposo"
[37] "agresto"	"ritmato"	"perfetto"	"colto"	"british"
[43] "artefatto"	"figurato"	"spartano"	"elegante"	"movimentato"
[49] "gattopardo"	"ermetico"	"sapiente"	"andante"	"dantesco"
[55] "narratore"	"ricco"	"ricercato"	"genuino"	"metaforico"
[61] "vivace"	"raro"	"cadenzato"	"curioso"	

Additional column (rightmost):

"attraente"
"emozionante"
"ineguagliabile"
"incantevole"
"grintoso"
"superbo"
"bizzarro"
"sexy"
"ideale"
"romanzato"

C3: Exact Sciences (N=33)

[1] "dinamico"	"statico"	"lineare"	"semplice"	"ibrido"	"usuale"
[7] "geometrico"	"calibrato"	"sofisticato"	"bilanciato"	"studiato"	"impostato"
[13] "percepibile"	"conciso"	"interpretabile"	"consonantico"	"iconico"	"scansionato"
[19] "eterogeneo"	"affidabile"	"approssimativo"	"schematico"	"discorsivo"	"riconoscibile"
[25] "istantaneo"	"obsoleto"	"spaziale"	"vocalico"	"frammentario"	"sintetico"
[31] "ordinato"	"accurato"	"ciclico"			

C4: Sarcasm (N=48)

[1] "caricaturale"	"sarcastico"	"enfatico"	"canzonatorio"	"irriverente"
[6] "parodistico"	"scanzonato"	"graffiante"	"macchiettistico"	"melodrammatico"
[11] "spassoso"	"sboccato"	"colloquiale"	"triviale"	"spigliato"
[16] "monocorde"	"sagace"	"burlesco"	"ansiogeno"	"stereotipato"
[21] "garbato"	"umoristico"	"goliardico"	"sciatto"	"verboso"
[26] "ironico"	"ridondante"	"incalzante"	"sgrammaticato"	"giullaresco"
[31] "frivolo"	"pretenzioso"	"arzigogolato"	"esilarante"	"scherzoso"
[36] "accentato"	"inflazionato"	"estroso"	"spiritoso"	"estroverso"
[41] "felliniano"	"sincopato"	"laconico"	"criptico"	"orecchiabile"
[46] "piacione"	"altisonante"	"riflessivo"	"forbito"	"comico"

C5: Argumentativity (N=33)

[1] "inaccettabile"	"evidente"	"comprensibile"	"decisivo"	"diffuso"	"artificioso"
[7] "incoerente"	"virtuoso"	"crescente"	"scorretto"	"inefficace"	"insostenibile"
[13] "estremo"	"chiaro"	"accettato"	"impreciso"	"espansivo"	"malinteso"
[19] "inesistente"	"anacronistico"	"intimidatorio"	"influenzato"	"accettabile"	"interclassista"
[25] "convincente"	"pragmatico"	"intellettuale"	"pleonastico"	"pronunciato"	"veritiero"
[31] "universale"	"capitale"	"forzato"			

(continued)

Appendix 1: (Continued)

C6: Food (N=38)

[1] "casereccio"	"affettato"	"crudo"	"fresco"	"mescolato"	"amalgamante"
[7] "casalingo"	"sfizioso"	"dolce"	"pregiato"	"mangiato"	"grasso"
[13] "spezzettato"	"rustico"	"insaporo"	"composto"	"mischiato"	"buongustaio"
[19] "tagliato"	"pizzaiolo"	"secco"	"ciociaro"	"capiente"	"pulito"
[25] "sciapo"	"tipico"	"caldo"	"acquatico"	"nostrano"	"fine"
[31] "magro"	"sbrodolato"	"confortevole"	"tenero"	"compito"	"caratteristico"
[37] "spumeggiante"	"corposo"				

C7: Arrogance (N=65)

[1] "frainteso"	"presuntuoso"	"ipocrita"	"arrogante"	"maleducato"	
[6] "supponente"	"spocchioso"	"volgare"	"stupido"	"ignorante"	
[11] "ridicolo"	"sensato"	"cafone"	"polentone"	"sopravvalutato"	
[16] "esagerato"	"sciocco"	"antipatico"	"autocompiaciuto"	"spicciolo"	
[21] "inutile"	"buzzurro"	"schizzinoso"	"strafottente"	"scurrile"	
[26] "petulante"	"indisponente"	"inelegante"	"noioso"	"insincero"	
[31] "sprovveduto"	"pirla"	"razzista"	"cacofonico"	"prolisso"	
[36] "irritante"	"banale"	"pessimo"	"confusionario"	"odioso"	
[41] "terrone"	"lagnoso"	"sfacciato"	"protervo"	"accomodante"	
[46] "scialbo"	"berlusconiano"	"spaccone"	"diminutivo"	"saccente"	
[51] "temporeggiante"	"antiquato"	"disgustoso"	"giusto"	"gorgia"	
[56] "bonaccione"	"pignolo"	"leghista"	"tedioso"	"sgradevole"	
[61] "frettoloso"	"disprezzante"	"incorretto"	"scocciato"	"polemico"	

C8: Space (N=30)

[1] "uguale"	"solare"	"anteriore"	"normale"	"raddoppiato"	"basso"	"verticale"
[8] "rigido"	"solido"	"marcato"	"usato"	"ascendente"	"bloccato"	"sospeso"
[15] "alto"	"naturale"	"variabile"	"nervoso"	"contaminato"	"medio"	"esteso"
[22] "pesante"	"neutro"	"omologato"	"isolato"	"posteriore"	"veloce"	"terrigeno"
[29] "arretrato"	"largo"					

C9: Agreeableness (N=65)

[1] "affettuoso"	"gentile"	"caloroso"	"lieto"	"cordiale"	"sincero"
[7] "adorabile"	"felice"	"orgoglioso"	"umile"	"cortese"	"amichevole"
[13] "gioviale"	"sentito"	"amabile"	"allegro"	"socievole"	"carino"
[19] "buono"	"sereno"	"bonario"	"simpatico"	"compiaciuto"	"spensierato"
[25] "sorridente"	"irreprensibile"	"bello"	"scontroso"	"focoso"	"gioioso"
[31] "burbero"	"guascone"	"perspicace"	"gagliardo"	"timido"	"bagordo"
[37] "convinto"	"chiocciante"	"donnaiolo"	"loquace"	"incasinato"	"sforzato"
[43] "regale"	"vispo"	"educato"	"tranquillo"	"anonimo"	"rassicurante"
[49] "rude"	"virile"	"soave"	"altezzoso"	"maltrattato"	"festaiolo"
[55] "cantato"	"sano"	"caciarone"	"partecipe"	"vivo"	"dubbioso"
[61] "chiassoso"	"indeciso"	"squillante"	"altolocato"	"figo"	

C10: Bad expression (N=60)

[1] "urlato"	"gridato"	"biascicante"	"gesticolato"	"lamentoso"	"gutturale"
[7] "fragoroso"	"scalpitante"	"stridulo"	"sospirato"	"martellante"	"rabbioso"
[13] "afono"	"trascinato"	"zoppicato"	"imperturbabile"	"troncato"	"stanco"
[19] "sordo"	"mellifluo"	"dolente"	"finto"	"concitato"	"sgraziato"
[25] "sibilante"	"smozzicato"	"storto"	"affannoso"	"balzante"	"truce"
[31] "cantilenante"	"ingessato"	"spavaldo"	"mozzato"	"impacciato"	"rassegnato"
[37] "atono"	"melodioso"	"duro"	"strascicato"	"stonato"	"flemmatico"
[43] "minaccioso"	"solito"	"svelto"	"tronfio"	"baldanzoso"	"vecchio"
[49] "effeminato"	"improvvisato"	"canterino"	"cascante"	"tosto"	"arcigno"
[55] "vicino"	"tamarro"	"stentato"	"strano"	"ganzo"	"povero"

(continued)

Appendix 1: (Continued)

C11: Inscrutability (N=56)

[1] "tragico"	"profondo"	"inquietante"	"oscuro"	"drammatico"	"caotico"
[7] "alieno"	"incerto"	"misterioso"	"strisciante"	"confuso"	"ambiguo"
[13] "vissuto"	"disordinato"	"esasperato"	"potente"	"improbabile"	"indistinto"
[19] "inaspettato"	"terribile"	"distorto"	"aggressivo"	"dimenticato"	"insuperabile"
[25] "imperfetto"	"sfuggente"	"tenace"	"quotidiano"	"complicato"	"puro"
[31] "irreale"	"angosciante"	"eloquente"	"impersonale"	"mediatico"	"sconosciuto"
[37] "claustrofobico"	"innaturale"	"onnipresente"	"spinto"	"infantile"	"simile"
[43] "inaccessibile"	"aspro"	"scandito"	"incostante"	"terreno"	"frenetico"
[49] "frammentato"	"ingarbugliato"	"decifrabile"	"mafioso"	"cupo"	"distante"
[55] "orrendo"	"aspirato"				

C12: Geography (N=30)

[1] "provinciale"	"partecipato"	"nazionale"	"locale"	"civile"	
[6] "centrale"	"regionale"	"ufficiale"	"internazionale"	"comune"	
[11] "straniero"	"diplomatico"	"dislocato"	"distaccato"	"rurale"	
[16] "onorevole"	"agricolo"	"coatto"	"urbano"	"protetto"	
[21] "ordinario"	"coinvolgente"	"unificato"	"materno"	"unico"	
[26] "informale"	"ammesso"	"associativo"	"pendente"	"radiotelevisivo"	

C13: Surface (N=65)

[1] "scuro"	"grigio"	"appuntito"	"opaco"	"spesso"	"tozzo"	"allungato"
[8] "arancione"	"tagliente"	"tondo"	"liscio"	"tronco"	"vaporoso"	"ruvido"
[15] "corto"	"cadente"	"sfumato"	"piatto"	"bucato"	"curvo"	"sciolto"
[22] "azzurro"	"robusto"	"colorato"	"sottile"	"scivolato"	"calcato"	"molle"
[29] "sbiadito"	"cristallino"	"rosso"	"scorrevole"	"piano"	"metallico"	"espirato"
[36] "lungo"	"limpido"	"leggero"	"spezzato"	"calante"	"diagonale"	"smussato"
[43] "guizzante"	"rotondo"	"arrotato"	"rudimentale"	"ripulito"	"morbido"	"trasparente"
[50] "pungente"	"avvolgente"	"spigoloso"	"nebbioso"	"livellato"	"gelido"	"pastoso"
[57] "eufonico"	"greve"	"intenso"	"alitato"	"grezzo"	"tonale"	"trasandato"
[64] "imbruttito"	"inespressivo"					

C14: Foreignness (N=49)

[1] "romano"	"longobardo"	"imperiale"	"spagnolo"	"illustre"	"portoghese"
[7] "francese"	"antico"	"papale"	"monastico"	"contadino"	"napoletano"
[13] "rumeno"	"medievale"	"brasiliano"	"milanese"	"montanaro"	"nobile"
[19] "toscano"	"prospero"	"popolare"	"meridionale"	"aristocratico"	"latino"
[25] "saggio"	"costruito"	"primitivo"	"arcaico"	"mondiale"	"famoso"
[31] "imponente"	"settentrionale"	"storico"	"nordico"	"siciliano"	"borghese"
[37] "istruito"	"autentico"	"estinto"	"borbone"	"dotto"	"fascista"
[43] "prezioso"	"signorile"	"elitario"	"maschile"	"paesano"	"illetterato"
[49] "campagnolo"					

C15: Arts (N=22)

[1] "musicale"	"teatrale"	"cinematografico"	"artistico"	"radiofonico"
[6] "letterario"	"creativo"	"filmico"	"dialettale"	"televisivo"
[11] "folkloristico"	"folcloristico"	"espressivo"	"originale"	"classico"
[16] "sonoro"	"variegato"	"ascoltabile"	"tradizionale"	"romanesco"
[21] "fanfarone"	"gergale"			

Appendix 2a: Contingency table for semantic domain associations per lect, by northern-Italian participants (.n).

	DIALOM.n	ITASTA.n	DIATOS.n	DIALAZ.n	DIACAM.n	ITATOS.n	ITAROM.n	ITAMIL.n	ITANAP.n
STRUCTURE/ FUNCTION	5	46	8	2	2	8	2	18	9
FASCINATION	2	22	23	2	2	15	10	5	6
EXACT SCIENCES	9	11	6	0	7	4	6	20	3
SARCASM	2	5	3	9	4	5	6	0	7
ARGUMENTATIVITY	7	19	5	3	4	3	9	11	12
FOOD	4	3	12	9	6	5	5	2	4
ARROGANCE	11	3	6	26	7	10	27	29	4
SPACE	4	17	5	3	8	5	8	14	9
AGREEABLENESS	13	8	42	27	14	45	19	7	18
BAD EXPRESSION	11	3	4	6	7	3	4	2	15
INSCRUTABILITY	2	5	0	2	10	2	4	3	21
GEOGRAPHY	7	1	0	2	2	1	3	2	2
SURFACE	14	9	4	5	8	8	8	10	5
FOREIGNNESS	28	0	7	7	9	6	6	5	7
ARTS	5	17	14	8	20	18	15	3	20

Appendix 2b: Contingency table for semantic domain associations per lect, by central-Italian participants (.c).

	DIALOM.c	ITASTA.c	DIATOS.c	DIALAZ.c	DIACAM.c	ITATOS.c	ITAROM.c	ITAMIL.c	ITANAP.c
STRUCTURE/FUNCTION	5	27	6	5	3	5	4	6	8
FASCINATION	3	11	12	2	4	11	6	6	8
EXACT SCIENCES	3	19	2	2	1	7	4	5	5
SARCASM	2	1	4	1	4	8	3	1	4
ARGUMENTATIVITY	2	23	13	16	0	10	17	5	10
FOOD	1	7	8	2	0	7	2	2	3
ARROGANCE	23	1	5	23	12	9	16	25	9
SPACE	0	4	3	3	2	1	4	4	4
AGREEABLENESS	5	6	21	18	18	22	23	4	15
BAD EXPRESSION	6	2	3	11	3	3	4	3	4
INSCRUTABILITY	2	2	3	2	4	1	1	4	0
GEOGRAPHY	2	3	1	3	4	1	2	4	1
SURFACE	3	7	5	1	3	5	5	4	5
FOREIGNNESS	4	2	3	4	4	3	3	2	4
ARTS	0	4	10	1	12	6	6	2	8

Appendix 2c: Contingency table for semantic domain associations per lect, by southern-Italian participants (.s).

	DIALOM.s	ITASTA.s	DIATOS.s	DIALAZ.s	DIACAM.s	ITATOS.s	ITAROM.s	ITAMIL.s	ITANAP.s
STRUCTURE/FUNCTION	7	34	8	1	4	15	8	18	10
FASCINATION	7	18	22	3	8	25	16	13	13
EXACT SCIENCES	6	23	12	10	4	6	10	17	11
SARCASM	3	0	3	5	2	4	6	0	2
ARGUMENTATIVITY	2	28	23	12	5	11	23	23	14
FOOD	4	10	6	5	2	6	3	1	5
ARROGANCE	16	4	4	36	10	7	20	18	7
SPACE	0	7	6	5	9	10	6	3	8
AGREEABLENESS	8	10	31	30	27	30	39	8	41
BAD EXPRESSION	7	4	4	7	8	4	1	6	4
INSCRUTABILITY	5	4	3	2	7	2	1	3	3
GEOGRAPHY	4	6	2	5	2	5	3	7	5
SURFACE	7	7	2	8	6	9	10	11	10
FOREIGNNESS	13	2	19	4	18	3	4	2	3
ARTS	7	6	7	7	10	1	10	5	25

Part III: Construction Grammar: Contact in and through more and less schematic form-meaning pairs

Bram Vertommen

8 Language alternation and the state-event contrast: A case-study of Dutch-Turkish and Dutch-Moroccan heritage speakers

Abstract: This paper investigates cognitive mechanisms underlying the alternating language choice in two fused (Dutch-Turkish and Dutch-Moroccan Arabic) lects. These lects are spoken by second generation heritage speakers in peer-group interactions (Nortier 1990; Backus 1996; Boumans 1998; Eversteijn 2012). It is argued that in these interactions the "alternations" between Turkish or Moroccan Arabic argument structures and Dutch argument structures occur on such a regular and intensive basis, that they cannot be exclusively attributed to extralinguistic contextual factors. Rather, the formal variation found in the data is hypothesized to reflect a distinction on the conceptual level: the speakers' choice between a Dutch or a Turkish/Moroccan Arabic argument structure is determined by a basic conceptual contrast between scenes that denote general states on the one hand, and scenes that represent events or temporally bounded states on the other. In this way, the paper shows how multilingual data can offer further empirical support for the pervasiveness of this contrast in languages around the world.

Keywords: bilingualism; language alternation; argument structure; event structure; conceptual scenes

1 Language alternation and fused lects

Most scholars in the field of contact linguistics acknowledge that there exist at least two different yet often intertwined types of juxtaposition strategies: (i) *insertions* and (ii) *alternations* (Backus 1996; Muysken 2000). Insertions take place when a single lexical item or phrase of source language A is embedded in the

---

Note: This project was supported by the *Research Foundation-Flanders* (FWO; Dutch: *Fonds voor Wetenschappelijk Onderzoek-Vlaanderen*) [grant number: 11G2812N]. I am particularly grateful to the researchers whom I got the bilingual (Dutch-Turkish and Dutch-Moroccan Arabic) data from: Ad Backus, Jacomine Nortier, Nadia Eversteijn and Louis Boumans.

Bram Vertommen, University of Antwerp

syntactic structure defined by source language B. Accordingly, source language A is called the "Embedded Language" (EL), whereas source language B is labeled as the "Matrix Language" (ML) (Myers-Scotton 1993b). For example, in (1) below the Dutch noun *arbeidsbureau* 'employment office' is embedded in a Turkish argument structure. In case of a switch of ML, then, an alternation takes place. Alternations involve switches that are more globally than locally defined: there is a shift of the source language which defines the argument structure of the sentence. In (1) the ML switches from (a) an argument structure defined by Turkish to (b) an argument structure defined by Dutch[1]:

(1a) **ON-DAN SONRA ŞEY-E GIT-TI-M**, *arbeidsbureau'*-**YA GIT-TI-M**.
that-ABL after thing-DAT go-PST-1SG employment.office-DAT go-PST-1SG
'After that, I went to the thing, to the employment office.'

(1b) *Die opleiding kost, ja, bijna tweeduizend gulden.*
that program cost.PRS.3SG yeah almost two.thousand guilders
'That [educational] program costs, yeah, almost two thousand guilders.'
(from the *Tilburg Cafe* data sample, see Backus 1996: 53–54, 59)

The example above instantiates only one out of the 146 alternations (105 intraturn, 41 interturn) produced by a single speaker, Ayhan, in the course of just one interaction. As the speaker produced 425 sentences during this interaction, this boils down to a ratio of 3.4 alternations (2.5 intraturn) in 10 sentences. A relatively high intensity of alternations is also found in the case of Ayhan's interlocutor, Hatice. She produced 62 alternations (24 intraturn, 38 interturn). Since her output comprises 277 sentences, this amounts to 2.3 alternations (0.9 intraturn) for every 10 sentences. This paper will exclusively focus on the systematic use of alternations throughout an interaction by multiple members of a speech community. More in particular, it will argue that the ML of (1a) and (1b) above (and most other sentences in the data sets under scrutiny) is not randomly chosen, but governed and constrained by considerations that are predominantly semantic in nature. Nevertheless, when it comes to alternations, the general image rather tends to be one in which the juxtaposition of MLs is a merely stylistic device which does not systematically occur. In line with such a view, most researchers interested in the use of alternations have adopted a descriptive sequential approach, with exclusive attention to local discursive

---

[1] The lay-out of the interlinear glosses in this paper is as follows. *Dutch morphemes* are only in italics, **Turkish morphemes** are in bold, in italics and in small capitals and MOROCCAN ARABIC MORPHEMES are in italics and in small capitals.

and conversational contextual factors that may trigger the use of alternations. Factors correspond to, amongst other things, changes of participant constellation, "mode" (activity type) shifts, or discourse topic switches (Gumperz 1982; Myers-Scotton 1993a; Auer 1998). Underlying this perspective on alternations is the thought that "what exactly a bilingual participant is doing when he or she switches languages is closely tied to the specific, never-identical circumstances in which alternation occurs" (Auer 1984: 3).

However, this perspective on alternations might be at least partially nourished by the subtype of bilingual data that have mainly been addressed. The relation between the use of alternations (as well as ML choice in multilingual speech) and ad hoc extralinguistic contextual factors can be seen as being characteristic for a particular subtype of multilingual behavior, "code-switching". In Auer's (1999) typology of bilingual speech, code-switching constitutes the initial stage in the potential development of a "fused lect". This development coincides with an increasing degree of "structural sedimentation" (Auer 1999: 310): the more conventionalized the meanings of ML choice (or of juxtapositions with another ML) are in bilingual language use, the closer this multilingual behavior resembles a fused lect. Accordingly, fused lects correspond to (semi-)autonomous varieties in which the meaning attached to such alternations, and to the use of one or the other MLs, is more or less stabilized or conventionalized (as opposed to inferential meanings that are only locally relevant). From that moment on, alternations occur with higher intensity and tend to become increasingly constrained by grammatical rules. In Auer's (1999: 321) words, in fused lects "the use of one "language" or the other for certain constituents [...] is part of their grammar, and speakers have no choice".

In the remainder of this paper I want to illustrate how the bilingual behavior of Dutch-Turkish and Dutch-Moroccan Arabic heritage speakers in the Netherlands can be seen as the manifestation of a fused lect and as rule-governed. Through a corpus-based analysis I will show that the speakers' preference for a particular ML at given points in discourse suggests the presence of underlying regularities imposed by the grammar of the bilingual variety. More precisely, speakers will be shown to systematically switch back and forth between Dutch and Turkish/Moroccan Arabic in accordance with a basic conceptual distinction between events and general states. A general state is defined by Michaelis (1998: xvi) as a state-of-affairs "which does not involve change over time and which does not have salient endpoints". For example, *being smart* or *being a dancer* are stable properties that, all things being equal, permanently apply to their holders (i.e., they are true throughout the entire lifetime (and beyond) of their holder). An event, by contrast, is characterized as a state-of-affairs "which involves change over time and/or which has salient points of inception and termination" (Michaelis

1998: xiii).[2] The events denoted by the VPs *being hungry* or *dancing* only last for a limited amount of time.

The structure of this article will be as follows. After I have introduced the Dutch-Turkish and Dutch-Moroccan Arabic corpora in Section 2, I will detail how I categorized my data in Section 3. Central to my analysis is a categorization of sentences, and their argument structures in particular, in terms of the basic conceptual scenes they express: association scenes, occurrence scenes, inception scenes and directionality scenes. Finally, in Section 4 I will show and discuss the results of the analysis. In Section 4.1 I will describe the quantitative analysis that tested the impact of conceptualization on language choice. In Section 4.2 I will illustrate (and nuance) the tendencies revealed by this analysis through a qualitative description of one selected fragment.

2 The corpus

In order to shed further light on the issues above I appealed to four corpora representative of two communities of heritage speakers in the Netherlands: (i) one Dutch-Turkish corpus from speech communities in Tilburg, Hilversum and Maastricht (see Backus 1996 for further details), (ii) one Dutch-Turkish corpus from the Lombok district in Utrecht (Eversteijn 2012), (iii) one Dutch-Moroccan Arabic corpus from Utrecht in general (Nortier 1990) and (iv) one Dutch-Moroccan Arabic corpus from the Lombok and Transvaal districts in Utrecht (Boumans 1998).

Despite their relative age, I selected these corpora for two main reasons. First, the juxtaposed languages in each language pair are relatively distant from each other from a typological point of view. Even in cases of early convergence of the two source languages this factor still facilitates the demarcation of the language which the argument structures are defined by. Second, during the compilation of the four corpora above the researchers in question were mostly not directly involved. They employed the technique of snowball sampling in order to gather the data: they relied on a few informants whom they were relatively acquainted with and requested them to tape-record interactions with people of their immigrant network. As the use of alternations is mainly a natural and spontaneous phenomenon, this sampling strategy provided the right environment for these alternations to occur.

---

2 It has been set forth by, amongst others, Boye (2010: 408–412, 2012: 188–194) that the (general) state-event distinction recurs under different headings in various subdomains: e.g., *"fact"* versus *"event"* (Vendler 1967) or *"propositional content"* versus *"state-of-affairs"* (Dik & Hengeveld 1991).

Within the chosen corpora I made further selections. First, my focus was on linguistic variation in contact settings. Accordingly, predominantly monolingual (Dutch, Turkish or Moroccan Arabic) interactions were not taken into account. Within the bilingual conversations I only singled out those speakers who exhibited enough variation between Dutch and Turkish/Moroccan Arabic to test the hypotheses above.

Second, in accordance with my research question I merely focused on those utterances which have descriptive function, such as statements, questions, promises and orders. This means that (minor) sentences constituted by so-called "expressives" (Langacker 2008: 475) were ruled out. Expressives correspond to linguistic elements such as response particles (e.g., *ja, evet, iyeh* 'yes', *nee, hayır, la* 'no'), exclamatives (e.g., *echt?, beşşeḥḥ?* 'really?', *wallah!* 'by God!', *ha!*) or backchannelling cues (e.g., *mhm, eh*). Such elements rather have an expressive, emotive or interactive value and do not conceptualize objective content.

The data set ultimately selected for analysis is presented in Table 1 below: The figures in the table refer to the number of sentences in one or the other language.

Table 1: Overview of the selected bilinguals and their output.

	DUTCH-TURKISH			
NAME SAMPLE	**SPEAKER**	**DUTCH**	**TURKISH**	**TOTAL**
Tilburg Café (Backus 1996)	Ayhan ♂	126	185	**311**
	Hatice ♀	140	48	**188**
Tilburg Women (Backus 1996)	Fulya ♀	39	88	**127**
	Müjgan ♀	27	91	**118**
Havva II.iii (Eversteijn 2012)	Ayşe ♀	26	9	**35**
	Fadime ♀	48	34	**82**
	Havva ♀	59	55	**114**
Havva IX–X (Eversteijn 2012)	Ayşe ♀	29	51	**80**
	Havva ♀	16	33	**49**
	DUTCH-MOROCCAN ARABIC			
NAME SAMPLE	**SPEAKER**	**DUTCH**	**TURKISH**	**TOTAL**
II.2a (Nortier 1990)	Morgan ♂	63	149	**212**
III.2b (Nortier 1990)	Moḥammed ♂	77	51	**128**
V.4a (Nortier 1990)	Souraya ♀	48	160	**208**
VI.4b (Boumans 1998)	Driss ♂	38	102	**140**
I.13a (Boumans 1998)	Hayat ♀	41	156	**197**

(continued)

Table 1 (continued)

II.9–II.9b (Boumans 1998)	Husayn ♂	133	263	**396**
	Samir ♂	60	281	**341**
IX.a–IX.b (Boumans 1998)	Abdullah ♂	94	85	**179**
	Samir ♂	69	120	**189**
VII.b–VIII.b (Boumans 1998)	Mahmoud ♂	36	144	**180**
	Samir ♂	110	334	**444**
X.11b–X.12a (Boumans 1998)	Maryam ♀	72	44	**116**
	Samir ♂	69	129	**198**

3 Conceptual scenes

3.1 Theoretical background

Conceptual scenes (e.g., transfer, (dynamic) activity, permanent state) are viewed as conventionalized mental scripts designed to categorize and structure thoughts according to the subtype of experiences or generalizations they pertain to. These subtypes are generally agreed to be based on a limited set of experientially-based parameters (or "archetypes") human beings deem as relevant (Goldberg 1995; Tomasello 2003), such as the (a)telicity of a state-of-affairs or the fact whether an event is oriented towards a specific goal or not. Given the general assumption that most language varieties show clear similarities in the basic set of conceptual scenes they give expression to (Goldberg 2006: 16–17), a well-defined set of conceptual scenes has a range of application that can span an entire multilingual data set, no matter whether an argument structure is ultimately defined by Dutch, Turkish or Moroccan Arabic grammar. In terms of formal correlates, conceptual scenes (e.g., transfers or permanent states) have been related to basic argument structure constructions such as ditransitive constructions or copula constructions (see Goldberg 1995 for further details).

Despite a large body of research on conceptual scenes (or similar concepts under different headings) and their formal correlates (Bybee 1988; Kemmer & Israel 1994; Goldberg 1995, 2006; Fauconnier & Turner 2002; Tomasello 2003; Croft 2012), the semantic criterion which is taken to be central to their classification is still very much under debate. In Levin and Rappaport Hovav (2005: 78–130) three main currents are distinguished: (i) the *localist approach*, (ii) the *(lexical) aspectual approach* and (iii) the *causal (force-dynamic) approach*. I would like to add a fourth influential current: (iv) the *systemic functional grammar approach*.

- The localist approach (Anderson 1971; Jackendoff 1972, 1983; Van Voorst 1988, 1993), starts from a basic conceptual contrast between location and motion "events",[3] either of them with their own set of participants. Location events are defined as states-of-affairs consisting of a thing (or a theme) and its location. This locative relation can apply to more eventive transitory states (e.g., *to remain on the shelf*) or to general states (e.g., states-of-affairs described by *to be* or other stative verbs). Motion events are described as states-of-affairs that imply a change-of-state (e.g., *to go from the warehouse to the store*.). They are constituted by an entity and a (metaphorical) path it goes along (i.e., *from the warehouse to the store*).
- The (lexical) aspectual approach (Vendler 1957; Verkuyl 1972; Dowty 1979; Smith 1997) takes the temporal and mereological properties of states-of-affairs into account. Combinations between the properties of [+/-stativity], [+/-dynamicity], [+/-telicity], [+/-punctuality] and, to a lesser extent, [+/-heterogeneity] lead to a classification of states-of-affairs into five well-known aspectual classes: accomplishments, achievements, activities, semelfactives (Smith 1997; Van Valin 2005) and states. Accomplishments (e.g., *to melt, to learn, to paint a portrait*) are defined as durative, inherently telic changes of state. Achievements (e.g., *to pop, to explode*) are punctual, inherently telic changes of state. Activities (e.g., *to walk, to swim, to snow*) refer to dynamic, durative and atelic states-of-affairs. Semelfactives (e.g., *to flash, to cough*) correspond to punctual states-of-affairs that do not lead to a change of state. Finally, states (e.g., *to be, to love, to know*) are temporally unbounded states-of-affairs that do not change over time (see Van Valin 2005: 32–33 for more examples).
- According to the causal (force-dynamic) approach (Croft 1991, 2012; Langacker 1987, 1991), many states-of-affairs can be segmented into more basal subevents that are causally connected to each other. More specifically, similar to how in a successful billiard shot the cue ball caroms off an object ball in order to strike another object ball, such states-of-affairs can be thought of as a chain of subevents that impact upon each other. For example, an event like *Sue broke the coconut for Greg with a hammer* (Croft 2012: 206, 209) consists of multiple segments that are interconnected and that impact upon each other: (i) Sue using a hammer, (ii) Sue causing a change of state (i.e., breaking) of the coconut and (iii) Sue performing this action for the benefit of Greg.
- The sextuple classification of process types in the transitivity system of systemic functional grammar (Halliday & Matthiessen 2004; Martin 1992; McGregor 1997;

---

[3] These concepts can be interpreted as merely physical, but they also allow more metaphorical meaning extensions (e.g., location in time, location as a permanent state).

Davidse 1999) is rooted in a distinction between three realms within which "experienced" processes can take place: the physical reality around us or the "outer experience" (e.g., *to happen, to prepare a dish*), the mental domain of consciousness or sensory impressions or the "inner experience" (e.g., *to see x, to understand x, to want x, to regret x*) and the abstract domain of generalizations drawn on the basis of the former two subtypes of experience (e.g., *to be, to have*).

3.2 Conceptual framework

The classification of conceptual scenes proposed in this study builds on the aforementioned general state-event distinction. It starts from the underlying rationale that conceptual scenes are "composite structures" (Langacker 2008: 162): they consist of smaller conceptual building blocks. These building blocks correspond to items stored in one's mind. Items like these may cover abstracted (i) *entities* (e.g., people, objects, categories, qualities), (ii) *processes* (e.g., activities, states-of-affairs) or (iii) *associative links* (e.g., possession, location, equation). In linguistic expressions these three subtypes of stored items either correlate (i) with (proper) nouns and adjectives, (ii) with verbs or (iii) with copula (specific verbs or juxtaposition structures), respectively.

General states consist of an associative link (abbreviated as A) and predominantly entail two entity nodes (abbreviated as E_1 and E_2) that are associated to each other through this link. Events, by contrast, center around a process node (abbreviated as 'P'). Following this reasoning, it would suffice to set up the corpus-based quantitative analysis by classifying two basic categories of states-of-affairs – i.e., general states and events – to test whether (and to what extent – their variation correlates with the language variation in the corpus data.

Nevertheless, it is important to note that the distinction between general states and events is not as sharp as it seems at first sight. Some events appear to be more closely related to general states than other ones. For example, similar to general states, events like *feeling disgusted, staying in the village* or even *training* and *speaking dialect* do not imply a participant's orientation (and inclination) towards a certain goal. Besides, in goal-oriented events there is a difference

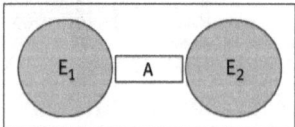

Figure 1: Schematic representation of association scenes (see Vertommen 2017).

between events the goal of which is (the inception) of a general state (e.g., *to become a househusband, to make life meaningful*) and events the goal of which is another event, in most cases a transitory state (e.g., *to watch a television program, to go to the employment office*). In order to reckon these subtle differences (and their potential impact on language choice), I will acknowledge and distinguish four (instead of two) basic categories of conceptual scenes: (section 3.2.1) *association scenes*, (section 3.2.2) *occurrence scenes*, (section 3.2.3) *inception scenes* and (section 3.2.4) *directionality scenes*.

3.2.1 Association scenes

Association scenes depict an association (A) between two items E_1 and E_2 (e.g., an entity and a quantity, or an entity and another entity). Such associations have the value of a permanent state: they do not correspond to time-bound states-of-affairs in physical (or virtual) reality, but to general patterns and tendencies mentally abstracted from this reality. Prototypical association scenes are the ones in which one item (E_1, see above) realizes (i.e., incorporates, personifies or further substantiates) the quality or entity accessed by the other item (E_2). This holds true for examples (2) and (3). Besides, the relation between two items can deal with *location* or *possession*: one item (E_1) can be viewed as being located in E_2 (see (4)) or as being physically (or mentally possessed) by E_2 (see (5)).

(2) *Die opleiding kost, ja, bijna tweeduizend gulden.*
 that program cost.PRS.3SG yeah almost two.thousand guilders
 'That [educational] program costs, yeah, almost two thousand guilders.'

(3) *L-HULANDIYA HIYA L-LUĠA LLI TƐELLEM-TI-HA,*
 DEF-Dutch she DEF-language REL learn-PFV.2SG-it
 N-QUL-U, RBEƐTAŠ SANA.
 IPFV.1PL$_1$-say-IPFV.1PL$_2$ fourteen year
 'Dutch is the language that you learnt for, let's say, fourteen years.'

(4) *Zij kwam niet uit Utrecht, zij kwam uit*
 she come.PST.(3)SG NEG from Utrecht she come.PST.(3)SG from
 Bergen-op-Zoom, Zeeland.
 Bergen-op-ZoomZeeland
 'She was not from Utrecht, she was from Bergen-op-Zoom, Zeeland.'

(5) **AMA HERKES-IN ÖY-LE FIKR-I VAR,** weet je.
    but everyone that-INS idea-POSS.3SG present know.PRS.(2)SG you
    'But everyone has ideas like that, you know.'

3.2.2 Occurrence scenes

Occurrence scenes conceptualize a stative or dynamic process (P) that takes place for an indefinite period of time without an inherent outcome or culmination point (i.e., they are continuous and do not lead up to a permanent or temporary effect). Depending on whether it is portrayed as having clearly discernible phases or not, this process corresponds to a *transitory state* (see (6) and (7)) or to a *dynamic activity* (see (8) and (9)).

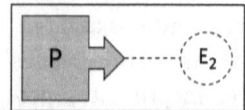

Figure 2: Schematic representation of occurrence scenes (see Vertommen 2017).

As visualized in Figure 2, occurrence scenes – both transitory states and dynamic activities – are centered around a process item (P). Very often (but not necessarily, as in (8)) this process is further modified by an entity item E_2 (i.e., a person, an object or a quality). This optional relationship of modification between E_2 and P is signaled through a dashed line between both items in the diagram in Figure 2. In such cases E_2 serves to further delineate P. This holds true for the feeling of anger (expressed by the Dutch informal proverb *over de zeik*) with respect to the transitory state indicated by the Dutch verb *zijn* 'to be' in (6). Likewise, in (7) the Moroccan Arabic prepositional phrase *feḍḍyuṛhum* (literally 'in their house') defines the setting in which the process P, denoted by the main verb *kan ikun* 'to be', is situated. In (9) the bare noun phrase *(ġir) qehwa* '(only) coffee' specifies the process verbalized by the Moroccan Arabic main verb *šṛeb* 'to drink'.

(6) De leerkracht, die was heel de tijd over de zeik.
    DEF teacher that be.PST.(3)SG whole DEF time over DEF piss
    'The teacher, he was pissed off the whole time.'

(7) HNA   F-Nederland   KA-Y-KUN-U   ĠIR   FE-Ḍ-ḌYUṚ-HUM
    here in-Netherlands DUR-IPFV.3PL₁-be-IPFV.3PL₂ only in-DEF-house.PL-their
    borrel-tje.
    drink-DIM
    '[During New Year's Eve, BV] here in the Netherlands they only stay at home, with a little drink.'

(8) DÜĞÜN-DE   OYNA-R-SIN.
    wedding-LOC   dance-AOR-2SG
    'At the wedding you are supposed to dance.'

(9) DABA   TE-MŠI   TE-ŠREB   ĠIR   QEHWA.
    now   IPFV.2SG(.M)-go   IPFV.2SG(.M)-drink   only   coffee
    'Right now you are going to drink only coffee.'

3.2.3 Inception scenes

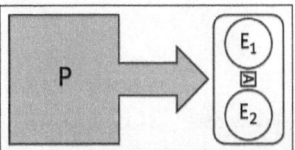

Figure 3: Schematic representation of inception (see Vertommen 2017).

Inception scenes portray a dynamic process that brings about the inception of (or the cancellation of) a permanent association (A) between two items (E_1 and E_2). Similar to occurrence scenes, the profiled center in inception scenes is a process P. This process is modified by the above-mentioned association in that it heads towards the actualization of that association. In order to accomplish this goal, P (gradually) meets an often indefinite set of conditions that warrant the validity of the association in question. For example, in (10) the association between the first person (E_1) and the category of househusbands (or "people who work at home") (E_2) can only obtain if some necessary prerequisites are complied with (e.g., being exclusively focused on the housekeeping (and often on the care of the children as well), not having a job outside the home because of this exclusive focus). In (12) the unspecified process P denoted by the Turkish verb *olmak* 'happen' brings about a permanent association between the category defined as *çiçek çalınması falan* 'flower-theft' (E_1) and one actual manifestion of this category in reality (as indicated by the demonstrative *o* 'that') (E_2).

The two remaining examples, (11) and (13), differ from the former in that they additionally conceptualize the external catalyst or agent who/which is responsible for the process of inception. In (11) Morgan's former girlfriend acts as the instigator of a process that gradually has led to an association between the first person (Morgan) (E_1) and the category of househusbands (E_2). In (13) the addressee (Mahmoud) is represented as an energy source who, through the process of writing (expressed by the Moroccan Arabic verb *kteb*), gradually effectuates a new instantiation of the category denoted by the Dutch borrowing *dictaat* 'lecture notes'. The instantiation itself is further verbalized through the Moroccan Arabic masculin far demonstrative *(ha)dak* 'that'.

(10) **WELLI-T**   XADAM   L-DAXAL   FE-Ḍ-ḌAṛ,   **WELLI-T**
become-PFV.1SG   work.PTCL   inside   in-DEF-house   become-PFV.1SG
huisman.
househusband
'I have become someone who works at home, I have become a househusband.'

(11) *Zij*   *heeft*   *een*   *huisman*   *van*   *mij*   *ge-maak-t.*
she   have-PRS.3SG   INDF   househusband   out.of   me   PTCL₁-make-PTCL₂
'She has made a househusband out of me.'

(12) **ON-DAN SONRA O**   ÇIÇEK   ÇAL-ıN-MA-SI   FALAN   NASıL
that-ABL after   that   flower   steal-PASS-NMLZ-POSS.3SG   stuff   how
OL-DU,   *eh* ...?
be-PST.3SG   eh
'After that, that stealing of the flower(s), well, how did it happen, eh ...?'

(13) *IWA*   *KIFAŠ*   *KA-TE-KTEB*   *DAK,*   *eh, dictaat?*   *B-HUḶANDIYA*
well   how   DUR-IPFV.2SG-write   that   eh   lecture.notes   with-Dutch
WELLA   *BE-L-FRANṢAWIYA*   *WELLA*   *BE-L-INGLISIYA*   *WELLA...?*
or   with-DEF-French   or   with-DEF-English   or
'Well, how do you write those lecture notes? In Dutch, in French, in English, or ...?'

3.2.4 Directionality scenes

Directionality scenes depict a dynamic process dealing with the selection of or the consequent orientation towards a specific goal. In Figure 4 this orientation is symbolized through a bold horizontal arrow. These scenes include processes dealing with selection or choice, resultative processes, (caused)

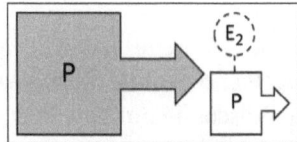

Figure 4: Schematic representation of directionality scene (see Vertommen 2017).

motion processes, processes of assistance or prevention, transfers (of goods, ownership or possession), processes of directed perception and conation processes.

The diagram in Figure 4 shows that, similar to occurrence scenes and inception scenes, the conceptual pivot in a directionality scene is a process P. This process is further modified by the goal it is consistently directed towards during its course. Goals like these mostly correspond to another process, and most often to a transitory state P modified by another entity (E_2): in (14) it refers to a transitory state of 'being located (P) at *the wedding of Fatoş (E_2)*', in (15) to a transitory state in which (a sheet of paper with) the others' contact details are possessed by the speaker and vice versa and in (16) to a transitory condition of being open (in the context of a door). In (17), however, the goal is an inception scene: it corresponds to the moment in which the one instance of a judiciary's decision that is relevant for the speaker takes place.

(14) **GEÇEN-DE   DÜĞÜN-E   GIT-TI-K,**   van   *Fatoş.*
     Recent-LOC   wedding-DAT   go-PST-1PL   of   Fatoş
     'Recently we went to a wedding, to the one of Fatoş.'

(15) ᶜṬA-W-NI   l'   adresse ANA ᶜṬI-T-L-HUM   l'   adresse
     give-PFV.3PL-me   DEF   address I   give-PFV.1SG-to-them   DEF   address
     'They gave me their address, I gave them my address.'

(16) U   HAD-I-K   wachtkamer   MA-TE-QDER-Š   T-ḤELL-HA
     and DEM-F-FAR   waiting.room NEG₁-IPFV.2SG-can-NEG₂   IPFV. 2SG-open-it
     ĠIR-MEN-BERRA.
     except-from-outside
     'And you can't open that waiting room, except from the outside.'

(17) Ik   wacht   op   de   beslissing   van   de [sic]   justitie.
     I   wait.PRS.1SG   for   DEF   decision   of   DEF   judiciary
     'I am waiting for the decision of the judiciary.'

4 Results and observations

Now that I have established the four categories that together constitute the independent variable of conceptualization, I will turn to a discussion of how they are distributed in the actual corpus data. As stated in the previous section, the corpus-based analysis covers 13 interactions and 17 speakers of the Dutch-Turkish and Dutch-Moroccan Arabic mixed varieties for which I divided every interaction into sentences (4035 in total) as primary units of analysis. Relying on the criteria outlined in Section 3 above, I further labeled these sentences according to whether they expressed an association scene, an occurrence scene, an inception scene or a directionality scene. For this specific purpose I relied on the core predicates (i.e., the [semantics of the] main verb and the argument structure it is embedded in) of the distinguished sentences. For more details about this coding scheme I refer to Vertommen (2017).

- For the expression of association scenes both Turkish and Moroccan Arabic tend to employ verbless juxtaposed sentence structures without a copula. Dutch, by contrast, necessarily employs a copula (i.e., *zijn* 'to be') in order to express an association scene, irrespective of whether the associative link is permanent (unbounded in time) and/or has a strong degree of modal force.[4]
- Both in Dutch, Turkish and Moroccan Arabic, occurrence scenes correlate (i) with simple intransitive argument structures without an explicit object or predicative complement (e.g., *qra iqra* 'to study (=the act of)', *eğlendirmek* 'to enjoy (oneself)') or with (ii) intransitive argument structures that contain an inherent argument (e.g., *Arabisch studeren* 'to study Arabic').
- Inception scenes formally correlate with a wide range of argument structures in Dutch, Turkish and Moroccan Arabic. If the external catalyst or agent is not conceptualized, inception scenes are prototypically realized by (i) pseudo-copula structures (with a language-specific variant of the light verb *to become*) or by (ii) simple intransitive argument structures (e.g., *wqeʕ* 'to appear, to happen'). If the external catalyst or agent is conceptualized, they are most typically realized by (iii) caused-motion argument structures (e.g., *ḥeṭṭ ʕliya waḥed onze* 'to give me an eleven' [literal interpretation: 'to put an eleven to me'), (iv) ditransitive argument structures (e.g., *het leven zin geven* 'to make life meaningful' [literal interpretation: 'to give life meaning']) or (v) transitive(-like) argument structures (e.g., *foto'yu yapmak* 'to make a picture').

---

[4] However, as soon as an association is conceptualized as temporally bounded, or as soon as a speaker intends to weaken his/her commitment to its truth (i.e., by toning down the degree of "modal force" of the proposition), the use of an explicit copula marker is obligatory.

– There are two dominant patterns with respect to the formal expression of directionality scenes in Dutch, Turkish and Moroccan Arabic: (i) a (transitive or intransitive) motion argument structure in which E_2 correlates with an oblique object (e.g., *başka bir yere gitmek* 'to go to another place') and (ii) a pseudo-copula structure or an (in)transitive structure in which E_2 is incorporated in the main verb (e.g., *büyümek* 'to grow', *ṭṭuwweṛ* 'to develop').

Table 2 represents the observed frequencies of the four categories per speaker, both their total number (in bold) and the number of attestations in the two matrix languages (Dutch or Turkish/Moroccan Arabic).

Before I go into the actual results, I briefly want to address one general remark about how I approached the quantitative analysis. It is obvious that the various heritage speakers in the corpus have contributed to a different extent to the overall amount of corpus data. For example, Samir's output accounts for 29.0% (1172 out of 4035 sentences) of the entire corpus, whereas Fadime's contributions only amount to 2.0% (82 out of 4035). It would therefore give a distorted image if I were to present quantitative results generalizing over the entire corpus, or even over one of the two language varieties. To redeem this issue, I present the results for each speaker individually, and show that within my corpus data a similar pattern recurs across these different speakers.[5] I also do not intend to generalize the pattern in my data to other varieties of Dutch-Turkish or Dutch-Moroccan Arabic than the ones that I have in the corpus.

A Pearson's chi-square test (with Yates' continuity correction) reveals that across the different Dutch-Turkish and Dutch-Moroccan Arabic heritage speakers conceptualization has a significant to highly significant effect on language choice.[6] Moreover, the accompanying Pearson residuals (see Table 3) point to a similar direction of this effect amongst the majority of the speakers:

The Pearson residuals in Table 3 indicate that, without exception, Dutch is strongly preferred in the case of association scenes while it is dispreferred in the case of directionality scenes. Occurrence scenes and inception scenes tend to follow the same pattern as directionality scenes amongst the majority of the speakers. In cases where they do not, the attested preference for Dutch is only weak. Overall it appears from the residuals that the observed binary contrast with respect to

---

[5] Due to the relatively small data set (and due to the relatively low number of hits for some speakers), I decided not to conduct a logistic regression analysis. However, a future issue should be to explore the possibility of these and other types of regression analyses in the compiled Dutch-Turkish and Dutch-Moroccan Arabic data sets.

[6] Even though it is true that Maryam does not entirely fit into this pattern, the chi-square test in her case still indicates a marginally significant effect ($\chi^2=5.7432$, df=3, p=0.1248).

Table 2: Observed frequencies for LANGUAGE CHOICE~CONCEPTUALIZATION (per speaker).

	ASSOCIATION			OCCURRENCE			INCEPTION			DIRECTIONALITY			TOTAL		
	DU	T/M	TOT	DU	T/M	TOT	DU	T/M	TOT	DU	T/M	TOT	DU	T/M	TOT
Ayhan	62	41	103	30	34	64	19	37	56	15	73	88	126	185	311
Ayşe	29	9	38	10	17	27	6	9	15	10	25	35	55	60	115
Fadime	18	5	23	13	10	23	9	11	20	8	8	16	48	34	82
Fulya	33	28	61	0	17	17	5	19	24	1	24	25	39	88	127
Hatice	88	15	103	13	12	25	22	11	33	17	10	27	140	48	188
Havva	40	20	60	12	16	28	11	12	23	12	40	52	75	88	163
Müjgan	14	18	32	1	25	26	7	26	33	5	22	27	27	91	118
DU-TU	284	136	420	79	131	210	79	125	204	68	202	270	510	594	1104
Abdullah	62	28	90	14	30	44	7	8	15	11	19	30	94	85	179
Driss	27	27	54	0	33	33	8	12	20	3	33	36	38	105	143
Hayat	27	45	72	1	32	33	5	31	36	8	48	56	41	156	197
Husayn	92	63	155	14	65	79	11	69	80	16	66	82	133	263	396
Mahmoud	26	54	80	3	27	30	7	26	33	0	37	37	36	144	180
Maryam	45	19	64	8	10	18	12	7	19	7	8	15	72	44	116
Mohammed	35	13	48	17	12	29	18	8	26	7	18	25	77	51	128
Morgan	32	44	76	14	25	39	11	37	48	6	43	49	63	149	212
Samir	212	318	530	28	199	227	40	135	175	28	212	240	308	864	1172
Souraya	32	51	83	9	26	35	3	28	31	3	56	59	47	161	208
Du-MA	590	662	1252	108	459	567	122	361	483	89	540	629	909	2022	2931
Total	874	798	1672	187	590	777	201	486	687	157	742	899	1419	2616	4035

Table 3: Pearson's chi-squared results (with residuals) for LANGUAGE CHOICE~CONCEPTUALIZATION (per speaker) (abbreviations: DF=degrees of freedom; SGF=significance level ('***'=highly significant, '**'=very significant, '*'=significant, '?'=marginally significant, ' '=not significant); φ^c=Cramer's V score; Du=Dutch, T/M=Turkish or Moroccan Arabic).

	X-SQUARE*	DF	P-VALUE	SGF	φ^c	PEARSON RESIDUALS							
						association		occurrence		inception		directionality	
						DU	T/M	DU	T/M	DU	T/M	DU	T/M
Ayhan	38.7461	3	1.964e-8	***	.353	3.1	-2.6	0.8	-0.7	-0.8	0.6	-3.5	2.9
Ayşe*	19.1886	3	.0002499	***	.408	2.5	-2.4	-0.8	0.8	-0.4	0.4	-1.6	1.6
Fadime	5.7155	3	.1263		.264	1.2	-1.5	-0.1	0.2	-0.8	0.9	-0.4	0.5
Fulya	32.6986	3	3.728e-7	***	.507	3.3	-2.2	-2.3	1.5	-0.9	0.6	-2.4	1.6
Hatice	16.0916	3	.001086	**	.293	1.3	-2.2	-1.3	2.2	-0.5	0.9	-0.7	1.2
Havva*	21.4582	3	8.455e-5	***	.363	2.4	-2.2	-0.2	0.2	0.1	-0.1	-2.4	2.3
Müjgan	13.5798	3	.003537	**	.339	2.5	-1.3	-2.0	1.1	-0.2	0.1	-0.5	0.3
Abdullah	20.4618	3	.0001362	***	.338	2.1	-2.3	-1.9	2.0	-0.3	0.3	-1.2	1.3
Driss	35.1174	3	1.151e-7	***	.496	3.3	-2.0	-3.0	1.8	1.2	-0.7	-2.1	1.3
Hayat	20.9919	3	.0001057	***	.326	3.1	-1.6	-2.2	1.1	-0.9	0.5	-1.1	0.5
Husayn	76.4499	3	<2.2e-16	***	.439	5.5	-3.9	-2.4	1.7	-3.1	2.2	-2.2	1.6
Mahmoud	18.9678	3	.0002776	***	.325	2.5	-1.3	-1.2	0.6	0.2	-0.1	-2.7	1.4
Maryam	5.7432	3	.1248		.223	0.8	-1.1	-0.9	1.2	0.1	-0.1	-0.8	1.0
Mohammed	14.9679	3	0.001844	**	.342	1.1	-1.4	-0.1	0.1	0.6	-0.7	-2.1	2.5
Morgan	14.5224	3	0.002274	**	.262	2.0	-1.3	0.7	-0.5	-0.9	0.6	-2.2	1.5
Samir*	101.7949	3	<2.2e-16	***	.295	6.2	-3.7	-4.1	2.4	-0.9	0.5	-4.4	2.6
Souraya	25.5817	3	1.167e-5	***	.351	3.1	-1.7	0.4	-0.2	-1.5	0.8	-2.8	1.5

Note: The data set for Selma was slightly too small to perform an entirely viable chi-square test.

matrix language use (i.e., Dutch versus Turkish/Moroccan Arabic) strongly reflects a binary distinction on the conceptual level between association scenes on the one hand, and occurrence, inception and directionality scenes on the other. It follows that the contrast above basically goes together with a distinction between atemporal (i.e., general or temporally unbounded) states and temporally bounded events.

4.2 Qualitative analysis

In order to make the tendencies and the observations laid bare by the descriptive statistical analysis more tangible, I will engage in a more detailed qualitative description of one fragment extracted from the data set. This fragment particularly gives an idea of how across a larger stretch of discourse, the variation between Dutch and Turkish(/Moroccan Arabic) argument structures mirrors the conceptual distinction outlined above. The sample discussed here corresponds to a fragment of Ayhan's (A) and Hatice's (H) Dutch-Turkish interaction at a pub in Tilburg (Backus 1996: 53–54). Ayhan considered himself obstructed by several authorities in terms of career prospects. The fact that he did not pass a Dutch exam with a deficit of only 0.1 point had far-reaching consequences with respect to his quest for a job: it specifically cost him a possible job as a lab assistant at a hospital.

(18)
A: 1 **ÇÜNKÜ** die kom-en van boven, die bevel-en enzo.
because these come-PRS.3PL from above these order-PL and so on
'Because they come from the powers that be, these orders and things like that.'

H: 2 *Ja,*
yes
'Yes,...'

3 *dè klop-t*
that be.right-PRS.3SG
'..., that is right.'

A: 4 **MESELA, ONLAR BAN-A ARA.SıRA TELEFON ED-IYOR-LAR:**
for.example they I-DAT sometimes telephone do-PROG-3PL
"*Hoe gaa-t het met jou?*"
how go-PRS.(3)SG it with you
'For example, they sometimes call me: "How are you doing?"'

H: 5 *Ooh, wat   leuk!*
       ooh (what)/how nice
       'Ooh, how nice!'

   6 *Je   had   wel   goed contact mee?*
       you   have.PST.(2)SG really good contact with
       'You really did have a good contact with them?'

A: 7 *Ja-wel*
       yes-EMP
       'Sure,...'

   8 **ÇÜNKÜ BEN ÇOĞ-UN-LAN   EV-İN-E   GİT-Tİ-M,**
       because I   many-POSS.3PL-INS   house-POSS.3PL-DAT   go-PST-1SG
       '... because I went to their house with many of them,...'

   9 **YEMEK FELAN   YE-Dİ-M.**
       dinner things.like.that eat-PST-1SG
       '... I had dinner and things like that.'

   10 *Zelfs met   de   ding-en, radiolog-en, daar   had   ik*
       even with DEF   thing-PL radiologist-PL these have.PST.1SG I
       goed-e   contact mee.
       good-INFL contact with
       'Even with the things, with the radiologists, (even) with them I had a good contact.'

   11 **ŞEY-DE   YILBAŞIN-DA   kaart   GÖNDER-MİŞ-LER** *met all-e*
       thing-LOC Christmas-LOC   postcard   send-INFER-3PL   with all-INFL
       iedereen foto-'s   daar-bij,   met   iedereen de   handtekening
       everyone   picture-PL   that-with   with everyone DEF signature
       daar-bij.
       that-with
       'At thing, at Christmas they sent a postcard with pictures of everyone included, with everyone's signature included.'

   12 *Het zijn   best.wel goei-e   collega-'s.*
       it   be.PRS.(3)PL actually good-INFL colleague-PL
       'In fact, they are good colleagues.'

The encounter above comprises ten main clause argument structures. Four of these argument structures are defined by Turkish ((18.4), (18.8), (18.9) and (18.11)), six of them are defined by Dutch ((18.1), (18.3), (18.5), (18.6), (18.10) and (18.12)). The utterances in (18.2) and (18.7) are interjections and therefore excluded from this analysis.

Each of the four Turkish argument structures in the excerpt above reflects a scene that either corresponds to a dynamic process or to a temporally bounded state. Accordingly, each of the scenes expressed by the Turkish argument structures shares the property of being centered around a potentially modified process item P. In (18.4) and (18.11) the scenes in question correspond to a directionality scene, and more specifically to a transfer scene. The foregrounded dynamic process is verbalized through the verb compound *telefon etmek* (literally 'to do/make a telephone (call)') and through the Turkish verb *göndermek* 'to send', respectively. In line with my characterization of directionality scenes set forth in Section 3.2.4 these processes are modified by a specific goal. This goal corresponds to a transitory state in which the first person (explicitly marked by the dative-case marked pronoun *ban-a* 'I' in (18.4), left implicit in (18.11)) is located within the attention span of the caller or of the sender, respectively. This attention span minimally covers the time it takes to produce the quoted message E_1 (*"Hoe gaat het met jou?"* '"How are you doing?"') or to send in the postcard (also E_1, expressed by the Dutch borrowing *kaart* 'postcard').

The conceptualized scene in (18.8) also deals with directionality. It corresponds to a motion scene in which the profiled process P is expressed by the Turkish verb *gitmek* 'to go'. This process is further oriented towards a transitory state in which the first person speaker, Ayhan, finds himself in the houses of his former colleagues. In (18.9) the Turkish argument structure in question formally reflects an occurrence scene. In this (dynamic) scene the item referred to by the bare NP *yemek felan* 'meal (dinner) and stuff like that' further specifies the central process P expressed by the Turkish verb *yemek* 'to eat'.

Importantly, the Dutch argument structures all represent scenes that correspond to general states. They are constituted by two entity items that either enter into a relation of realization (incorporation, personification or substantiation) or of location (possession) with each other (see section 2.2.1 above). In this relation the realizing or the located entity, E_1, holds a more prominent place than the other one (E_2). The conceptual scenes expressed by (18.3), (18.5) and (18.12) form part of the subclass of "realizing associations": in (18.3) Ayhan's previous statement (E_1) is qualified as an instance of "true statements" (E_2), in (18.5) the anecdote described in the previous turn (E_1) is labelled as an example of the category "nice stories or events" (E_2), and in (18.12) Ayhan's former colleagues (E_1) personify the category of "good colleagues" (E_2). The associative link with E_2 in these cases can be expressed through the use of a stative verb (*kloppen* 'to be right' in 18.3) or through a predicative complement: e.g., an adjective (*leuk* 'nice' in (18.5)) or a predicative NP (*goeie collega's* 'good colleagues' in (18.12)).

The other scenes expressed by Dutch argument structures conceptualize *locative or possessive associations*. In (18.1) the entity E_2 denoted by the adverb *boven* 'above' provides a setting for the entity E_1 referred to by *die bevelen enzo* 'these orders and things like that'. In (18.6) and (18.10) the notion of location has a more metaphorical interpretation: the former colleagues and the radiologists referred to by the pronominal adverbs *er ... mee* 'herewith' in (18.6) and *daarmee* 'therewith' in (18.10) both function as domains which the inherent possession expressed by *een goed contact hebben* 'to have a good contact' applies to.

5 Concluding remarks

This paper yields two key observations. First, it demonstrates that the use of alternations, as well as the choice of a particular ML in multilingual speech, does not always have to index aspects of the interactive context or of the speakers that are involved in it. In specific bilingual contexts it can also serve to signal conceptual distinctions. More in particular, the reason why the heritage speakers under scrutiny (unconsciously or otherwise) opt to use a Dutch or a Turkish/Moroccan Arabic argument structure is related to the types of conceptual scenes these argument structures express. For almost every speaker in the data set the majority of the formal variation between Dutch and Turkish/Moroccan Arabic can be explained in terms of a conceptual contrast between general states on the one hand, and events on the other.

The second observation in this paper supports Auer's (1999) claim that, apart from being attached to locally relevant (inferential) meanings, the meanings that are paired with alternations can also be highly conventionalized or encoded. The quantitative analysis of the correlation between ML choice and the general state-event contrast shows that this correlation is a recurrent pattern in the output of the analyzed Dutch-Turkish and Dutch-Moroccan Arabic speakers. As suggested by the highly intensive and consistent use of alternations, ML choice in the datasets under scrutiny is primarily governed by the grammatical system of the bilingual variety heritage speakers use amongst peers. Both observations in this paper shed new light on how (and to what extent) bilingual varieties – used by heritage speakers as a device in its own right for flagging their 'bilingual or multilingual identity' – can be internally (i.e., grammatically) organized.

However, there are some caveats. Even though the language choice of the Dutch-Turkish and the Dutch-Moroccan Arabic heritage speakers reveals a binary conceptual distinction that matches a general state-event contrast, the observations based on the chi-squared results and the accompanying Pearson residuals deserve a closer examination. Cramer's V scores[7] in between .223 (Maryam) and .507 (Fulya) signal a moderate effect size: i.e., the nature of conceptual scenes has a visible impact on language choice in the speakers' language use, but it does not account for all the formal variation in the corpus data.

One explanation for some of the counterexamples would be that the use of alternations (and ML choice) in the interactions under scrutiny is not entirely governed by grammatical rules, and that the analyzed speakers additionally use this device in order to contextualize aspects of the local social or interactive environment. However, according to Auer (1999: 321), the more frequently alternations occur in an interaction, the weaker their contextualization value. This is because alternations can only function as contextualization cues if they are to some extent salient, e.g., in interactions in which one (matrix) language is dominant. Given my focus on speakers who exhibited enough variation between Dutch and Turkish or Moroccan Arabic (as a result of which a dominant ML is not easily discernible), this condition is not fulfilled. It therefore seems less likely that in the data sets at hand considerations dealing with ad hoc social or interactive factors trigger the use of alternations and the choice of a particular ML. Rather this paper turns out to elaborate on Auer's (1999: 321) suggestion that, once alternations become more intensive and less attached to ad hoc meanings, they tend to be associated with discourse-structuring functions such as the contrast between personal versus objective passages or between information of high or low relevance.

Vertommen (2017) proposes a cognitively oriented explanation for the moderate impact of the general state-event contrast on the ML variation in the data sets. The outlined relationship between association scenes and general states on the one hand, and between occurrence, inception and directionality scenes and

---

[7] A Cramer's V score (also denoted as φc) indicates the strength of association between two independent nominal variables by means of a value varying from 0 (no association) to 1 (complete association). Although there does not really exist a univocal interpretation of Cramer's V values, certainly not in the case of spoken linguistic data that are often exposed to and affected by an extensive set of independent variables, we will use the following standard for evaluating the scores: a score of 0.1 sets the lower limit of a *minimal association*, a score of 0.3 is required in order to have a *medium association*, and a score of 0.5 counts as the threshold of a *large association* (Janda 2013: 10-11).

time-bound events on the other only amounts to the default construal of these conceptual scenes. This default construal coheres with the specificities of the specific item (i.e., associated entities or a process) that constitutes the center of these conceptual scenes (see section 3.2). Nevertheless, in specific semantic contexts association scenes can be construed as time-bound, or as "eventive", whereas the other three conceptual scenes can be sometimes construed as atemporal states.

Nevertheless, the explanations above still do not answer the question why Dutch is preferred for the verbalization of general states and Turkish or Moroccan Arabic for events (and not the other way around). One avenue for further research therefore would be to explore this particular issue. Is Dutch, in terms of grammatical tools and complexity, considered to be "better equipped" for the expression of general states than Turkish or Moroccan Arabic? Are the latter two languages, because of their grammatical peculiarities, seen as better candidates for the expression of events than Dutch? Or can the speakers' preference for one or the other language in the case of general states and events be explained by the age when (and the social or psychological circumstances in which) these people acquired these languages? Whatever the exact answer will be, research on this matter requires an interdisciplinary perspective, in which insights from cognitive (contact) linguistics must be cross-fertilized with evidence from sociolinguistic, psychological, and even neurolinguistic studies.

References

Anderson, John M. 1971. *The Grammar of Case*. Cambridge: Cambridge University Press.
Auer, Peter. 1984. *Bilingual Conversation*. Amsterdam: John Benjamins Publishing Company.
Auer, Peter (ed.). 1998. *Code-Switching in Conversation: Language, Interaction and Identity*. London: Routledge.
Auer, Peter. 1999. From codeswitching via language mixing to fused lects: toward a dynamic typology of bilingual speech. *International Journal of Bilingualism* 3. 309–332.
Backus, Ad. 1996. *Two in One: Bilingual Speech of Turkish Immigrants in the Netherlands*. Tilburg: Tilburg University Press.
Boumans, Louis. 1998. *The Syntax of Codeswitching: Analyzing Moroccan Arabic/Dutch Conversations*. Tilburg: Tilburg University Press.
Boye, Kasper. 2010. Reference and clausal perception-verb complements. *Linguistics* 48(2). 391–430.
Boye, Kasper. 2012. *Epistemic Meaning: A Crosslinguistic and Functional-Cognitive Study*. Berlin: Mouton de Gruyter.
Bybee, Joan. 1988. Morphology as lexical organization. In Hammond, Michael & Michael Noonan (eds). *Theoretical Morphology*, 119–141. San Diego: Academic Press.
Croft, William. 1991. *Syntactic Categories and Grammatical Relations. The Cognitive Organization of Information*. Chicago: The University of Chicago Press.

Croft, William. 2012. *Verbs: Aspect and Causal Structure*. Oxford: Oxford University Press.
Davidse, Kristin. 1999. *Categories of Experiential Grammar*. Nottingham: University of Nottingham.
Dik, Simon C. & Hengeveld, Kees. 1991. The hierarchical structure of the clause and the typology of perception-verb complements. *Linguistics* 29. 231–259.
Dowty, David R. 1979. *Word Meaning and Montague Grammar*. Dordrecht: D. Reidel Publishing Company.
Eversteijn, Nadia. 2012. *"All at once": Language Choice and Code Switching by Turkish-Dutch Teenagers*. Saarbrücken: Lap Lambert Academic Publishing AG & Co. KG.
Fauconnier, Gilles & Mark Turner. 2002. *The Way we Think: Conceptual Blending and the Mind's Hidden Complexities*. New York: Basic Books.
Goldberg, Adele. 1995. *Constructions: A Construction Grammar Approach to Argument Structure*. Chicago: The University of Chicago Press.
Goldberg, Adele. 2006. *Constructions at Work: The Nature of Generalization in Language*. Oxford: Oxford University Press.
Gumperz, John J. 1982. *Discourse Strategies*. Cambridge: Cambridge University Press.
Halliday, Michael A.K. & Christian M.I.M. Matthiessen. 2004. *An Introduction to Functional Grammar*. 3rd edition. London: Hodder Arnold.
Jackendoff, Ray S. 1972. *Semantic Interpretation in Generative Grammar*. Cambridge, MA: The MIT Press.
Jackendoff, Ray S. 1983. *Semantics and Cognition*. Cambridge, MA: The MIT Press.
Janda, Laura A. (ed.). 2013. *Cognitive Linguistics: The Quantitative Turn*. Berlin: Mouton de Gruyter.
Kemmer, Suzanne & Michael Israel. 1994. Variation and the usage-based model. In Beals, Katharine, Denton, Jeannette, Knippen, Robert, Melnar, Lynette, Suzuki, Hisami & Zeinfeld, Erica (eds). *CLS 30: Papers from the 30th Regional Meeting of the Chicago Linguistic Society*, Vol. 2: *Parasession on Variation and Linguistic Theory*, 165–179. Chicago: CLS.
Langacker, Ronald W. 1987. *Foundations of Cognitive Grammar*, Volume 1: *Theoretical Prerequisites*. Stanford, CA: Stanford University Press.
Langacker, Ronald W. 1991. *Foundations of Cognitive Grammar*, Volume 2: *Descriptive Application*. Stanford, CA: Stanford University Press.
Langacker, Ronald W. 2008. *Cognitive Grammar: A Basic Introduction*. Oxford: Oxford University Press.
Levin, Beth & Malka Rappaport Hovav. 2005. *Argument Realization*. Cambridge: Cambridge University Press.
Martin, James R. 1992. *English text: System and Structure*. Amsterdam: John Benjamins Publishing Company.
McGregor, William B. 1997. *Semiotic Grammar*. Oxford: Oxford University Press.
Michaelis, Laura A. 1998. *Aspectual Grammar and Past-Time Reference*. London: Routledge.
Muysken, Pieter. 2000. *Bilingual Speech: A Typology of Code-Mixing*. Cambridge: Cambridge University Press.
Myers-Scotton, Carol. 1993a. *Social Motivation for Codeswitching: Evidence from Africa*. Oxford: Clarendon Press.
Myers-Scotton, Carol. 1993b. *Duelling Languages: Grammatical Structure in Codeswitching*. Oxford: Clarendon Press.
Nortier, Jacomine. 1990. *Dutch-Moroccan Arabic Code Switching*. Dordrecht: Foris Publications.

Smith, Carlota S. 1997. *The Parameter of Aspect*. 2nd edition. Dordrecht: Kluwer Academic Publishers.
Tomasello, Michael. 2003. *Constructing a Language: A Usage-Based Theory of Language Acquisition*. Cambridge, MA: Harvard University Press.
Van Valin, Robert D. Jr. 2005. *Exploring the Syntax-Semantics Interface*. Cambridge: Cambridge University Press.
van Voorst, Jan. 1988. *Event Structure*. Amsterdam: John Benjamins Publishing Company.
van Voorst, Jan. 1993. A localist model for event semantics. *Journal of Semantics* 10(1). 65–111.
Vendler, Zeno. 1957. Verbs and times. *The Philosophical Review* 66(2). 143–160.
Vendler, Zeno. 1967. *Linguistics in Philosophy*. Ithaca, NY: Cornell University Press.
Verkuyl, Henk J. 1993. *A Theory of Aspectuality. The Interaction between Temporal and Atemporal Structure*. Cambridge: Cambridge University Press.
Vertommen, Bram. 2017. *Coding Cognition: A Case-Study of Dutch-Turkish and Dutch-Moroccan Arabic Language Users in the Netherlands*. Unpublished Ph.D dissertation, University of Antwerp.

Antje Endesfelder Quick, Ad Backus and Elena Lieven
9 Partially schematic constructions as engines of development: Evidence from German-English bilingual acquisition

Abstract: This paper investigates code-mixing (CM) in the speech of a young German-English bilingual child at the ages of 2;3, 3;0 and 3;11. The child grew up in an environment characterized by a 'One Parent One Language' mode of communicating. The child's recordings were analyzed for the amount and types of mixing that occurred. We specifically aimed to find out whether instances of CM can be accounted for with reference to ease of activation, which will sometimes favor units from the other language. To do this, we made use of the 'Traceback method', which searches for evidence that the units a child produces were already entrenched in his mental representation or primed by previous discourse. We report on several findings. First, German, the language of the wider environment and of the mother, was clearly dominant, as shown by its higher use and higher Mean Length of Utterance (MLU). Second, after a period of increased exposure to English-speaking environments, the proportion of English went up considerably. Third, CM went from predominantly German-based to predominantly English-based. Fourth, CM often involved the filling in of an open slot in a partially schematic construction by functional and lexical material from the other language. Finally, much of the CM turned out to be primed by occurrence of the same forms in the immediately preceding discourse. We conclude that the child's output follows principles of ease of activation, the levels of which are determined in large part by input and previous usage.

Keywords: Code-mixing, German – English bilingual child, partially schematic units, discourse priming

1 Introduction

Code-mixing (CM) is probably the most salient aspect of bilingual speech. It is broadly defined as "the alternative use by bilinguals of two or more languages in the same conversation" (Milroy and Muysken 1995: 7) and has been investigated

---

Antje Endesfelder Quick, University of Leipzig
Ad Backus, Tilburg University
Elena Lieven, University of Manchester

in many speech communities around the world. Data are often from adult or adolescent speakers, as the main interest has been in how speakers combine their languages and why they do so. A smaller body of work has looked at CM in the speech of young children growing up in bilingual families, and the current study adds to this tradition (e.g. Bernardini and Schlyter 2004, Cantone 2007, Deuchar and Quay 2000).

Like much recent work on language acquisition, we adopt a usage-based approach. Usage-based work on contact data, whether from children or from adults, is relatively rare (cf. Backus 2014). Until recently, most studies adopted a fairly theory-neutral, structuralist approach, documenting common patterns, extrapolating from that to claim that some patterns were apparently difficult or impossible, and turning to general linguistic, generative, or psycholinguistic theories to find explanations. While this work has given rise to fairly robust empirical generalizations that seem to hold more or less universally, the search for an explanation of these generalizations within a linguistic theory (whether descriptive-structuralist or generative) does not appear to have produced wide consensus. From a usage-based perspective, no account would be complete that does not make reference to the cognitive mechanisms that lead to the attested speech that underlies these generalizations.

Applying a usage-based approach to bilingual acquisition data, we will examine the CM patterns of a young German-English bilingual child. German-English data (e.g. Clyne 1987) do not always support the main descriptive generalizations, nor do data from other language pairs in which the typological distance is small. We will, therefore, not test any pre-existing expectations about how German and English can be combined in bilingual speech. Instead, we do explore whether the overall prediction of the usage-based approach that children build up their linguistic competence on the basis of usage and innate cognitive skills, finds support in our data.

1.1 Child bilingual code-mixing

Language acquisition in bilingual children has been an area of long-standing interest. Reflecting perhaps the dominant Western language ideology of seeing individual languages as more or less strictly separated entities, the question that has dominated research is how children who grow up with two languages manage to keep them separate. Parents who speak two different mother tongues likewise often show keen interest in training their children to learn both languages but not to mix them. The strategy they often settle on is that each parent exclusively speaks his or her native language to the child. The children are expected to learn this language choice pattern and to accommodate to it, by always addressing each parent in the expected language. This One Parent One Language ('OPOL') strategy is most common in middle class expatriate families, and data from such environments dominate the literature on bilingual acquisition (e.g. Döpke 2000), in striking contrast to most of the literature on adult CM, which is largely based on data from bilingual or multilingual communities in which CM is an unmarked way of speaking (Gardner-Chloros 2009).

Issues prominent in child bilingualism studies have been identifying the age at which children learn to keep their languages separate, and the path through which they get there (e.g. Petitto, Katerlos, Levy, Gauna, Tétrault, and Ferraro 2001, De Houwer 1990). However, in a usage-based perspective, additional questions come to the fore. The default focus on separation is frequently motivated first by theory-internal questions in generative linguistics about the degree to which a child can learn two complete syntactic systems with native proficiency, and, second, by questions in psycholinguistics about the organization of the bilingual mental lexicon (as opposed to structure) in the mind. In our approach, in line with most of the work in the usage-based tradition, we focus not so much on the higher-order level of language choice (German or English) but on the choice of individual words and constructions, which may be German, English or mixed. The child may or may not have known at the time that individual words and structures were 'German' or 'English', and may or may not have been sensitive to the pressure to pay attention to language choice. Be that as it may, here we focus on the acquisition of individual multiword combinations and schematic constructions, and will assume that the degree to which these are monolingual and thus support language separation is a by-product of word and construction learning. This view may require some argumentation, however.

Child CM is often analyzed in relation to unequal proficiency levels in the two languages, often referred to through the concept of 'Language Dominance'. Children are thought to use CM because they need to fill lexical and syntactic gaps in their weaker language with items from the stronger language (e.g. Petersen 1988, Quay 1995, Bernardini and Schlyter 2004, Gawlitzek-Maiwald and Tracy 1996). There are many proposals that account in different ways for the most common empirical observation, that functional elements tend to be from the stronger language (e.g. Bernardini and Schlyter's 2004). This generalization is also the centerpiece of much of the theorizing about adult CM (e.g. Myers-Scotton's 2002).

Clearly there is a correlation between language dominance and CM but the argument can easily become circular if dominance is used to predict CM patterns, so an independent criterion for determining dominance is needed. Many researchers, e.g. Bernardini and Schlyter (2004), determine the stronger language as the one with the longer Mean Length of Utterance (MLU) or as the language that grammatically frames the longest utterances ('Upper bound'). However, language dominance is sometimes quite difficult to establish using these criteria, for example because language choice and CM patterns may change across utterances, topics, and interlocutors. Other factors besides proficiency play a role in bringing about CM. For example, a child may demonstrably know the translation equivalent of a particular word from the other language, yet not use it and produce CM instead. This may be because the word from the other language is better entrenched for that particular child, and hence activation of that word may be easier. The same may hold for the entrenchment and ease of activation of constructions. Differences in language proficiency, we will argue, are the automatic by-product if constructions and word combinations that derive from one language systematically have higher degrees of entrenchment and are therefore retrieved and activated more easily than units from the other language.

What is typical for almost all studies is that they assume dominance ranges across the entire syntactic domain. However, when looked at from a usage-based point of view, there is no reason to assume that dominance in Language A entails that each and every syntactic structure will be framed by that language. Since language is suggested to consist of a large number of constructions (e.g. Tomasello 2003), some schematic and others partially schematic (i.e. containing a lexically fixed part together with one or more open slots), there may well be constructions from language B that are at least as entrenched in a particular speaker's mind as individual constructions from Language A, despite perhaps an overall impression that for that speaker Language A is the better mastered language. We will account for just this kind of variability in the speech of the child we studied, as well as changes in CM patterns across the time period in which we studied him.

1.2 A usage-based approach to CM

The usage-based perspective has made major contributions to the study of first language acquisition; for this reason we argue that it is important to extend its empirical reach to bilingual acquisition, given that a large percentage of children in the world grows up with two languages. Below, we briefly outline the basic characteristics of this approach.

Communication is a cooperative act that is grounded in 'usage events' (Grice 1975, Langacker 2008, Tomasello 2008). Language is seen as the collection of units that combine a specific form and its symbolically associated specific meaning. Both 'form' and 'meaning' are defined broadly. Forms include words as well as patterns, while meanings can be semantic, pragmatic or social in nature, and often are all of that at the same time. Usage-based grammar does not assume that children are born with a priori linguistic categories such as word classes or phrases, but rather aims to show that children's learning is based on a set of biologically inherited basic (social-) cognitive processes that are domain general (e.g. *rapid temporal order processing, intention-reading* and *pattern-finding)* (Tomasello 2003). Therefore, what children acquire is a growing inventory of units which differ in complexity and level of abstractness. Units can range from completely lexically fixed (individual words and morphemes, and conventional multiword expressions such as *'What's that')* to partially schematic or low-scope slot-and-frame patterns (*I want x*), and on to wholly schematic (or 'abstract', 'syntactic') patterns (*NP VP NP*). Schematic patterns emerge on the basis of an abstraction process, in which the child's representations become connected through structural similarities across a number of lexically fixed expressions (e.g. Theakston and Lieven 2017).

As children are just language beginners, their emerging language is characterized by a large proportion of lexically specific units which are initially processed as unanalyzed ensembles (e.g., Bannard and Matthews 2008). This feature complicates the distinction between lexical and functional items, as a functional item (e.g. a definite article) will often be an integral part of a larger whole rather than a separate element that was used in a productive way (e.g. in the combination *in the car*). On their way to full mastery of their language(s) children acquire a structured inventory of constructions. Starting with a few concrete words and constructions, they move from lexically specific units to more abstract constructions. In between lexically fixed units and abstract constructions are partially schematic constructions. These are marked by a lexically fixed part and one or more open slots into which the child productively inserts novel items, e.g. *I want x* (Lieven, Salomo, and Tomasello 2009). However, even in these slot-and-frame patterns children have been shown to be productive only in limited ways. They create their abstract categories and schematic constructions gradually, in piecemeal fashion (Brooks and Tomasello 1999, Lieven, Salomo and Tomasello. 2009).

This development was analyzed, for example, in a corpus study of four two-year-old English speaking children by Lieven, Salomo and Tomasello (2009), who showed that there is a close relationship between what a child says and previous utterances said by or to the child. The authors applied the so-called 'Traceback method' to investigate how children generated new utterances by tracing back the individual parts to their own previous utterances. Results showed that a large proportion of the utterances could be traced back, either as exact repeats or as partially schematic constructions with an open slot. However, the more proficient the children became, as indicated by a higher MLU, the fewer exact repetitions they produced, and the more operations were required to trace back the individual parts. This method is conservative in identifying existing schemas, as any corpus, even a dense one, captures at most 10% of daily speech. Therefore, the results probably underestimate the extent to which partially schematic constructions make up a speaker's competence.

Characteristics of the input play a crucial role in usage-based accounts of what children learn (Stoll, Abbot-Smith, and Lieven 2009). Child directed speech (CDS) has been shown to be highly repetitive, which aids the child in acquiring the partially schematic units and the lexically specific units that can be used to fill in the open slots. It has a shaping role: the more frequent a construction is in the input, the more likely it is it gets established as a cognitive "routine" (Langacker 1987). Frequent items become better entrenched and, therefore, are more easily activated. Consequently, high frequency strengthens the representations of words, phrases or partially schematic units and makes it easier to access and process them as a whole. Another influence on the ease with which words and constructions are activated is priming, i.e. occurrence in the immediately prior ongoing discourse, to be discussed below.

1.3 Influence of discourse context

Input-Output effects play a special role in functional approaches, particularly in the occurrence of priming situations. Priming is a form of repetition, and refers to the tendency people have to repeat an action or structure that was performed or uttered just before, despite the availability of alternative actions or structures. Priming studies are often used to obtain insight into mental representation, particularly how people process syntax (e.g. Bock 1986).

It stands to reason that priming and frequency have something to do with one another. A unit that is frequent in someone's linguistic experience is better entrenched for that person, therefore more easily activated, therefore continues to be used often, and therefore will often be in a position to prime further use. Studies often examine frequency effects at a global level, showing for example that higher frequency structures are acquired earlier than lower frequency structures. But immediate discourse effects have also been shown to play an important role in the production of constructions; either supporting or impeding them (e.g. Theakston and Lieven 2008, Kirjavainen and Theakston 2011). For example, Kirjavainen and Theakston (2011) investigated the influence of immediate discourse on the production of correct and erroneous *to*-infinitive constructions in 13 English children's corpora at the age of two to three. Children's production of WANT-*to*-VP and WANT-X constructions was significantly predicted by the presence or absence of the respective construction in the immediately prior discourse, providing strong support for discourse priming on production. If structures compete for production, both discourse context and frequency will affect their realization. Thus, parts of a code-mixed utterance might be primed by contextual persistence, especially at a younger age when children are less proficient in their language(s) and degrees of entrenchment are correspondingly low. Consequently, one could hypothesize that younger children will produce more chunks, and that these in turn will be more often primed. Older children are more proficient, therefore their language knowledge will contain more constructions, and production will rely less often on immediate discourse priming.

1.4 The current study

In this paper we trace back antecedents of the units that appear in the bilingual utterances of one German-English bilingual child. For the reasons outlined above, we use individual utterances and the constructions they instantiate as our basic descriptive unit, rather than for example the overall roles of German and English. Nevertheless, most of the time the elements that make up the bilingual utterances will be recognizable as belonging to either German or English. This holds for constructions as well as words, by virtue of the language origin of the functional elements in the individual constructions. However, lumping these constructions together in order to establish that the child is either English- or German-dominant would miss important information about the acquisition of the constructional knowledge that ultimately leads to this impression of dominance. In addition, knowing about the productivity of these individual constructions, dramatically illustrated by their openness to slot fillers from the other language, tells us something about where creativity in language resides. This holds for data from bilingual children as much as it does for monolingual children (as studied in for example Lieven, Salomo and Tomasello 2009). The research question we attempt to answer is which constructions in either language tend to attract CM, and we will demonstrate that most CM involves the use of a partially schematic unit from one language in which the open slot is filled with lexical material from the other language, that the shifting German or English origin of these constructions reflects shifts in the amount of input the child received in each language, and that discourse priming indeed is an important determinant for what the bilingual child produces at any given moment.

2 Method

2.1 Participant

Fion is the second child in a middle-class family. He grew up in a German city. The mother is a native speaker of German and the father of English. The parents aimed to follow the one parent – one language approach but in reality were very inconsistent in their use of their respective mother tongues. Both parents speak their non-native language quite well and occasionally code-mix themselves. Fion has an older brother who was also raised according to the OPOL strategy. Unfortunately, we have no information concerning the age of the brother. From the recordings we can tell that the brother produced code-mixes as well. Fion went to a monolingual German-speaking daycare from 18 months onwards for about 4 hours per day. At the age of two, Fion started a German-speaking kindergarten where he spent on average 6–8 hours, 5 days per week.

2.2 Data

Fion's data consist of audiotape recordings of spontaneous speech in the home environment. The recordings cover a span from 2;3 – 3;11. Recordings were made on average two hours per week, adding up to a total of 205 hours for the whole period. For the purpose of the present study we analyzed 3 months (22 hours) of Fion's data (at the ages of 2;3, 3;0, and 3;11). Most of the time both parents were present, which resulted in a bilingual context. Often the brother was also present and as he sometimes code-mixes, he presents another source of bilingual language use.

All recordings were transcribed and coded in SONIC CHAT format (MacWhinney 2000) by a bilingual research assistant.

2.3 Analysis

2.3.1 Basic measurements

The first analyses were concerned with the amount of CM, as in all bilingualism studies, and utterance lengths, as in all acquisition studies. We therefore first coded all multiword utterances for the language they were in: English monolingual, German monolingual and mixed. The corpus contained 5443 utterances, of which 321 contained material from both languages ('mixed'), and these will be further analyzed below (see Quick, Lieven, Backus and Tomasello, 2018, for an analysis of the entire data set). As is customary in language acquisition research, we calculated the MLU in words. Studies of bilingual acquisition usually present MLU separately for each language, but note that in most OPOL cases, the actual recording contexts tend to be monolingual, or at least more so than in our case. In order to see whether there were proficiency differences between the two languages, and how bilingual utterances relate to these differences, we calculated the MLU separately for the English, German and mixed utterances.

2.3.2 Partially schematic units in code-mixing

Central to the present paper is the issue of schematicity in the code-mixing of this German-English bilingual child. This makes it crucially important that we operationalize partial schematicity in an unambiguous way. Perhaps the best operationalization available at the moment is the 'Traceback' method (Lieven, Behrens, Speares and Tomasello 2003, Lieven, Salomo and Tomasello 2009). The underlying rationale is that entrenched words, chunks and schemas should only be identified as such if they can be related ('traced back') to previous utterances in the recordings. Accordingly, we coded for each mixed utterance whether it constituted a fully lexically specific chunk, a combination of two or more fixed lexical chunks, a partially schematic construction, or a novel construction. A partially schematic construction is a recurring schema that contains one or more fixed lexical elements. Although child utterances are usually very short, an utterance may occasionally contain other things, for example a discourse marker, but these do not influence the coding. Each utterance gets one code. Therefore, all code-mixed utterances were given one of the following codes:
i.   Chunks: lexically fixed items which have occurred before
ii. Partially schematic constructions which contain a chunk in the open slot
iii. Partially schematic constructions in which the open slot is filled by a word or sequence not found in earlier recordings in this slot
iv. Utterances which fit neither of these categories ('other').

A sequence containing CM was identified as a mixed chunk if it constituted an exact repetition of something said earlier by the child and contained material from both languages. For example, the child repeated the German-English combination _und this_ 'and this'[1] a number of times, so it was coded as a chunk.

---

[1] Chunks are underlined throughout the paper

If the code-mixed utterance contained a monolingual sequence we looked for exact occurrences of that sequence in the monolingual portions of the data, and coded it as a chunk if previous occurrences were found. As a result, if the open slot in a partially schematic construction was filled by a lexically fixed chunk, this was coded as category 'ii'. For example the utterance *nein big one* 'no big one' (2;3) is a creative utterance containing two units, *nein X* and *big one*. *Nein x* is a partially schematic construction and was supported by other occurrences at the age of 2;3, such as *nein ask mama*, *nein blue*, *nein seven*. In *nein big one*, the open slot is filled by the lexically fixed chunk *big one*, supported by other occurrences at 2;3, such as *big one* and *big one little one*. Similarly, *nein you* is also coded as category ii, since the word *you* occurs outside of this particular instance. *Nein seven*, on the other hand, is coded as category iii, since in this recording the word *seven* only occurs in this particular instance. Similarly, in *nein ask mama*, the open slot is filled by a sequence *ask mama* that does not occur elsewhere in the data. Therefore, the utterance *nein ask mama* is also coded as instantiating Category iii: a partially schematic construction that, as far as we can tell on the basis of the data, is filled in a creative way.

Finally, if an utterance fit neither of these coding schemes it was classified as other, e.g. *fighter helm an* 'fighter helmet on'. Outside of this example, there are no occurrences of *fighter* plus noun, noun plus *helm* or noun plus *an* in either CM utterances or monolingual German utterances.

Additionally, we were also interested in the types of elements that instantiated the fixed part and that filled the open slots in the partially schematic constructions. For example, the utterance *was is breakfast* 'what is breakfast' (3;0) contains the partially schematic unit *was is x* 'what is x' which was supported by *was is hedge* 'what is hedge', *was is yuck* 'what is yuck', *was is this fuer eine zahnpasta?* 'what is this for a toothpaste', all uttered at 3;0. The open slot is usually filled with a lexical element such as *breakfast*, but also sometimes with more complex sequences, as in *was is this fuer eine zahnpasta?* 'what is this for a toothpaste'.

2.3.3 Discourse priming

Since we were further interested in whether any part of a code-mixed utterance was primed by immediately previous discourse we also checked the 20 previous utterances in the same recording, from both child and interlocutor. Input priming was categorized as either self-priming by the child or discourse priming by the interlocutor (Table 1).

Table 1: Example discourse priming.

Fion discourse, age 2;3	Fixed part	Open slot	
FAT: I see a helicopter, do I?	English	English	input
CHI: I see helm 'I see helmet' I see a Kelle 'I see a ladle'	German I see x	German/English helm a Kelle	output

Table 1 shows an example of discourse priming by the father. In this example the fixed part (*I see*) as in the *I see x* schema was primed by the previous utterance of the father.

In a second step we analyzed whether the prime was a chunk, a fixed part of a partially schematic construction or the word that had filled an open slot in a partially schematic construction.

25% of the code-mixed utterances were coded by a second person and reliability for the categories was good (Kappa 0.83).

3 Results

3.1 Quantitative results

Figure 1 shows the proportion of the three language 'types' across the three months of recordings. Whereas Fion used mostly German monolingual utterances at the ages of 2;3 and 3;0, the distribution pattern shows an increase of English at the

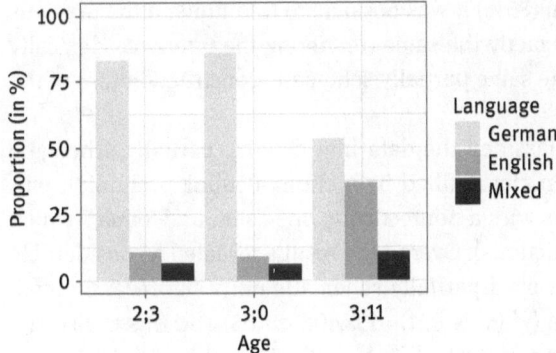

Figure 1: Language proportions.

age of 3;11. This presumably reflects the combined effects of a trip to Ireland that took place before the third measurement and a visit from monolingual English-speaking grandparents. In general, Fion's data reflect the input he receives. As a result, Fion produces mostly monolingual utterances but not exclusively so.

MLU was calculated individually for language type and age (Figure 2). Results show that throughout development the German MLU is higher than the English MLU. However, the mixed MLU significantly exceeds the monolingual MLU in all three months (U=1362882, *p*<.001).

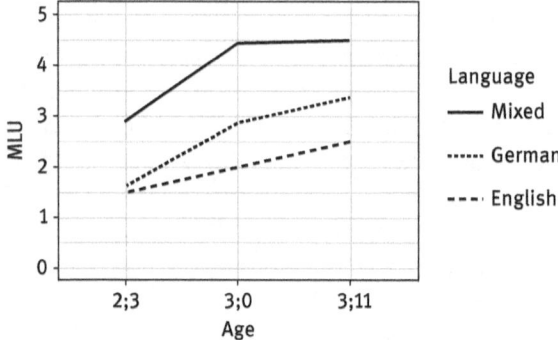

Figure 2: MLU across age.

There are various possible reasons why mixed utterances are longer. These will be discussed in Section 4.

3.2 Partially schematic units in code-mixing

Our main analysis was concerned with the level of schematicity in the code-mixed utterances. For many of them (85%) it was possible to find units in the previous recordings that were either exactly the same (rendering the utterances lexically fixed chunks) or that used the same partially schematic construction (276 of the 321 utterances, Figure 3).

As detailed above, we classified the data into chunks, partially schematic utterances in which the open slot is filled by a chunk ('chunk + chunk'), partially schematic constructions with a nonrecurring open slot, and 'other' (which would likely be novel constructions). Overall the results revealed a considerable reliance on fixed items. Fion used partially schematic units significantly more often than all the other types (χ^2 (6, N=321)= 13.4506, *p*<.05) and this is also significant for each individual month (2;3: χ^2 (3, N=150)= 73.0933, *p*<.001, 3;0: χ^2 (3, N=121)= 77.3802, *p*<.001, and 3;11: χ^2 (2, N=50)= 44.92, *p*<.001). This suggests he

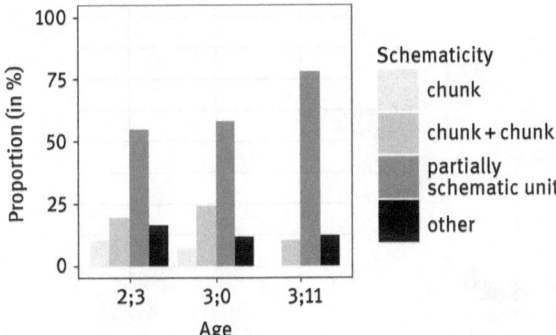

Figure 3: Levels of schematicity in code-mixing.

strongly relies on low-level syntactic schemas, i.e. patterns built around one or more lexical elements.

The proportion of utterances that as a whole instantiated a chunk, including ones that Fion most likely created himself considering they instantiate CM, such as *lid kaput* 'lid broken', *ander frog* 'other frog' and *und this* 'and this', slowly decreased over time, showing that Fion became more creative as he grew older. This creativity largely involves the productive use of partially schematic units. For example, the utterances <u>nein</u> *a fireman* 'no a fireman', <u>nein</u> *mein phone* 'no my phone', <u>nein</u> *in a wall* 'no in a wall' were all classified as the *nein x* 'no x' partially schematic construction. At the age of 3;11, Fion relies a lot on familiar partially schematic units.

3.3 Language distribution across slots

The next step in the analysis was to investigate the distribution of partially schematic units across the two languages. The fixed part was coded as German, English or mixed (see Figure 4). Results show a correlation of age and language of the fixed part (χ^2 (4, N=277)= 65.1439, *p*<.001) with an interesting shift from German schemas to English schemas which ties in with the proportional shift towards more English at the age of 3;11. At the age of 2;3, Fion overwhelmingly produced more German partially schematic constructions, e.g. <u>da</u> *motorbike* 'there motorbike', *nein in a wall* 'no in a wall', <u>das</u> *time out* 'this time out' (χ^2 (2, N=126)= 57.1905, *p*<.001). At age 3;0, this pattern has changed: we see a transition towards more English schemas and fewer German schemas (χ^2 (2, N=107)= 18.243, *p*<.001). Age 3;11 shows that most of his partially schematic units have an English schema, e.g. <u>and that's</u> *groesser* 'and that is bigger', <u>or</u> *als vampir* 'or as

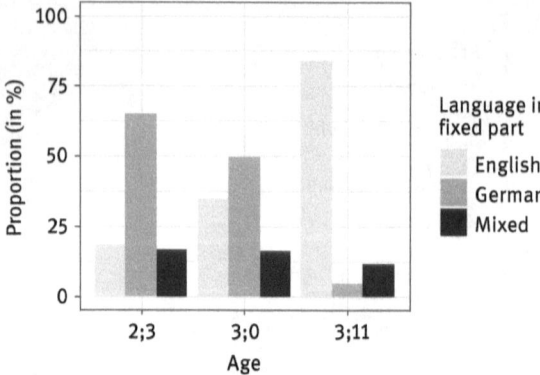

Figure 4: Language distribution in the frames across age.

vampire', <u>and</u> schwarz <u>there</u> 'and black there' (χ^2 (2, N=44)= 51.3182, $p<.001$). It is again difficult to establish the exact reason for this, but tentatively we suggest that this too reflects Fion's linguistic experience. He spends more time in monolingual German environments (especially his day care center) than in monolingual English ones, and hence he suppresses CM more easily when speaking German, or simply experiences the need less.

Partially schematic constructions have, by definition, a fixed and an open part. Therefore, in our next analyses we determined the language of the open slots. Results basically mirrored the findings of the fixed part (Figure 5). Again, we found a correlation of language of the open slot and age (χ^2 (4, N=245)= 44.4512, $p<.001$). At the age of 2;3 the language of the frame is overwhelmingly German and consequently the open slot is either filled with English material or mixed material, see examples above (2;3: χ^2 (2, N=126)= 57.1905, $p<.001$, 3;0: χ^2 (2, N=107)= 18.243, $p<.001$, 3;11: χ^2

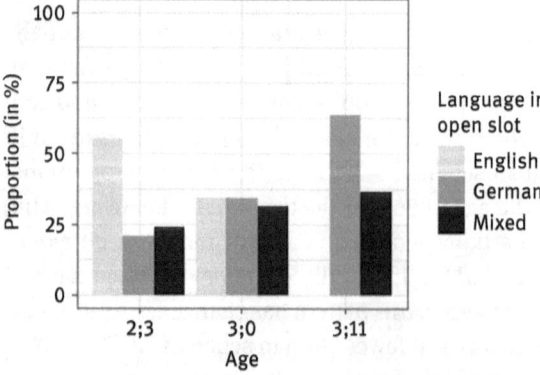

Figure 5: Language distribution of open slots across age.

(2, N=44)= 51.3182, *p*<.001). The same shift which was observed for the language of the fixed part is also present in the language of the open slot, with more English slot fillers at age 2;3, a transition at age 3;0 with nearly equal amount of English or German slot fillers and finally at age 3;11 the majority of slot fillers are in German.

Note that at age 3;0 open slots are equally filled with either German, English or mixed constituents, e.g. *this is* ein loewe 'this is a lion', *this little piggy* had bread und butter 'this little piggy had bread and butter', *du* a big one 'you a big one', *aber ich will* mit this fahren 'but I want to drive with this', *und this* eine eisenbahn 'and this a train', *mit this* musst du gruen 'with this you must green'.

3.4 Functional and lexical items in fixed and open parts

To get some more insight into the properties of the partially schematic constructions, we analyzed the distribution of functional and lexical items in the fixed parts. Lexical items were defined as any verb, noun, adjective or adverb. The distribution of functional and lexical material in these fixed parts is given in Figure 6. Some constructions contain functional items only, e.g. the preposition and demonstrative in *mit this* musst du gruen 'with this you must green' (*mit this x*). Others combine lexical and functional elements, such as the demonstrative and copula in *this is* deins 'this is yours' (*this is x*). Note that the lexical part here is fairly 'functional'; in our coding scheme all verbs were coded as 'lexical', including copulas and auxiliaries. Finally, fixed parts could be lexical, e.g. the verb in *look* eine schlange 'look a snake' (*look x*). Results showed that there is a correlation of category and age (χ^2 (4, N=277)= 27.2937, *p*<.001). At the age of two the fixed parts contained mostly functional elements thus providing the grammatical frame of the utterances (χ^2 (2, N=126)= 42.0476, *p*<.001). At the age

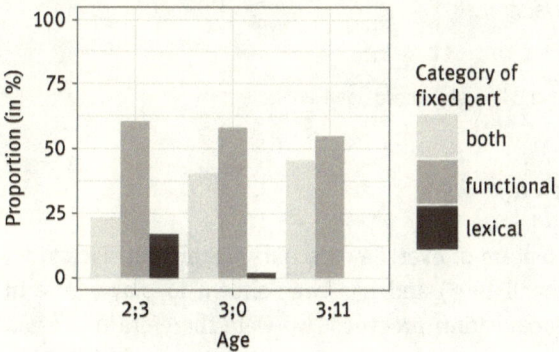

Figure 6: Distribution of functional and lexical items in fixed parts.

of 3;0 we see that fixed parts are again mostly functional items (χ^2 (2, N=107)= 52.729, $p<.001$) but also contain both functional and lexical items sometimes. At the age of 3;11 this shifts to schemas more often containing lexical in addition to functional items (χ^2 (2, N=44)= 22.5455, $p<.001$). Purely lexical frames play only a minor role throughout and do not occur at all at age 3;11. All told, the data suggest that in language acquisition the schemas used become more complex with age.

One way to look at these partially schematic units is that they represent what is traditionally called 'syntax', and thus it is not surprising that they consist of fixed functional elements and variable lexical ones. Turning our attention to what fills the open slots, it is clear that results mirror those for the fixed parts (Figure 7). The open slots are mainly filled with lexical items or a combination of functional and lexical elements, e.g. _nein_ big one 'no big one', _or_ a prinz 'or a prince' (χ^2 (6, N=321)= 20.6164, $p=0.00215$). However, the distribution also shows that functional items are often part of the slot filler for which Fion has the translation equivalent available. This could be interpreted as suggesting that the code-mixing is not just a matter of filling gaps in Fion's vocabulary in either language, since in that case one would expect a larger share of lexical elements (at 3;0: χ^2 (3, N=121)= 34.7355, $p<.001$, at 3;11: χ^2 (3, N=50)= 27.28, p<.001).

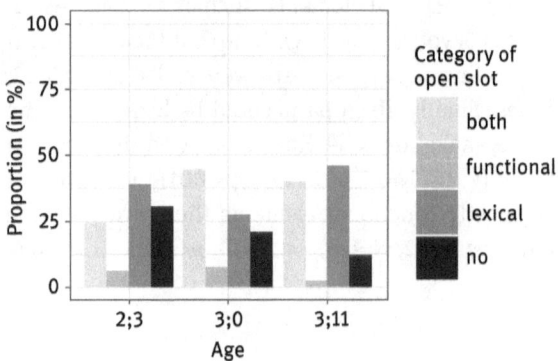

Figure 7: Distribution of functional and lexical items in open slots.

3.5 Discourse priming

Priming is a very pervasive feature of everyday discourse (Branigan, Pickering, Liversedge, Stewart and Urbach 1995) and has been shown to play a role in determining how language acquisition proceeds; we were therefore interested in whether priming plays a role in the code-mixed utterances of this child. Code-mixed utterances which contained a fixed string (n=277) were included into

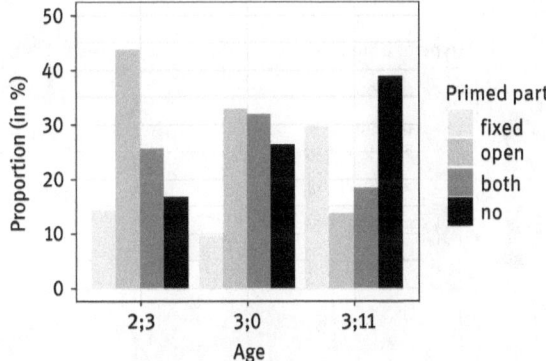

Figure 8: Influence of priming on code-mixing.

the analyses, leaving out utterances which belonged to the 'other' category. 211 of the 277 utterances contained parts which occurred in the immediately prior discourse (recall we set the limit at twenty preceding utterances), either provided by the interlocutor or by the child itself. Priming differs across age (χ^2 (6, N=277)= 26.6187, p<.001). Figure 8 shows that priming has a greater effect at the ages of 2;3 and 3;0 (2;3: χ^2 (3, N=126)= 26.8254, p<.001, 3;0: χ^2 (3, N=107)= 15.0561, p<.001, 3;11: χ^2 (3, N=44)= 6.7273, p=0.08. There is also a qualitative difference: the open slot is primed more often at the younger age and fixed parts more often at 3;11.

Although priming decreases we still see that it plays an important role at the age of 3;11 (Figure 9).

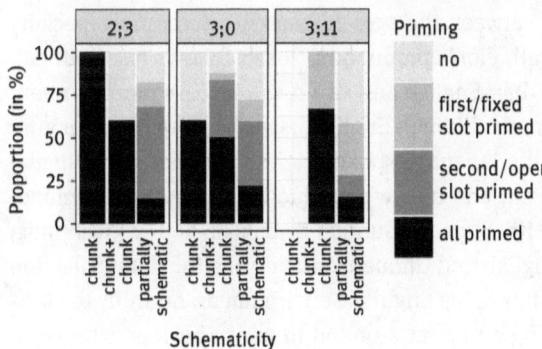

Figure 9: Effect of priming on schematicity and age.

Finally, we were also interested in the type of the prime. Priming could either happen through speech by others, a combination of speech by others and self-priming, or through self-priming. Figure 10 shows that, at the age of 2;3, Fion

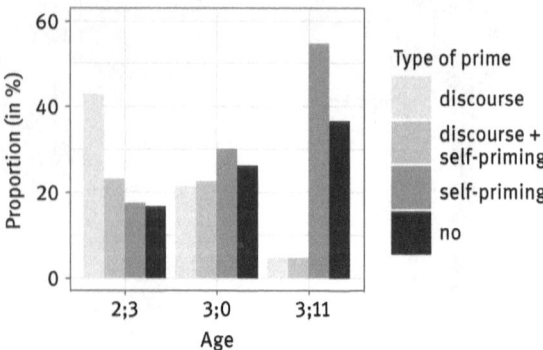

Figure 10: Type of priming on code-mixing.

relied more on discourse priming (χ^2 (3, N=126)= 22.6349, $p<.001$). Again, at the age of 3;00 we seem to have a transition phase in which no specific type of prime seemed to dominate. However, at the age of 3;11 most priming happens through self-priming in that Fion himself has uttered parts of the code-mix immediately before the target utterance (χ^2 (3, N=44)= 32.3636, $p<0.001$); in addition the share of non-primed utterances has gone up.

4 Discussion

In this contribution, we have analyzed the language production of the German-English bilingual child Fion, between the ages 2;3 and 3;11, focusing especially on his language mixing. Overall, Fion's production closely follows his input patterns. He hears more German than English and as a result he uses more German, and his MLU is higher in German, although English becomes more frequent after increased exposure. Most of the language spoken to him is either monolingual German or monolingual English, and his own production is also largely monolingual, in the sense that he either speaks German or English at any given time. The relative distribution of English and German shifts during the data collection period, and this mirrors a change in his linguistic environment: he shifts towards increased use of English during and after a period in which he was exposed to monolingual English more (see Slavkov 2015 for a similar example).

However, Fion also produces quite a lot of mixed language. In itself, this is not surprising, since his parents are fairly relaxed about CM, he has a brother who produces code-mixes, and it is frequently observed that even children growing up with two languages that are kept rigorously separate in the input will mix them, up to a point (Müller, Arnaus Gil, Eichler, Geveler, Hager, Jansen, Patuto, Repetto and Schmeißer 2015). Presumably this has to do with ease of activation, itself influenced by factors such as the high degree of entrenchment of particular words and constructions in each language, and priming by immediately prior discourse. We will explore these factors in some more detail below; it is not our intention to explain why Fion produces CM at all, but why it has the characteristics that it has.

A child growing up with two languages naturally has to acquire words and structures from both. A crucial aspect of language knowledge, from a usage-based perspective at least, is that more than knowing or not knowing a particular linguistic unit, speakers know units to a particular degree: units are more or less entrenched, and for every unit this differs from speaker to speaker, and it is likely that acquisition is characterized by ever-changing, mostly increasing, entrenchment of individual words, word combinations, and constructions. It is very likely that for Fion, many German units will be entrenched better than their English equivalents, but that there will also be English units that are better entrenched than their German equivalents. For some words, this will simply be because they exist only in English form. Decades of research on CM and loanwords have made clear that languages contain lexical gaps that get filled with foreign words: these convey concepts for which the borrowing language simply had no words, and in many cases had no need either. Similarly, some concepts may be lexicalized in both languages but are always talked about in just one of the languages (Backus 2014). In these cases, it is likely that CM simply originates in semantic appropriateness: the concept has to be named and the child uses the best available word for it. Recall, further, that Fion was growing up in a family that was not very strict about the OPOL strategy; whenever Fion produced CM he was not called on it. On the other hand, by far the most of Fion's utterances were monolingual, reflecting the relatively low amount of CM in his everyday linguistic environment, and supporting the broad usage-based hypothesis that competence and output reflect input.

Better entrenchment means easier activation, and thus well entrenched German lexical and constructional units may get activated in utterances that ostensibly seem to be in English and vice versa. If this line of argumentation is true, it may account for two aspects of our data. One is that CM occurs in the first place. The second one relates to the finding that the MLU was significantly higher for mixed utterances than for German or English utterances, confirming earlier findings by Quick, Lieven, Carpenter and Tomasello 2018 for another German-English bilingual child. When Fion constructs a German utterance and finds it difficult to finish it, for example because he does not know a particular word well or at all, he might simply abort the utterance, or get interrupted by a parent. As a result, the utterance stays relatively short. If, however, that particular concept is well entrenched in its English form, he might insert the English word or chunk in the already produced German frame, producing an instance of CM. As a result, the utterance is longer than if it had been aborted. For example at age 3;11, the partially schematic unit *I need x* as in *I need my topf to pee pee* 'I need my pot to pee', has the open slot x filled with German and English material and thus is more complex and longer than the monolingual phrase *I need* containing no open slot, which was also found in the same recordings. The same applies for partially schematic utterances that contain CM such as in *this is kein taxi* 'this is no cab' (instantiating *this is x*) versus the monolingual fragment *this* (used as a simple deictic). Both were found in the data at 3;0.

In order to support this interpretation, we should engage more deeply with the concept of entrenchment. However, that would go beyond the empirical scope of the current work, since the only data we have are Fion's recordings. Degree of entrenchment is often assumed to be reflected by corpus frequency, but in a very imprecise way, given the spotty data coverage of corpora, especially in relation to an actual individual language user's language experience. Entrenchment is also often assessed through a participant's responses to suitable experimental tasks, for example lexical decision. The latter type of data is obviously unavailable for Fion. The frequency data we have are not ideal, given that even our intensive data collection procedure cannot avoid missing a lot of relevant language use. However, the relatively sizable data set and the inbuilt conservativeness of the Traceback method allow some conclusions about Fion's lexical and constructional competence. The general tendency is that Fion's output links up nicely with his presumed competence: more German than English, initially more CM from a German than from an English base, and a shift towards increased use of English at the end of the data period, when the degree of entrenchment of his English units will have gotten a boost from his increased usage of, and exposure to, English in the period immediately before.

Our analysis focused in particular on partially schematic units. Following the competence model commonly adopted in usage-based accounts, we characterize any speaker's linguistic competence as the inventory of specific, partially schematic and schematic units (e.g. Tomasello 2000; Theakston and Lieven 2017). Cross-cutting the traditional modules of lexicon, morphology and syntax, these correspond, respectively, to words and expressions (or 'chunks'), constructions with some fixed elements, and completely schematic templates ('syntactic constructions'). Partially schematic units are interesting because, first, they have been left out of traditional accounts which contain only lexicon and syntax with nothing in between, and, second, they allow insight into the early beginnings of a child's syntactic knowledge. If being a proficient speaker means that one has an extensive vocabulary ('specific units') and a good command of constructions in which to use them (partially and completely 'schematic units'), then one would expect Fion to use more schematic units (whether partial or not) as he grows older. It is clear that no speaker produces only fully rote-learned utterances. In our approach, it is equally clear that speakers also do not produce full grammatical frames first and then fill them in with lexical material, including the desired function words and grammatical morphemes. Partially schematic constructions fill in the middle ground between these two extremes, and understanding how they are used is crucial for understanding linguistic competence and linguistic production. As in anybody else's production, Fion's data exhibit constant interplay between the ease of activation that favors the use of well entrenched units and the creativity needed to produce utterances that convey as precisely as possible what one wants to say. This interplay requires the overlapping use and productive filling out of partially and completely schematic constructions.

However, identifying whether a particular utterance, or rather any part of an utterance, was lexically fixed, completely novel, or the instantiation of a partially schematic construction is not easy. Currently, the Traceback method (Lieven, Salomo and Tomasello 2009) is perhaps the best available way of identifying the overall degree of schematicity in an individual's constructicon, and this is what we used in our analysis to identify whether Fion's mixed utterances were complete or partial repetitions of earlier utterances.

A full 85% of Fion's mixed utterances were either complete or partial repetitions, the latter far outnumbering the former. This should not come as a surprise. If native speaker language production proceeds chunk-by-chunk (Christiansen and Chater 2015), and utterances consists of several chunks combined together in overlapping fashion, it stands to reason that when a child's utterances get longer, they will more and more resemble this adult pattern. As long as utterances are not much longer than a single chunk, one could expect a lot of completely fixed phrases (identified as verbatim repetition by the Traceback method), but as soon as the child's competence allows longer utterances, these fixed phrases get embedded into larger structures, creating slot-and-frame patterns (Bannard and Lieven 2012, Bannard and Matthews 2008, Abbot-Smith and Tomasello 2006).

We mentioned above that Fion's output fairly closely matched his input, with a quantitative shift towards increased use of English in the final stage of data collection mirroring an increase of English input. This shift also shows in the distribution of partially schematic units throughout the data set. In CM analyses, it is usually assumed that if a lot of the mixing is insertional, the language that functions as the 'Matrix Language' is the dominant language for the speaker, the language of highest proficiency (e.g. Bernardini and Schlyter 2004). While dominance is a problematic issue (see Cantone, Kupisch, Müller, and Schmitz 2008), it could be argued that the shift from more German to more English and a shift from more German-based partially schematic units to more English-based ones are both indicators of a shift towards English dominance in Fion's bilingualism.

However, this cannot be the quite true, since Fion produces more German than English throughout, and his MLU is consistently higher for German. What it suggests is that as his English proficiency increases, and he produces more English frames, activation of these frames does not block activation of well-entrenched German lexical elements. The reverse does not happen, suggesting that the increasing entrenchment of English chunks and schematic units in his competence does not reach degrees high enough for them to get activated quicker than their German equivalents, as these are even more entrenched.

The Traceback method identifies whether or not an utterance or a chunk was produced at any prior point in the data collection, but we also investigated whether or not the previous occurrence was in the immediately prior discourse, here operationalized as the previous twenty utterances by any speaker. We defined units repeated within this window as primed (either self- or other-primed). Roughly two thirds of the code-mixed units turned out to be primed. This suggests priming plays a substantial role in determining the usage that is instrumental in building up competence, and that it plays a larger role at a younger age, especially in relation to chunks and combinations involving a chunk. This suggests that at a younger age, Fion's proficiency is still low enough for him to 'just try to get' whatever he can to compensate for the relatively low ease of activation that holds for most of the units in his inventory. Priming never fades out as it still plays an important role at 3;0 and 3;11. This persistence should not surprise us, as it is assumed that priming plays a role in all everyday discourse throughout life (as argued by Pickering and Garrod 2004). The fact that at 3;11 priming is found most for the fixed part of partially schematic units, i.e. for the functional elements in it (e.g. '*mit this x*') or a chunk within it that includes functional elements (such as '*I see x*') suggests that Fion has started to frequently use common grammatical patterns. They show up as priming thanks to our operationalization, in which an occurrence in the past twenty turns is sufficient. Whether all these instances of common constructions are indeed primed, or whether at least some of them instead reflect easy activation of entrenched structures, is hard to tell at this point.

Summing up the priming data, at least three interesting tendencies emerged from the data. First, the incidence of discourse priming went down with age. Second, what was primed moved from predominantly lexical to predominantly functional material with increasing age. We interpret this to mean that as lexical and grammatical competence grows with age, utterance formation increasingly relies on the productive use of partially schematic templates. As Fion commands an ever larger range of partially schematic constructions, he also produces more of them, and some of these are so common that they end up primed according to our definition, but overall the variation in constructions is large enough to bring the overall proportion of priming down. However, the lower incidence of lexical priming at 3;11 would require a more detailed and qualitative analysis of the data. The third notable tendency was that the main source of priming shifted from parent to self. This suggests that with increasing age and therefore increasing proficiency, Fion became less dependent on imitating what he heard, and became better at constructing his own discourse.

5 Conclusion

Our analysis of the bilingual conversational data of a German-English bilingual child has shown that increasing proficiency in acquisition is mostly a matter of the increased use of partially schematic constructions. It is possible that at later stages of acquisition and in adult usage, the use of partially schematic constructions in turn gives way to the employment of fully schematic constructions, though whether or not fully schematic constructions are indeed prominently present in adult competence and form the basis of everyday language use remains to be seen. Both the increasing degree of entrenchment of partially schematic constructions and their priming by recent use in ongoing discourse contribute to the ease of activation that underlies their use. Although the child we investigated hears relatively little CM around him, he did produce mixed utterances, in which he combined German and English material, around 8% of the time. We suggest that entrenchment and priming of individual words and constructions is the trigger for the use of English lexical material in German constructions and vice versa, and for the occasional alternate use of English and German partially schematic constructions side-by-side. As in comparable studies of monolingual development, we saw that Fion moved in piecemeal fashion from relying on lexical chunks to partially schematic constructions, which then act as a gateway to more abstract syntactic patterns. In bilingual development, these developments are equally visible, with the added aspect that these constructions are sometimes filled with foreign lexical material, giving rise to the phenomenon we know as CM.

References

Abbot-Smith, Kirsten & Michael Tomasello. 2006. Exemplar-learning and schematization in a usage based account of syntactic acquisition. *The Linguistic Review* 23. 275–290. DOI 10.1515/TLR.2006.011

Backus, Ad 2014. Towards a usage-based account of language change: Implications of contact linguistics for linguistic theory. In Robert Nicolai (ed.), *Questioning Language Contact: Limits of Contact, Contact at its Limits*, 91–118. Leiden/Boston: Brill.

Bannard, Colin & Elena Lieven. 2012. Formulaic language in L1 acquisition. *Annual Review of Applied Linguistics* 32. 3–16. DOI: 10.1017/S0267190512000062.

Bannard, Colin & Danielle Matthews. 2008. Stored word sequences in language learning: The effect of familiarity on children's repetition of four-word combinations. *Psychological Science* 19(3). 241–248. doi:10.1111/j.1467-9280.2008.02075.x

Bernardini, Petra & Suzanne Schlyter. 2004. Growing syntactic structure and code-mixing in the weaker language: The Ivy Hypothesis. *Bilingualism: Language and Cognition* 7. 49–69. doi: 10.1017/S1366728904001270.

Bock, J. Kathryn. 1986. Syntactic persistence in language production. *Cognitive Psychology* 18. 355–387.

Branigan, Holly P., Martin J. Pickering, Simon P. Liversedge, Andrew J, Stewart & Thomas P. Urbach. 1995. Syntactic priming: Investigating the mental representation of language. *Journal of Psycholinguistic Research* 24(6). 489–506.

Brooks, Patricia J. & Michael Tomasello. 1999. Young children learn to produce passives with nonce verbs. *Developmental Psychology* 35(1). 29–44.

Cantone, Katja F. 2007. *Code-switching in Bilingual Children*. Dordrecht: Springer.

Cantone Katja F., Tanja Kupisch, Natascha Müller & Katrin Schmitz. 2008. Rethinking language dominance in bilingual children. *Linguistische Berichte* 215. 307–343.

Christiansen, Morten H. & Nick Chater. 2015. The language faculty that wasn't: A usage-based account of natural language recursion. *Frontiers in Psychology* 6, 1182. doi: 10.3389/fpsyg.2015.01182.

Clyne, Michael. 1987. Constraints on code switching: How universal are they? *Linguistics* 25. 739–764.

De Houwer, Annick 1990. *The Acquisition of Two Languages from Birth: A Case Study*. Cambridge: Cambridge University Press.

Deuchar, Margaret & Suzanne Quay. 2000. *Bilingual Acquisition: Theoretical Implications of a Case Study*. Oxford: Oxford University Press.

Döpke, Susanne. 2000. *Crosslinguistic Structures in Simultaneous Bilingualism*. Amsterdam: John Benjamins.

Gardner-Chloros, Penelope. 2009. *Code-Switching*. Cambridge: Cambridge University Press.

Gawlitzek-Maiwald, Ira & Rosemary Tracy. 1996. Bilingual bootstrapping. *Linguistics* 34. 901–926.

Grice, Herbert P. 1975. Logic and conversation. In P. Cole and J. Morgan (eds.), *Syntax and Semantics* (Vol. 3), 41–58. New York: Academic Press.

Kirjavainen, Minna & Anna Theakston. 2011 Are infinitival to omission errors primed by prior discourse? The case of WANT constructions. *Cognitive Linguistics* 22(4). 629–657.

Langacker, Ronald W. 1987. *Foundations of Cognitive Grammar*, vol. 1. Palo Alto: Stanford University Press.

Langacker, Ronal W. 2008. *Cognitive Grammar: A Basic Introduction*. New York: Oxford University Press.

Lieven, Elena, Dorothé Salomo & Michael Tomasello. 2009. Two-year-old children's production of multiword utterances: A usage-based analysis. *Cognitive Linguistics* 20(3). 481–507. doi: 10.1515/COGL.2009.022

Lieven, Elena, Heike Behrens, Jennifer Speares & Michael Tomasello. 2003. Early syntactic creativity: a usage-based approach. *Journal of Child Language* 30(02). 333–370. doi: 10.1017/S0305000903005592

MacWhinney, Brian 2000. *The CHILDES Project: Tools for Analyzing Talk*. Mahwah, NJ: Lawrence Erlbaum Associates.

Milroy, Leslie & Pieter Muysken. 1995. *One Speaker, Two Languages: Cross-Disciplinary Perspectives on Code-Switching*. Cambridge, UK: Cambridge University Press.

Müller, Natascha, Laia Arnaus Gil, Nadine Eichler, Jasmin Geveler, Malin Hager, Veronika Jansen, Marisa Patuto, Valentina Repetto & Anika Schmeißer (2015). *Code-Switching: Spanisch, Italienisch, Französisch. Eine Einführung*. Tübingen: Narr.

Myers-Scotton, Carol. 2002. *Contact Linguistics Bilingual Encounters and Grammatical Outcomes*. Oxford: Oxford University Press.

Petersen, Jennifer. 1988. Word-internal code-switching constraints in a bilingual child's grammar. *Linguistics* 26. 479–493.

Petitto, Laura Ann, Marina Katerelos, Bronna Levy, Kristine Gauna, Katrine Tétrault & Vittoria Ferraro. 2001. Bilingual signed and spoken language acquisition from birth: Implications for mechanisms underlying bilingual language acquisition. *Journal of Child Language* 28(2). 1–44.

Pickering, Martin J. & Simon Garrod. 2004. Toward a mechanistic psychology of dialogue. *Behavioral and Brain Sciences* 27(2). 169–190.

Quay, Susanne. 1995. The bilingual lexicon: implications for studies of language choice. *Journal of Child Language* 22. 369–387.

Quick, Endesfelder A., Lieven, E., Carpenter, M., Tomasello, M. (2018). Identifying partially schematic units in the code-mixing of an English and German speaking child. *Linguistic Approaches to Bilingualism*. 8(4). 477–501. https://doi.org/10.1075/lab.15049.qui.

Quick, Endesfelder Antje, Elena Lieven, Ad Backus & Michael Tomasello. 2018. Constructively combing languages: The use of code-mixing in German-English bilingual children. *Linguistic Approaches to Bilingualism* 8(3). 393–409. https://doi.org/10.1075/lab.17008.qui.

Slavkov, Nikolay. 2015. Language attrition and reactivation in the context of bilingual first language acquisition. *International Journal of Bilingual Education and Bilingualism* 18(6). 715–734.

Stoll, Sabine, Kirstin Abbot-Smith & Elena Lieven. 2009. Lexically Restricted Utterances in Russian, German, and English Child-Directed Speech. *Cognitive Science* 33. 75–103. doi:10.1111/j.1551-6709.2008.01004.x

Theakston, Anna & Elena Lieven. 2008. The influence of discourse context on children's provision of auxiliary BE. *Journal of Child Language* 35. 129–158.

Theakston Anna & Elena Lieven. 2017. Multiunit sequences in first language acquisition. *Topics in Cognitive Science* 9(3). 588–603.

Tomasello, Michael. 2000. The item-based nature of children's early syntactic development. *Trends in Cognitive Sciences* 4. 156–163.

Tomasello, Michael. 2003. *Constructing a Language: A Usage-Based Theory of Language Acquisition*. Cambridge: Harvard University Press.

Tomasello, Michael. 2008. *Origins of Human Communication*. MIT Press.

Dirk Noël and Timothy Colleman
10 Constructional renovation: The role of French legal language in the survival of the nominative-and-infinitive in Dutch

Abstract: This chapter presents a case of contact-induced "constructional renovation", which is a new term for an under-researched phenomenon where a construction that is disappearing from a language gets revived. It offers an explanation for the current presence of the (micro)construction *geacht worden te* 'be considered / supposed to' in the Dutch constructicon, as a semasiologically changed remnant of a nominative-and-infinitive (NCI) schema which used to be instantiated much more diversely from the 17th to the 19th century. While English probably played a major role in the survival and change in meaning of another such remnant, *verondersteld worden te* 'be supposed to' (Colleman and Noël 2014), it is argued here that the entrenchment of *geacht worden te* received a boost in the 19th century through contact with legal French. Frequency evidence for its regeneration is drawn from a new historical Dutch corpus extracted from the newspaper component of the Delpher text archive, while proof for the influence of French is sought in a number of early-19th-century Dutch translations of French legal texts. Important theoretical conclusions are that the consequence of language contact for the evolution of constructicons is not limited to constructional borrowing and that genre is a determining factor in contact-induced constructional change.

Keywords: contrastive diachronic construction grammar; constructional attrition; constructional renovation; nominative-and-infinitive; *geacht worden te*; Dutch-French contact; legal language

1 Introduction

This study[1] on the Dutch nominative-and-infinitive is framed in a "contrastive diachronic construction grammar" perspective, as was our earlier joint work on

---

[1] Dirk Noël's contribution to the research reported on was supported by an allocation from the General Research Fund of the Hong Kong Research Grants Council for the project 'Construc-

---

Dirk Noël, The University of Hong Kong
Timothy Colleman, Ghent University

https://doi.org/10.1515/9783110619430-011

this morphosyntactic configuration (Noël and Colleman 2009, 2010; Colleman and Noël 2012, 2014). As the historical morphosyntactic branch of "the cognitive linguistic enterprise" (Langacker 1999: 13), diachronic construction grammar – sometimes written with three initial capitals to insist on its disciplinary credentials – concerns itself with "the historical study of constructions" (Barðdal and Gildea 2015: 42), with the "principles of constructional change" (Fried 2013), or, more broadly, with the study and theory of the evolution of the constructional resources of languages, i.e. the sociohistorical, or phylogenetic, evolution of "constructicons",[2] conceived of as cognitively relevant "network[s] of constructions" (Goldberg 2003: 219), which "may grow, be reorganized, and contract" (Traugott and Trousdale 2013: 46). *Contrastive* diachronic construction grammar always considers more than one constructicon, either to bring out interesting differences or similarities in the way they have developed, or to account for how changes in one constructicon are effected by another constructicon in a language contact situation. The latter research strand includes work on "constructional borrowing", a term introduced by Adele Goldberg in a reflection on a number of originally Yiddish constructions that "have been assimilated by a group of native English speakers", like the ones illustrated by *What's to forgive / to lose / not to like?*, *She's a crazy! / That is a funny*, and *Milk, shmilk / Papers, shmapers* (Goldberg 1990: 2). Some of the other contributions so far to this strand of work in diachronic construction grammar are Mithun (2008), Noël (2008), Doğruöz and Backus (2009), Pietsch (2010), Van de Velde and Zenner (2010), Höder (2012, 2014), Backus, Demirçay, and Sevinç (2013), Fischer (2013), Colleman and Noël (2014), and Colleman (2016, submitted).

Constructional borrowing leads to constructional innovations, which can in turn, as the innovative uses subsequently spread to larger portions of the linguistic community, turn into actual cases of established constructional change, i.e. where new constructions get added to the target constructicon (see, e.g., Backus, Doğruöz and Heine 2011 on salient stages in contact-induced constructional change) or where extant constructions develop new conventionalized uses on

---

tional attrition in a (contrastive) diachronic construction grammar perspective' (Project No. HKU748213H). Timothy Colleman's contribution was carried out within the framework of two research projects on 'Productivity, constructionalization and "expressive" constructions: Tracking productivity shifts in 19th- to 21st-century Belgian and Netherlandic Dutch' (FWO-Flanders & Ghent University) and 'Grammatical alternation, register and explicitation in original and translated Dutch' (Ghent University Special Research Fund). We are grateful for the feedback received from two reviewers on an earlier version of this text.

2 The term "constructicon" can be traced back to Daniel Jurafsky's UC Berkeley PhD dissertation (Jurafsky 1991); also see Jurafsky (1992: 302).

the basis of a foreign model (for the latter kind of contact-induced constructional innovation, see, e.g., Colleman submitted on new clusters of uses of selected Afrikaans argument structure constructions).[3] The theoretical point we want to make in this chapter, however, is that the effects of contact on the evolution of a constructicon can be more subtle than that. The case we will look at is one of an extant construction that was on the verge of extinction but which received a new lease of life as a result of language contact. In other words, we will provide an illustration of what one could call contact-induced "constructional renovation", to bring out the difference with constructional innovation.

The study builds on, and complements, Colleman and Noël (2014), which attributed the residual presence of the evidential and the deontic nominative-and-infinitive (or "NCI") in present-day Dutch to influence from English. The evidential NCI construction having lost the competition with other evidential constructions in the Dutch constructicon, the only Dutch NCI patterns occurring with any frequency today are those which, next to their evidential and other uses, are predominantly used as deontic modal expressions, most prominently *geacht worden te* 'be considered / supposed to' and, though considerably less frequently, *verondersteld worden te* 'be supposed to'. Judging a simple reanalysis of an evidential NCI as a deontic one to be no more likely in Dutch than it had been argued to be for similar English constructions (in Noël and van der Auwera 2009), we concluded it to be a plausible hypothesis, on the basis of the evidence considered, that the Dutch NCI patterns had "copied" the polysemy of a similar English pattern, *be supposed to*. In other words, our argument was that Dutch still has the NCI today because of contact-induced constructional innovation: the deontic NCI was borrowed from English as a semantic loan (Weinreich [1953] 1968: 48; Haugen 1950: 220) and the extant lexically substantive constructions survived as a result, or so we thought.

Two considerations have since led us to believe that this is unlikely to be the complete picture. First, while working very well for *verondersteld worden te*, the account is somewhat less probable in the case of *geacht worden te* because the latter is less obvious as a translational equivalent of *be supposed to*. Second, and more importantly, there is a problem with timing: the Dutch deontic NCI only

---

3 We do not address the question of whether changes of the latter kind are actually deserving of the label constructional *borrowing* here. On a narrow conception of borrowing as change involving the transfer of *phonetic substance* – or at least of ready-made form / meaning-pairings – they would not. However, in practice, the distinction between a brand-new construction being imported into the language and an existing construction being extended to new meanings or functions under the influence of language contact is not always straightforward. We refer to Colleman (2016) for further thoughts on the demarcation of constructional borrowing.

started proliferating near the end of the 20th century, while the non-deontic NCI had already become a marginal pattern by the start of that century. It needs to be explained, therefore, how come *geacht worden te* and *verondersteld worden te* stayed around as non-deontic constructions before they became deontic, and why the less straightforward translational equivalent of *be supposed to* is so much more frequent than the more obvious one.

To find an answer to these questions we will in this contribution revisit the 19th- and 20th-century history of *geacht worden te* and *verondersteld worden te* using a new historical corpus extracted from the online Delpher digital text archive (http://www.delpher.nl). In the next section we will elaborate on what was said in the third and fourth paragraphs of this introduction, illustrating the constructions referred to and briefly summarizing the findings of our research to date on the history of the NCI in both English and Dutch, as well as formulate and justify our research questions for the present study in greater detail. In section 3, besides introducing a few additional data sources, we will describe the new Delpher corpus, how we searched it and the other sources, and how we processed the query results. Section 4 will present quantitative data extracted from the data sources and discuss which hypotheses they are supportive of. Section 5, finally, will summarize the descriptive findings and reiterate how they feed into diachronic construction grammatical theory.

2 Background and problem

2.1 Nominative-and-infinitive constructions in Dutch

The nominative-and-infinitive, or NCI, short for *nominativus-cum-infinitivo*, is more generally known, both within and outside formalist paradigms, as a *believe*-type "raising-to-subject" pattern (see, e.g., Postal 1974 and, for an example of a functionalist using the term, Givón 1993). Barring the title of one of our contributions to its study we have consistently referred to it with the term inspired by Latin grammar, however, to underscore the Latin origin of this morphosyntactic configuration. It is often considered to be the passive construal of the "raising-to-object" pattern that also goes by the older name of ("genuine" / "learned" / "Latin-type") accusative-and-infinitive, or ACI for *accusativus-cum-infinitivo*. However, while the ACI used to be more frequent than the NCI, it has now all but disappeared from Dutch (Fischer 1994; Noël and Colleman 2010), with only the very occasional occurrence of archaic-sounding instances, like the one presented in (1).

(1) Onder aanroeping van het subsidiariteitsprincipe *achten* de meeste Nederlanders het voor de hand te liggen dat elke lidstaat zijn eigen infrastructuur moet financieren. (*Liberaal Reveil*, from the INL 38-million-word corpus)
'Referring to the principle of subsidiarity, most Dutchmen consider it to go without saying that each member state should finance its own infrastructure.'

The current and one-time presence of the NCI and ACI in the grammar of Dutch is ultimately attributable to two waves of Latin influence, a medieval one, at the start of the Middle Dutch period (1200 to 1500), and a late 16th- and 17th-century one, in the early stages of Modern Dutch (Duinhoven 1991). *Geacht worden te* and *verondersteld worden te*, two of the three NCI patterns that still occur with any frequency today,[4] are remnants of a once more productive pattern resulting from this second wave which until the start of the 20th century also still included patterns such as *bevonden worden te* 'be found to', *gehouden worden te* 'be held to', *gerekend worden te* 'be reckoned to', and, most prominently among these, *gezegd worden te* 'be said to' (Noël and Colleman 2009). This last pattern particularly became quite common as an evidential construction at one time, its frequency peaking in the 18th century, but in the 19th century, like most of the other patterns, it faded away and all but disappeared in the first half of the 20th century (Colleman and Noël 2012).

The surviving patterns *geacht worden te* and *verondersteld worden te* can today instantiate a diverse set of constructions. To begin with, they are now predominantly used as auxiliary-like deontic modal constructions signalling a medium-strength[5] moral desirability of the state of affairs expressed in the utterance[6] (Colleman and Noël 2014: 224–225). Two recent examples are presented in (2) and (3).[7, 8]

---

[4] The third lexical NCI pattern occurring (sporadically) in the present-day language is *verwacht worden te* 'be expected to', which is briefly discussed below.
[5] This qualification is inspired by Collins' (2009: 80) description of *be supposed to* as "a medium strength lexico-modal with semantic affinities to *should* and *ought to*". Collins, in turn, borrowed "strength of modality" from Huddleston and Pullum (2002: 175), who employ it as one of three dimensions in their description of the meanings and use of the English modal auxiliaries.
[6] The last part of this semantic characterization was extracted from Nuyts's (2016: 36) general definition of deontic modality "as an indication of the degree of moral desirability of the state of affairs expressed in the utterance, typically but not necessarily on behalf of the speaker (speakers can report on others' deontic assessments [...])".
[7] Unless otherwise indicated, the Dutch corpus examples in this section are from the 1988 or 1989 volumes of the *Leeuwarder courant* and were culled from a corpus extracted from the Dutch newspaper collection of the National Library of the Netherlands available through www.delpher.nl. We refer to section 3 for more information about this corpus.
[8] In all corpus examples, we have italicized the lexically-fixed parts of the two patterns, i.e. the passive auxiliary *worden* or *zijn*, the participle *geacht* or *verondersteld* and the infinitival particle *te*. In the older NCI examples featuring other instantiating verbs than *achten* and *veronderstellen*

(2) Voetballen bij FC Groningen houdt ook het doen van concessies in. Piet Wiersma *wordt geacht* sober *te* spelen, de bal moet bij de Vedetten ingeleverd worden.
'Playing for FC Groningen also entails making concessions. Piet Wiersma is expected to play soberly, the ball has to be handed over to the Stars.'

(3) Het college wil dat het enkele weken geleden opgezegde vertrouwen in Smallenbroek, na de berisping door minister Van Dijk, wordt bekrachtigd. Daarnaast moet de raad uitspreken dat samenwerking onmogelijk is en dat de burgemeester *verondersteld wordt* thuis *te* blijven. Tenslotte moet de raad Smallenbroek zijn vertegenwoordigende functies ontnemen.
'The board of aldermen desires that the withdrawal of confidence from [Mayor] Smallenbroek a few weeks ago, following the reprimand by Minister Van Dijk, be confirmed. Furthermore, the council has to state that collaboration is impossible and that the mayor is supposed to stay at home. Finally, the council has to strip Smallenbroek of his representative functions.'

As such, these patterns with cognition verbs very much resemble combinations of mandative verbs with *te*-infinitives like the ones illustrated in (4)–(6) and it remains to be explored – but this will not be our focus here – whether, in the deontic modal domain of present-day Dutch speakers' mental constructicons, they exist as the only microconstructions licensed by a weak DEONTIC NCI schema, or whether they should currently be subsumed under a more general schema of the form [SBJ *worden* / *zijn*-TNS VERB-PA.PPL *te* VERB-INF], possibly as a subschema.[9]

(4) Maar Noriega zal niet *worden gedwongen* uit de ambassade weg *te* gaan, en het Vatikaan is zeker niet van plan de gewezen dictator aan de Verenigde Staten uit te leveren.
'But Noriega will not be forced to leave the embassy, and the Vatican definitely does not intend to extradite the former dictator to the United States.'

(5) "Omdat het college weigert het schadebedrag door een advocaat te laten narekenen, *ben* ik wel *genoopt* mij aan mijn eerdere uitspraak *te* houden", aldus Post.

---

quoted later in this chapter, the participle is in italics as well, as it is in the English and French examples quoted below.

9 "Schema", "subschema" and "microconstruction" are terms adopted from Traugott and Trousdale (2013: 14). A simple explanatory example found there is that "*may* is a microconstruction of the subschema modal; modal is a subschema of the schema auxiliary". The term "construct", employed below, refers to an instance of use, i.e. a token, not a type.

'"Since the board of aldermen refuses to have the insurance claim verified by a solicitor, I am compelled to stay with my original claim", Post said.'

(6) Het restaurant *is* niet *verplicht* de doorslagen *te* bewaren.
'The restaurant is not obliged to keep the copies.'

Unlike the patterns exemplified in (4)–(6), however, *geacht worden te* and *verondersteld worden te* also instantiate a very different construction which we have called the EVIDENTIAL NCI construction. Two examples are (7) and (8). More specifically, they are "generic hearsay" evidentials, which report information without specifying the source (cf. Squartini 2016: 58). Unlike the DEONTIC NCI, and the "plain passive" one which we will discuss next, this one is a "qualificational" construction (cf. Aijmer 1972: 39; Nuyts 2001: 113), i.e. it can be omitted without affecting the propositional content of the sentence.

(7) De mens *wordt geacht* een logisch denkend wezen *te* zijn. In ieder geval word je als kind al door ouders, opvoeders en onderwijzers getraind in het onderdrukken van emoties, terwijl verstandig nadenken wordt bevorderd.
'Man is thought to be a logically thinking creature. In any event, already as a child, one is trained by parents, educators, and teachers to suppress one's emotions, while rational thinking is promoted.'

(8) Hervormer Gorbatsjov *wordt* sinds zijn bezoek aan Bukarest vorig jaar *verondersteld* de nodige weerzin *te* hebben tegen Ceausescu's persoon en opvattingen.
'Since his visit to Bucharest last year, reformer Gorbachev is supposed to feel a measure of disgust for Ceausescu's person and opinions.'

We can be reasonably sure that in the constructional networks of most current speakers of Dutch who have the EVIDENTIAL NCI construction it is a largely substantive node of the form [SBJ *worden*-TNS *geacht / verondersteld te* VERB-INF], instantiated by only two microconstructions, while for many educated speakers from the 17th to the 19th century it was a much more schematic construction (see Colleman and Noël 2012).

Used as plain passives, as in (9) and (10), *geacht worden te* and *verondersteld worden te* are far from auxiliary-like. What we have here instead are cognition matrix verbs which are complemented by an infinitive and whose meaning is very much part of the proposition expressed by the sentence. We have termed this the "plain passive" NCI because its use is motivated by the same information packaging principles that prompt the use of the passive generally. It therefore does not constitute a construction in its own right, even though its active counterpart, the ACI, is now virtually non-existent in Dutch. Plain passive constructs inherit characteristics from the PASSIVE construction and the ACI construction (the latter's function was described in Noël 2003).

(9) Enige kopman Gölz *werd* door Raas *geacht* tot het selecte groepje kanshebbers *te* behoren uit de groep van 191 renners, van wie er 75 gistermiddag finishten. Aan de vooravond van de start in Spa legde Raas daarom het onvoorwaardelijke kopmanschap in Gölz' handen.
'The only leader Gölz was considered by [team manager] Raas to belong to the small group of favourites from the pack of 191 riders, 75 of whom would eventually finish yesterday afternoon. That is why on the evening before the start in Spa he unconditionally put the leadership in Gölz's hands.'

(10) In de film speelt Derek de Lint een Zwitser. De Zweedse Lena Olin, française Juliette Binoche en Engelsman Daniel Day Lewis *worden verondersteld* alle drie Tsjechoslowaken *te* zijn en spreken daartoe Engels met een soort Tsjechisch accent.
'In the film, Derek de Lint is playing a Swiss. Swedish Lena Olin, française Juliette Binoche and the Englishman Daniel Day Lewis are all three supposed to be Czechoslovakian and therefore speak English with a kind of Czech accent.'

(11) and (12) illustrate a qualificational construction we have named as the DESCRIPTIVE NCI construction. It connects a description with a descriptum.[10] The difference with the plain passive is that in this case there is no reference to a spatio-temporally locatable judgement.

(11) Zouden de stemmen tijdens een volgende vergadering weer staken, dan kan het voorstel *worden geacht te* zijn afgewezen.
'If it were to happen in the next meeting that the votes are equally divided again, then the proposal can be considered to have been rejected.'

---

[10] Goossens (1991) discussed this use of the NCI in a study of English *be said to* which was prompted by what is listed as sense 11 of the verb *say* in the *Oxford English Dictionary*: "To call or refer to by a specified name or description; to designate, define, or categorize as. Chiefly in *pass.*" ("say, v.1 and int.". OED Online. September 2016. Oxford University Press. http://www.oed.com/view/Entry/171590; accessed 31 October 2016).

(12) Een aantal afspraken binnen de gedragscode kan *worden verondersteld te* gelden voor iedereen. (www.vlaamseschermbond.be, accessed 16 January 2017)
'Some provisions in the code of conduct can be supposed to apply to everyone.'

Finally, (13) and (14) are examples of what we have termed the COUNTERFACTUAL NCI construction. It signals that a state of affairs was expected to occur but did not materialize in the end.[11] This construction as well is instantiated by only two microconstructions.

(13) Ook deze week aandacht voor de waanzin aan 'light'-produkten, die de verbaasde consument nu weer *geacht wordt* naar binnen *te* werken.
'This week as well, we will pay attention to the insane profusion of 'lite' products that the astounded customer is now supposed to ingest.'

(14) De aanklager *werd verondersteld* de kinderen *te* verdedigen. (ConDiv-Standaard)
'The prosecutor was supposed to defend the children.' (but it is clear from the context that he did not)'

2.2 Nominative-and-infinitive constructions in English

English has all of these NCIs as well. In fact, they were all first discerned and discussed either in studies of the English NCI generally (Noël 2001, 2008) or in more specific investigations of English *be supposed to* (Mair 2004; Ziegeler 2003; Visconti 2004; Berkenfield 2006; Moore 2007; Noël and van der Auwera 2009). The difference with Dutch is that the English NCI is exponentially more frequent than the Dutch one and, at least in the case of the evidential and plain passive NCIs, immensely more productive in terms of type frequency (Noël and Colleman 2009). The following are the twenty most frequent English NCI patterns (with utterance, cognition and perception verbs) in descending frequency order, based on a count in the British National Corpus (Noël 2008: 328): *be expected to, be said to, be supposed to, be thought to, be found to, be seen to, be known to, be believed to, be*

---

[11] Visconti (2004: 185) termed a similar use of *be supposed to* "epistemic", because it "evokes a possible world, a state of affairs which would be expected to occur but does not", often in combination with "counterfactual signals" like *but, in fact, in reality,* ... In our opinion, though, "counterfactual" is the operative word here, rather than "epistemic", because no judgement of the (un)certainty or (im)probability of a proposition (cf. van der Auwera and Plungian 1998: 81) is involved.

reported to, be shown to, be considered to, be held to, be deemed to, be assumed to, be taken to, be estimated to, be claimed to, be understood to, be alleged to and *be felt to*. We will here also illustrate the English evidential and plain passive NCIs with examples of *be supposed to* and *be expected to* only, though, in view of their immediate relevance to the specific concern of this chapter.

Examples (15) and (16) illustrate the EVIDENTIAL NCI construction.¹²

(15) THE herb echinacea *is supposed to* boost the immune system naturally, helping to ward off winter ailments and alleviating the symptoms of colds and flu –and now is the right time of year to start taking it.

(16) The stun gun – the M26 Air Taser – is being studied by the Home Office as well as by the Metropolitan and Northants forces. London's Met *are expected to* be the first to use it on the streets later this year.

Plain passives are rare but (17) and (18) clearly qualify as such.

(17) One native observer alleged that the foreign governors were just as brutal as the local chiefs. [...] They have the advantage of administering districts naturally rich [and] they also have the benefit, as foreigners, of *being supposed* by the people *to* be more protected by the court, and by the court to *be supposed to* be cared for by the British.

(18) Engineers from the NASA Orbital Debris Program Office were tasked to calculate the risk to human population should the HST [Hubble Space Telescope] reenter the Earth's atmosphere in an uncontrolled manner. [...] Based upon the latest configuration and orbit of HST and on solar activity projection, HST *is expected to* reenter Earth's atmosphere around the year 2020.

Neither *be supposed to* nor *be expected to* appear to be used descriptively and it remains to be seen which, if any, patterns can instantiate the DESCRIPTIVE NCI construction in addition to *be said to*, for which it was originally distinguished (see note 10). We are illustrating it with *be said to* in (19).

(19) Whereas I believe all activities which are not play may *be said to* be work, most of my work was not of a commercial kind.

---

12 All English examples were sourced from the *Wordbanks Online: English* corpus (wordbanks.harpercollins.co.uk).

More important for one part of the argument that will be presented below, however, is that *be supposed to* (20) and *be expected to* (21) are the only two of the NCI patterns listed above which can instantiate the DEONTIC NCI construction, and only the former can realize the COUNTERFACTUAL NCI construction (22).

(20) Arriving at the Court Restaurant, it is not immediately clear where you *are supposed to* go.

(21) Being a minister brings responsibility and we *are expected to* behave ourselves, so I was a little bit nervous.

(22) "I had one of the happiest times of my life in this division 10 years ago at Leeds. I left Manchester United and you *are supposed to* curl up and die when you leave. But we went up at Leeds and it was enjoyable."

Like the Dutch deontic NCI constructions, *be supposed to* and *be expected to* can be connected with formally and semantically similar *be+Ven+to*-inf patterns containing mandative verbs, like the ones exemplified in (23)–(26). In fact, Noël and van der Auwera (2009) have argued that deontic *be supposed to* and *be expected to* can be traced back to volitive / deontic meanings of the verbs *suppose* and *expect* combined as active verbs with switch-subject infinitival complements, contra the argument that they grammaticalized from evidential NCI constructions, and this makes for a close connection with the patterns illustrated in (23)–(26). Disney (2016), while disputing the need to recognize additional meanings for *suppose*, emphasizes the role of a schematic deontic construction which covers such forms as are illustrated here as an analogical source for deontic *be supposed to*.

(23) "I am also a guest here, Adrina, and I'*m compelled to* abide by the wishes of my hosts."

(24) Male doctors *are forbidden to* touch female patients.

(25) The Post Office *is obliged to* charge exactly the same for every letter, even though everyone knows that it costs far more to send a postcard from Land's End to John o' Groats than it does to mail a letter from one part of London to another.

(26) Successful applicants will *be required to* organise and pay for their own travel insurance.

2.3 The role of language contact in the subsistence of the Dutch nominative-and-infinitive

Returning to the Dutch NCI, a more schematic deontic [SBJ *worden* / *zijn*-TNS VERB-PA.PPL *te* VERB-INF] construction, illustrated in (4)–(6) above, might well have played a "coercive" role in the innovation and propagation of deontic *geacht worden te* and *verondersteld worden te* as well. However, while the diachronics of such a construction remains to be investigated, this is not our objective in the current chapter. There would in any case need to have been a catalyst for such an attraction and what we will do instead in this chapter is further explore to what extent that catalyst is attributable to language contact, specifically in the case of *geacht worden te*.

2.3.1 Previous findings

In Colleman and Noël (2014), based on data from three historical corpora covering the 17th to the 20th centuries and two synchronic ones with texts from the late 20th century, we situated the introduction of deontic *geacht worden te* and *verondersteld worden te* into Dutch usage in the second half of the twentieth century, "a period of unprecedented potential for contact influence of English on Dutch because of the enormous increase in the 'consumption' of English by speakers of Dutch" (Colleman and Noël 2014: 229). We also pointed to the "unproblematic" interlingual identification of Dutch *geacht worden te* and *verondersteld worden te* with English *be supposed to*: not only did these patterns match formally and could all be used evidentially, "the active Dutch verbs *achten* / *veronderstellen* and English *suppose* also display an important overlap in lexical meaning" (2014: 229). The English NCI pattern also had a deontic meaning, which had proliferated in the late 19th century (Moore 2007), and which the Dutch patterns only developed later, and we proposed that speakers of Dutch started using the Dutch patterns in the same way as the English one as a result of "polysemy copying" (Heine and Kuteva 2003: 555–561; 2005: 100–103) or "semantic map / distributional assimilation" (Gast and van der Auwera 2012), which in effect are more operational terms for Weinreich's and Haugen's older concept "semantic loans", already referred to in section 1. We also proposed that *verwacht worden te* 'be expected to', as a much newer and still very rare, not even generally accepted, expression, was not a remnant of a once more productive NCI pattern, but a recent wholesale calque of the cognate English pattern *be expected to*, the most common English NCI pattern (see section 2.2).

2.3.2 Unanswered questions, a new hypothesis, and possible evidence for it

One of the questions we did not address in our previous study is why the Dutch pattern which is the least prototypically equivalent with English *be supposed to*, *geacht worden te*, is considerably more frequent than the most straightforward translation *verondersteld worden te*. Indeed, *veronderstellen*, like *suppose*, means 'to believe or assume as true' (an epistemic judgement), while *achten* means 'to consider / deem to be as described in the complement' (an opinion), and while translation dictionaries (like *van Dale*) translate *suppose* with *(ver)onderstellen* and vice versa, they do not mention *achten* in connection with *suppose*. Nor did we ask why *geacht worden te* had already become more frequent in the first half of the 19th century as a non-deontic pattern, while the frequency of all other NCI patterns was dwindling then, including that of *verondersteld worden te*, though it rebounded later (Noël and Colleman 2009). Both these facts suggest that some factor ensuring the survival of, first of all, non-deontic *geacht worden te*, but indirectly perhaps also of the Dutch NCI generally, is likely to have preceded the influence from English, which must first and foremost have been important for *verondersteld worden te*.

To find clues to solve the problem of the dominance of *geacht worden te* we turned to the Delpher text archive, which because of its vastness provided a much richer source of historical data than the smallish corpora we had been using previously.[13] An initial impressionistic qualitative examination of instances of *geacht worden te* extracted from several 19th- and 20th-century data points in its newspaper component revealed that many of the 19th-century examples had an official administrative or juridical context and that these were either plain passive or descriptive in nature (Noël and Colleman 2014). (27) and (28) are two representative examples.

(27) De generaal-majoor Klerck is eervol ontheven van het tot dus verre door hem tijdelijk waargenomen oppercommandement in de vesting Breda,

---

[13] The data in our previous study on the development of the Dutch deontic NCI were sourced from a suite of four corpora, the largest one of which totals 17 million words and the smallest sub-corpus of which counts only 1.2 million words (for details, see Colleman and Noël 2014: 223). The size of the Delpher *text archive* – not to be confused with the *corpus* we extracted from it (see section 3) – cannot be expressed in terms of number of words but is advertised on its website as "over 60 million pages from Dutch newspapers, books and magazines" (http://www.delpher.nl/; accessed 9 June 2017; our translation). Its newspaper component is said to comprise "over 11 million pages" (http://www.delpher.nl/nl/kranten; accessed 9 June 2017).

welk oppercommandement tevens zal *worden geacht te* zijn opgeheven. (*Algemeen Handelschblad*, 1840)

'Major general Klerck has been honourably discharged from his interim supreme command of the garrison of Breda, and this supreme command will also be considered to have been abolished.'

(28) Bij staking der stemmen *wordt* het voorstel *geacht te* zijn verworpen. (*Nederlandsche Staatscourant*, 1863)

'In the event of an equality of votes the proposal is considered to have been rejected.'

We thought this typical statutory context could well be the key to why we still have *geacht worden te* in Dutch while most other NCI patterns have disappeared: the influence of French on Dutch legal and administrative language may have played a crucial role. At the start of the 19th century the Netherlands were under French rule and the French civil code, or *Code Napoléon*, which was introduced during that time, has had a lasting effect on the way laws are formulated in Dutch. The current Dutch civil code (*Burgerlijk Wetboek*) contains numerous instances of *geacht worden te*. (29) and (30) are two random examples.

(29) Het kind waarvan een vrouw zwanger is wordt als reeds geboren aangemerkt, zo dikwijls zijn belang dit vordert. Komt het dood ter wereld, dan *wordt* het *geacht* nooit *te* hebben bestaan. (*Burgerlijk Wetboek Boek 1, Personen- en familierecht*, Artikel 2.[14])

'The child a woman is pregnant of is held to have already been born whenever this serves its interests. If it is stillborn, it is considered to have never existed.'

(30) Wanneer de volgorde waarin twee of meer personen zijn overleden niet kan worden bepaald, *worden* die personen *geacht* gelijktijdig *te* zijn overleden en valt aan de ene persoon geen voordeel uit de nalatenschap van de andere ten deel. (*Burgerlijk Wetboek Boek 4, Erfrecht*, Artikel 2, lid 1.[15])

'In case the order in which two persons are deceased cannot be established, they are considered to be deceased at the same time and neither person can reap benefit from the estate of the other.'

---

[14] http://wetten.overheid.nl/BWBR0002656/2016-08-01, accessed 18 December 2016.
[15] http://wetten.overheid.nl/BWBR0002761/2016-09-01, accessed 18 December 2016.

The Napoleonic Code contained many instances of the equivalent French expression *être censé* + adjective / past participle / infinitive. (31) and (32) are examples of the construction with the infinitival complement.

(31) L'héritier qui renonce *est censé* n'*avoir* jamais été héritier. (*Code civil des français, édition originale et seule officielle*, 1804, Article 785)
'The heir who renounces a succession is considered never to have been heir.'

(32) Le fossé *est censé appartenir* exclusivement à celui du côté duquel le rejet se trouve. (*Code civil des français, édition originale et seule officielle*, 1804, Article 668)
'The ditch is considered to belong exclusively to him on whose side the earth thrown up from it is found.'

The hypothesis we will explore in this contribution is that the survival of *geacht worden te*, in the face of a general attrition of the NCI in Dutch, was due to the commonality of such plain passive / descriptive uses in legal texts and official documents, as well as in journalism texts reporting on administrative decisions, as a result of it being a straightforward translational equivalent of French *être censé*. Evidence that could support this hypothesis would first and foremost be a salient use of *geacht worden te* as a translation of *être censé* in early Dutch translations of French legal texts, as well as, less directly, an increase in the occurrence of plain passive / descriptive *geacht worden te* in early 19th-century texts that report on what goes on in the public sphere. We will also revisit the timing of the ascent of both deontic *geacht worden te* and deontic *verondersteld worden te*, which on the basis of a smaller and different data source we previously situated in the second half of the 20th century (Colleman and Noël 2014). If the initial survival of *geacht worden te* is not attributable to its use as a deontic construction, there should – in contrast to the decrease of other NCI patterns – be an exceptional *in*crease in the frequency of the form *before* it came to be used deontically.

3 Methodology

To test for the possibility of direct influence of the use of *être censé* in French legal language on the use of *geacht worden te* in Dutch legal language we looked at early Dutch translations of 19th-century codes of law. The territory largely corresponding to what is now called The Netherlands was a client state of France from 1795 to 1810 (first as the Batavian Republic, then, from 1806, as the Kingdom of Holland) and in 1810 was formally annexed by the First French Empire, after which French law came into full effect in the territory. While the French text of the various codes of law was the only official one from then until the end of French rule in 1813, two distinguished lawyers produced integral translations, published in 1811 by Johannes Allart in Amsterdam in parallel with the original French text (for further legal-historical background, see Bellefroid 1932 and Lokin 2004). Joannes van der Linden (1756–1835) translated the *Code Napoléon* (officially the *Code civil des français*) in two volumes under the title *Wetboek Napoléon* and Willem Bilderdijk (1756–1831), who was not only a practicing lawyer but also a well-known man of letters, translated the *Code pénal* (*Wetboek van het Strafregt* 'Criminal Code'), the *Code d'instruction criminelle* (*Wetboek van Strafvordering* 'Code of Criminal Procedure') and the *Code de procédure civile* (*Wetboek van Civiele Regtspleging*, 'Code of Civil Procedure').[16] All of these translations are freely digitally available through the Google Books Digital Library Project, as OCR-converted text files. We searched all of them for NCIs by lexical queries for *geacht* 'considered' as well as the participle forms of other Dutch verbs of cognition that we knew from Noël and Colleman (2010) to be eligible for use with the NCI around the turn of the 19th century and established which French expressions they were equivalent with in the corresponding sentences in the original texts. Subsequently we looked at it from the other end and determined the variety in the translations for the most frequent source expressions for NCIs in the Dutch translations.

To ascertain whether evolution in the frequency of *geacht worden te* might throw up indirect evidence of French influence we made use of a newly created

---

16 Present-day Belgium was under direct French rule for a somewhat longer period, viz. from 1795 to 1814, and during this period, several official and unofficial Dutch translations of the Napoleonic Codes were also produced in Flanders (i.e., in the northern, Dutch-speaking half of present-day Belgium). However, in view of the different status of Dutch in both parts of the language area throughout the 19th century, it made more sense to focus on Netherlandic Dutch legal sources for the present investigation; in Bellefroid's (1932: 89) terms, the Flemish translations have not contributed to the formation of the modern Dutch legal language ("De officieele en niet officieele wetsvertalingen ten gebruike van de Vlaamsche departementen hebben op de vorming der Nederlandsche rechtstaal geen duurzamen invloed uitgeoefend"). We leave it to future research to establish the presence of NCI patterns in 19th-century Flemish legal sources directly or indirectly based on the Napoleonic codes, the most likely hypothesis being that they were at least equally present there as in the Netherlandic translations investigated here.

corpus that was extracted from the newspaper component of the Delpher text archive.[17] Law and the public sphere being very much interconnected and with newspapers primarily reporting on all aspects of the public sphere, they are a good place to start looking for indications for the adoption of legal / administrative language beyond its proper domain. A sub-corpus was compiled consisting of material from three newspapers which each span a substantial part of the 19th and 20th centuries, viz. the general regional newspapers *Leeuwarder courant* and *Middelburgsche courant* and the Amsterdam-based general and business newspaper *Algemeen Handelsblad*. More precisely, we started in the 1820s and defined nine snapshots of two consecutive years, viz. 1828–29, 1848–49, 1868–69, etc. to 1988–89.[18] The sub-corpus thus created, which, in all, consisted of 389.6 million words of running text, was searched for all instances of *geacht* followed by the infinitival particle *te* within a span of 15 words. The NCI instances were manually extracted from the query hits and categorized in three semantic classes: 1. plain passive / descriptive, 2. evidential, or 3. deontic. The same procedure was repeated for *verondersteld* and the participles of a number of other verbs of cognition or utterance (see section 4.2 for details).

4 Results and discussion

4.1 Legal texts

There turn out to be big differences both in the incidence of *geacht worden te* in the translations and in the incidence of *être censé* in the source texts. In Van der Linden's translation of the civil code *geacht worden te* occurs 41 times (see Table 1 for an overview).[19] In 12 cases of these it matches *être censé* followed by an

---

[17] This corpus was made available for research purposes to the second author as part of an agreement between the National Library of the Netherlands and Ghent University, and consists of the OCR-converted text files of a sample of the 19th- and 20th-century Dutch newspaper collections available through the Delpher website (www.delpher.nl). The earliest texts in the corpus date from 1813 and the most recent ones from 1995.

[18] The *Leeuwarder courant* is the only of the three sources which covers the *entire* period. For the *Middelburgher courant*, there are no data for 1888–1889, nor for 1929 and later years. Similarly, for *Algemeen Handelsblad*, we have no data for the post-World War II period.

[19] This figure rises to 62 occurrences if instances in the index at the end of Part II are added. These additional 21 instances are not included in the frequencies reported in Tables 1 and 2. The same applies to the other verbs.

infinitive in the original text, as in (33). In 9 more it matches related patterns in which *être censé* is followed by a past participle, a noun phrase, or an adjectival phrase – which, in lexicographic sources of present-day French, are presented as rare uses involving ellipsis of the infinitive *être*[20] – see (34) for an example.

(33) Art. 525
    a. Le propriétaire *est censé avoir* attaché à son fonds des effets mobiliers à perpétuelle demeure, quand ils y sont scellés en plâtre, ou à chaux ou à ciment, ou lorsqu'ils ne peuvent être détachés sans être fracturés et détériorés, ou sans briser ou détériorer la partie du fonds à laquelle ils sont attachés.
    b. De eigenaar *wordt geacht*, zoodanige goederen tot een blijvend gebruik bij zijn erf gevoegd *te* hebben, wanneer dezelve daar aan gehecht zijn met pleister, kalk of cement, of wanneer zij daar van niet kunnen losgemaakt worden, zonder dezelven te breken en te beschadigen, of zonder een gedeelte van den grond, waar aan zij vastgehecht zijn, te breken of te beschadigen.
    'A proprietor is considered to have attached moveable effects to his estate for ever, when they are fastened thereto by plaster, lime, or cement, or when they cannot be separated without being broken and damaged, or without breaking or injuring that part of the estate to which they are attached.'[21]

(34) Art. 1758
    a. Si rien ne constate que le bail soit fait à tant par an, par mois ou par jour, la location *est censé faite* suivant l'usage des lieux.
    b. Indien niet blijkt, dat de huur voor zoo veel in het jaar, in de maand, of bij den dag is aangegaan, *wordt* dezelve *geacht* volgens plaatselijk gebruik *te* zijn aangegaan.
    'If there be nothing to show that the lease was made at so much a year, a month, or day, the hiring is deemed to have been made according to the custom of the place.'[22]

---

20 See, e.g., the lemma for *censé* in the *Trésor de la langue française informatisé* available at http://atilf.atilf.fr/tlf.htm, accessed 16 January 2017.
21 English translation from http://www.napoleon-series.org/research/government/code/book2/c_title01.html#chapter1, accessed 31 December 2016.
22 English translation from http://www.napoleon-series.org/research/government/code/book3/c_title08.html#section1, accessed 16 January 2017.

In addition, in one case the original expression is *être réputé* with an infinitive, and in 11 more it is *être réputé* complemented by a past participle, a noun phrase or an adjectival phrase. Féron and Coltier (2009) comment on the close semantic similarity between *être censé* and *être réputé*, both of which, among other uses, display a specialized sub-sense that, in their corpus, "est attestée dans des textes à caractère juridique" (p. 160), where the pattern is used in the formulation of laws and regulations, with the legislator as the implicit agent. For instance, for the 19th-century instance from the Code civil in (31) above, repeated here for convenience, they propose the paraphrase 'nous posons que X doit désormais être considéré comme' (p. 156) (i.e., 'we stipulate that X should from now on be considered to be').

(31) L'héritier qui renonce *est censé* n'*avoir* jamais été héritier. (*Code civil des français, édition originale et seule officielle*, 1804, Article 785)
'The heir who renounces a succession is considered never to have been heir.'

In a follow-up study which looks into the semantics of *être censé* from a diachronic perspective, Féron and Coltier (2012: 104) provide further discussion of this specialized use in legal language, which is part of a broader sense that is "lié à la notion de convention". Here they distinguish between two usage types, both of which could be subsumed under what we have termed "descriptive". One is the kind typical of juridical texts in that it is "déclaratif", i.e. it creates a convention. It can be glossed by "il est décidé que (quoi qu'il en soit de la réalité)" – a gloss using our own terms could be: 'it is decided that a description applies to a descriptum'. The other type merely signals the existence of a convention: "le locuteur n'est donc pas celui qui fixe la convention". In sum, there is reason enough to connect *être censé* and *être réputé* with legal language.

As shown in Tables 1 and 2, other NCI patterns occur as well in the Dutch translations, most frequently *geoordeeld worden te* 'be judged to' (12 instances), followed by *gerekend worden te* 'be reckoned to' (11 instances), *gehouden worden te* 'be held to' (5 instances) and *verondersteld worden te* (3 instances). These all occur as matches for *être censé* too, but fact is that *geacht worden te* is the most frequently used NCI pattern in the translations and that it most frequently translates *être censé*, the match between *être censé* + infinitive and *geacht worden te* being specifically salient (see Table 2). For the related patterns in which *être censé / réputé* is combined with a past participle, adjectival or noun phrase, *geacht worden te* is the most frequently chosen translation, too, though *gerekend worden te*, *geoordeeld worden te* and *gehouden worden te* all occur several times as well.

Table 1: NCI patterns in Van der Linden's translation of the Code Napoléon and their corresponding expressions in the source text (INF = infinitive; PART = past participle).

	geacht worden te (41)	geoordeeld worden te (12)	gerekend worden te (11)	gehouden worden te[a] (6)	verondersteld worden te (3)
NCI in source text	être censé INF (12)	être censé INF (2)	être censé INF (1)		être censé inf (1)
	être réputé INF (1)	être jugé INF (1)	être réputé INF (1)		être présumé INF (2)
Related pattern with PART / NP / AdjP in source text	être censé (9)	être censé (4)	être censé (4)	être censé (3)	
	être réputé (11)	être réputé (2)		être réputé (2)	
		être présumé (1)			
Other pattern in source text	8	2	5	1	0

Note:

a The verb *houden* 'hold' also occurs in a mandative construction similar to the one illustrated in (4) to (6) above, i.e. *gehouden zijn te* for 'to be obliged to', usually as a translation for *être tenu de*. Such uses have not been counted as instances of the NCI. See (i) below for an example of this alternative mandative pattern, and see (ii) for an example of *gehouden worden te* exemplifying the (descriptive) NCI.

(i) De verkooper *is gehouden* duidelijk uit *te* drukken, waar toe hij zich verbindt. (Article 1602) 'The seller is bound to explain clearly what it is he binds himself to.' (English translation from http://www.napoleon-series.org/research/government/code/book3/c_title06.html#section1a, accessed 17 January 2017.)

(ii) De giften en legaten, gedaan en gemaakt aan den echtgenoot van iemand, die het regt van erfvolging heeft, *worden gehouden* geschied *te* zijn met vrijstelling van inbreng. (Article 849) 'Donations and legacies made to the husband or wife of a party succeeding, are deemed to have been made with dispensation of restitution.' (English translation from http://www.napoleon-series.org/research/government/code/book3/c_title01.html#section2b.)

The three translations by Bilderdijk present a somewhat different picture. Not only is *être censé / réputé* + infinitive used much less often in their source texts – only two times in all three texts combined – but Bilderdijk also never used *geacht worden te* to translate it. When he used an NCI pattern at all, it was *gerekend worden te*, which occurs five times: in one of the two cases where the French text had *être censé* + infinitive, and in four more cases where the French text had a related pattern with *être censé / réputé* + past participle or NP. In addition, there

Table 2: The translations of the most frequently occurring source text matches for NCI patterns in Van der Linden's translation of the Code Napoléon.

être censé INF (16)	être réputé INF (2)	être censé PART / ADJP / NP (22)	être réputé PART / ADJP / NP (24)
geacht worden te (12)	geacht worden te (1)	geacht worden te (9)	geacht worden te (11)
gerekend worden te (1)	gerekend worden te (1)	gerekend worden te (4)	geoordeeld worden te (2)
geoordeeld worden te (2)		geoordeeld worden te (4)	gehouden worden te (2)
verondersteld worden te (1)		gehouden worden te (3)	other (9)
		other (2)	

is a single occurrence of *gehouden worden te*, in a translation of *être réputé* + past participle. Little should be concluded from such small frequencies, of course, though they might suggest that *geacht worden te* was not the default translation equivalent for *être censé / réputé* for *everyone*, but experienced some competition from *gerekend worden te*.[23] That both lexical patterns enjoyed some degree of popularity in 19th-century legal language, is confirmed by the post-Napoleonic *Burgerlijk Wetboek 1838* ('Civil code 1838'), a synthesis of pre-Napoleonic Roman-Dutch law and the French civil code which remained in effect until the late 20th century. In this source, *geacht worden te* occurs 29 times, compared to 16 occurrences of *gerekend worden te*. *Gehouden worden te*, *geoordeeld worden te* and *verondersteld worden te* do not occur.

The next sub-section turns to newspaper language. Prototypical equivalence is not only relevant in direct translations: if *geacht worden te*, and to a lesser extent also *gerekend worden te*, functioned as prototypical equivalents for French *être censé* + infinitive in the legal language of 19th-century Dutch, we may expect them

---

[23] The observed difference between Van der Linden and Bilderdijk is potentially interesting in view of recent work by Schmid and Mantlik (2015) and Petré (2016, 2017) on the linguistic behaviour of sets of individual speakers in cases of ongoing constructional change. If the translations are anything to go by, both authors seem to differ with respect to the types of schema formed: whereas Van der Linden has a clear preference for the *geacht worden te* subschema but also uses the (descriptive / plain passive) NCI with several other verbs, which is indicative of the existence of a higher-level schema, Bilderdijk's translation suggests a strongly entrenched *gerekend worden te* subschema with little evidence of a higher-level schema.

to occur with some frequency beyond literal translations of the original French code, too, in texts that make reference to the code text or to legal matters in general.

4.2 Newspaper texts

Newspapers do not create legal and administrative conventions, but they do report on them. A positive difference between the frequency evolution of *geacht worden te* in 19th-century newspapers and the post-18th-century downward evolution of the Dutch NCI generally would consequently be suggestive of French influence as well, albeit possibly only an indirect one, and depending on the nature of the bulk of the examples.

The frequencies reported in Noël and Colleman (2010) already suggested that the frequency evolution of NCI *achten* over the 19th century was exceptional compared to that found with other verbs of perception, cognition and utterance: in an (admittedly rather small) corpus of literary prose divided in four 70-year subperiods, we found *achten* to be the only verb for which the NCI frequency kept increasing *after* the subperiod 1710–1780, at a time when the overall frequency of the NCI had already started dwindling and many lexical patterns had already virtually fallen out of use.[24] In this respect, we can also refer to the steadily declining frequency of the lexical pattern *gezegd worden te* 'be said to' during the course of the 19th century which we reported on in Colleman and Noël (2012). The question now is whether the much larger newspaper corpus extracted from Delpher corroborates this trend.

The data presented in Table 3 show that, abstracting from differences between the individual data sources, there was indeed an increase in the frequency of the use of *geacht worden te* in Dutch newspapers in the first three quarters of the 19th century, the regional newspapers *Leeuwarder Courant* and *Middelburgher Courant* seemingly catching up with the Amsterdam business newspaper *Algemeen Handelschblad* to reach a level of incidence the latter publication already had in the first data period. In terms of normalized frequency, the peak of *geacht worden te* is to be situated in 1868–69, with over 13 instances per million words of text. Subsequently, in the third quarter of the century, the pattern's frequency diminished again, which is consistent with our hypothesis as well in that a frequency boost resulting from a very temporary intense contact situation is likely to subside with the dwindling of the intensity of the contact. This decreasing trend continued over the 20th century: the normalized frequency

---

24 Unfortunately, in the published version of Noël and Colleman (2010), the row for *achten* in Table 2 on page 168 was inadvertently deleted in the production process. See https://hub.hku.hk/bitstream/10722/65696/1/Content.pdf for a version with the correct table.

Table 3: Frequency evolution of *geacht worden te* in three Dutch newspapers. In the data cells the top figures represent absolute frequencies and the bottom figures frequencies per million words (the figure in the middle of each cell is the token-size of the sub-corpus).

	Leeuwarder Courant	Middelburgher Courant	Algemeen Handelschblad	TOTAL
1828–1829	6 2,512,649 2.39	2 1,152,512 1.74	31 2,378,177 13.03	39 6,043,338 6.45
1848–1849	24 2,453,238 9.78	21 1,356,046 15.49	149 12,061,589 12.35	194 15,870,873 12.22
1868–1869	32 4,225,028 7.57	89 3,886,119 22.90	219 17,408,556 12.58	340 25,519,703 13.32
1888–1889	120 13,097,677 9.16		297 29,412,448 10.10	417 42,510,125 9.81
1908–1909	185 17,739,688 10.43	73 9,635,400 7.58	589 52,517,688 11.22	847 79,892,776 10.6
1928–1929	221 25,328,336 8.73	38 5,026,949 7.56	545 81,488,400 6.69	804 111,843,685 7.19
1948–1949	63 14,842,692 4.24			63 14,842,692 4.24
1968–1969	112 36,582,844 3.06			112 36,582,844 3.06
1988–1989	174 56,526,396 3.08			174 56,526,396 3.08

of about 3 occurrences per million words of text found in the two most recent sub-periods is comparable to the normalized frequency of 3.52 observed in a corpus of Dutch and Flemish newspaper text from the 1990s in Noël and Colleman (2009).

By way of comparison, Table 4 shows the frequency evolutions over the 19th century, i.e. until the sub-period 1888–1889, of the NCI patterns of six other verbs, viz. *bevinden* 'find', *bewijzen* 'prove', *beweren* 'claim', *rekenen* 'reckon', *oordelen* 'judge', and *veronderstellen* 'suppose', all of which we knew from the corpus investigations reported on in Noël and Colleman (2010) and / or Colleman and Noël (2012) to have still been possible (if not necessarily frequent) in the NCI in

19th-century Dutch (the table aggregates the results for the three newspapers). For *rekenen* and *veronderstellen*, we also compiled frequency data for the 20th century.

Table 4: Frequency evolution of six verb-specific NCI patterns in three Dutch newspapers. In the data cells the top figures represent absolute frequencies and the bottom figures frequencies per million words.

	bevinden	bewijzen	beweren	oordelen	rekenen	veronder-stellen
1828–1829 6,043,338	27 4.47	4 0.66	1 0.17	5 0.83	40 6.62	6 0.99
1848–1849 15,870,873	51 3.21	10 0.63	0 0	18 1.13	76 4.79	13 0.82
1868–1869 25,519,703	40 1.57	7 0.27	2 0.08	8 0.31	94 3.68	19 0.74
1888–1889 42,510,125	36 0.85	2 0.05	7 0.16	4 0.09	92 2.16	31 0.73
1908–1909 79,892,776					208 2.60	28 0.35
1928–1929 111,843,685					56 0.50	59 0.53
1948–1949 14,842,692					8 0.54	12 0.81
1968–1969 36,582,844					3 0.08	23 0.63
1988–1989 56,526,396					1 0.02	24 0.42

None of these other NCI patterns displays a frequency increase similar to *geacht worden te*: if a trend can be observed at all, which is only possible in case of the more frequently occurring verbs, viz. *bevinden* and *rekenen*, it is a downward trend. Note that in the first subperiod, *gerekend worden te* was still equally frequent as *geacht worden te*, in line with the suggestion in the previous sub-section that *geacht worden te* may have experienced some competition from *gerekend worden te* as a functional equivalent of *être censé* + infinitive. Indeed, both lexical patterns are used in very similar ways in the newspaper data, the context often being one of regulations, provisions or law sections, see (35) and (36) for typical examples.

(35) Ieder, die zijne acceptatie onder eenen Wissel stelt, kent of behoort het Wisselregt te kennen, en heeft zich daardoor tot de bepalingen van dat Regt

verpligt, of kan *geacht worden* zich daartoe *te* hebben willen verbinden. (*Algemeen Handelschblad* 1828–29)
'Anyone who signs their acceptance on a bill of exchange knows or should know the law on negotiable instruments, and thereby undertakes to abide by the provisions of this law, or can be considered to have undertaken to do so.'

(36) Overwegende, dat de eenige reden, waarom bij hetzelve besluit de invordering dier regten provisioneel is opgeschort, door de voltooijing der werken te Ter Neuzen, en de opening van het Kanaal op den 18 November laatstleden, is komen te vervallen, en alzoo met dat tijdstip die provisionele vrijstelling van regten moet *gerekend worden te* hebben opgehouden. (*Middelburgsche courant*, 1828–1829)
'Considering that the only reason why by this same decree the reclamation of those rights had provisionally been suspended has come to expire with the completion of the works in Terneuzen and the opening of the canal on November 18th, and that, thus, the provisional exemption of rights must be considered to have ended.'

Geacht worden te soon won out, however, the frequency of *gerekend worden te* showing a steady decline, which in fact, as is also shown in Table 4, continued in the 20th century: in the latter half of the 20th century, the frequency dwindled to the point of virtual non-existence. If, at the onset of the 19th century, *gerekend worden te* experienced a boost from its association with *être censé*, too, this was too weak to keep the pattern into existence until the later 20th century.

In the cases of the four remaining verbs included in Table 4 the observed normalized frequencies never rise above a single instance per one million words of text – barring *geoordeeld worden te* in 1848-49, which has a normalized frequency marginally over 1 – which indicates that their NCI uses were already marginal in the early 19th century and remained so in the remainder of the century. This includes *veronderstellen*, and this, too, is consistent with our general hypothesis in that we restricted it to French influence on the incidence of *geacht worden te* (and possibly to a lesser extent on *gerekend worden te*) only. While *verondersteld worden te* does occur in Van der Linden's translation (see Table 1) and while its frequency does not drop in the 19th-century newspaper data, unlike that of most of the other patterns considered (see the top half of Table 4), the numbers are too small to draw any confident conclusions about French influence here.

For a closer look into the semantics of *geacht worden te*, it is obvious from the data that the descriptive use is the dominant one until well into the 20th century – (35) above and (37) below provide two typical examples.

(37) Geschrevene aanplakkings-biljetten zonder naam-onderteekening zijn vrij van zegel, doch indien zij geteekend zijn, *worden* dezelve *geacht* aan het gewoon formaatzegel onderhevig *te* zijn. (*Leeuwarder Courant* 1828–29)
'Written posters with no signature are exempt from stamp duty, but when signed they are considered to be subject to the standard stamp duty.'

The evidential NCI occurs as well, as in (38), but the first potentially deontic example, presented in (39), only turns up in the 1868–69 sample.

(38) De bevolking van Europisch Turkije wordt op 9,660,000 zielen geschat. Aziatisch Turkije grenst ten noorden aan de Zwarte Zee en de Zee van Marmara; ten oosten aan Perzië, ten zuiden aan Arabië en ten westen aan de Middelandsche Zee en den Archipel. De bevolking *wordt geacht* 10,000,000 *te* bedragen. (*Algemeen Handelschblad* 1828–29)
'The population of European Turkey is estimated at 9,660,000 souls. Asiatic Turkey borders on the Black Sea and the Sea of Marmara to the north, Persia to the east, Arabia to the south and the Mediterranean and the Archipelago to the west. Its population is believed to amount to 10,000,000.'

(39) Sluit de Grondwet de toelating van capaciteiten uit? vraagt Spr[eker]. [Z]oo ja, dan kan bij wijze van fictie aan officieren, ambtenaren, enz. toch wel eene plaats onder het kiespersoneel gegeven worden, door te bepalen dat zij *geacht worden* eene zekere som *te* betalen. (*Algemeen Handelschblad* 1868–69)
'Does the Constitution preclude introducing merit-based voting, the Speaker asks. If so, then theoretically officers, civil servants, etc. could still be offered a place among the electorate by stipulating that they are expected to pay a certain sum.'

The numbers for potentially deontic instances increase a little in later samples but they remain very low until the second half of the 20th century. In the 1968–69 sample, about one in eight instances are potentially deontic. An unambiguous example is (40). In the 1988–89 sample almost half of all tokens are either potentially or unambiguously deontic.

(40) Als coach van de club in Yallourn *werd* hij *geacht* zijn medeleden niet *te* verslaan maar eenmaal overgegaan naar de Newborough Club – in de plaats waar hij nu al jarenlang woont – was die verplichting er niet meer. (*Leeuwarder Courant* 1968–69)
'As coach of the [athletics] club in Yallourn he was not supposed to beat his fellow members but after he had moved to the Newborough Club – in the

place where he has been living for years now – this constraint no longer existed.'

This not only confirms our earlier finding that the Dutch deontic NCI did not start proliferating in earnest until the second half of the 20th century, it is also confirmation that *geacht worden te* must have survived the 19th century for a different reason than its usefulness as a deontic construction.

In the case of *verondersteld worden te* more or less the same picture emerges with regard to the occurrence of the deontic construction, though a bigger proportion of its tokens allow a deontic interpretation slightly earlier. This is already the case for half of all tokens in the 1968–69 sample. There appears to be nothing in these new data that contradicts our previous suggestion (in Colleman and Noël 2014) that the example of English *be supposed to* played a role in its survival.

Did *geacht worden te* come to be used as a deontic expression after the example of *verondersteld worden te*, given that the latter was more saliently deontic earlier than the former? Possibly the best answer is that for some speakers the polysemy of *verondersteld worden te* is likely to have been a causal factor in their assumption, or acceptance, of a similar polysemy for *geacht worden te*, but also that the latter would probably not have needed much help from the other pattern for it to get used deontically. While "iedere burger wordt geacht de wet te kennen" (cf. the similar French expression "Nul n'est censé ignorer la loi") only means that, for legal purposes, everyone is considered to know the law, rather than that everyone is expected to learn it, such a misconception can easily come about, given that legal texts prescribe conventions. In other words, the salient administrative / legal context of use of *geacht worden te* may for some have been enough of a prompt to assign a deontic meaning to it. Therefore, contrary to what we argued previously (in Colleman and Noël 2014), semantic reanalysis of the form *geacht worden te* is not unlikely to have played a part in the development of its use as a deontic construction.

Did French play a direct role in the development of deontic *geacht worden te*? This is not very likely. While Féron and Coltier (2012: 105) do not themselves separate a deontic meaning for *être censé* in their diachronic study of its meaning development, they do mention in a footnote that the *Dictionnaire de l'Académie française* only inserted the verb *devoir* 'must' in the definition of *censé* in its 9th edition, which dates from 1992, the previous edition being from 1932–35. *Être censé* appears to have developed a similar polysemy to *geacht worden te*, therefore, but this also seems to have happened well into the 20th century, at a time when influence from French on Dutch language users had become much less obvious than it was in the first half of the 19th century.

5 Conclusion

To somewhat adjust the sweeping characterization of one of the two major strands of research in contrastive diachronic construction grammar offered at the start of this contribution, changes in *the* constructicon of a language cannot, of course, be effected by the constructicon of another in any literal sense, for the simple reason that such constructicons only exist as abstractions from what communities of speakers do and what individual members of these communities can, but in no way must, know. In a usage-based perspective, people's linguistic behaviour and knowledge is determined by their experience of language and ultimately, therefore, so is constructional change. Naturally, this may include more than one language: linguistic experience knows no linguistic borders. Crucially for contact-induced constructional change, Höder (2012, 2014) has argued in favour of a lack of clear boundaries between constructicons in the minds of bilingual speakers even. In his "diasystematic" model, such speakers develop a common system for all their languages, which involves "interlingual links" between constructions. In such a view, to help explain the development described here, one could hypothesize that target language constructions with a low level of entrenchment receive a saliency boost if they are linked up with cognate source language constructions that have a higher entrenchment level, leading to increased usage of the target construction.

The formulation of a hard cognitive theory of contact-induced constructional renovation, as part of an all-encompassing radically usage-based theory of constructional change, must await further reflection, however. Our descriptive argument in this paper has been that, in certain contexts, groups of speakers of Dutch at some point started to use a particular existing Dutch NCI pattern, *geacht worden te*, more than had been the case previously, as a result of their experience *with* a specific kind of French discourse and their experience *of* a functionally equivalent and formally very similar French expression, and that in so doing they ensured the survival of a construction suffering from attrition. As such, this is a corrective to our earlier suggestion that the Dutch NCI survived through contact with English and that it was specifically due to the copying of the polysemy of *be supposed to*, though this hypothesis remains intact as an account of why *verondersteld worden te* continued as a Dutch microconstruction.

Summarizing the descriptive details of the role of French with regard to *geacht worden te* in more specific terms: The Dutch NCI pattern *geacht worden te* saw a rise in its frequency that lasted for the biggest part of the 19th century, at a time when the Dutch NCI was very much on the decline generally. Its repeated occurrence in an early 19th-century translation of the French civil code, which was the law in the Netherlands at the time, as the most frequently occurring translational match of French *être censé*, combined with its recurrence in a later civil code which was partially based on the French code, as well as the fact that in 19th-century newspapers it often occurred in texts reporting on sections of laws and administrative regulations, all conspire to suggest that at a particular moment in history French legal language played a significant, direct as well as indirect, role in its survival. This happened before *geacht worden te* came to be used as a deontic construction, a constructional innovation which probably would not have happened if the French-induced constructional *re*novation had not occurred.

The theoretical significance for diachronic construction grammar, as well as for Cognitive Contact Linguistics, is that the effect of language contact on the evolution of constructicons is not restricted to constructional borrowing, not even if constructional borrowing is broadly construed to also include cases where an existing construction develops a new meaning or function. Hilpert (2013: 16) defines constructional change as any change that "selectively seizes a conventionalized form-meaning pair of a language, altering it in terms of its form, its function, any aspect of its frequency, its distribution in the linguistic community, or any combination of these." The present paper documents a case where the frequency of an existing microconstruction that was licensed by, amongst others, the Dutch DESCRIPTIVE NCI construction and which would very probably have followed other such microconstructions into near-obsolescence otherwise was boosted by its interlingual identification with a French construction that was popular in the highly influential legal language of the Napoleonic codes. Thus, in a language contact situation, the perceived equivalence of constructions in the source and target constructicons can impact on the entrenchment of extant target constructions, bringing to a halt an ongoing contraction of specific branches of constructional networks. Furthermore, the case discussed here illustrates the relevance of genre-specific conventions for contact-induced constructional change, in that our argument is not simply that the fate of Dutch *geacht worden te* was influenced by Dutch speakers' experience with French *être censé*, but, more specifically, with their experience of the use of this source language expression in a specific type of French discourse, or even in a specific, highly influential (set of) French text(s).

The search is now on for other cases of contact-induced constructional renovation. One found in the literature so far nicely complements the case presented here in that it concerns a much more schematic construction, viz. the Old English DATIVE ABSOLUTE construction, which van de Pol (2012) shows had all but disappeared when it was revived through contact with Latin. There must be many more such cases remaining to be detected.

References

Aijmer, Karin. 1972. *Some Aspects of Psychological Predicates in English*. Stockholm: Almqvist & Wiksell.
Backus, Ad, Derya Demirçay & Yeşim Sevinç. 2013. *Converging Evidence on Contact Effects on Second and Third Generation Immigrant Turkish* (Tilburg Papers in Culture Studies 51). Tilburg: Tilburg University.
Backus, Ad, Seza Doğruöz & Bernd Heine. 2011. Salient stages in contact-induced grammatical change: Evidence from synchronic vs. diachronic contact situations. *Language Sciences* 33 (5). 738–752.
Barðdal, Jóhanna & Spike Gildea. 2015. Diachronic Construction Grammar: Epistemological context, basic assumptions and historical implications. In Jóhanna Barðdal, Elena Smirnova, Lotte Sommerer & Spike Gildea (eds.), *Diachronic Construction Grammar*, 1–49. Amsterdam & Philadelphia: John Benjamins.
Bellefroid, Paul. 1932. De code-vertalingen in den Franschen tijd. *Verslagen en Mededelingen van de Koninklijke Vlaamse Academie voor Taal- en Letterkunde*, januari 1932. 87–108.
Berkenfield, Catie. 2006. Pragmatic motivations for the development of evidential and modal meaning in the construction 'be supposed to X'. *Journal of Historical Pragmatics* 7(1). 39–71.
Colleman, Timothy. 2016. A reflection on constructionalization and constructional borrowing, inspired by an emerging Dutch replica of the 'time'-*away* construction. *Belgian Journal of Linguistics* 30. 91–113.
Colleman, Timothy. Submitted. Distributional assimilation in constructional semantics: On contact-related semantic shifts in Afrikaans three-argument constructions.
Colleman, Timothy & Dirk Noël. 2012. The Dutch evidential NCI: A case of constructional attrition. *Journal of Historical Pragmatics* 13(1). 1–28.
Colleman, Timothy & Dirk Noël. 2014. Tracing the history of deontic NCI patterns in Dutch: A case of polysemy copying. In Irma Taavitsainen, Andreas H. Jucker & Jukka Tuominen (eds.), *Diachronic Corpus Pragmatics*, 213–236. Amsterdam & Philadelphia: John Benjamins.
Collins, Peter. 2009. *Modals and Quasi-Modals in English*. Amsterdam: Rodopi.
Disney, Steve. 2016. Another visit to BE *supposed to* from a diachronic constructionist perspective. *English Studies* 97(8). 892–916.
Doğruöz, Seza & Ad Backus. 2009. Innovative constructions in Dutch Turkish: An assessment of on-going contact induced change. *Bilingualism: Language and Cognition* 12(1). 41–63.
Duinhoven, A. M. 1991. Dat siet men wit ende reine wesen. A.c.i.-constructies in het Nederlands. *Nieuwe Taalgids* 84. 409–430.
Féron, Corinne & Danielle Coltier. 2009. Etude sémantique des unites *censé / réputé / supposé* + infinitif: les limites de la synonymie. *Pratiques* 141 / 142. 150–164.
Féron, Corinne & Danielle Coltier. 2012. Etude diachronique d'une unité lexicale polyphonique: *censé* dans les définitions du *Dictionnaire de l'Académie française* (1er, 4e, 5e, 6e, 8e, 9e éditions). In Céline Guillot, Bernard Combettes, Alexei Lavrentiev, Evelyne Oppermann-Marsaux and Sophie Prévost (eds.), *Le changement en français: Etudes de linguistique diachronique*, 103–117. Bern: Peter Lang.
Fischer, Olga. 1994. The fortunes of the Latin-type accusative and infinitive construction in Dutch and English compared. In Toril Swan, Endre Mørck & Olaf Jansen Westvik (eds.),

Language Change and Language Structure: Older Germanic Languages in a Comparative Perspective, 91–133. Berlin & New York: Mouton de Gruyter.

Fischer, Olga. 2013. The role of contact in English syntactic change in the Old and Middle English periods. In Daniel Schreier & Marianne Hundt (eds.), *English as a Contact Language*, 18–40. Cambridge: Cambridge University Press.

Fried, Mirjam. 2013. Principles of constructional change. In Thomas Hoffmann & Graeme Trousdale (eds.), *The Oxford Handbook of Construction Grammar*, 419–437. Oxford: Oxford University Press.

Gast, Volker & Johan van der Auwera. 2012. What is 'contact-induced grammaticalization'? Examples from Mayan and Mixe-Zoquean languages. In Björn Wiemer, Bernhard Wälchli & Björn Hansen (eds.), *Grammatical Replication and Borrowability in Language Contact*, 381–426. Berlin & New York: Mouton de Gruyter.

Givón, Talmy. 1993. *English Grammar: A Function-Based Introduction*, vol. 2. Amsterdam & Philadelphia: John Benjamins

Goldberg, Adele E. 1990. Constructional borrowing and the process of factorization. Unpublished manuscript. *www.princeton.edu/~adele/papers/Papers/Finished/Yiddish. doc (accessed 10 October 2016)*.

Goldberg, Adele E. 2003. Constructions: A new theoretical approach to language. *Trends in Cognitive Sciences* 7(5). 219–224.

Goossens, Louis. 1991. FG reflections on 'Tobacco is said to be harmful'. *Cahiers de l'Institut de Linguistique de Louvain* 17. 65–74.

Haugen, Einar. *1950. The analysis of linguistic borrowing. Language* 26. 210–231.

Heine, Bernd & Tania Kuteva. 2003. On contact-induced grammaticalization. *Studies in Language* 27(3). 529–572.

Heine, Bernd & Tania Kuteva. 2005. *Language Contact and Grammatical Change*. Cambridge: Cambridge University Press.

Hilpert, Martin. 2013. *Constructional Change in English: Developments in Allomorphy, Word Formation, and Syntax*. Cambridge: Cambridge University Press.

Höder, Steffen. 2012. Multilingual constructions: a diasystematic approach to common structures. In Kurt Braunmüller & Christoph Gabriel (eds.), *Multilingual Individuals and Multilingual Societies*, 241–257. Amsterdam & Philadelphia: John Benjamins.

Höder, Steffen. 2014. Constructing Diasystems: Grammatical Organisation in Bilingual Groups. In Tor A. Åfarli & Britt Mæhlum (eds.), *The Sociolinguistics of Grammar*, 137–152. Amsterdam & Philadelphia: John Benjamins.

Huddleston, Rodney & Geoffrey K. Pullum. 2002. *The Cambridge Grammar of the English Language*. Cambridge: Cambridge University Press.

Jurafsky, Daniel. 1991. *An On-Line Computational Model of Human Sentence Interpretation: A Theory of the Representation and Use of Linguistic Knowledge*. Berkeley, CA: University of California dissertation. http://digitalassets.lib.berkeley.edu/techreports/ucb/text/CSD-92-676.pdf.

Jurafsky, Daniel. 1992. An on-line computational model of human sentence interpretation. *AAAI-92 Proceedings*. 302–308.

Langacker, Ronald W. 1999. Assessing the cognitive linguistic enterprise. In Theo Janssen & Gisela Redeker (eds.), *Cognitive Linguistics: Foundations, Scope, and Methodology*, 13–59. Berlin & New York: Mouton de Gruyter.

Lokin, Johannes H. A. 2004. De receptie van de Code Civil in de Noordelijke Nederlanden. *Groninger Opmerkingen en Mededelingen* XXI. 1–15.

Mair, Christian. 2004. Corpus linguistics and grammaticalization theory. In Hans Lindquist & Christian Mair (eds.), *Corpus Approaches to Grammaticalization in English*, 121–150. Amsterdam & Philadelphia: John Benjamins.

Mithun, Marianne. 2008. Borrowed rhetorical constructions as starting points for grammaticalization. In Alexander Bergs & Gabriele Diewald (eds.), *Constructions and Language Change*, 196–230. Berlin: Mouton de Gruyter.

Moore, Colette. 2007. The spread of grammaticalized forms: The case of *be+supposed to*. *Journal of English Linguistics* 35(2). 117–131.

Noël, Dirk. 2001. The passive matrices of English infinitival complement clauses: Evidentials on the road to auxiliarihood? *Studies in Language* 25(2). 255–296.

Noël, Dirk. 2003. Is there semantics in all syntax? The case of accusative and infinitive constructions vs. *that*-clauses. In Günter Rohdenburg & Britta Mondorf (eds.), *Determinants of Grammatical Variation in English*, 347–377. Berlin & New York: Mouton de Gruyter.

Noël, Dirk. 2008. The nominative and infinitive in Late Modern English: A diachronic constructionist approach. *Journal of English Linguistics* 36(4). 314–340.

Noël, Dirk & Timothy Colleman. 2009. The nominative and infinitive in English and Dutch: An exercise in contrastive diachronic construction grammar. *Languages in Contrast* 9(1). 144–181.

Noël, Dirk & Timothy Colleman. 2010. *Believe*-type raising-to-object and raising-to-subject verbs in English and Dutch: A contrastive investigation in diachronic construction grammar. *International Journal of Corpus Linguistics 15(2)*. 157–182.

Noël, Dirk & Timothy Colleman. 2014. Same formal pattern, different contact situation, different propagation: evidential vs. deontic NCI constructions in Dutch (contrasted with English). Paper presented at the workshop on Grammatical Hybridization and Social Conditions, Max Planck Institute for Evolutionary Anthropology, Leipzig, 16–18 October.

Noël, Dirk & Johan van der Auwera. 2009. Revisiting *be supposed to* from a diachronic constructionist perspective. *English Studies* 90(5). 599–623.

Nuyts, Jan. 2001. *Epistemic Modality, Language and Conceptualization: A Cognitive-Pragmatic Perspective*. Amsterdam & Philadelphia: John Benjamins.

Nuyts, Jan. 2016. Analyses of the modal meanings. In Jan Nuyts & Johan van der Auwera (eds.), *The Oxford Handbook of Modality and Mood*, 31–49. Oxford: Oxford University Press.

Petré, Peter. 2016. Unidirectionality as a cycle of convention and innovation: Micro-changes in the grammaticalization of [be going to INF]. *Belgian Journal of Linguistics* 30. 115–146.

Petré, Peter. 2017. The extravagant progressive: An experimental corpus study on the history of emphatic [BE V*ing*]. *English Language and Linguistics* 21(2). 227–250.

Pietsch, Lukas. 2010. What has changed in Hiberno-English: Constructions and their role in contact-induced change. *Sprachtypologie und Universalienforschung* 63. 118–145.

Postal, Paul M. 1974. *On Raising: One Rule of English Grammar and its Theoretical Implications*. Cambridge, Mass.: The MIT Press.

Schmid, Hans-Jörg & Annette Mantlik. 2015. Entrenchment in historical corpora? Reconstructing dead authors' minds from their usage profiles. *Anglia* 133(4). 583–623.

Squartini, Mario. 2016. Interactions between modality and other semantic categories. In Jan Nuyts & Johan van der Auwera (eds.), *The Oxford Handbook of Modality and Mood*, 50–67. Oxford: Oxford University Press.

Traugott, Elizabeth Closs & Graeme Trousdale. 2013. *Constructionalization and Constructional Changes*. Oxford: Oxford University Press.

van de Pol, Nikki. 2012. Between copy and cognate: The origin of absolutes in Old and Middle English. In Johanson Lars & Martine Robbeets (eds.), *Copies versus Cognates in Bound Morphology*, 297–322. Leiden & Boston: Brill.
van der Auwera, Johan & Vladimir Plungian. 1998. Modality's semantic map. *Linguistic Typology* 2(1). 79–124.
Van de Velde, Freek & Eline Zenner. 2010. Pimp my Lexis: het nut van corpusonderzoek in normatief taaladvies. In Els Hendrickx, Karl Hendrickx, Willy Martin, Hans Smessaert, William Van Belle & Joop van der Horst (eds.), *Liever meer of juist minder? Over normen en variatie in taal*, 51–68. Gent: Academia press.
Visconti, Jacqueline. 2004. Conditionals and subjectification: Implications for a theory of semantic change. In Olga Fischer, Muriel Norde & Harry Perridon (eds.), *Up and Down the Cline: The Nature of Grammaticalization*, 169–192. Amsterdam & Philadelphia: John Benjamins.
Weinreich, Uriel. 1968 [1953]. *Languages in Contact: Findings and Problems*. The Hague: Mouton.
Ziegeler, Debra. 2003. On the generic origins of modality in English. In David Hart (ed.), *English Modality in Context: Diachronic Perspectives*, 33–69. Bern: Peter Lang.

Index

After perfect 161, 169
Agentivity
– RL-agentivity 28
– SL-agentivity 28
Alternations 253–254, 273–274
Ambiguity 109, 113–114
– perceptive ambiguity 83, 114
Analogical activation 40–41
Anglicism 83–85, 87–88, 91, 93, 102, 116, 118–119, 121
Arabic 164
Association task 192, 194–196, 199–200, 202–203, 205–207
Attachment 166
Attitudes 216, 220–221, 235–237
Attribute-listing task 189

Bilingual
– BIA+ (Bilingual Interactive Activation Plus) Model 33
– bilingual child 279
– bilingual variety 273
Blending 6, 189–190, 208
Borrowability 6, 7
Borrowing 26–28, 36, 38–40, 44
– constructional borrowing 306–307, 333
British English 190–193, 195–209

Calques 27, 42
– calquing 42–43
Catachrestic reinterpretation 99, 117, 119, 122–123
Causal (force-dynamic) approach 259
Citétaal 127, 130–131, 137, 141, 146, 154
Code alternation 58
Code-copying 51
Code-mixing (cm) 279
Codeswitching 4, 26, 34, 36, 38–40, 255
Cognates 34
Cognitive Anthropology 216
Cognitive Linguistics 128, 161
Cognitive Sociolinguistics 3, 9, 128
Composite structures 260

Conceptual Metaphor Theory (CMT) 6, 160, 183
– cross-cultural 160
– variation in metaphor 183
– within-culture variation 160
Conceptual scenes 258, 260
– association scenes 261, 266–269, 274
– associative links 260
– directionality scenes 264, 266–269, 274
– entities 260
– inception scenes 263, 266–269, 274
– occurrence scenes 261, 266–269, 274
– processes 260
Conscious activation 36, 41
Construction Grammar 7, 24
– constructional attrition 319, 332
– constructional change 306, 325, 332
Contact phenomena 188, 190, 192, 209–210
Contact-induced grammaticalization 28
Contact-induced variation and change 1, 3–4, 8, 10–11, 129, 214
Contact jargon 170
Contact Linguistics 161
CONTAINMENT 160, 162–163, 165–166, 168, 171, 178, 179
Contiguity 85–86, 88, 92–95, 99, 103–105, 110, 120–121
Conventionalization 61, 255, 273
Copying 51
Critical discourse analysis 214–215
Cross-cultural 164
Crosslinguistic influence 30
– crosslinguistic homonyms 34
– crosslinguistic interaction(s) 25, 41
– crosslinguistic priming 34, 40
Cultural models 9, 191, 194, 205, 209, 214–217, 222, 225, 228, 234–237
Cultural values 183
Culture-specific 164

Dative of Disadvantage 171, 177
De Bot's Bilingual Production Model 33
Deontic modality 307, 309–310, 315, 330

Diachronic Construction Grammar 306, 333
    See also Construction Grammar
– Contrastive Diachronic Construction
    Grammar 305, 332
Dialect contact 161
Diasystematic Construction Grammar 8, 24,
    31–33 *See also* Construction Grammar
Discourse particles 66
Discourse priming 279
Discourse 128, 137, 145–147, 151
Discursive analyses 131, 132, 134, 136–137,
    144, 151, 154, 220
Distributional networks 33
Dutch 162–163, 305
Dutch-Moroccan Arabic 256, 265
Dutch-Turkish 256, 265
Dynamic Systems Theory 33

Ease of activation 279
Ellipsis/truncation 86, 88, 92, 95, 98,
    101–109, 121, 123
Embedded Language (EL) 253 *See also*
    Matrix Language (ML)
English 160–161, 163–164, 167, 172, 182,
    307, 313, 331
English-based pidgins and creoles 29
Entrenchment 6, 56
Equivalence 73
Estonian 52
Eventive 258
Events 255, 259–260, 273, 275
Evidentiality 307, 309, 311, 314, 316, 330
Executive control 34, 38
Expressives 257

Family resemblance 129–130, 149, 153
Figure-Ground
– figure 162–163
– ground 162, 163
Finnish 162
Form-meaning units 34, 36, 38–39
Free association(s) 213, 215, 222,
    224, 237
French 318
Functional geometry 162
Fused lect 255
Fuzzy boundaries 127–128, 153–154

General states 255, 258–260, 272–274
Genre 333
German-English 279
Global copying 28
Graded membership 149
Grammatical interference 161

Habitualization 61
Hungarian 164
Hybrids
– hybrid compounds 26, 44
– hybrid forms 43, 44
Hyphenation 90, 109, 116, 123

Ideology 214, 216–217
Imperfect learning 27
Imposition 28
Inanimate possession 171
Indian English 190–192, 195–197, 199–208
Inhibition 34
Inner circle 164
Insertions 253
Interaction 127, 128, 131–132, 134–138,
    140, 142, 144–145, 147, 150–151,
    153–154
Intercultural 164
Interference 26–27, 34
Interlingual homophone 26
Interlingual identification 26, 32, 34
Irish 160–161, 164–165, 167, 169–171, 176,
    178, 181–183
Irish English 160–161, 164, 169,–171,
    176–177, 182–183
– prepositions 170
Italo-Romance dialects 213–214, 218
Item-linking task 192–194, 197, 199,
    201–202, 204–206

Language attitudes 215
Language change 54
Language contact
– language contact phenomena 36, 81–126
– modern contact linguistics 25
Language dominance 28
Language mode(s) 34, 36, 38–40, 42, 44
Latin 309, 333
Legal language 319, 333

Levelt speaking model 33
(Lexical) aspectual approach 259
Lexical borrowing 4
Lexifier language 29
Loan creations 27, 42
Loan formations 27
Loan rendition(s) 27, 42
Loan translation(s) 27, 42–43
Loanblends 27
Loanshifts 27
Loanword(s) 5, 27, 41, 83–85, 87, 89, 91–93, 96–97, 100–101, 116, 118
Localist approach 258
Localist networks 33
Locations 162, 168
Luxury loans 7 *See also* Necessary loans

Matrix Language (ML) 253, 273 *See also* Embedded Language (EL)
Matter replication 8, 28 *See also* Replication
Meaning of variation *See* Social meaning
Mental lexicon 6
Mental network 31, 33–36, 39, 41–42, 44
Metaphor 100, 122, 163–164, 183
– culture-specific 163
– metaphorical similarity 85, 88, 99
– universal 163
Metonymy 6, 92–95, 114, 120, 122–123
Mixed methods 131
Multi-competence 55
Multi factorial statistical analysis 145
Multilectal repertoire 32
Multilingualism
– multilingual mind 33
– multilingual repertoire 31, 33, 41
Multi-word items 58

Necessary loans 7 *See also* Luxury loans
Neuronal network 32
Nigerian English 189–192, 195–209
Nominative and infinitive 305, 307–308
Nonce borrowings 26, 39

Old English 333
Onomasiology 5–7, 188 *See also* Semasiology

Parallel activation 34
Partially schematic construction 279 *See also* Construction Grammar
Pattern replication 8, 28 *See also* Replication
Perceived-strength-of-connection task 193–194, 197–199, 201–202, 204–207
Permanency 169
Polysemy copying 316 *See also* Copying
Practice 128
Proper names 89
Prototype theory 9, 127–130, 145, 147, 149, 151, 153–154
– prototype analysis 153
– prototype-based classifications 149
– prototype representation 152
– prototype structure(s) 127, 149–154
– prototype-theoretical representation 153
– prototypicality 5
Pseudo anglicisms 43
Pseudo loan 43

Qualitative discursive methods 129, 153
Quantitative variationist analyses 128, 153
Questionnaire 173

Raising 308
Reanalysis 82, 83, 91, 109–110, 112–117, 120–124
Recontextualising trend 216
Regional Italian varieties 213
Replication 28, 36, 41–44
– matter replication 8, 28
– pattern replication 8, 28
– Yélî Dnye 163
Revised Hierarchical Model 34
RL-agentivity *See* Agentivity

Salience 6, 60, 94, 109, 118–120, 122–123, 130, 149–150, 154
Second language acquisition 41
Selective copying 28
Semantic change 82, 86–88, 91–96, 98, 100, 104–105, 107, 110, 117, 119, 122
Semantic domain 84, 91, 99, 117, 123
Semantic loans 316

Semasiology 7, 13, 111 *See also* Onomasiology
Semiotics 82, 109–112, 119–120, 123
– semiotic model 82
Shift-induced interference 28 *See* Interference
Sibilant palatalization 129
SL-agentivity *See* Agentivity
Snowball effect 173
Social meaning 8, 127–132, 145, 147, 149–154
– meaning of variation 213–214, 217
Social profiling 131
Social psychology 216
– social psychology of language 215
Sociolinguistic interview 173
Stereotypes 9
Substrate 29, 161, 169
Superstrate influence 29, 161
SUPPORT 160, 162–163, 165–166, 178
Surfaces 168, 179

Systemic functional grammar 259
– transitivity 259

Taxonomic subordination 85, 88, 91–93, 95–97, 99, 104, 117, 119–120, 122, 123
Third wave sociolinguistics 127–128, 132, 151–154
Transfer 29, 34, 36, 40–44
Translation 38
Transmutation 41
Transparency 89–90, 92, 104, 110–111, 115–116, 121–123

Unconscious activation 36
Urban vernacular 127, 130, 132
Usage-based approach 3–4, 8, 10, 280, 332

Variationist analyses 129, 131, 134, 136, 147, 151, 154, 163–164

World Englishes 190, 208

www.ingramcontent.com/pod-product-compliance
Lightning Source LLC
Chambersburg PA
CBHW031755220426
43662CB00007B/410